NEGIMA!

36

Ken Akamatsu

TRANSLATED AND ADAPTED BY
Alethea Nibley and Athena Nibley

LETTERING AND RETOUCH BY
Scott O. Brown

KC
KODANSHA
COMICS

A word from the author

IF YOU ONLY BUY ONE LIMITED EDITION, PLEASE BUY THE ONE FOR THE NEXT VOLUME (37).*

IT'S A COMMEMORATIVE VOLUME.

*AKAMATSU IS REFERRING TO THE LIMITED EDITION VOLUME 37 RELEASED IN JAPAN.

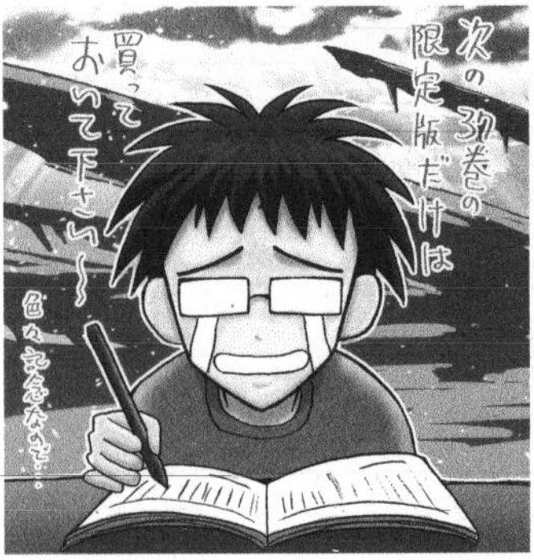
次の37巻の限定版だけは
買っておいて下さい〜
色々記念なので…。

THIS VOLUME BRINGS US AT LAST TO THE CONCLUSION OF THE MAGICAL WORLD ARC! WHAT WILL BE THE FATE OF NEGI, ASUNA, AND THE OTHERS!?

WE PRESENT THIS VOLUME WITH ELEVEN CHAPTERS--THE GREATEST NUMBER OF CHAPTERS CONTAINED IN A VOLUME TO THIS POINT. (USUALLY IT'S NINE CHAPTERS PER VOLUME.)

...And because of that, there are zero bonus pages. I think this might be the first time that's ever happened (laugh).

Incidentally, the limited edition for the next volume will come with the Ken Akamatsu Cut of the Negima! movie. It was created based on my "ending B" plan--how the series would have ended if it stopped at volume 37. In other words, you could say it's an official parallel universe ending.

It's several minutes longer than the movie that played in theaters, and it's chock-full of other surprising bonuses, so please reserve your commemorative copy today.

Ken Akamatsu's home page address*
http://www.ailove.net/

*Please note the webpage is in Japanese.

Honorifics Explained

Throughout the Kodansha Comics books, you will find Japanese honorifics left intact in the translations. For those not familiar with how the Japanese use honorifics and, more important, how they differ from American honorifics, we present this brief overview.

Politeness has always been a critical facet of Japanese culture. Ever since the feudal era, when Japan was a highly stratified society, use of honorifics—which can be defined as polite speech that indicates relationship or status—has played an essential role in the Japanese language. When addressing someone in Japanese, an honorific usually takes the form of a suffix attached to one's name (example: "Asuna-san"), is used as a title at the end of one's name, or appears in place of the name itself (example: "Negi-sensei," or simply "Sensei!").

Honorifics can be expressions of respect or endearment. In the context of manga and anime, honorifics give insight into the nature of the relationship between characters. Many English translations leave out these important honorifics and therefore distort the feel of the original Japanese. Because Japanese honorifics contain nuances that English honorifics lack, it is our policy at Kodansha Comics not to translate them. Here, instead, is a guide to some of the honorifics you may encounter in Kodansha Comics.

- **-san:** This is the most common honorific and is equivalent to Mr., Miss, Ms., or Mrs. It is the all-purpose honorific and can be used in any situation where politeness is required.

- **-sama:** This is one level higher than "-san" and is used to confer great respect.

- **-dono:** This comes from the word "tono," which means "lord." It is an even higher level than "-sama" and confers utmost respect.

- **-kun:** This suffix is used at the end of boys' names to express familiarity or endearment. It is also sometimes used by men among friends, or when addressing someone younger or of a lower station.

- **-chan:** This is used to express endearment, mostly toward girls. It is also used for little boys, pets, and even among lovers. It gives a sense of childish cuteness.

- **Bozu:** This is an informal way to refer to a boy, similar to the English terms "kid" and "squirt."

Sempai/Senpai: This title suggests that the addressee is one's senior in a group or organization. It is most often used in a school setting, where underclassmen refer to their upperclassmen as "sempai." It can also be used in the workplace, such as when a newer employee addresses an employee who has seniority in the company.

Kohai: This is the opposite of "sempai" and is used toward underclassmen in school or newcomers in the workplace. It connotes that the addressee is of a lower station.

Sensei: Literally meaning "one who has come before," this title is used for teachers, doctors, or masters of any profession or art.

-[blank]: This is usually forgotten in these lists, but it is perhaps the most significant difference between Japanese and English. The lack of honorific means that the speaker has permission to address the person in a very intimate way. Usually, only family, spouses, or very close friends have this kind of permission. Known as *yobisute*, it can be gratifying when someone who has earned the intimacy starts to call one by one's name without an honorific. But when that intimacy hasn't been earned, it can be very insulting.

Ken
Akamatsu

NEGIMA!

MAGISTER NEGI MAGI

36

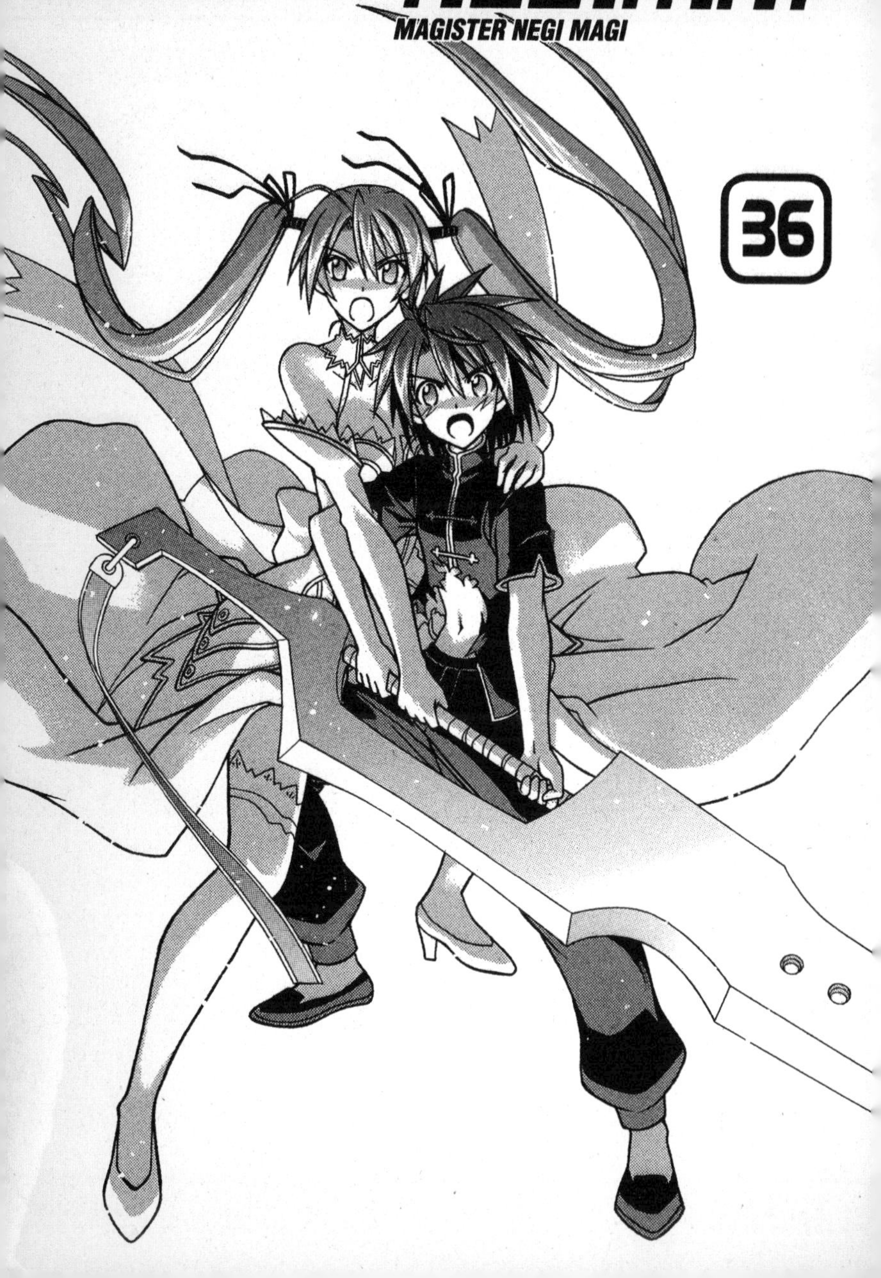

CONTENTS

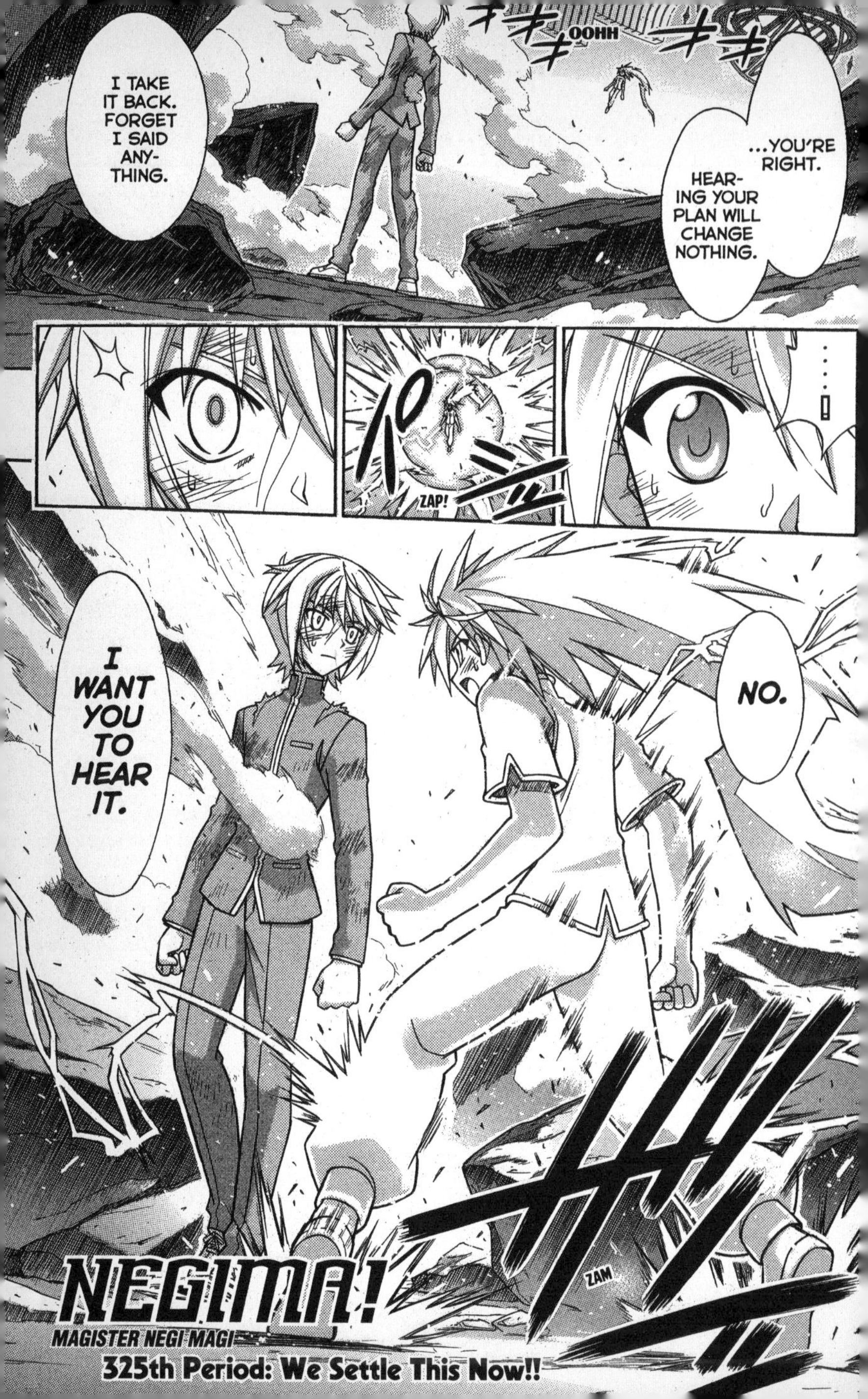
OOHH
...YOU'RE RIGHT. HEARING YOUR PLAN WILL CHANGE NOTHING.
I TAKE IT BACK. FORGET I SAID ANYTHING.
.....!
ZAP!
NO.
I WANT YOU TO HEAR IT.
ZAM
NEGIMA!
MAGISTER NEGI MAGI
325th Period: We Settle This Now!!

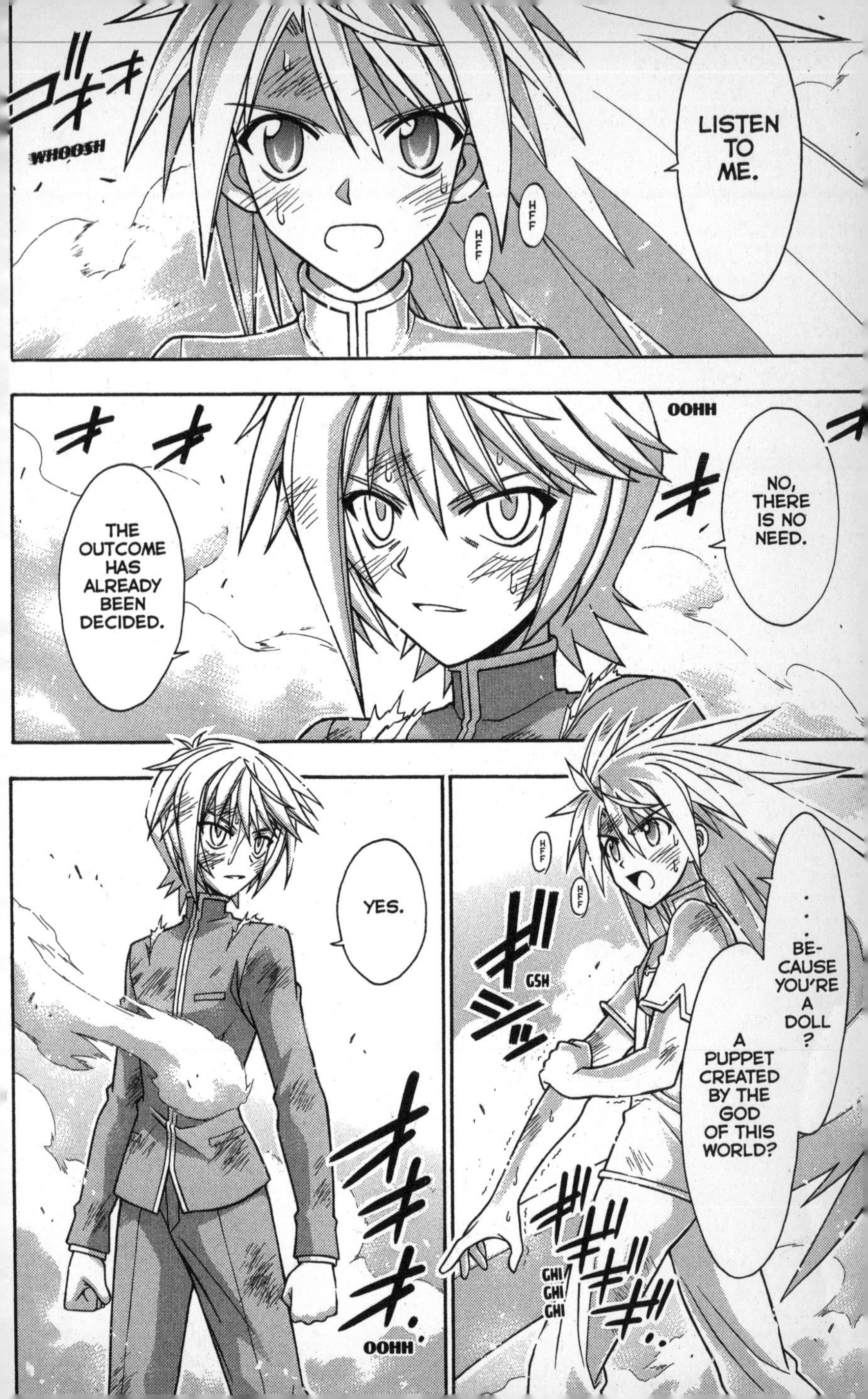
LISTEN TO ME.
HFF
HFF
WHOOSH
OOHH
NO, THERE IS NO NEED.
THE OUTCOME HAS ALREADY BEEN DECIDED.
HFF
HFF
GSH
. . . BE-CAUSE YOU'RE A DOLL?
A PUPPET CREATED BY THE GOD OF THIS WORLD?
GHI GHI GHI
YES.
OOHH

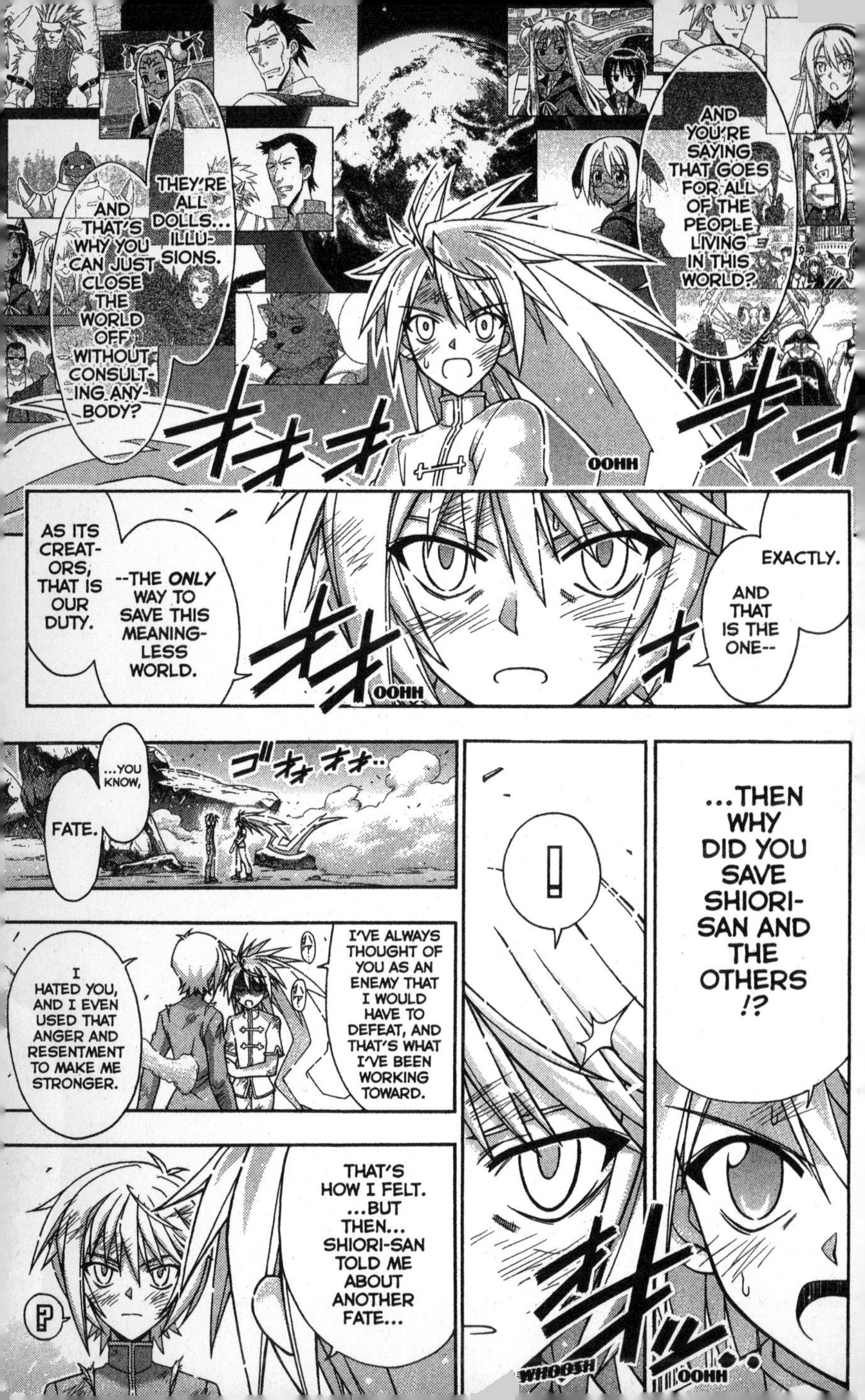
AND YOU'RE SAYING THAT GOES FOR ALL OF THE PEOPLE LIVING IN THIS WORLD?
THEY'RE ALL DOLLS... ILLUSIONS.
AND THAT'S WHY YOU CAN JUST CLOSE THE WORLD OFF WITHOUT CONSULTING ANYBODY?
OOHH
EXACTLY.
AND THAT IS THE ONE--
--THE *ONLY* WAY TO SAVE THIS MEANINGLESS WORLD.
AS ITS CREATORS, THAT IS OUR DUTY.
OOHH
...THEN WHY DID YOU SAVE SHIORI-SAN AND THE OTHERS!?
WHOOSH
OOHH
!
...YOU KNOW,
FATE.
I'VE ALWAYS THOUGHT OF YOU AS AN ENEMY THAT I WOULD HAVE TO DEFEAT, AND THAT'S WHAT I'VE BEEN WORKING TOWARD.
I HATED YOU, AND I EVEN USED THAT ANGER AND RESENTMENT TO MAKE ME STRONGER.
THAT'S HOW I FELT. ...BUT THEN... SHIORI-SAN TOLD ME ABOUT ANOTHER FATE...
?

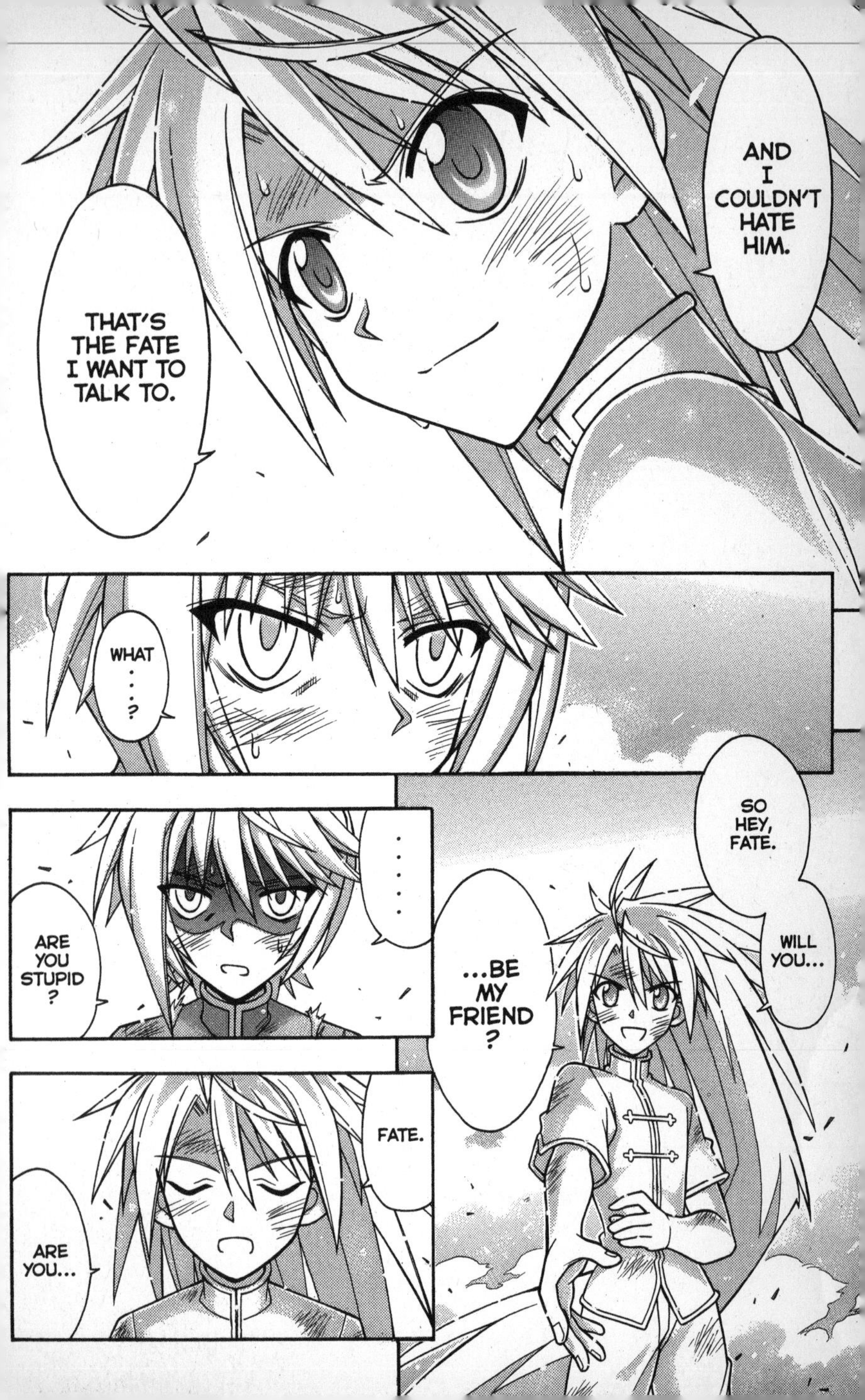
AND I COULDN'T HATE HIM.
THAT'S THE FATE I WANT TO TALK TO.
WHAT ...?
SO HEY, FATE.
WILL YOU...
...BE MY FRIEND?
......
ARE YOU STUPID?
FATE.
ARE YOU...

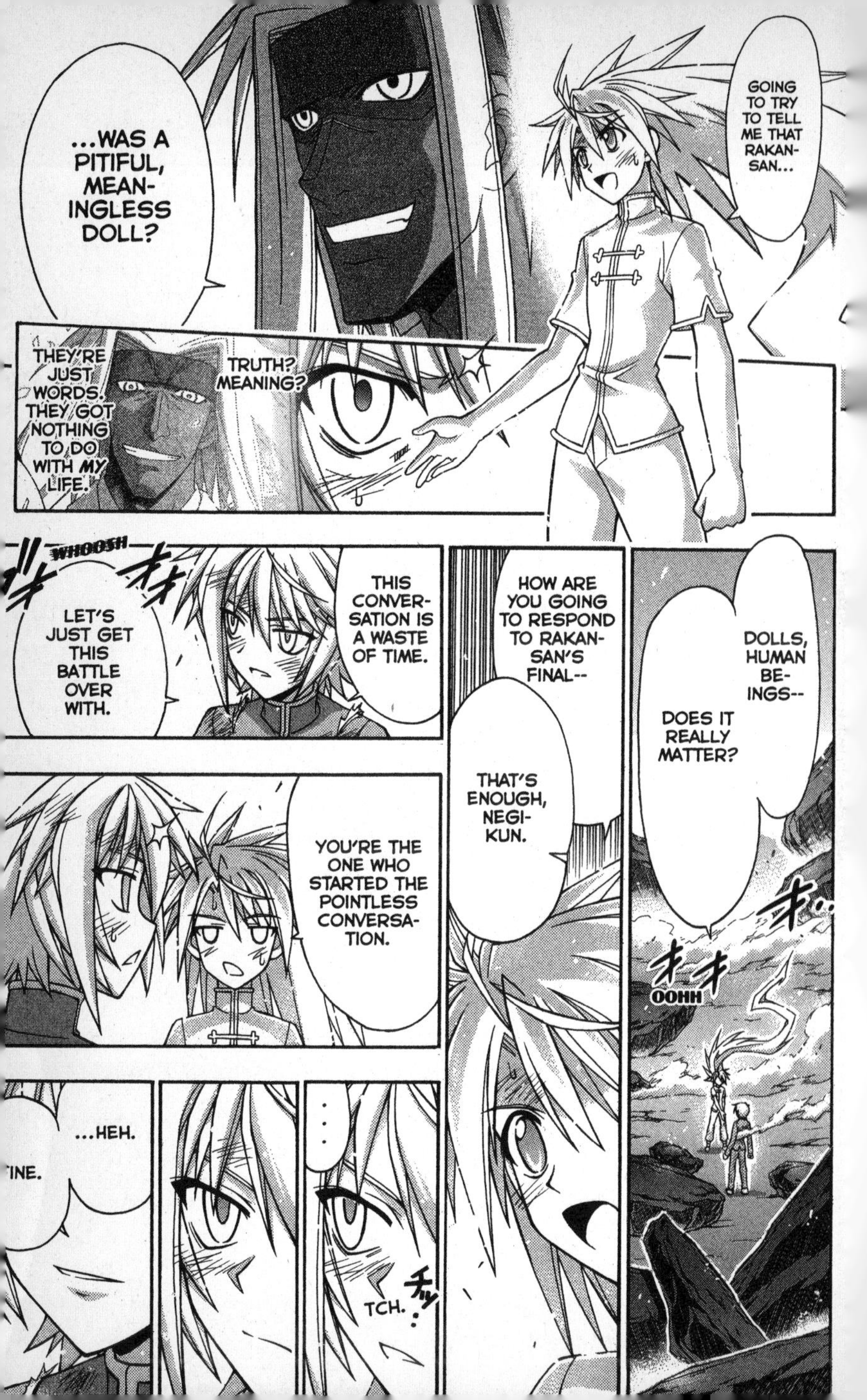
GOING TO TRY TO TELL ME THAT RAKAN-SAN...
...WAS A PITIFUL, MEAN-INGLESS DOLL?
TRUTH? MEANING?
THEY'RE JUST WORDS. THEY GOT NOTHING TO DO WITH MY LIFE.
DOLLS, HUMAN BEINGS--
DOES IT REALLY MATTER?
OOHH
HOW ARE YOU GOING TO RESPOND TO RAKAN-SAN'S FINAL--
THAT'S ENOUGH, NEGI-KUN.
THIS CONVER-SATION IS A WASTE OF TIME.
WHOOSH
LET'S JUST GET THIS BATTLE OVER WITH.
YOU'RE THE ONE WHO STARTED THE POINTLESS CONVERSA-TION.
....
TCH.
...HEH.
INE.

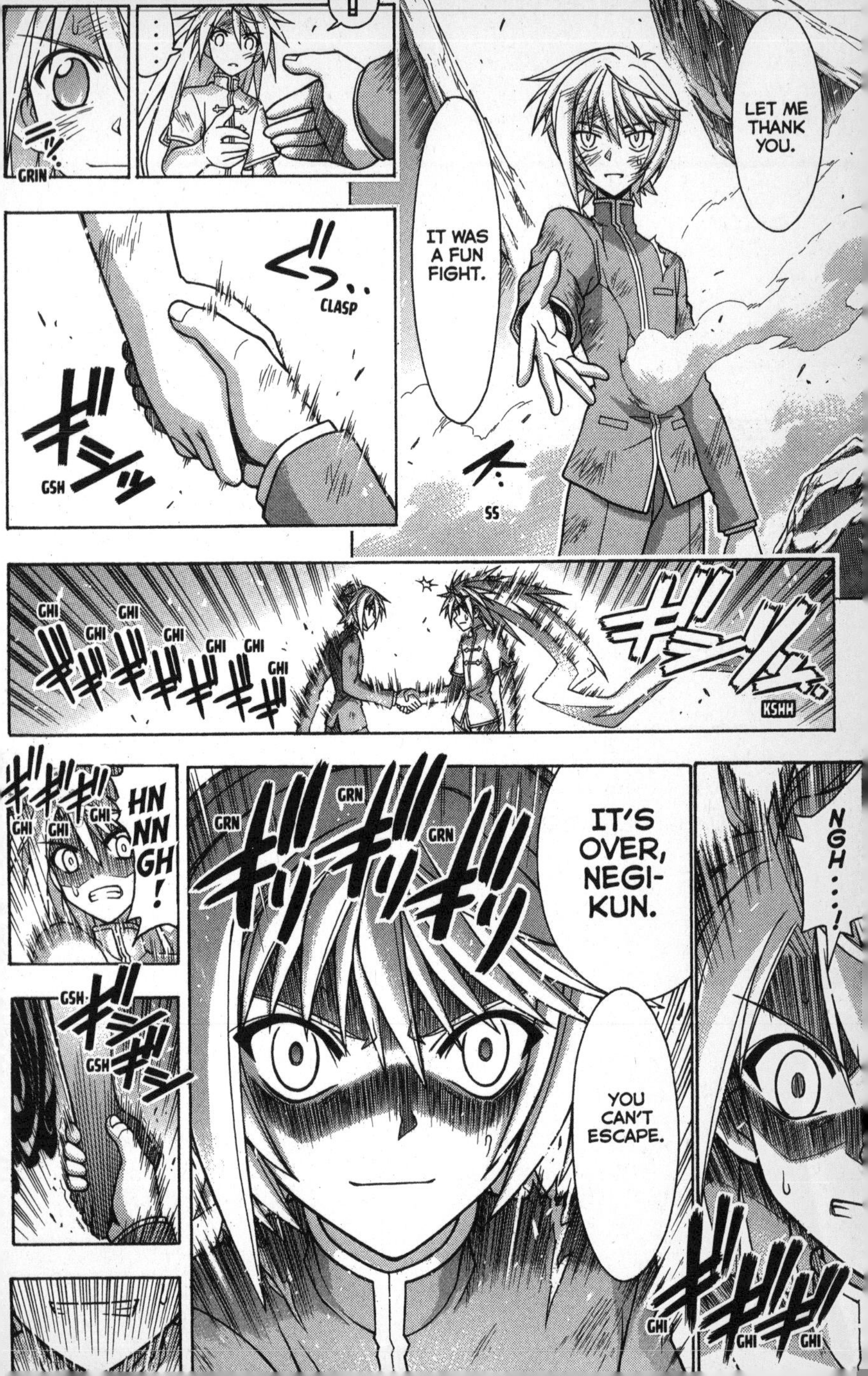
LET ME THANK YOU.
IT WAS A FUN FIGHT.
SS
!
...
GRIN
CLASP
GSH
KSHH
GHI GHI GHI GHI GHI GHI GHI
NGH...!
GHI GHI GHI
IT'S OVER, NEGI-KUN.
YOU CAN'T ESCAPE.
GRN GRN GRN
HNNNGH!
GHI GHI GHI
GSH GSH

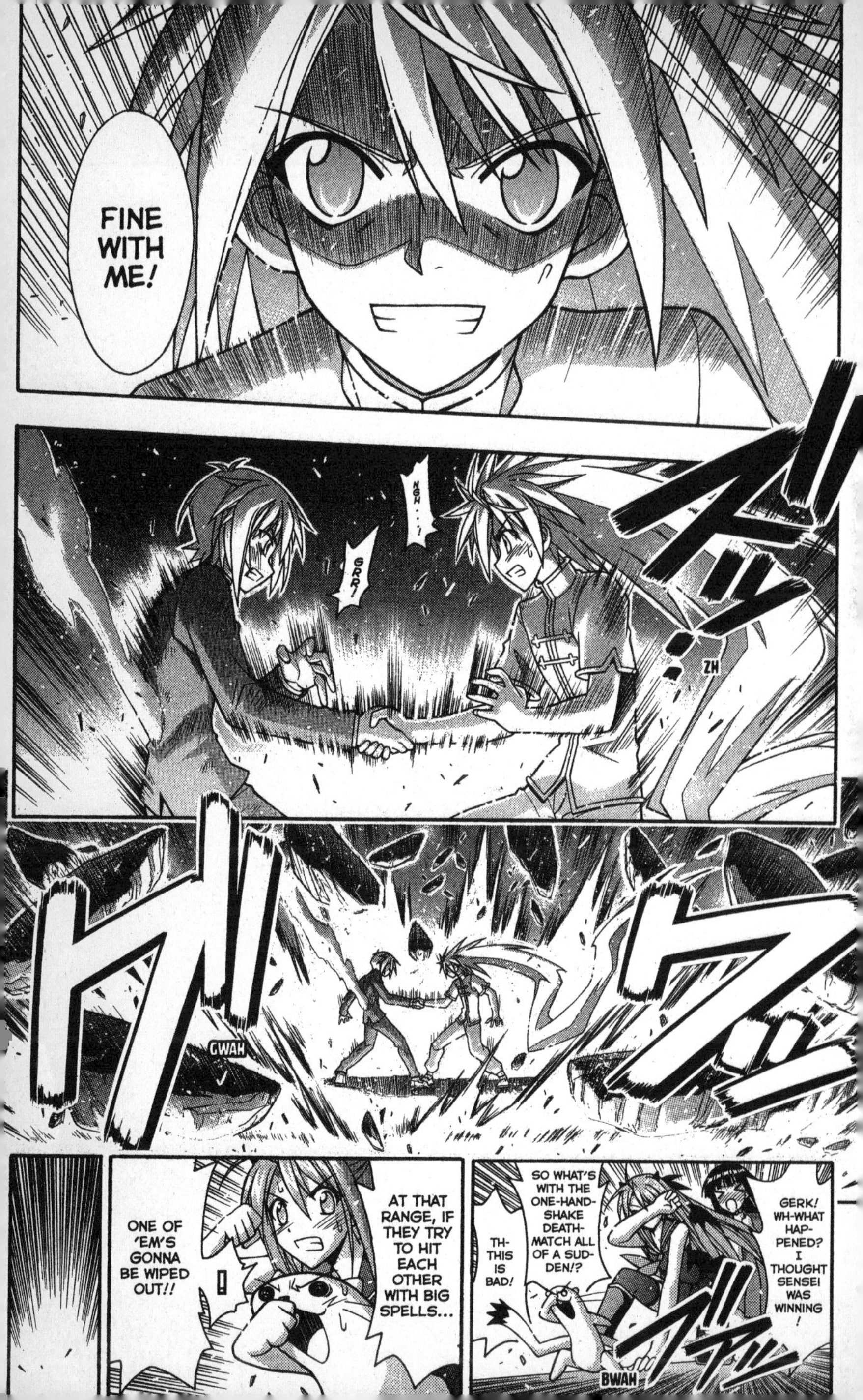
FINE WITH ME!
ZH
NGH...!
GRR!
GWAH
GERK! WH-WHAT HAPPENED? I THOUGHT SENSEI WAS WINNING!
SO WHAT'S WITH THE ONE-HAND-SHAKE DEATH-MATCH ALL OF A SUDDEN!?
TH-THIS IS BAD!
BWAH
AT THAT RANGE, IF THEY TRY TO HIT EACH OTHER WITH BIG SPELLS...
!
ONE OF 'EM'S GONNA BE WIPED OUT!!

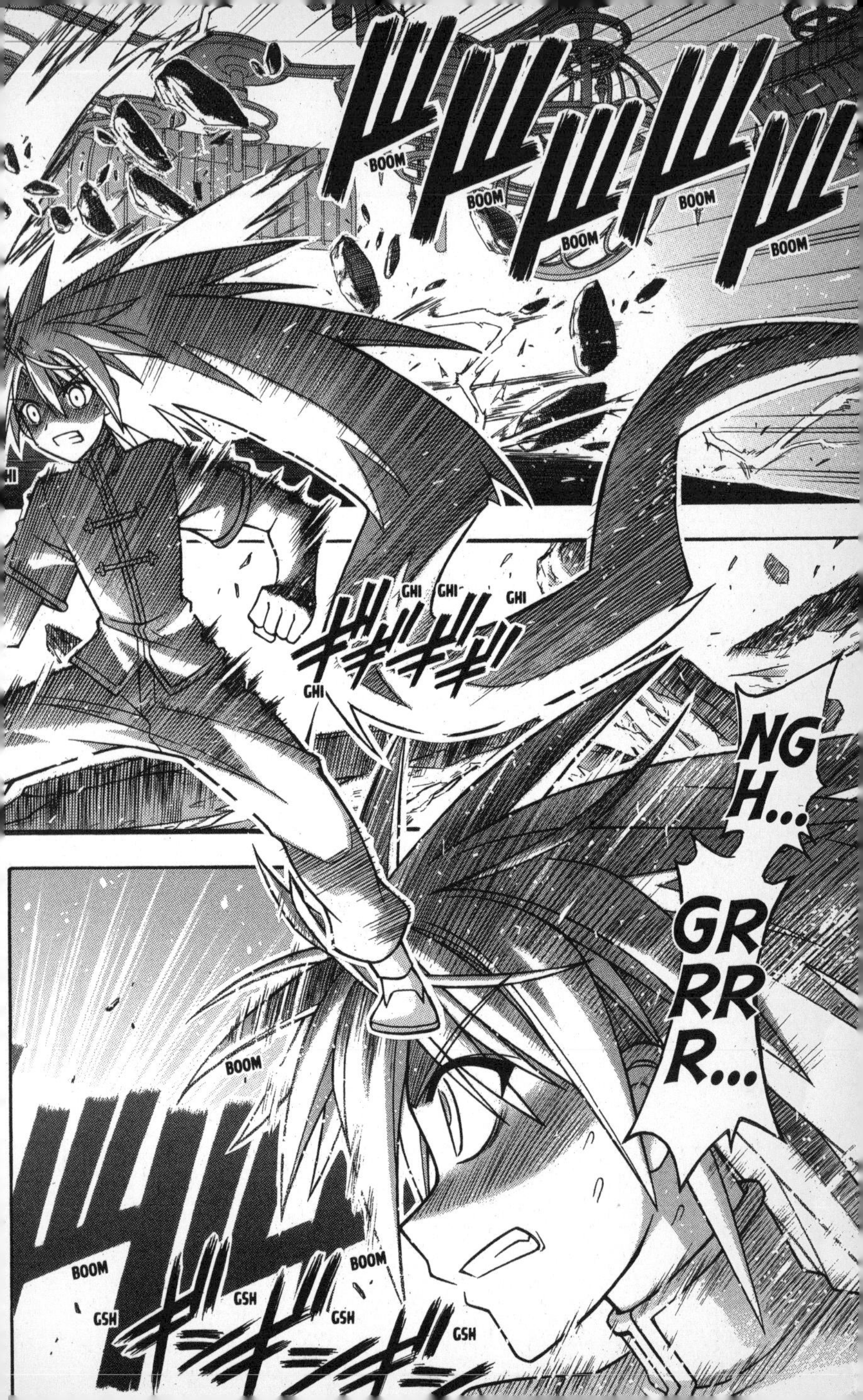
BOOM
BOOM
BOOM
BOOM
BOOM
GHI
GHI
GHI
GHI
NGH...
GRRRR...
BOOM
BOOM
BOOM
GSH
GSH
GSH
GSH

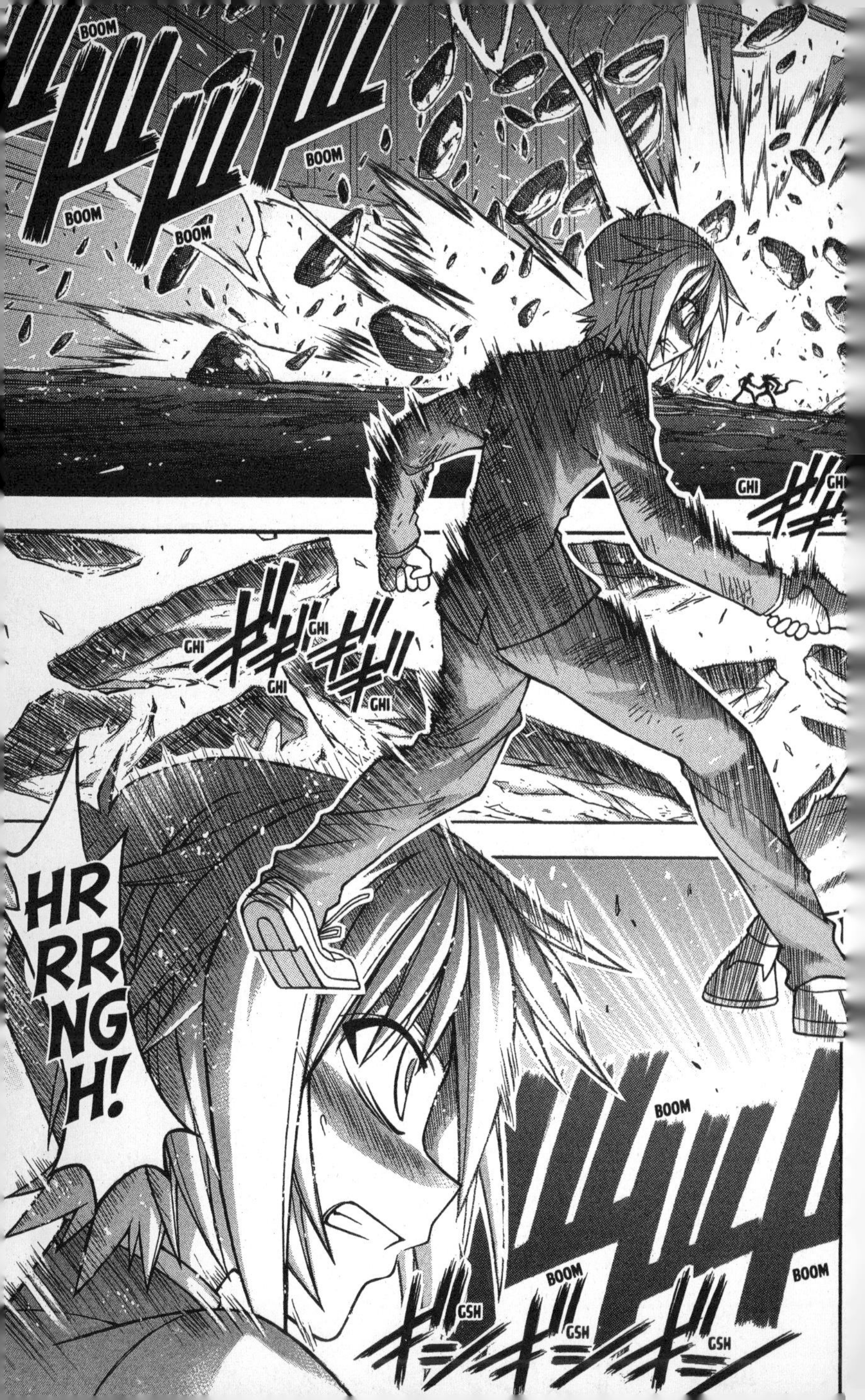
BOOM
BOOM
BOOM
BOOM
GHI
GHI
GHI
GHI
GHI
HRRRNGH!
BOOM
BOOM
BOOM
GSH
GSH
GSH

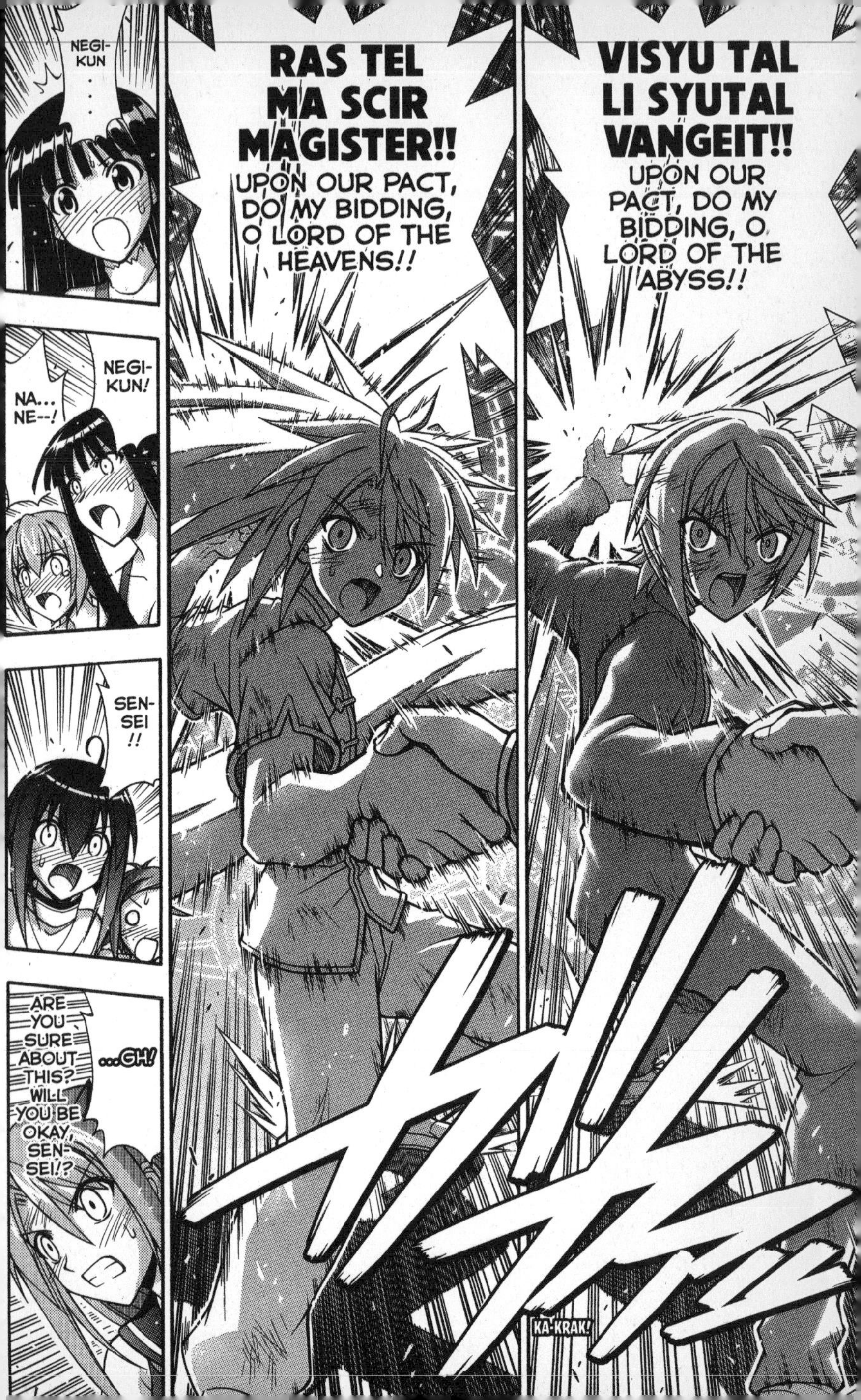

VISYU TAL LI SYUTAL VANGEIT!!
UPON OUR PACT, DO MY BIDDING, O LORD OF THE ABYSS!!
KA-KRAK!
RAS TEL MA SCIR MAGISTER!!
UPON OUR PACT, DO MY BIDDING, O LORD OF THE HEAVENS!!
NEGI-KUN
NEGI-KUN!
NA... NE--!
SEN-SEI!!
...GH!
ARE YOU SURE ABOUT THIS? WILL YOU BE OKAY, SEN-SEI!?

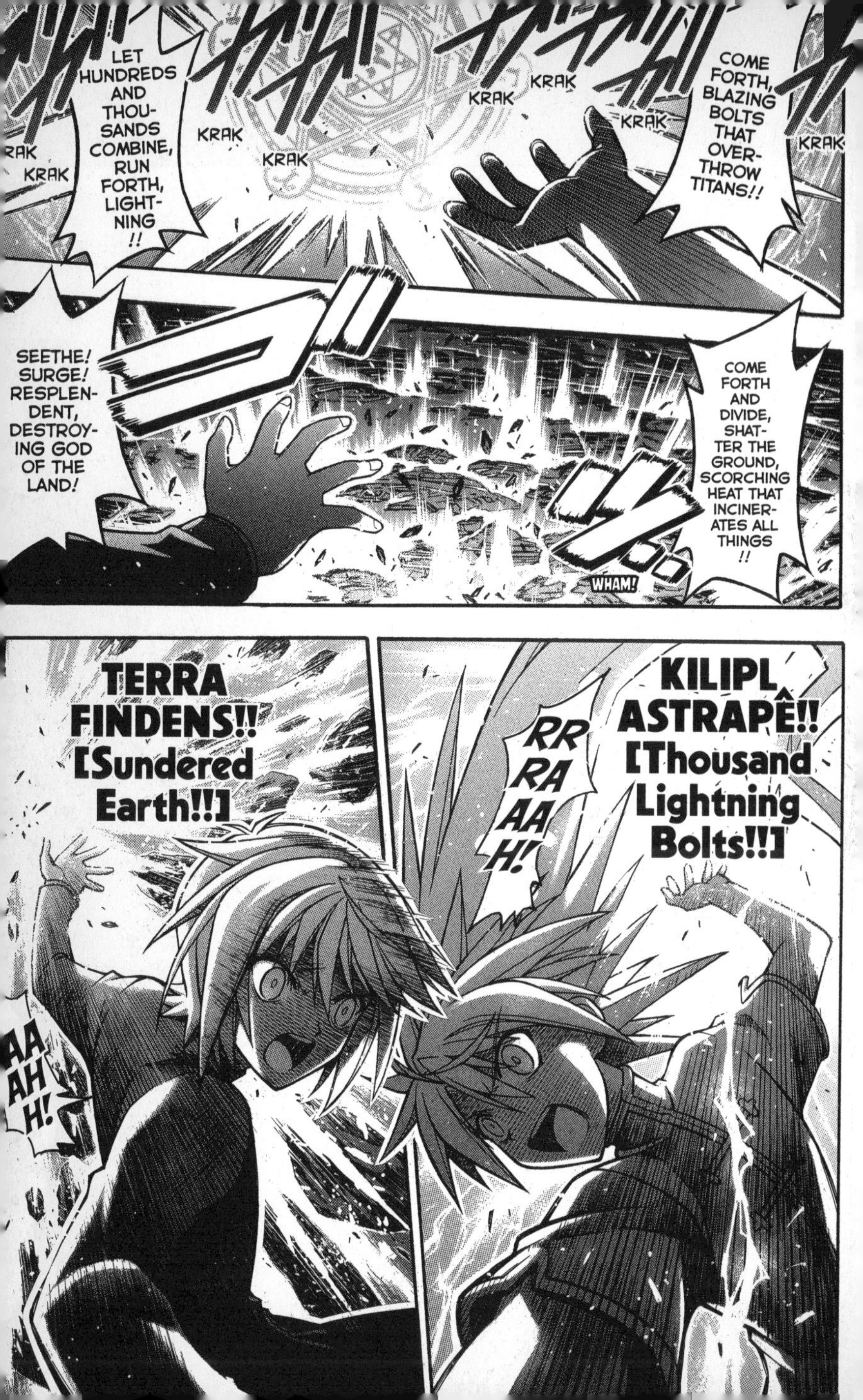
KRAK
KRAK
KRAK
COME FORTH, BLAZING BOLTS THAT OVER-THROW TITANS!!
KRAK
KRAK
KRAK
LET HUNDREDS AND THOU-SANDS COMBINE, RUN FORTH, LIGHT-NING!!
RAK
KRAK
COME FORTH AND DIVIDE, SHAT-TER THE GROUND, SCORCHING HEAT THAT INCINER-ATES ALL THINGS!!
WHAM!
SEETHE! SURGE! RESPLEN-DENT, DESTROY-ING GOD OF THE LAND!
KILIPL ASTRAPÊ!! [Thousand Lightning Bolts!!]
RRRAAAH!
TERRA FINDENS!! [Sundered Earth!!]
AAAHH!

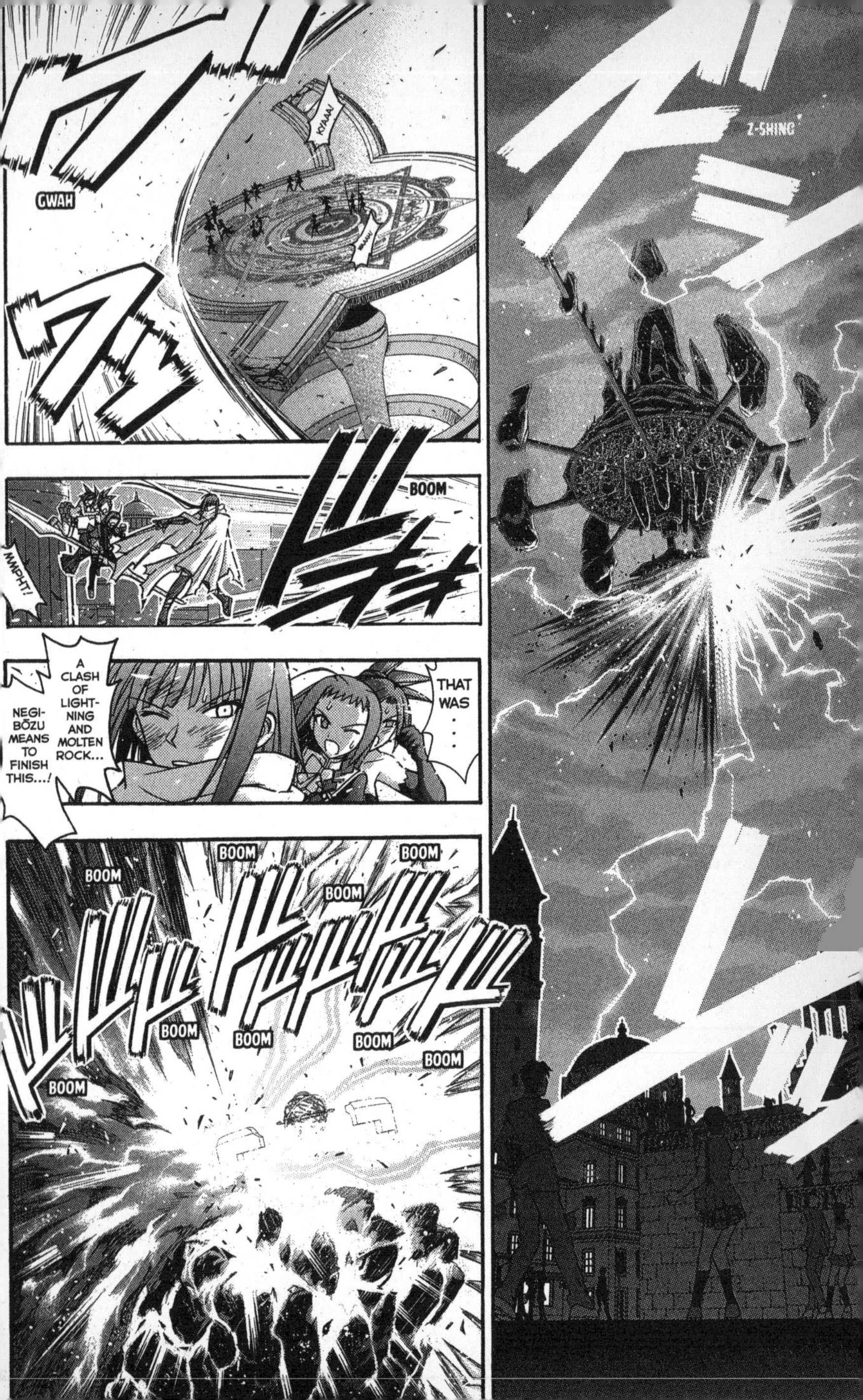
Z-SHING
KYAAA!
WAAAH!
GWAH
BOOM
MMPHT!
THAT WAS...
A CLASH OF LIGHTNING AND MOLTEN ROCK...
NEGI-BŌZU MEANS TO FINISH THIS...!
BOOM
BOOM
BOOM
BOOM
BOOM
BOOM
BOOM
BOOM
BOOM

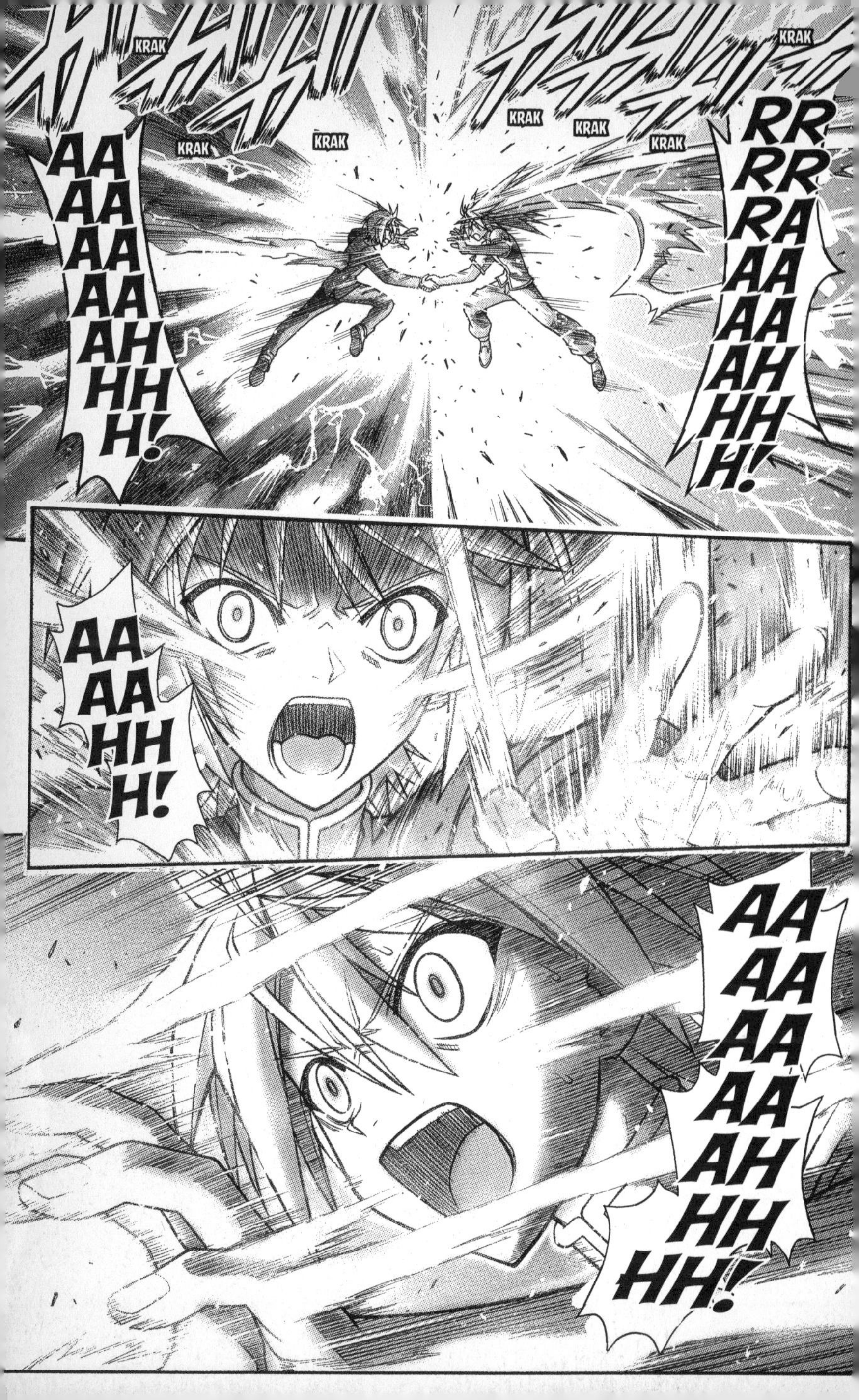
KRAK
KRAK
KRAK
KRAK
RRRRRAAAAAAAAHHHH!
KRAK
KRAK
KRAK
AAAAAAAAAHHHH!
AAAAHHH!
AAAAAAAAAHHHHH!

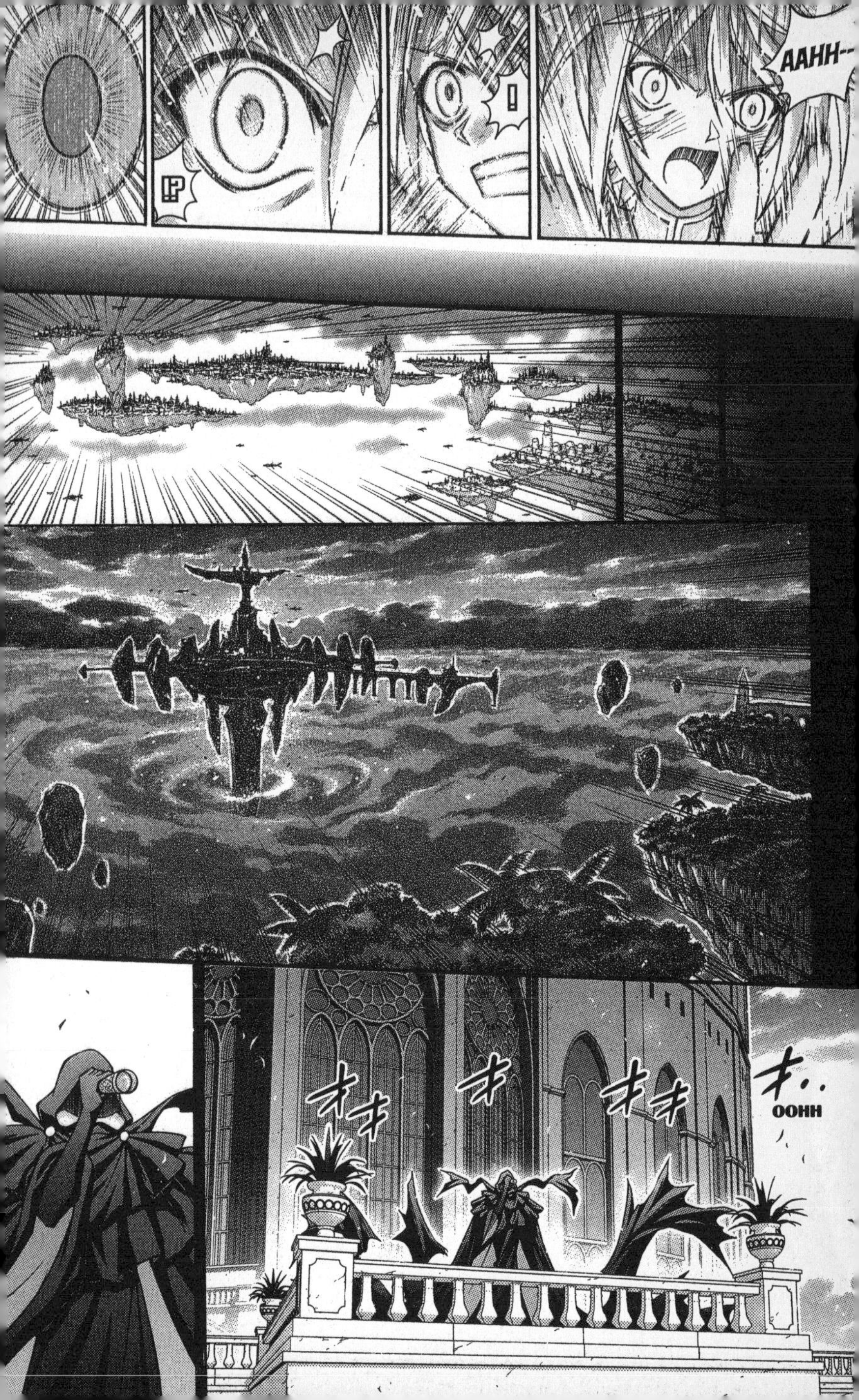
AAHH--
!
!?
オ..
OOHH
オオ
オオ
オオ

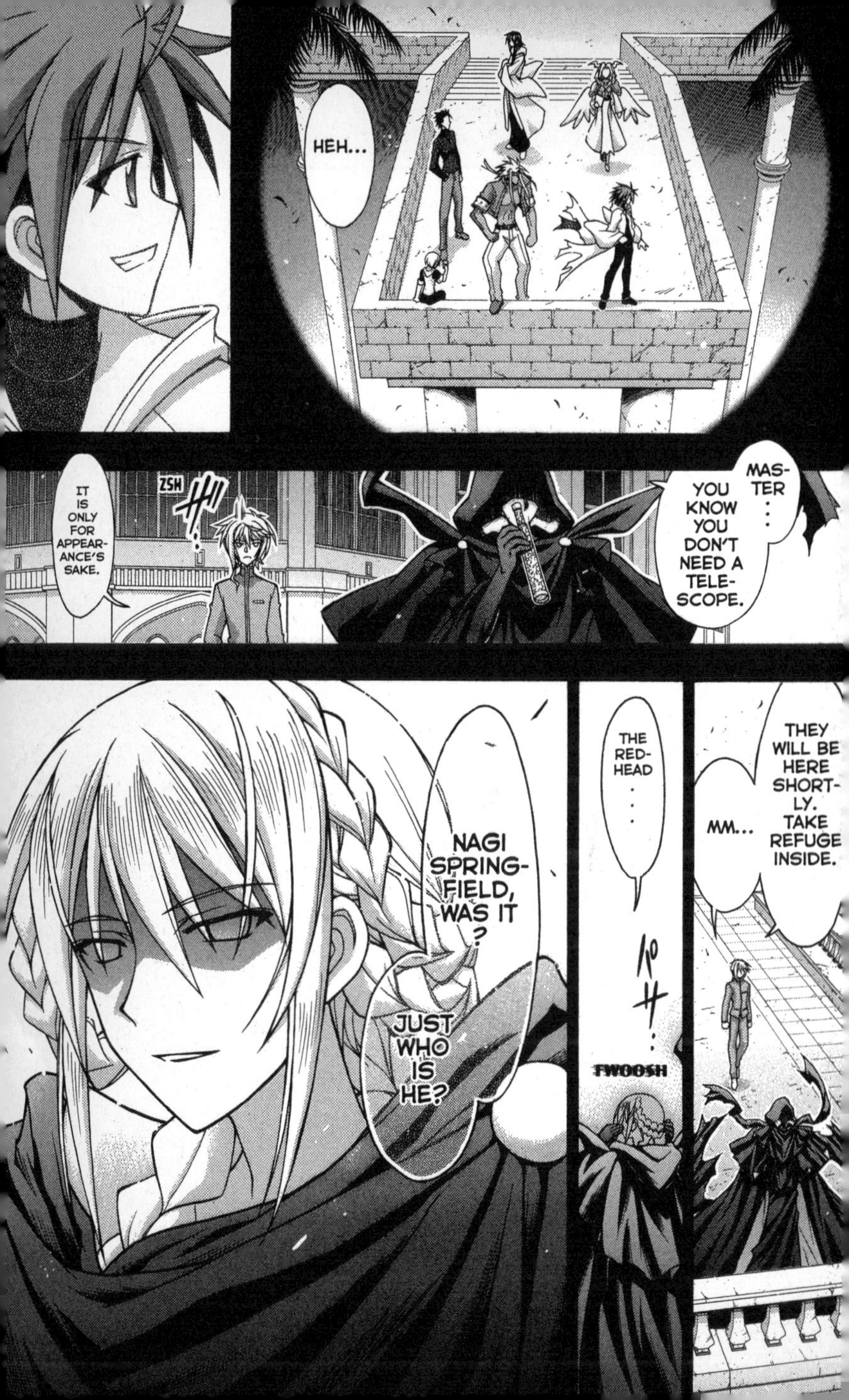
HEH...
MASTER... YOU KNOW YOU DON'T NEED A TELESCOPE.
ZSH
IT IS ONLY FOR APPEARANCE'S SAKE.
THEY WILL BE HERE SHORTLY. TAKE REFUGE INSIDE.
MM...
THE REDHEAD...
FWOOSH
NAGI SPRINGFIELD, WAS IT?
JUST WHO IS HE?

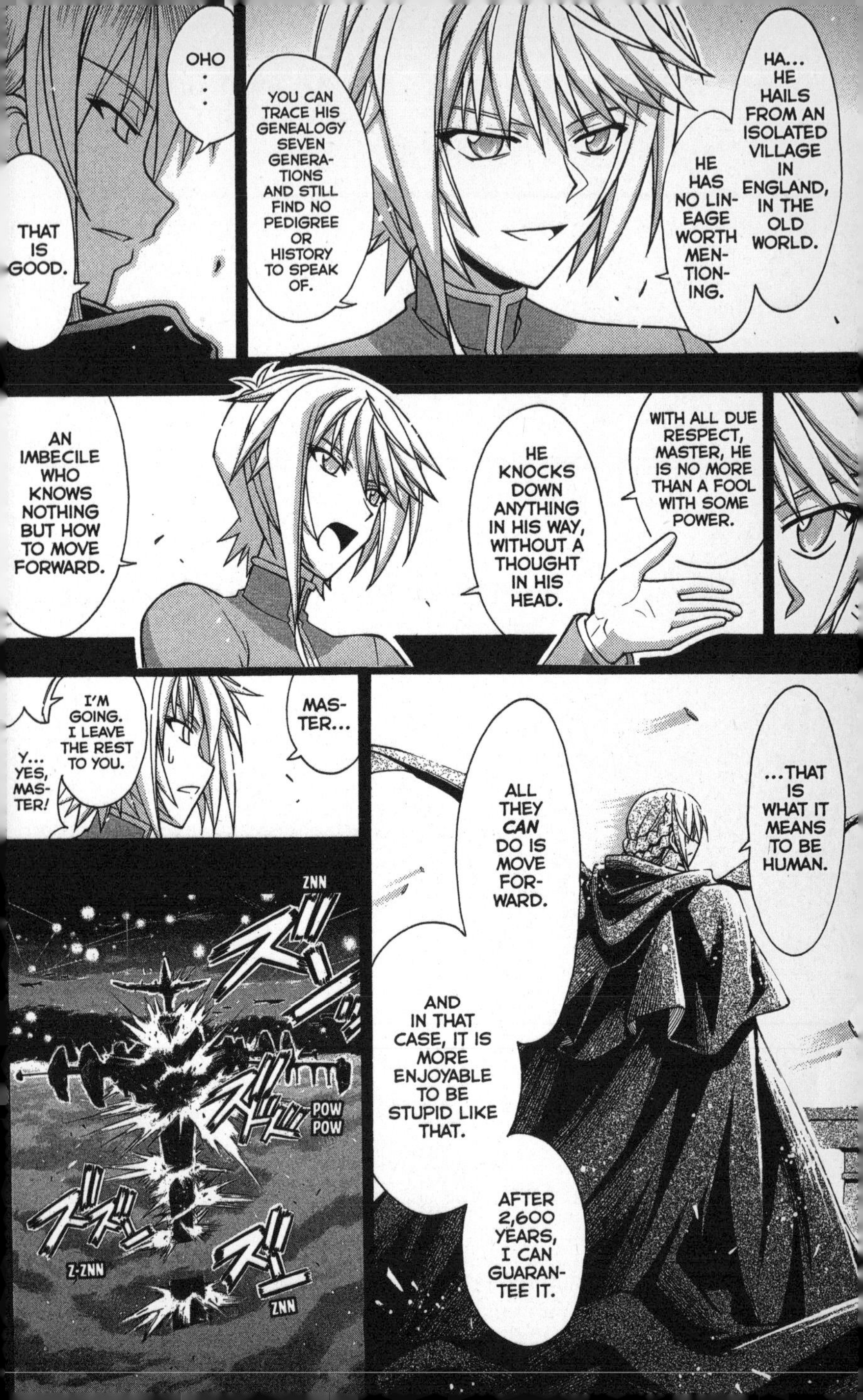
HA... HE HAILS FROM AN ISOLATED VILLAGE IN ENGLAND, IN THE OLD WORLD.
HE HAS NO LINEAGE WORTH MENTIONING.
YOU CAN TRACE HIS GENEALOGY SEVEN GENERATIONS AND STILL FIND NO PEDIGREE OR HISTORY TO SPEAK OF.
OHO...
THAT IS GOOD.
WITH ALL DUE RESPECT, MASTER, HE IS NO MORE THAN A FOOL WITH SOME POWER.
HE KNOCKS DOWN ANYTHING IN HIS WAY, WITHOUT A THOUGHT IN HIS HEAD.
AN IMBECILE WHO KNOWS NOTHING BUT HOW TO MOVE FORWARD.
...THAT IS WHAT IT MEANS TO BE HUMAN.
ALL THEY *CAN* DO IS MOVE FORWARD.
AND IN THAT CASE, IT IS MORE ENJOYABLE TO BE STUPID LIKE THAT.
AFTER 2,600 YEARS, I CAN GUARANTEE IT.
MASTER...
I'M GOING. I LEAVE THE REST TO YOU.
Y... YES, MASTER!
ZNN
POW POW
Z-ZNN
ZNN

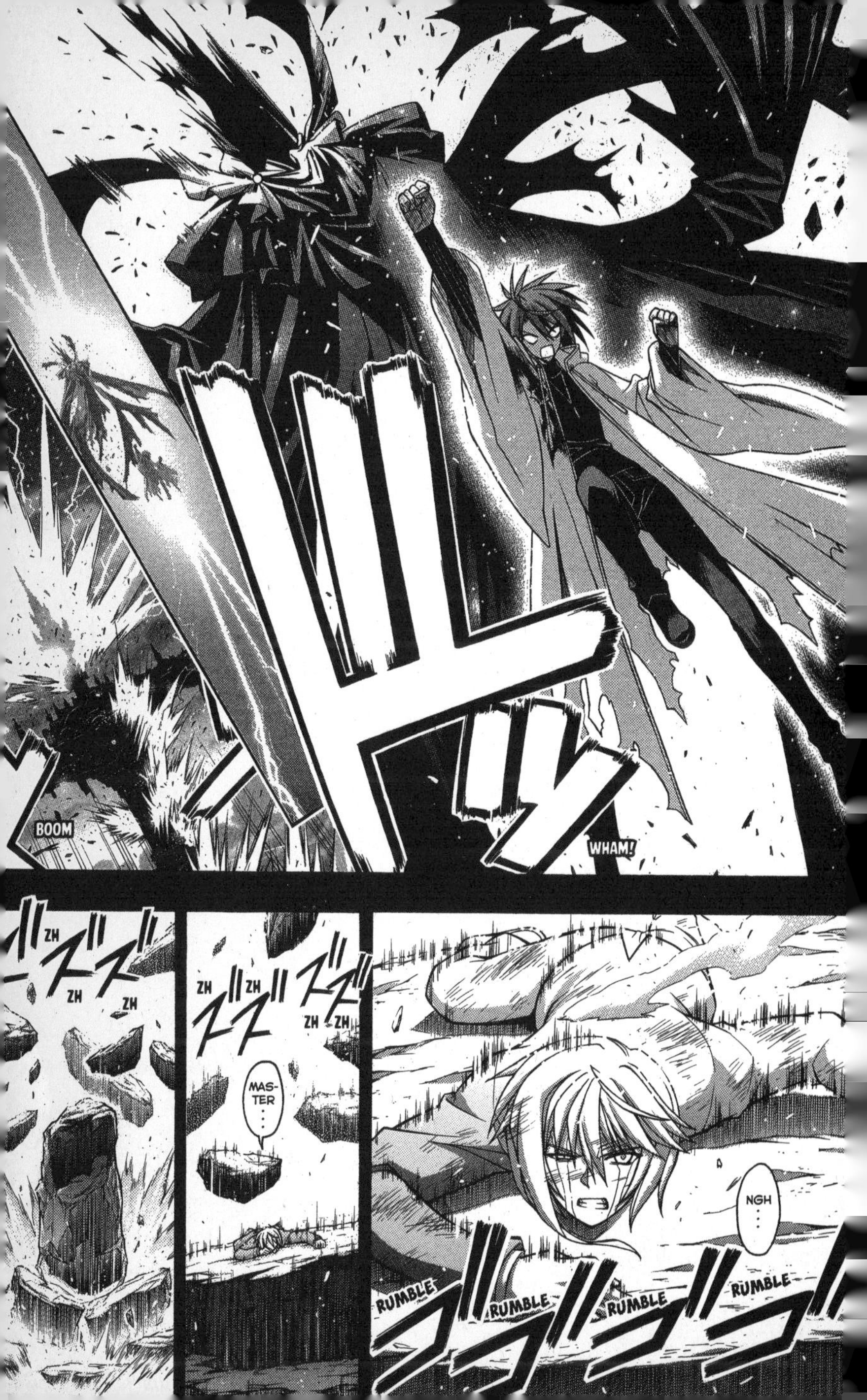
WHAM!
BOOM
NGH...
RUMBLE
RUMBLE
RUMBLE
RUMBLE
ZH
ZH
ZH
ZH
MASTER...
ZH
ZH
ZH

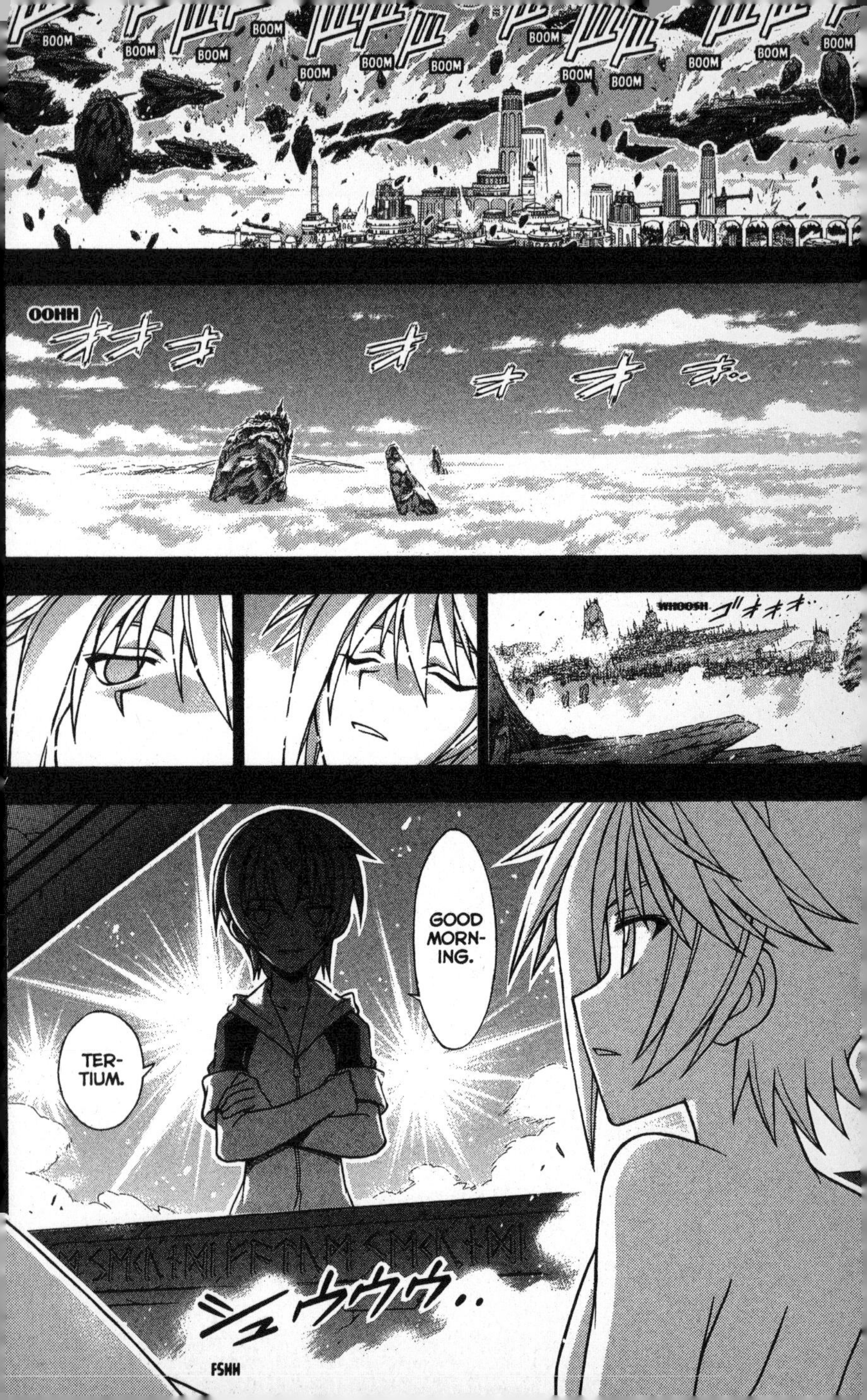
BOOM
BOOM
BOOM
BOOM
BOOM
BOOM
BOOM
BOOM
BOOM
BOOM
BOOM
BOOM
BOOM
OOHH
WHOOSH
GOOD MORNING.
TERTIUM.
FSHH

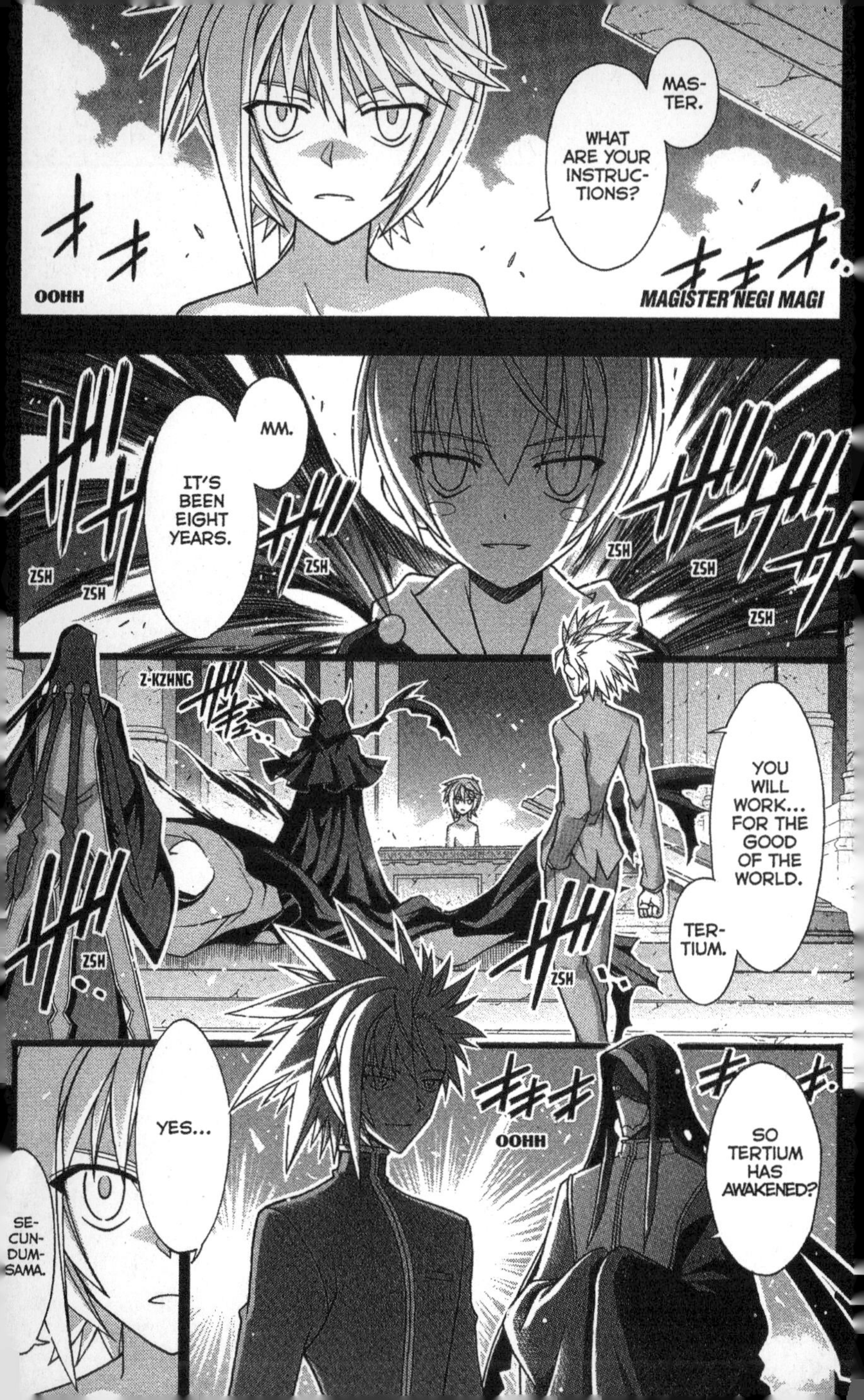
MAGISTER NEGI MAGI
MAS-TER.
WHAT ARE YOUR INSTRUCTIONS?
OOHH
ZSH
ZSH
ZSH
MM.
IT'S BEEN EIGHT YEARS.
ZSH
ZSH
ZSH
YOU WILL WORK... FOR THE GOOD OF THE WORLD.
TER-TIUM.
Z-KZHNG
ZSH
ZSH
SO TERTIUM HAS AWAKENED?
OOHH
YES...
SE-CUN-DUM-SAMA.

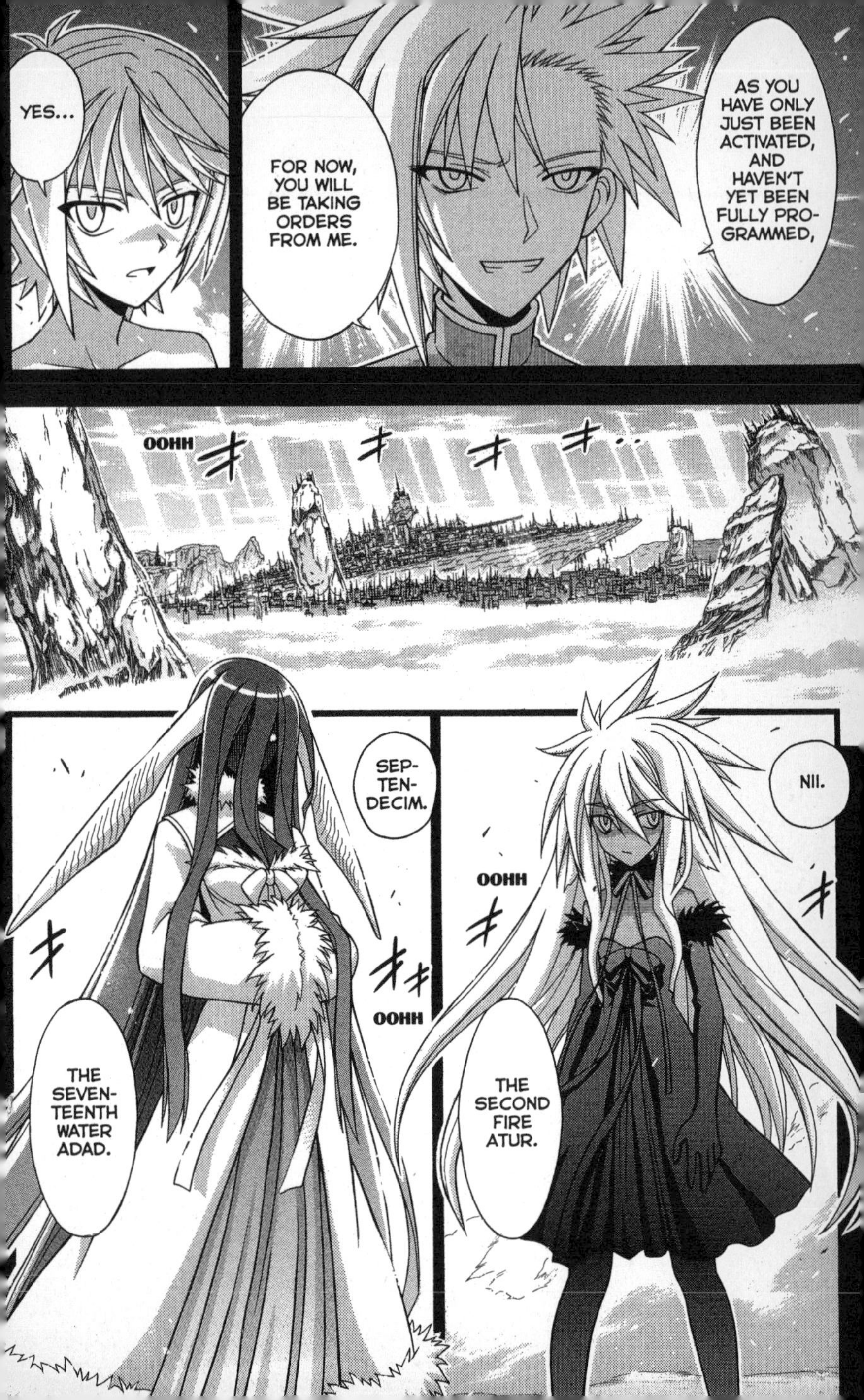
AS YOU HAVE ONLY JUST BEEN ACTIVATED, AND HAVEN'T YET BEEN FULLY PRO-GRAMMED,
FOR NOW, YOU WILL BE TAKING ORDERS FROM ME.
YES...
OOHH
NII.
OOHH
THE SECOND FIRE ATUR.
SEP-TEN-DECIM.
OOHH
THE SEVEN-TEENTH WATER ADAD.

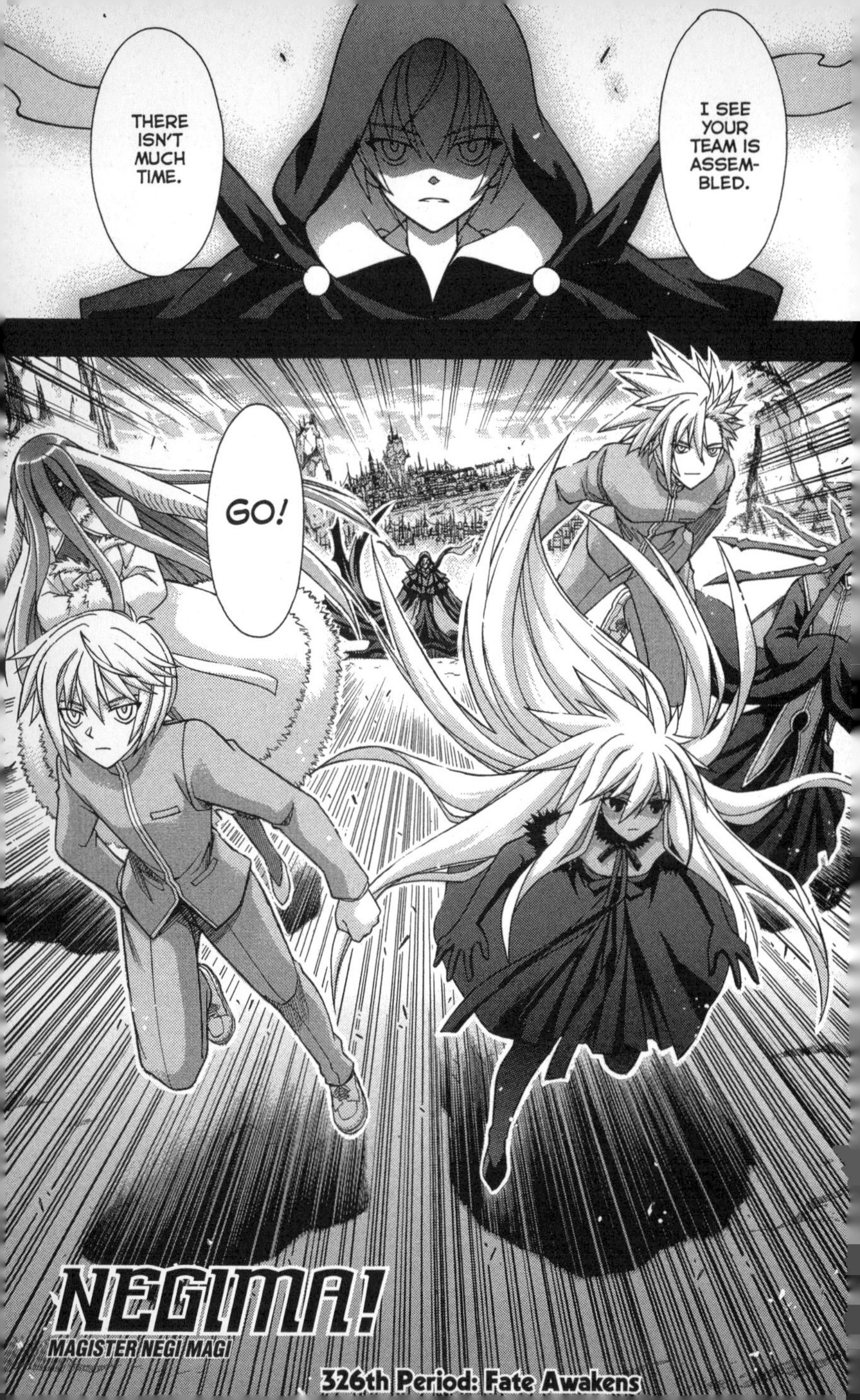
I SEE YOUR TEAM IS ASSEMBLED.
THERE ISN'T MUCH TIME.
GO!
NEGIMA!
MAGISTER NEGI MAGI
326th Period: Fate Awakens

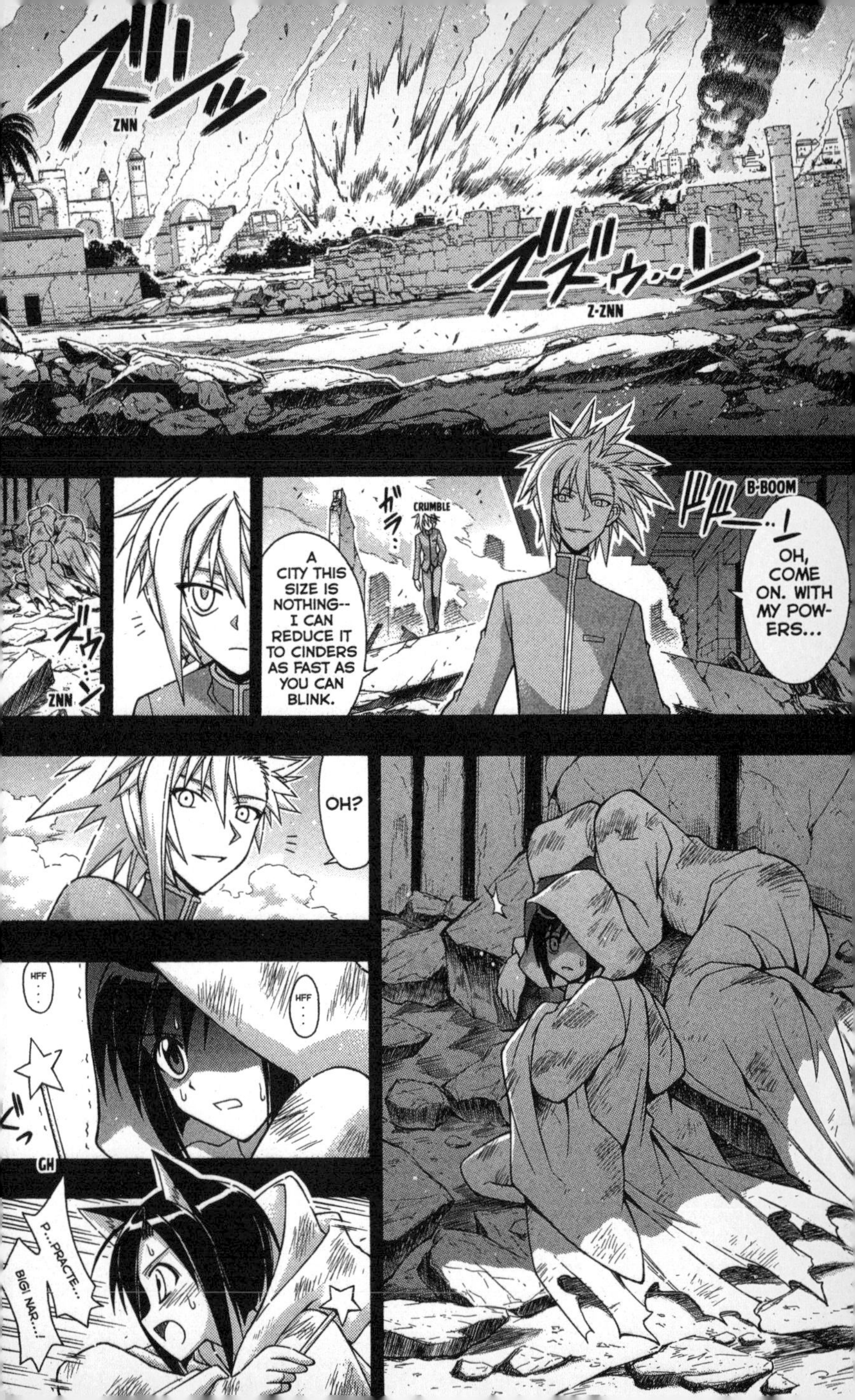
ZNN
Z-ZNN
B-BOOM
OH, COME ON. WITH MY POWERS...
CRUMBLE
A CITY THIS SIZE IS NOTHING-- I CAN REDUCE IT TO CINDERS AS FAST AS YOU CAN BLINK.
ZNN
OH?
HFF...
HFF...
GH
P...PRACTE... BIGI NAR...!

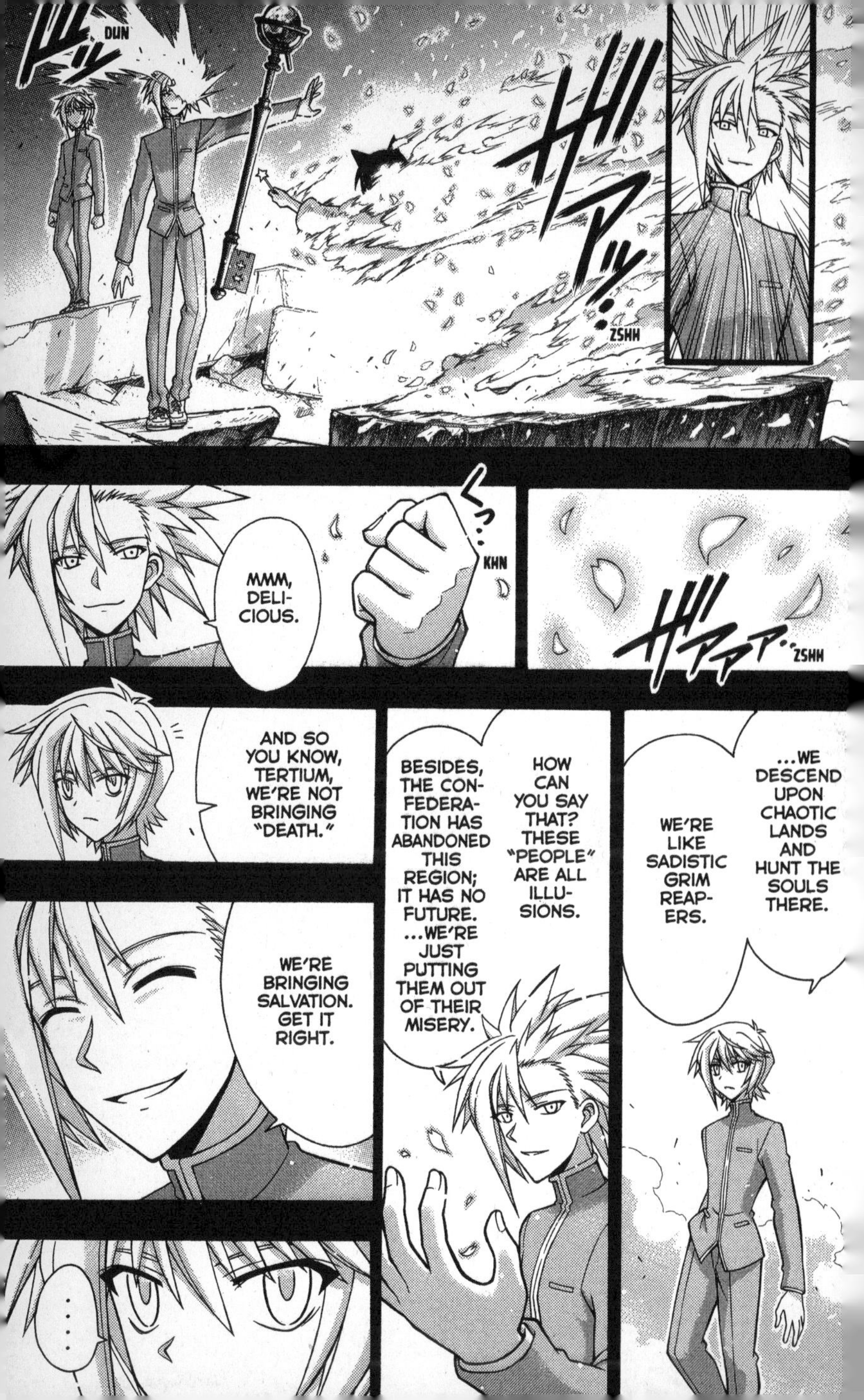
DUN
ZSHH
ZSHH
KHN
MMM, DELICIOUS.
WE'RE LIKE SADISTIC GRIM REAPERS.
...WE DESCEND UPON CHAOTIC LANDS AND HUNT THE SOULS THERE.
HOW CAN YOU SAY THAT? THESE "PEOPLE" ARE ALL ILLUSIONS.
BESIDES, THE CONFEDERATION HAS ABANDONED THIS REGION; IT HAS NO FUTURE. ...WE'RE JUST PUTTING THEM OUT OF THEIR MISERY.
AND SO YOU KNOW, TERTIUM, WE'RE NOT BRINGING "DEATH."
WE'RE BRINGING SALVATION. GET IT RIGHT.
...

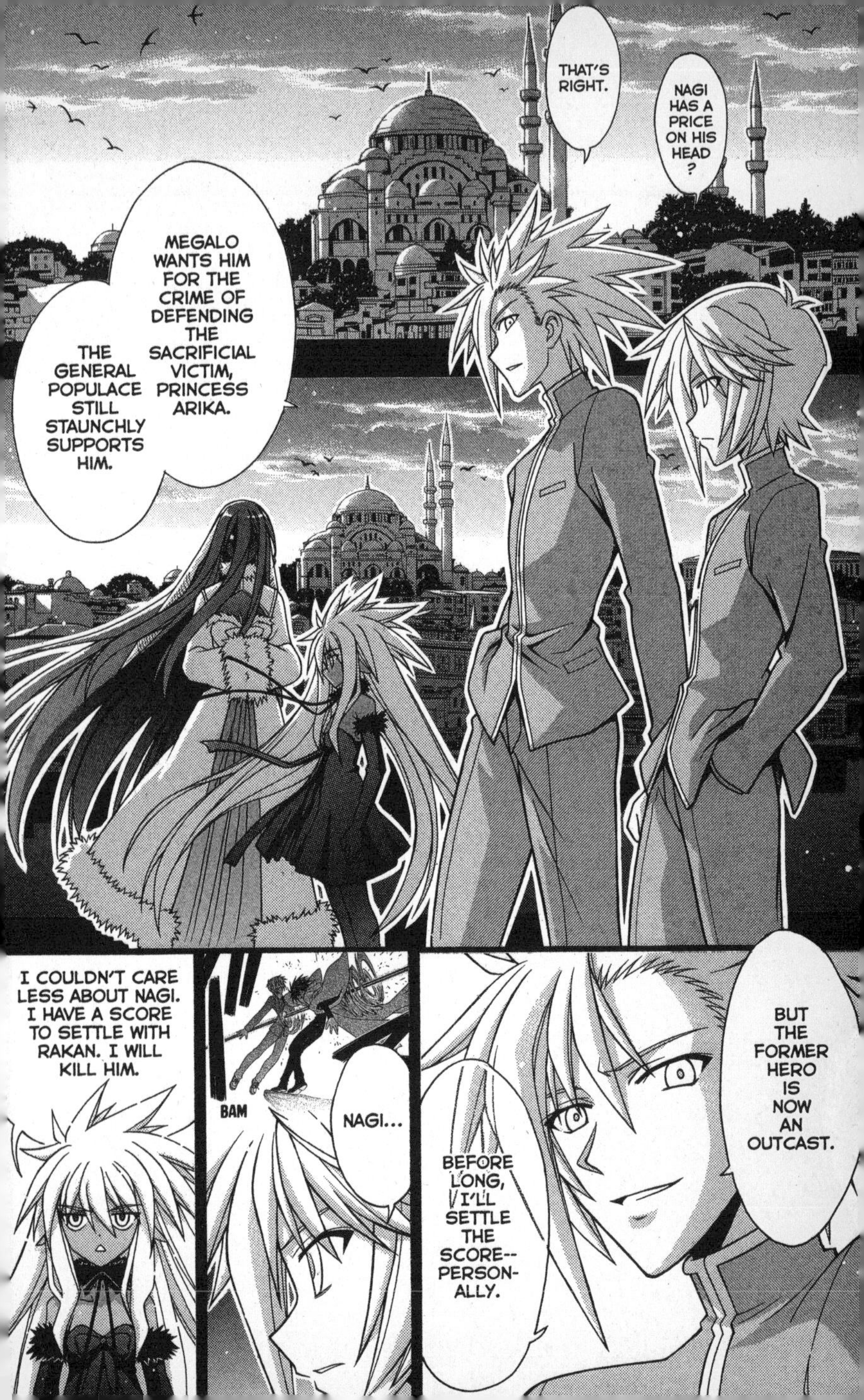
NAGI HAS A PRICE ON HIS HEAD?
THAT'S RIGHT.
MEGALO WANTS HIM FOR THE CRIME OF DEFENDING THE SACRIFICIAL VICTIM, PRINCESS ARIKA.
THE GENERAL POPULACE STILL STAUNCHLY SUPPORTS HIM.
BUT THE FORMER HERO IS NOW AN OUTCAST.
BEFORE LONG, I'LL SETTLE THE SCORE--PERSONALLY.
NAGI...
BAM
I COULDN'T CARE LESS ABOUT NAGI. I HAVE A SCORE TO SETTLE WITH RAKAN. I WILL KILL HIM.

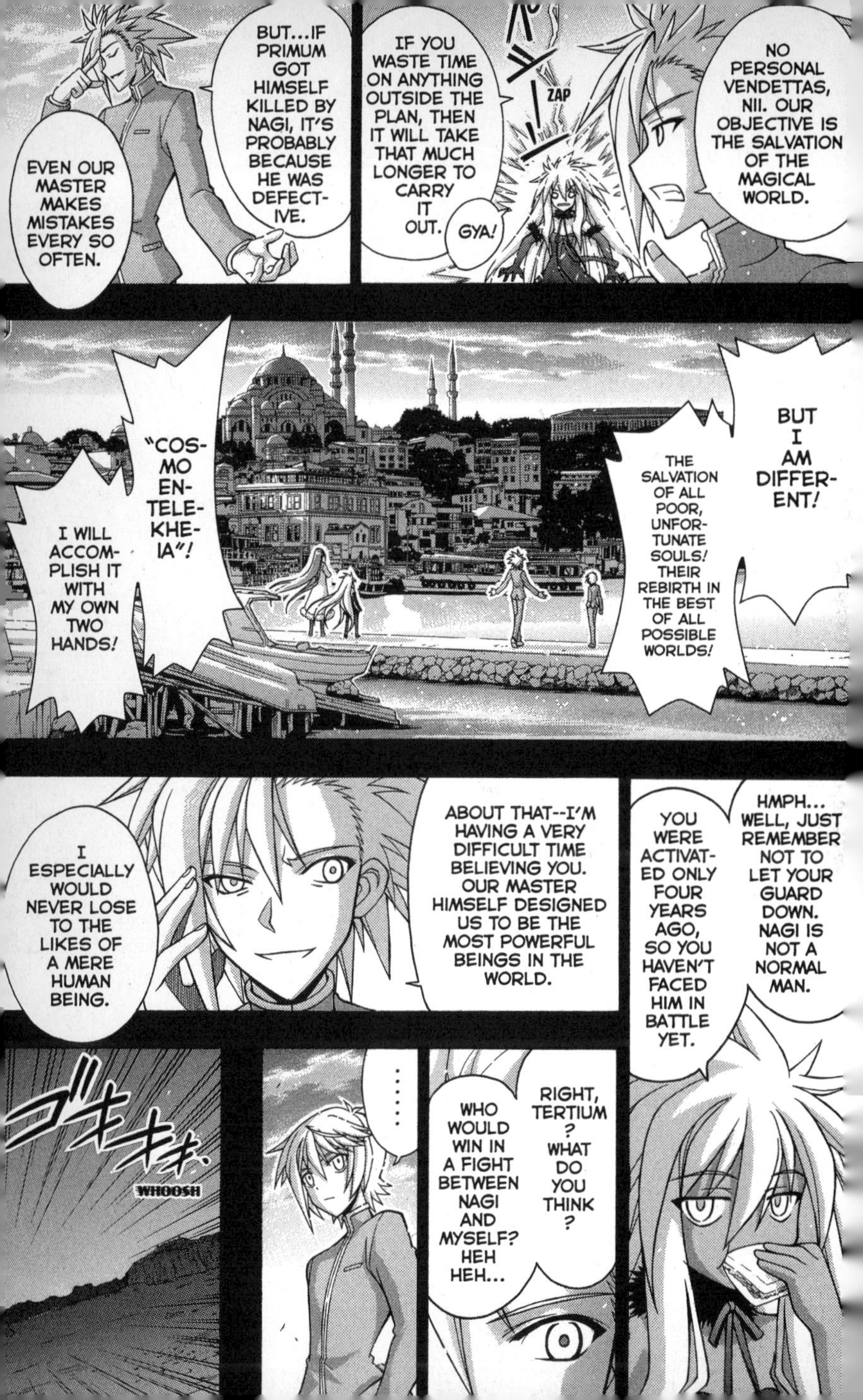
NO PERSONAL VENDETTAS, NII. OUR OBJECTIVE IS THE SALVATION OF THE MAGICAL WORLD.
ZAP
GYA!
IF YOU WASTE TIME ON ANYTHING OUTSIDE THE PLAN, THEN IT WILL TAKE THAT MUCH LONGER TO CARRY IT OUT.
BUT...IF PRIMUM GOT HIMSELF KILLED BY NAGI, IT'S PROBABLY BECAUSE HE WAS DEFECTIVE.
EVEN OUR MASTER MAKES MISTAKES EVERY SO OFTEN.
BUT I AM DIFFERENT!
THE SALVATION OF ALL POOR, UNFORTUNATE SOULS! THEIR REBIRTH IN THE BEST OF ALL POSSIBLE WORLDS!
"COSMO ENTELEKHEIA"!
I WILL ACCOMPLISH IT WITH MY OWN TWO HANDS!
HMPH... WELL, JUST REMEMBER NOT TO LET YOUR GUARD DOWN. NAGI IS NOT A NORMAL MAN.
YOU WERE ACTIVATED ONLY FOUR YEARS AGO, SO YOU HAVEN'T FACED HIM IN BATTLE YET.
ABOUT THAT--I'M HAVING A VERY DIFFICULT TIME BELIEVING YOU. OUR MASTER HIMSELF DESIGNED US TO BE THE MOST POWERFUL BEINGS IN THE WORLD.
I ESPECIALLY WOULD NEVER LOSE TO THE LIKES OF A MERE HUMAN BEING.
RIGHT, TERTIUM? WHAT DO YOU THINK?
WHO WOULD WIN IN A FIGHT BETWEEN NAGI AND MYSELF? HEH HEH...
......
WHOOSH

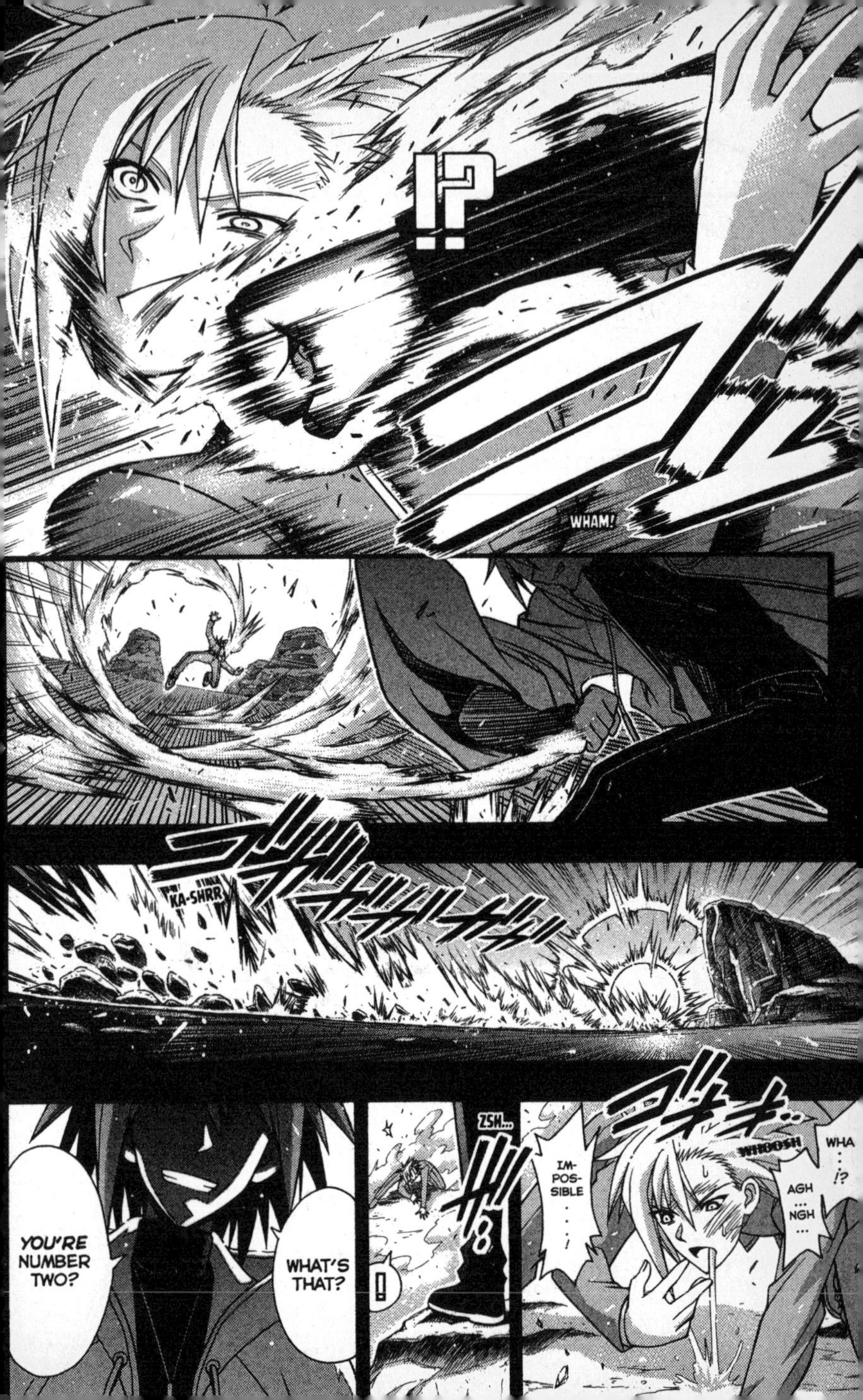
!?
WHAM!
KA-SHRR
WHOOSH
WHA...!?
AGH... NGH...
IM-POSSIBLE......
ZSH...
!
WHAT'S THAT?
YOU'RE NUMBER TWO?

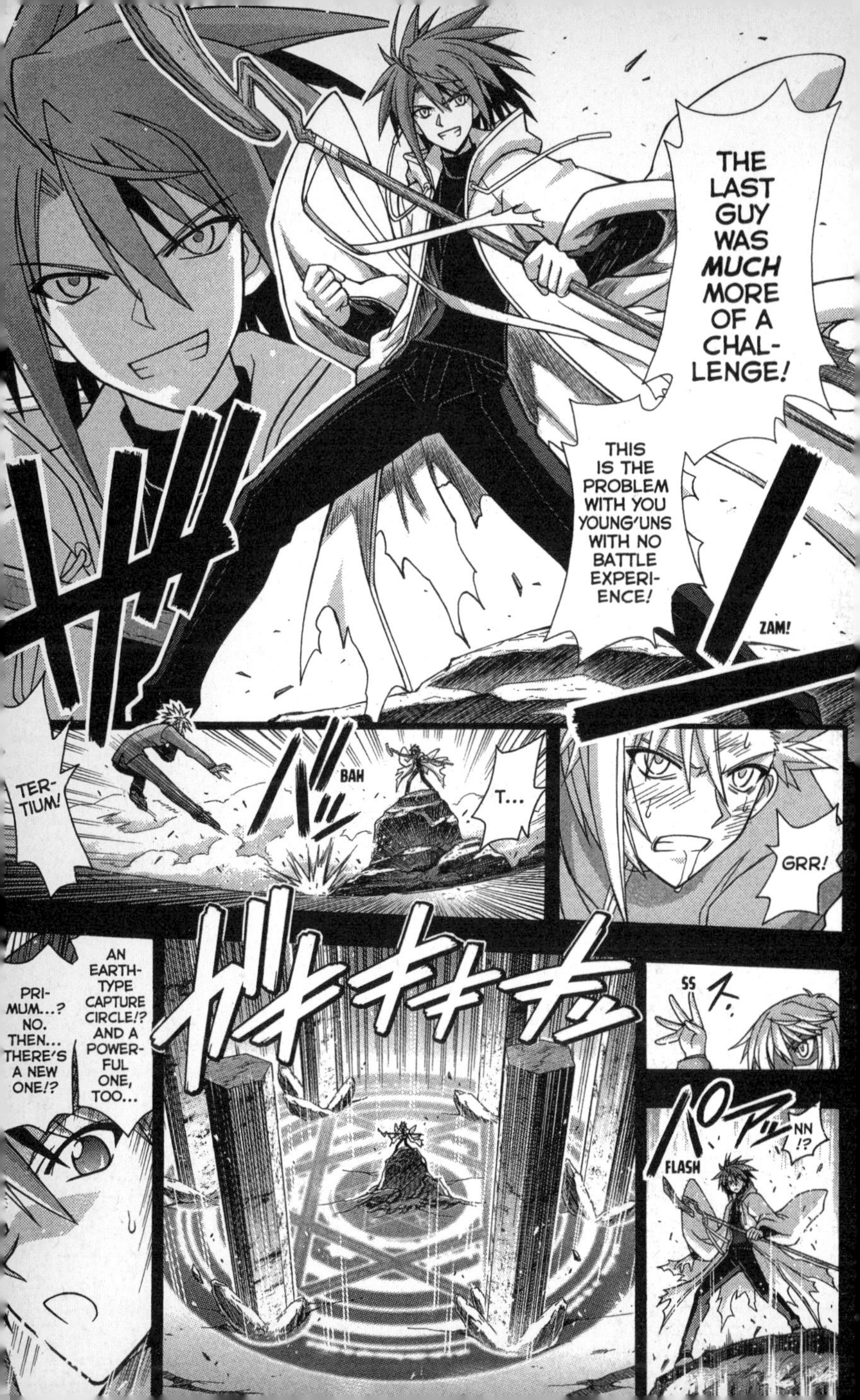
THE LAST GUY WAS MUCH MORE OF A CHALLENGE!
THIS IS THE PROBLEM WITH YOU YOUNG'UNS WITH NO BATTLE EXPERIENCE!
ZAM!
GRR!
T...
BAH
TER-TIUM!
SS
NN!?
FLASH
AN EARTH-TYPE CAPTURE CIRCLE!? AND A POWERFUL ONE, TOO...
PRI-MUM...? NO. THEN... THERE'S A NEW ONE!?

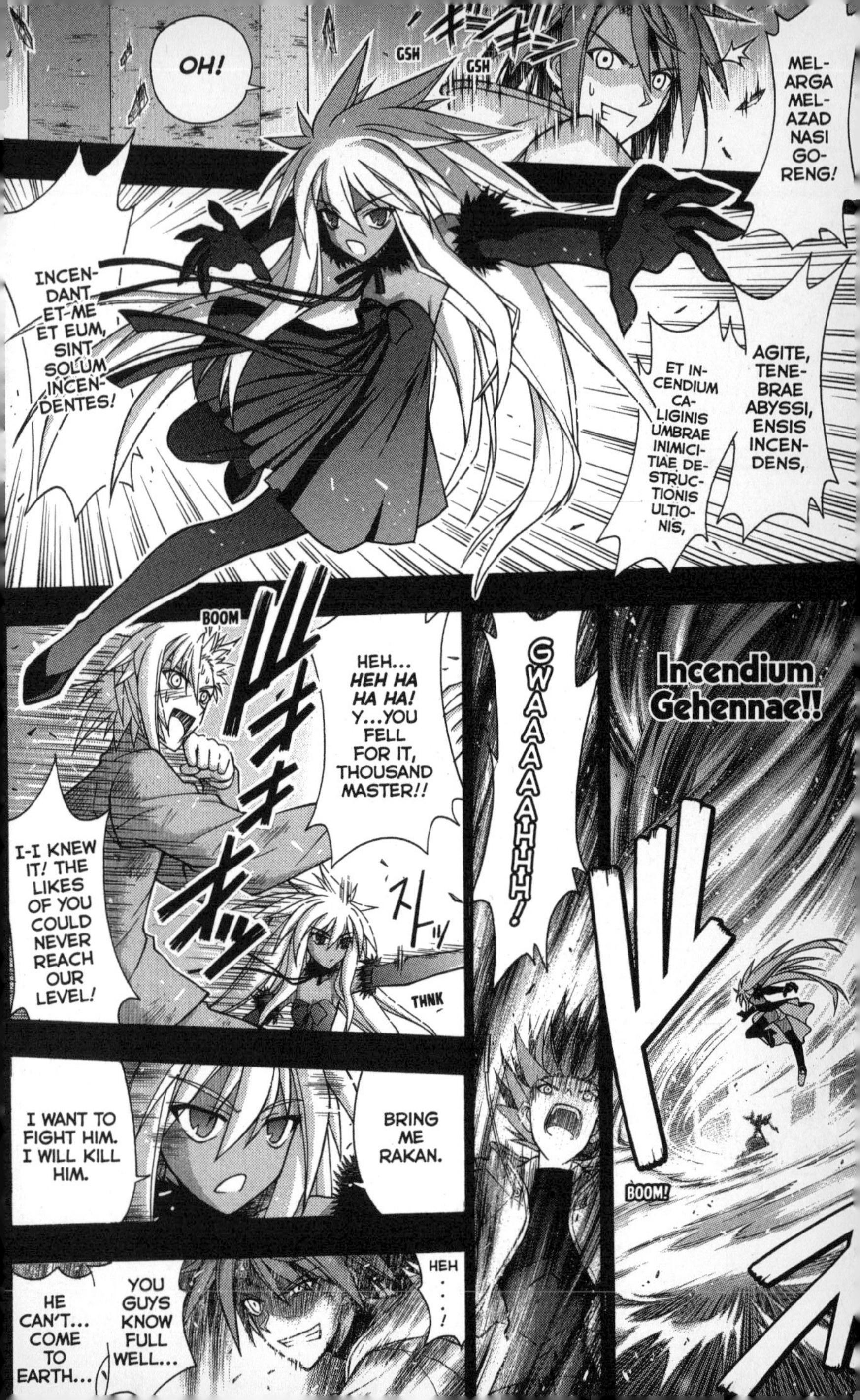

MEL-ARGA MEL-AZAD NASI GO-RENG!
GSH
GSH
OH!
AGITE, TENEBRAE ABYSSI, ENSIS INCENDENS,
ET INCENDIUM CALIGINIS UMBRAE INIMICITIAE DESTRUCTIONIS ULTIONIS,
INCENDANT ET ME ET EUM, SINT SOLUM INCENDENTES!
Incendium Gehennae!!
GWAAAAAAAHHHH!
BOOM!
HEH... HEH HA HA HA! Y...YOU FELL FOR IT, THOUSAND MASTER!!
BOOM
I-I KNEW IT! THE LIKES OF YOU COULD NEVER REACH OUR LEVEL!
THNK
BRING ME RAKAN.
I WANT TO FIGHT HIM. I WILL KILL HIM.
HEH...!
YOU GUYS KNOW FULL WELL...
HE CAN'T... COME TO EARTH...

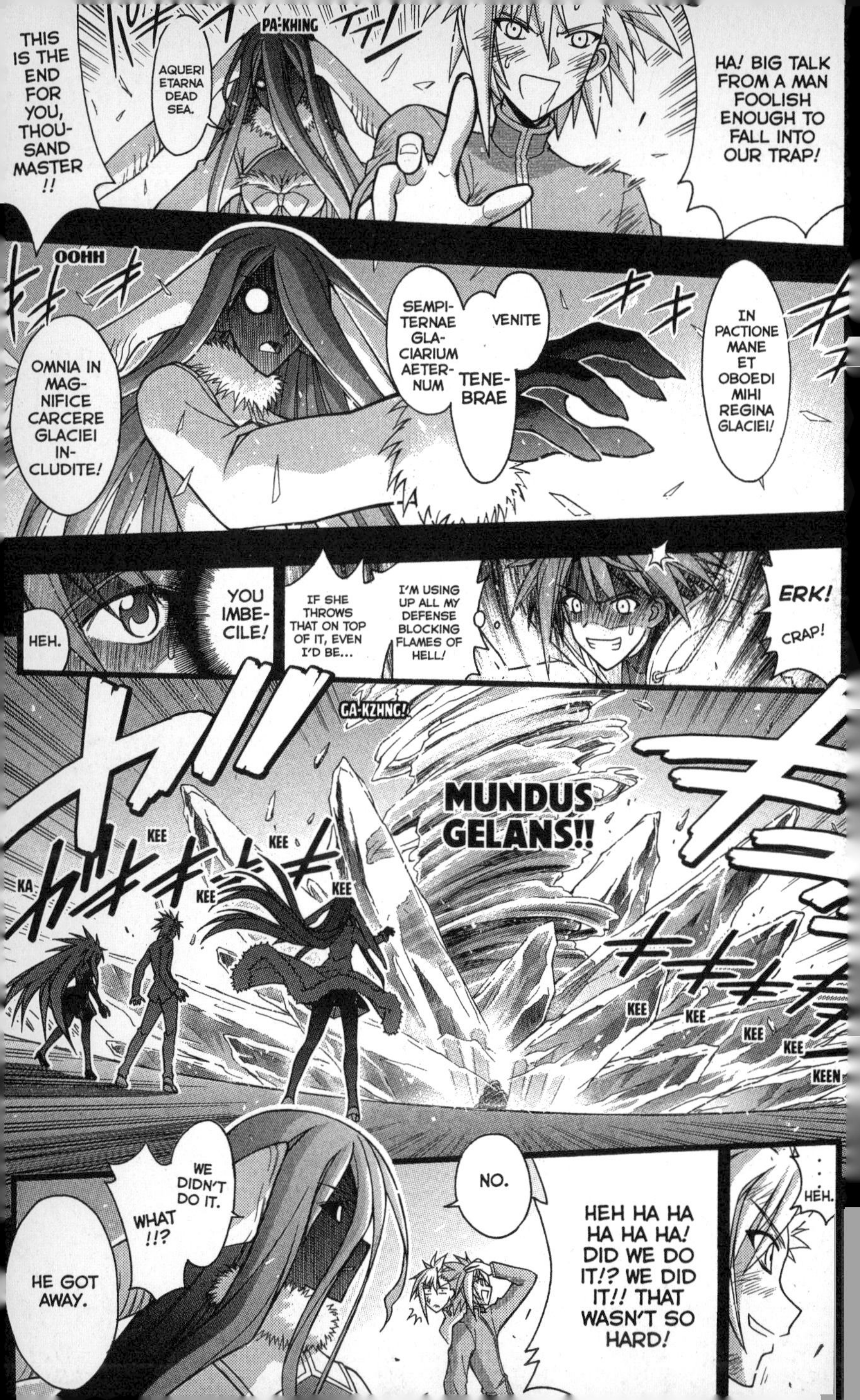
HA! BIG TALK FROM A MAN FOOLISH ENOUGH TO FALL INTO OUR TRAP!
PA-KHING
AQUERI ETARNA DEAD SEA.
THIS IS THE END FOR YOU, THOUSAND MASTER!!
IN PACTIONE MANE ET OBOEDI MIHI REGINA GLACIEI!
VENITE
TENEBRAE
SEMPITERNAE GLACIARIUM AETERNUM
OOHH
OMNIA IN MAGNIFICE CARCERE GLACIEI INCLUDITE!
ERK!
CRAP!
I'M USING UP ALL MY DEFENSE BLOCKING FLAMES OF HELL!
IF SHE THROWS THAT ON TOP OF IT, EVEN I'D BE...
YOU IMBECILE!
HEH.
GA-KZHNG!
MUNDUS GELANS!!
KEE KEE KEE KEE KEEN
KEE KEE KEE KEE
KA
HEH.
HEH HA HA HA HA HA! DID WE DO IT!? WE DID IT!! THAT WASN'T SO HARD!
NO.
WE DIDN'T DO IT.
WHAT!!?
HE GOT AWAY.

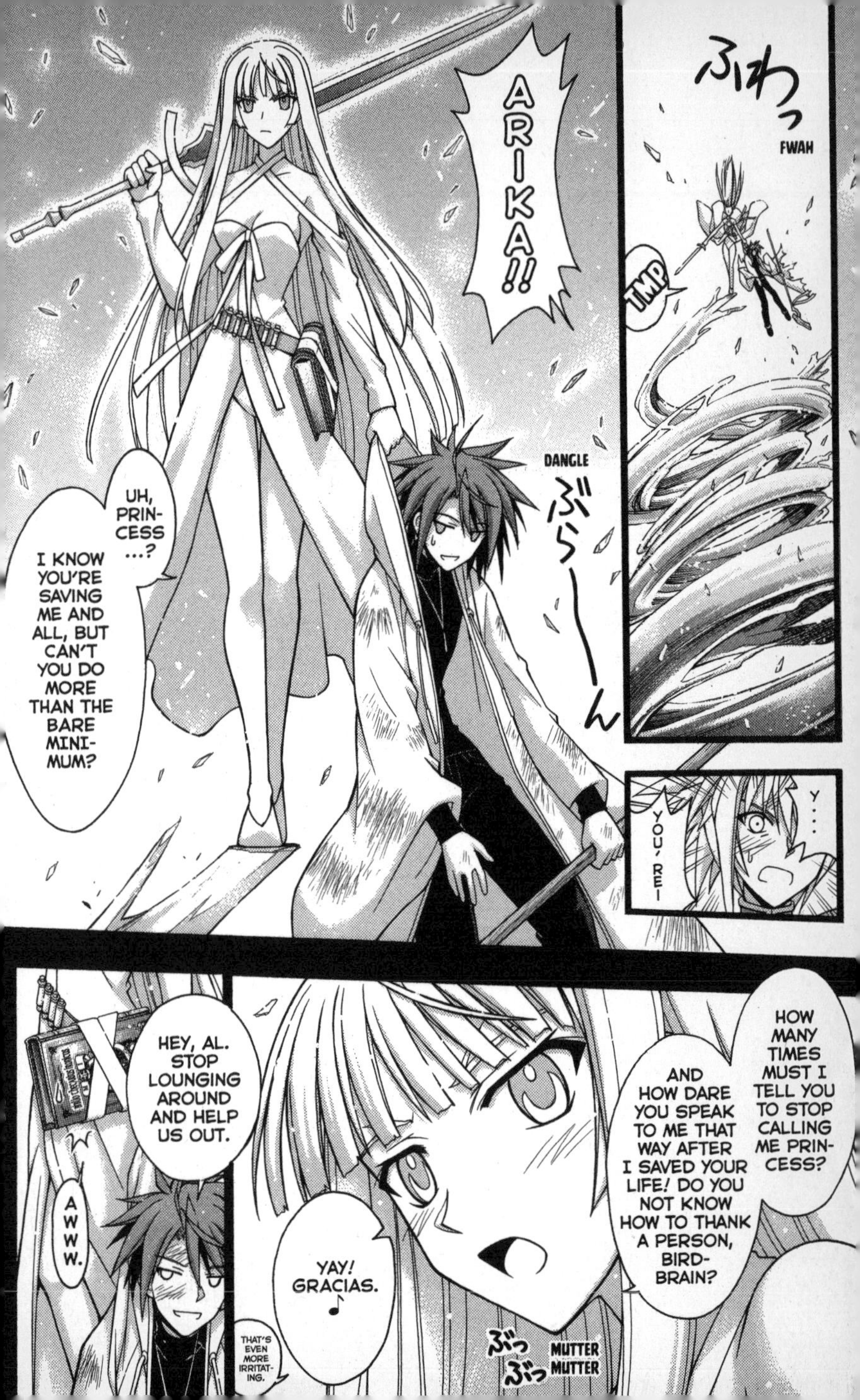
ふわっ
FWAH
TMP
Y... YOU'RE!
ARIKA!!
DANGLE
ぶらーーん
UH, PRINCESS...?
I KNOW YOU'RE SAVING ME AND ALL, BUT CAN'T YOU DO MORE THAN THE BARE MINIMUM?
HOW MANY TIMES MUST I TELL YOU TO STOP CALLING ME PRINCESS?
AND HOW DARE YOU SPEAK TO ME THAT WAY AFTER I SAVED YOUR LIFE! DO YOU NOT KNOW HOW TO THANK A PERSON, BIRD-BRAIN?
YAY! GRACIAS. ♪
ぶつぶつ
MUTTER MUTTER
THAT'S EVEN MORE IRRITATING.
HEY, AL. STOP LOUNGING AROUND AND HELP US OUT.
AWWW.

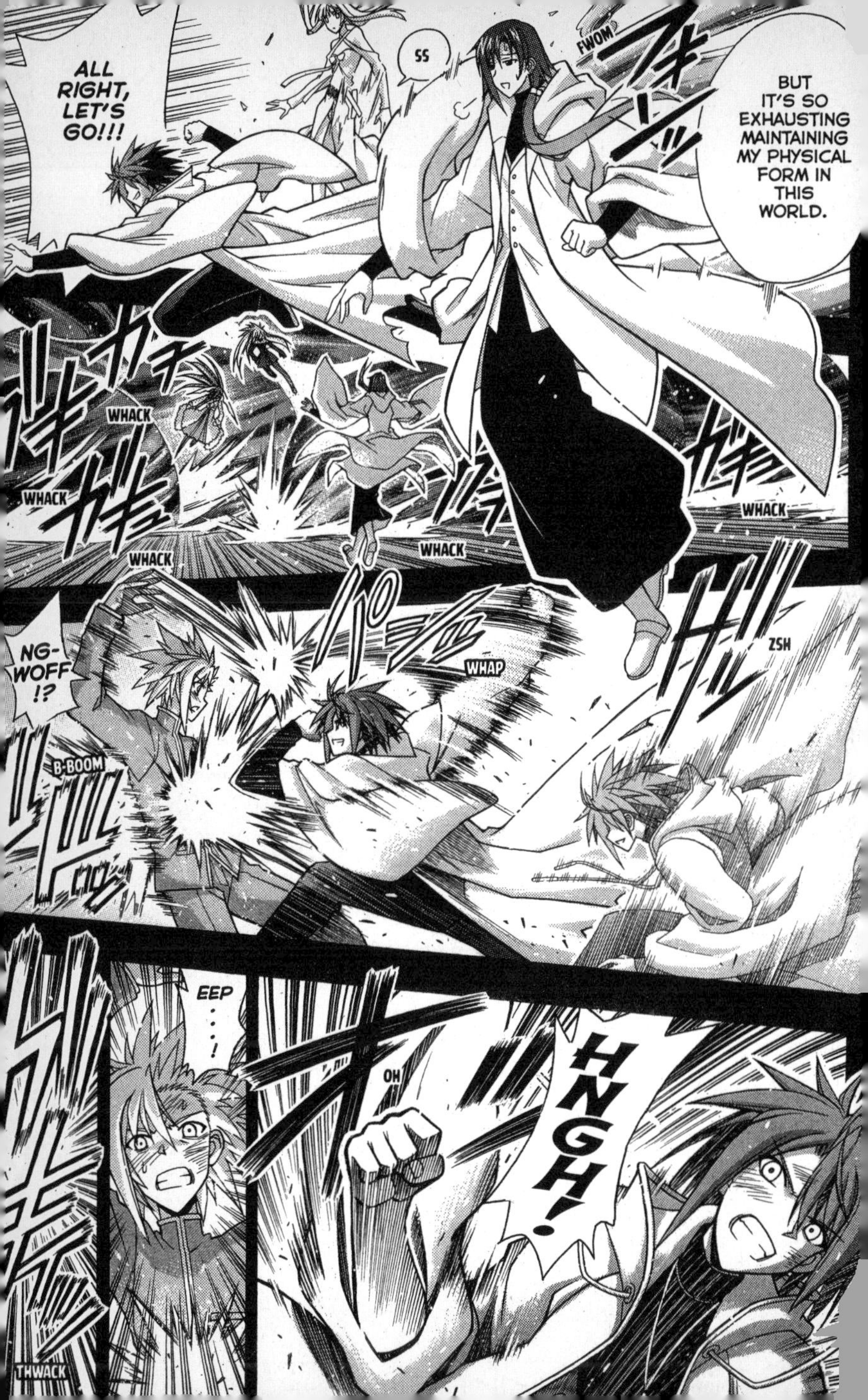
BUT IT'S SO EXHAUSTING MAINTAINING MY PHYSICAL FORM IN THIS WORLD.
FWOM
SS
ALL RIGHT, LET'S GO!!!
WHACK
WHACK
WHACK
WHACK
WHACK
ZSH
WHAP
NG-WOFF!?
B-BOOM
HNGH!
OH
EEP...!
THWACK

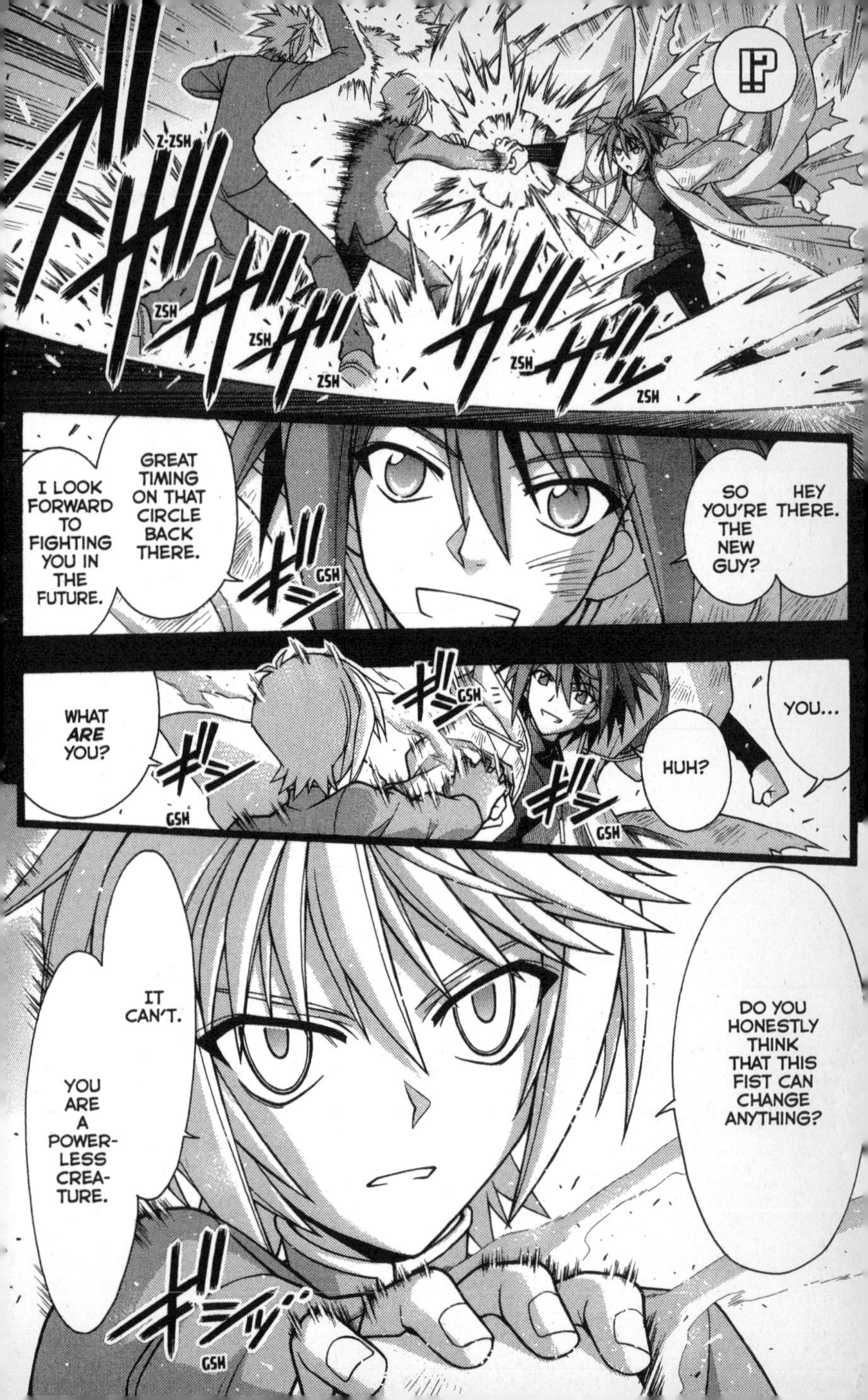
!?
ZSH
ZSH
ZSH
ZSH
ZSH
Z-ZSH
HEY THERE.
SO YOU'RE THE NEW GUY?
GSH
GREAT TIMING ON THAT CIRCLE BACK THERE.
I LOOK FORWARD TO FIGHTING YOU IN THE FUTURE.
YOU...
HUH?
GSH
GSH
GSH
WHAT *ARE* YOU?
DO YOU HONESTLY THINK THAT THIS FIST CAN CHANGE ANYTHING?
IT CAN'T.
YOU ARE A POWERLESS CREATURE.
GSH

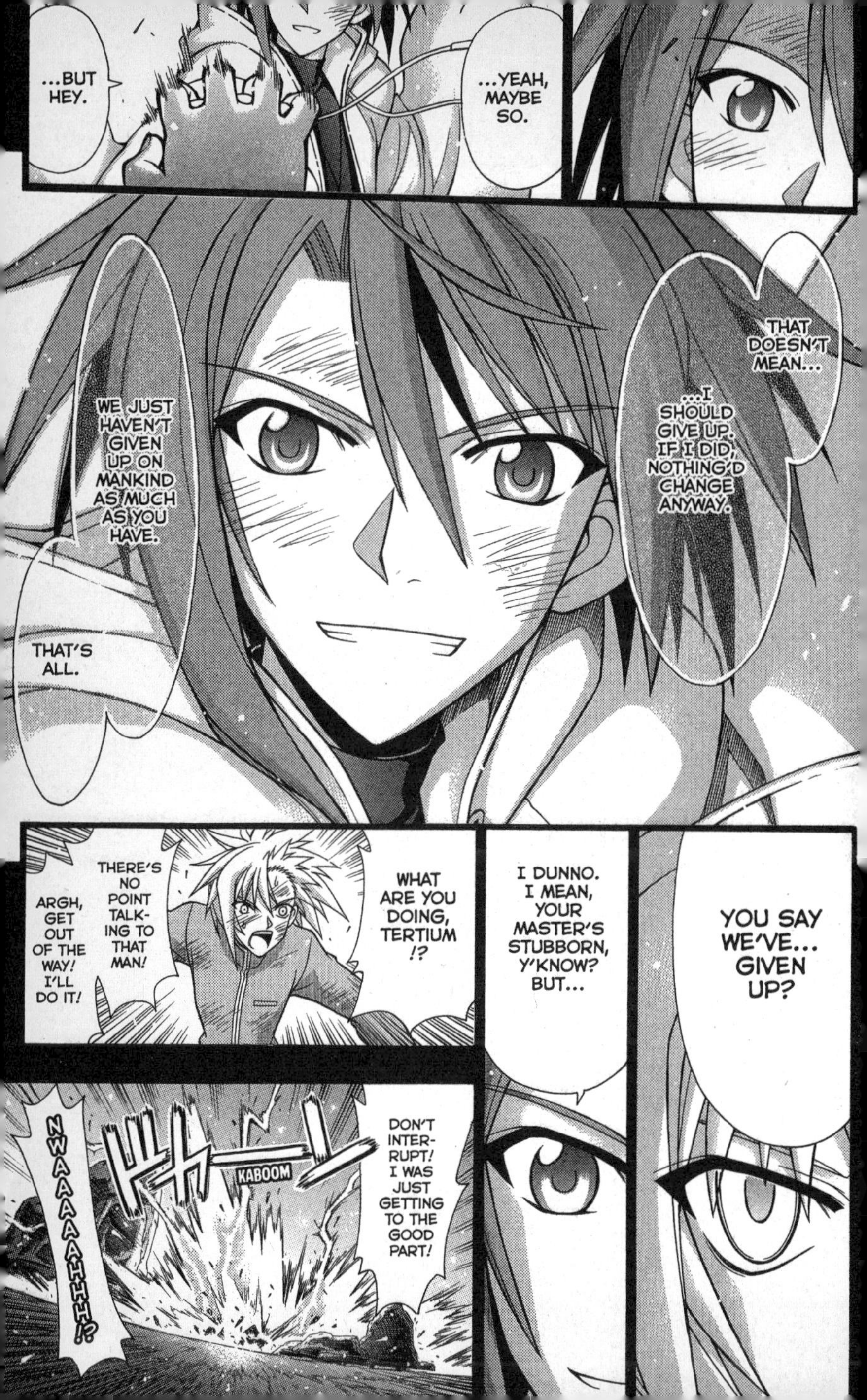
...YEAH, MAYBE SO.
...BUT HEY.
THAT DOESN'T MEAN...
...I SHOULD GIVE UP. IF I DID, NOTHING'D CHANGE ANYWAY.
WE JUST HAVEN'T GIVEN UP ON MANKIND AS MUCH AS YOU HAVE.
THAT'S ALL.
YOU SAY WE'VE... GIVEN UP?
I DUNNO. I MEAN, YOUR MASTER'S STUBBORN, Y'KNOW? BUT...
WHAT ARE YOU DOING, TERTIUM!?
THERE'S NO POINT TALKING TO THAT MAN!
ARGH, GET OUT OF THE WAY! I'LL DO IT!
DON'T INTERRUPT! I WAS JUST GETTING TO THE GOOD PART!
KABOOM
NWAAAAAAHHH!?

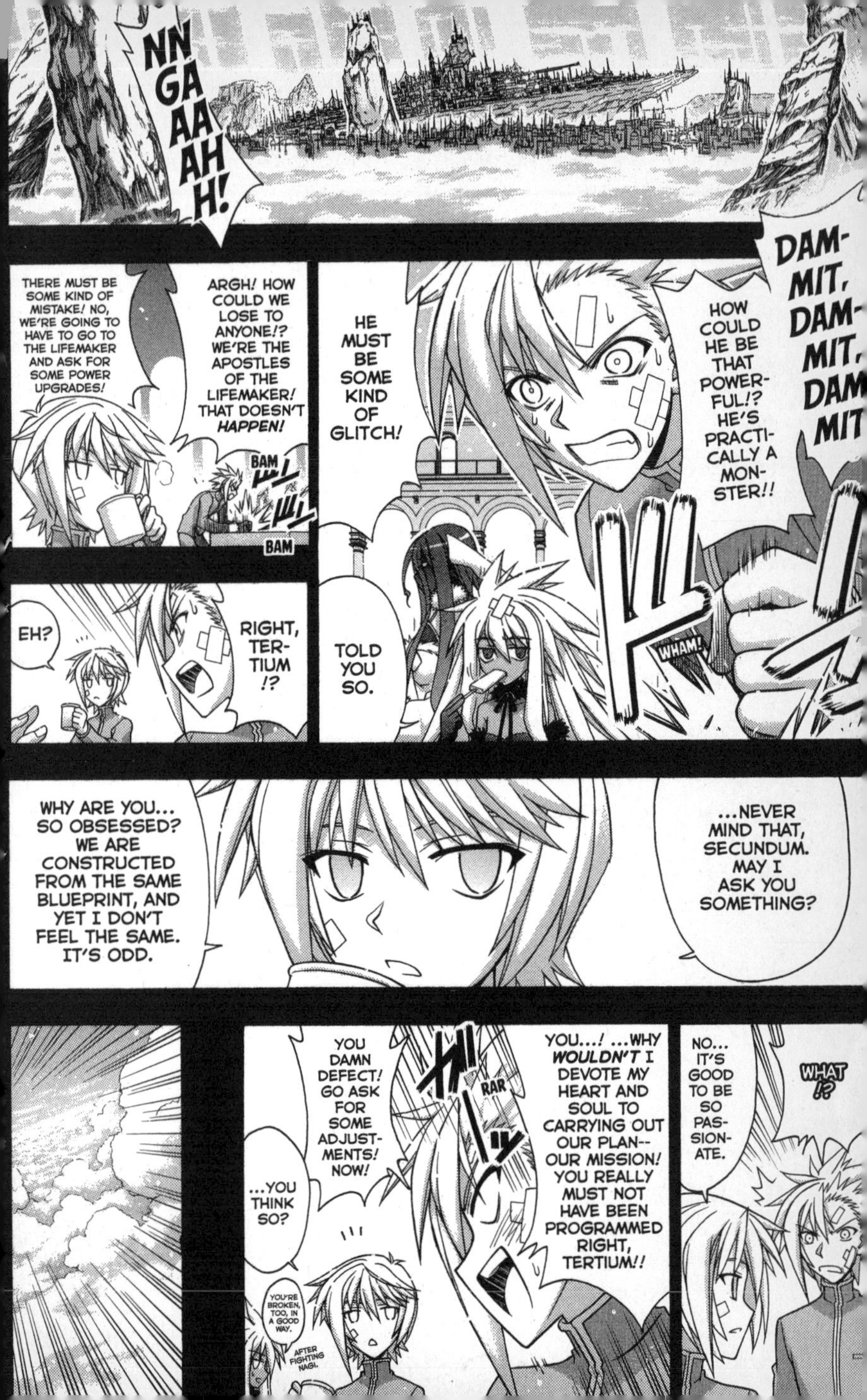

NNGAAAAH!
DAMMIT, DAMMIT, DAMMIT
HOW COULD HE BE THAT POWERFUL!? HE'S PRACTICALLY A MONSTER!!
HE MUST BE SOME KIND OF GLITCH!
WHAM!
TOLD YOU SO.
ARGH! HOW COULD WE LOSE TO ANYONE!? WE'RE THE APOSTLES OF THE LIFEMAKER! THAT DOESN'T *HAPPEN!*
THERE MUST BE SOME KIND OF MISTAKE! NO, WE'RE GOING TO HAVE TO GO TO THE LIFEMAKER AND ASK FOR SOME POWER UPGRADES!
BAM
BAM
RIGHT, TERTIUM !?
EH?
...NEVER MIND THAT, SECUNDUM. MAY I ASK YOU SOMETHING?
WHY ARE YOU... SO OBSESSED? WE ARE CONSTRUCTED FROM THE SAME BLUEPRINT, AND YET I DON'T FEEL THE SAME. IT'S ODD.
WHAT !?
NO... IT'S GOOD TO BE SO PASSIONATE.
YOU...! ...WHY *WOULDN'T* I DEVOTE MY HEART AND SOUL TO CARRYING OUT OUR PLAN--OUR MISSION! YOU REALLY MUST NOT HAVE BEEN PROGRAMMED RIGHT, TERTIUM!!
RAR
YOU DAMN DEFECT! GO ASK FOR SOME ADJUSTMENTS! NOW!
...YOU THINK SO?
YOU'RE BROKEN, TOO, IN A GOOD WAY.
AFTER FIGHTING NAGI.

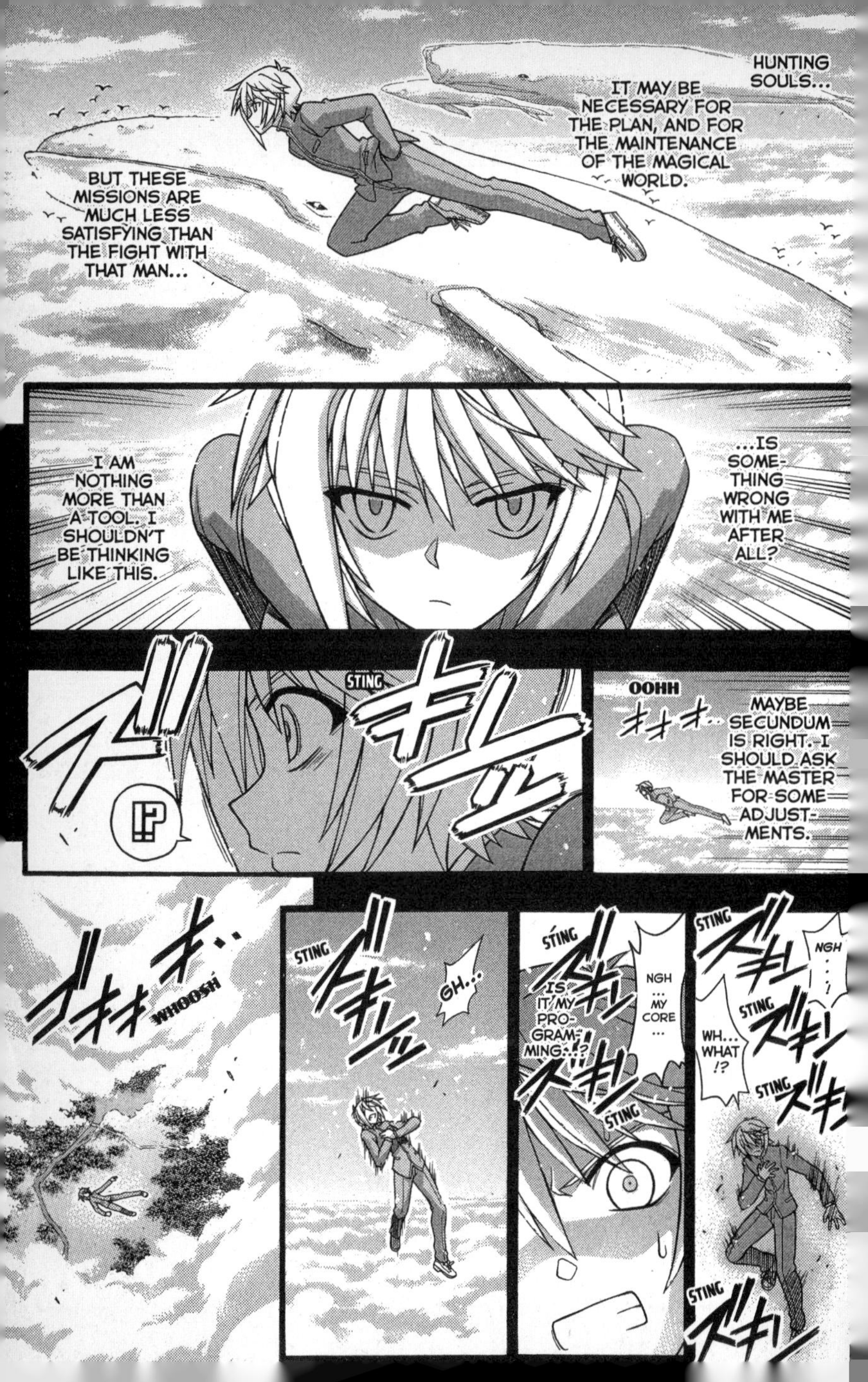
HUNTING SOULS...
IT MAY BE NECESSARY FOR THE PLAN, AND FOR THE MAINTENANCE OF THE MAGICAL WORLD.
BUT THESE MISSIONS ARE MUCH LESS SATISFYING THAN THE FIGHT WITH THAT MAN...
...IS SOMETHING WRONG WITH ME AFTER ALL?
I AM NOTHING MORE THAN A TOOL. I SHOULDN'T BE THINKING LIKE THIS.
OOHH
MAYBE SECUNDUM IS RIGHT. I SHOULD ASK THE MASTER FOR SOME ADJUSTMENTS.
STING
!?
STING
NGH...!
STING
WH... WHAT!?
STING
STING
STING
NGH... MY CORE...
IS IT MY PROGRAMMING...!?
STING
STING
GH...
WHOOSH

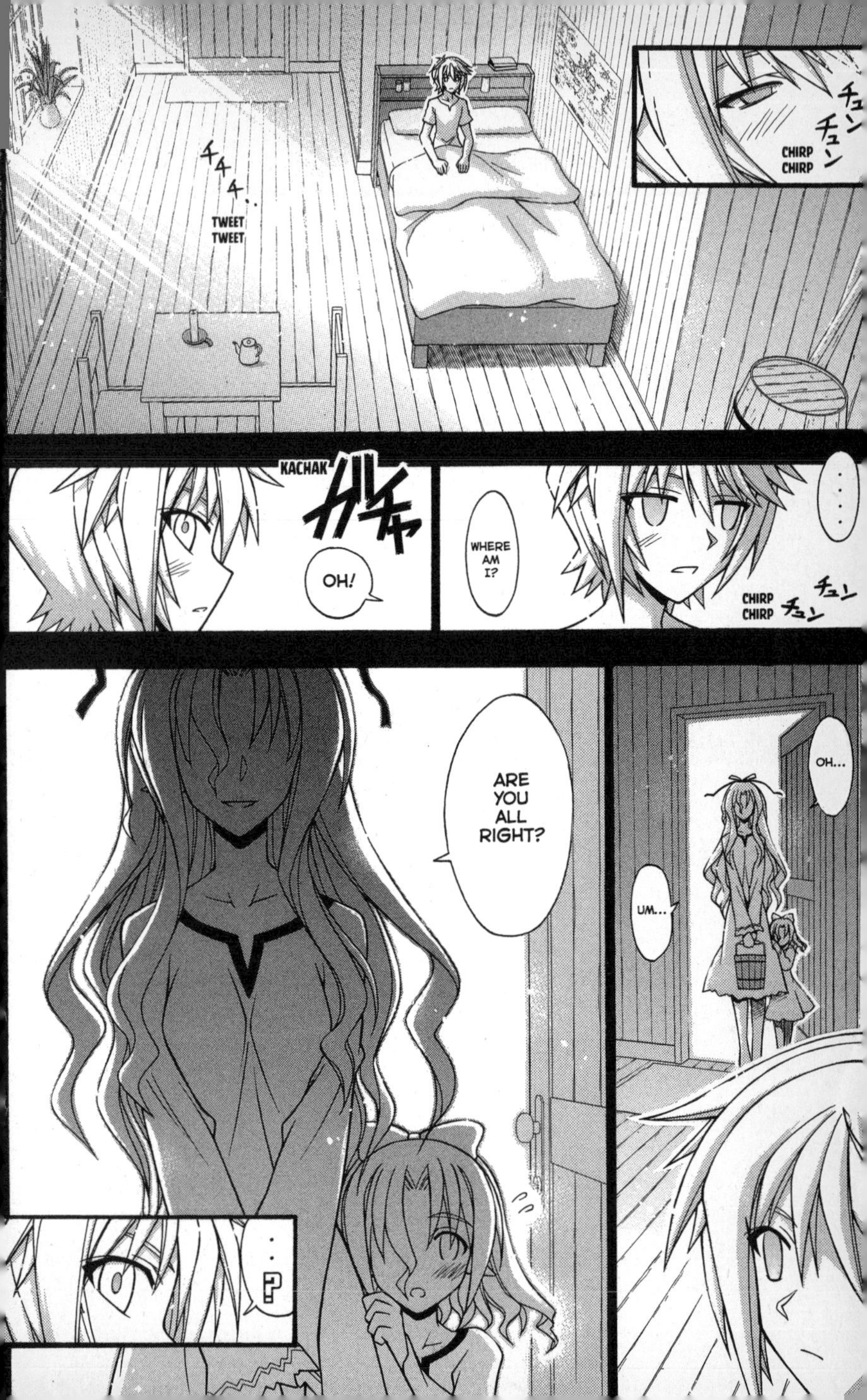

チュンチュン
CHIRP CHIRP
チチチ..
TWEET TWEET
...
WHERE AM I?
チュンチュン
CHIRP CHIRP
KACHAK
ガチャ
OH!
OH...
UM...
ARE YOU ALL RIGHT?
...
?

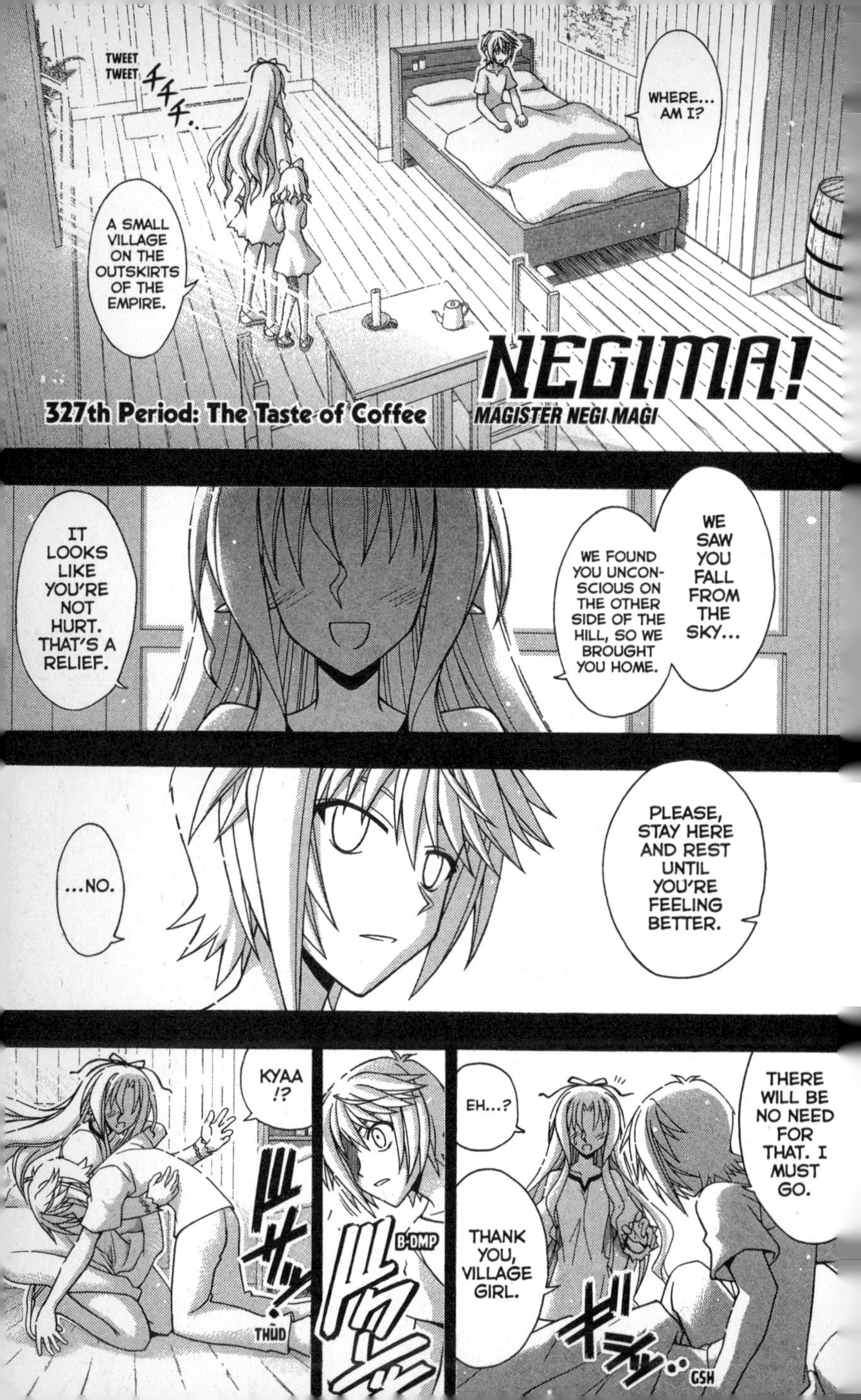
WHERE... AM I?
TWEET TWEET
チチチ..
A SMALL VILLAGE ON THE OUTSKIRTS OF THE EMPIRE.
NEGIMA!
MAGISTER NEGI MAGI
327th Period: The Taste of Coffee
WE SAW YOU FALL FROM THE SKY...
WE FOUND YOU UNCONSCIOUS ON THE OTHER SIDE OF THE HILL, SO WE BROUGHT YOU HOME.
IT LOOKS LIKE YOU'RE NOT HURT. THAT'S A RELIEF.
PLEASE, STAY HERE AND REST UNTIL YOU'RE FEELING BETTER.
...NO.
THERE WILL BE NO NEED FOR THAT. I MUST GO.
EH...?
THANK YOU, VILLAGE GIRL.
GSH
B-DMP
KYAA !?
THUD

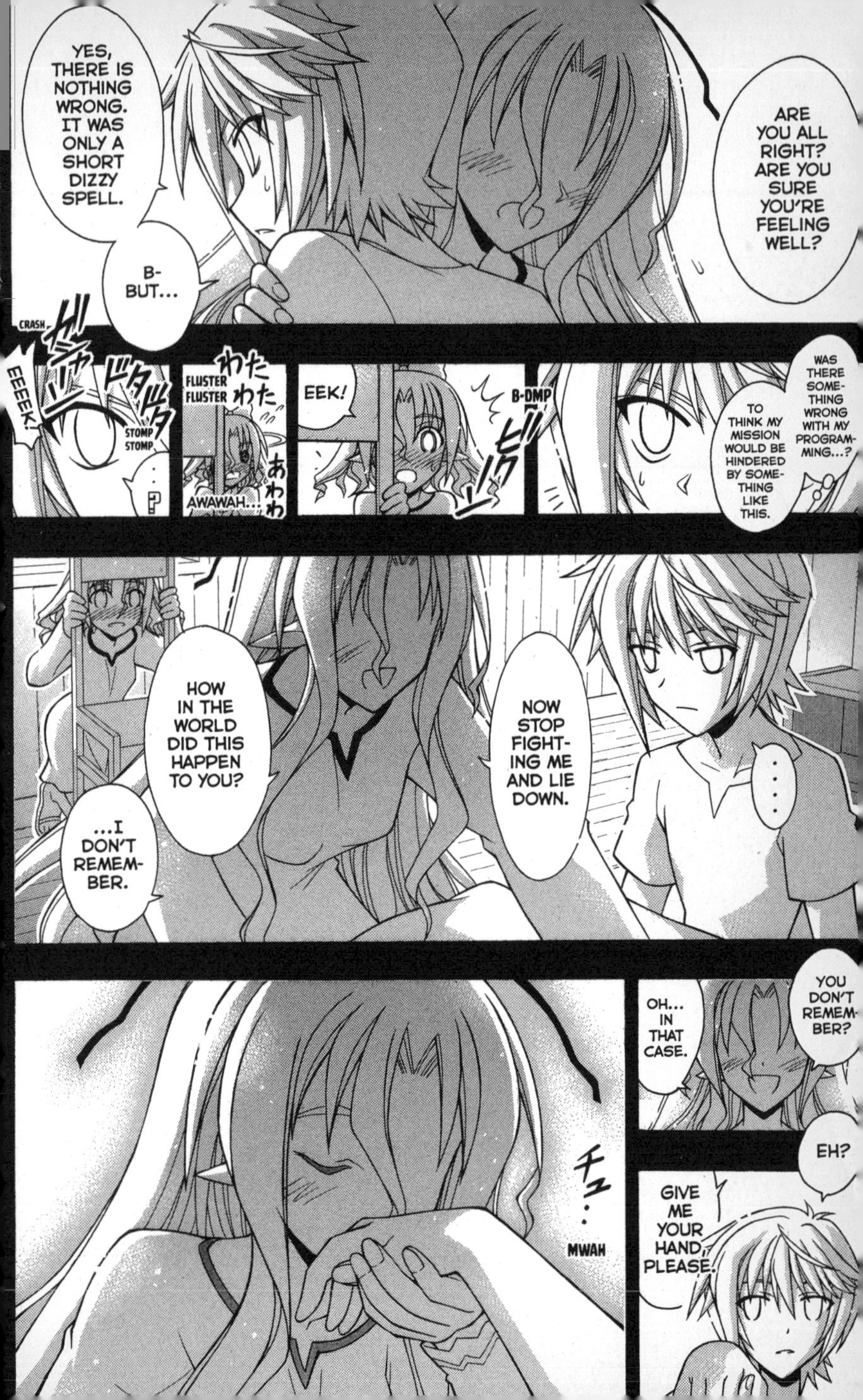
ARE YOU ALL RIGHT? ARE YOU SURE YOU'RE FEELING WELL?
YES, THERE IS NOTHING WRONG. IT WAS ONLY A SHORT DIZZY SPELL.
B-BUT...
WAS THERE SOMETHING WRONG WITH MY PROGRAMMING...?
TO THINK MY MISSION WOULD BE HINDERED BY SOMETHING LIKE THIS.
B-DMP
EEK!
わたわた
FLUSTER FLUSTER
あわわわ
AWAWAH...
CRASH
EEEEK!
STOMP STOMP
...?
...
NOW STOP FIGHTING ME AND LIE DOWN.
HOW IN THE WORLD DID THIS HAPPEN TO YOU?
...I DON'T REMEMBER.
YOU DON'T REMEMBER?
OH... IN THAT CASE.
EH?
GIVE ME YOUR HAND, PLEASE.
チュ...
MWAH

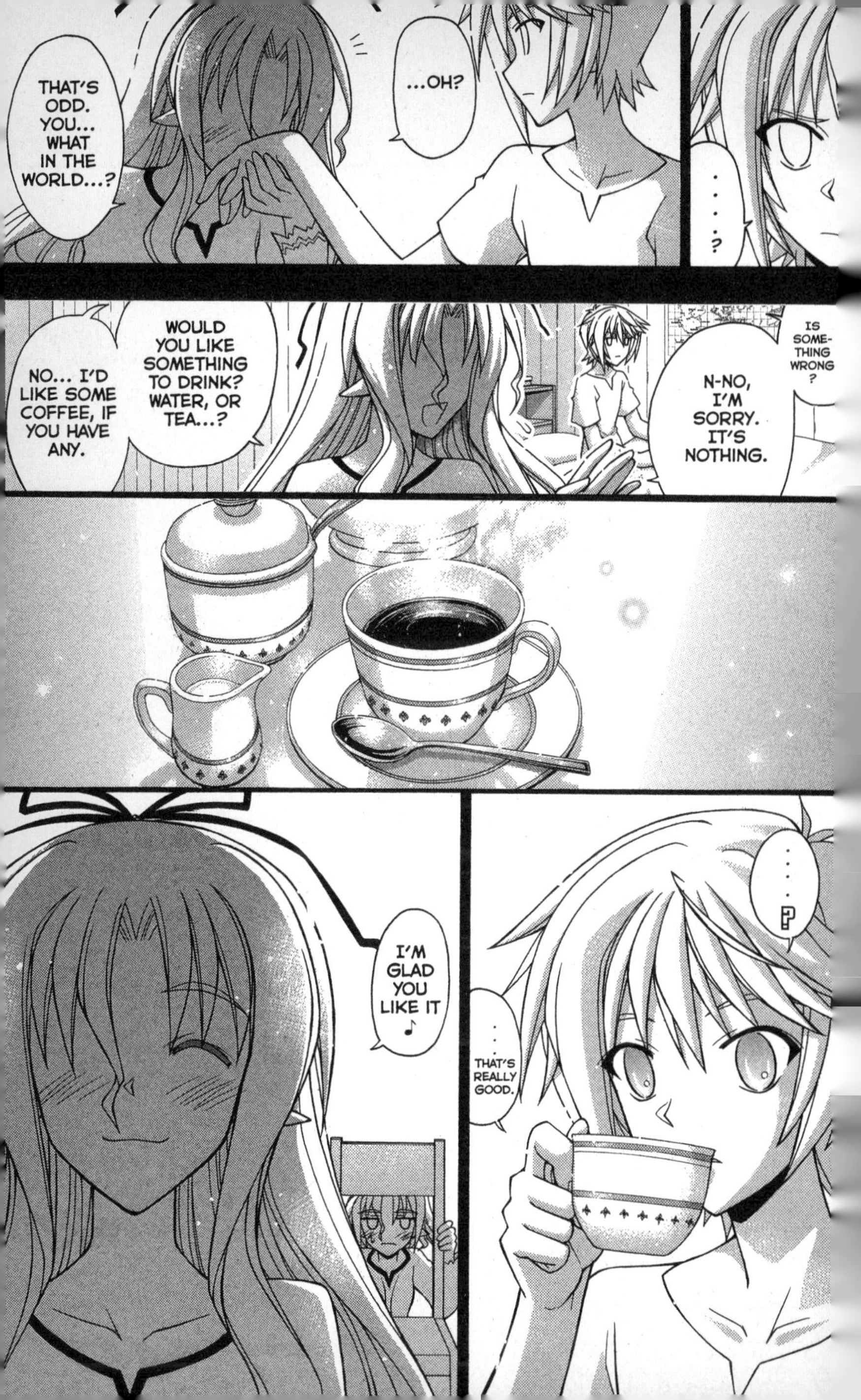
......?
...OH?
THAT'S ODD. YOU... WHAT IN THE WORLD...?
IS SOMETHING WRONG?
N-NO, I'M SORRY. IT'S NOTHING.
WOULD YOU LIKE SOMETHING TO DRINK? WATER, OR TEA...?
NO... I'D LIKE SOME COFFEE, IF YOU HAVE ANY.
......?
...THAT'S REALLY GOOD.
I'M GLAD YOU LIKE IT ♪

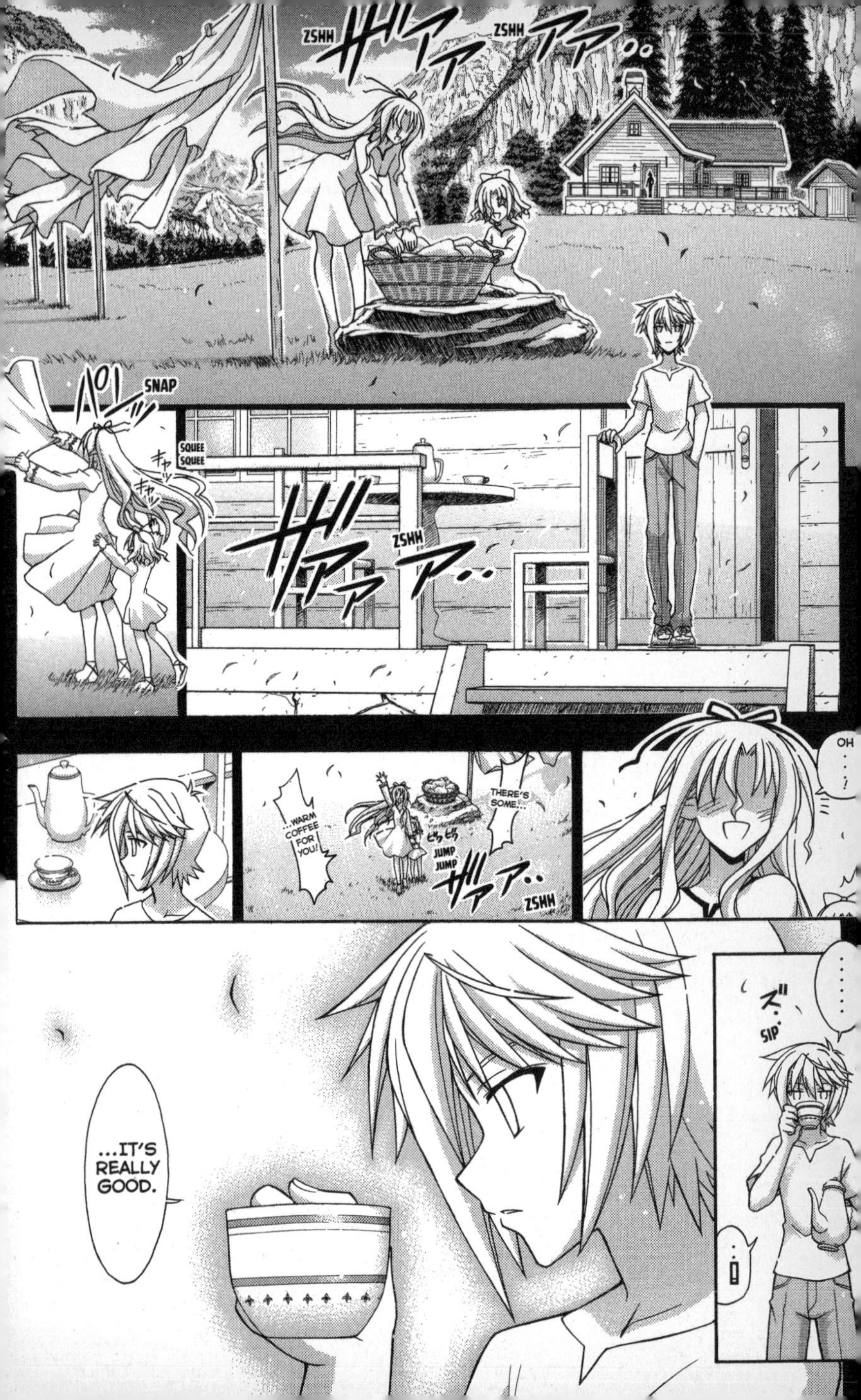
ZSHH
ZSHH
ZSHH
SNAP
SQUEE SQUEE
OH...!
THERE'S SOME...
...WARM COFFEE FOR YOU!
JUMP JUMP
ZSHH
......
SIP
...!
...IT'S REALLY GOOD.

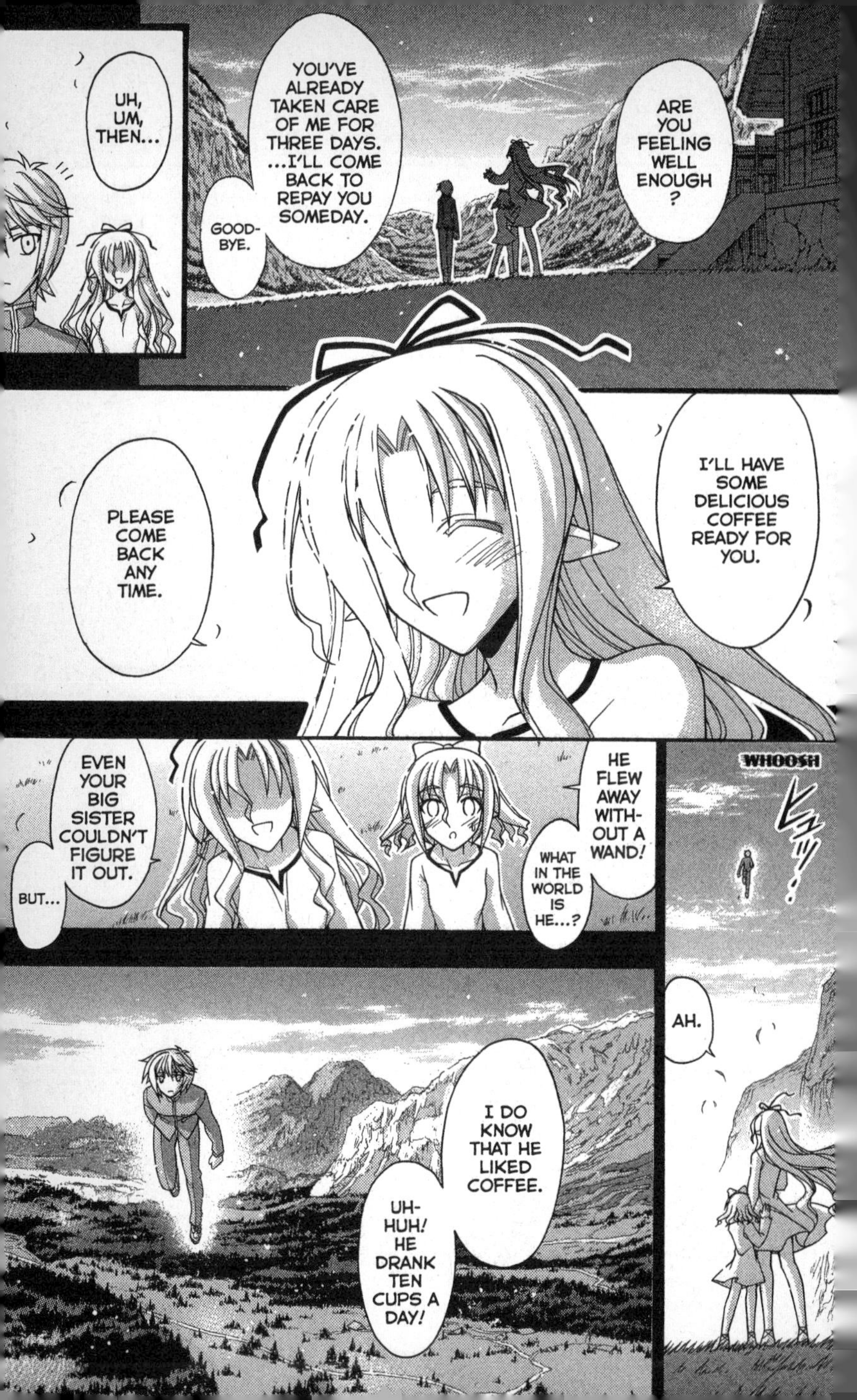
ARE YOU FEELING WELL ENOUGH?
YOU'VE ALREADY TAKEN CARE OF ME FOR THREE DAYS. ...I'LL COME BACK TO REPAY YOU SOMEDAY.
GOOD-BYE.
UH, UM, THEN...
I'LL HAVE SOME DELICIOUS COFFEE READY FOR YOU.
PLEASE COME BACK ANY TIME.
WHOOSH
AH.
HE FLEW AWAY WITHOUT A WAND!
WHAT IN THE WORLD IS HE...?
EVEN YOUR BIG SISTER COULDN'T FIGURE IT OUT.
BUT...
I DO KNOW THAT HE LIKED COFFEE.
UH-HUH! HE DRANK TEN CUPS A DAY!

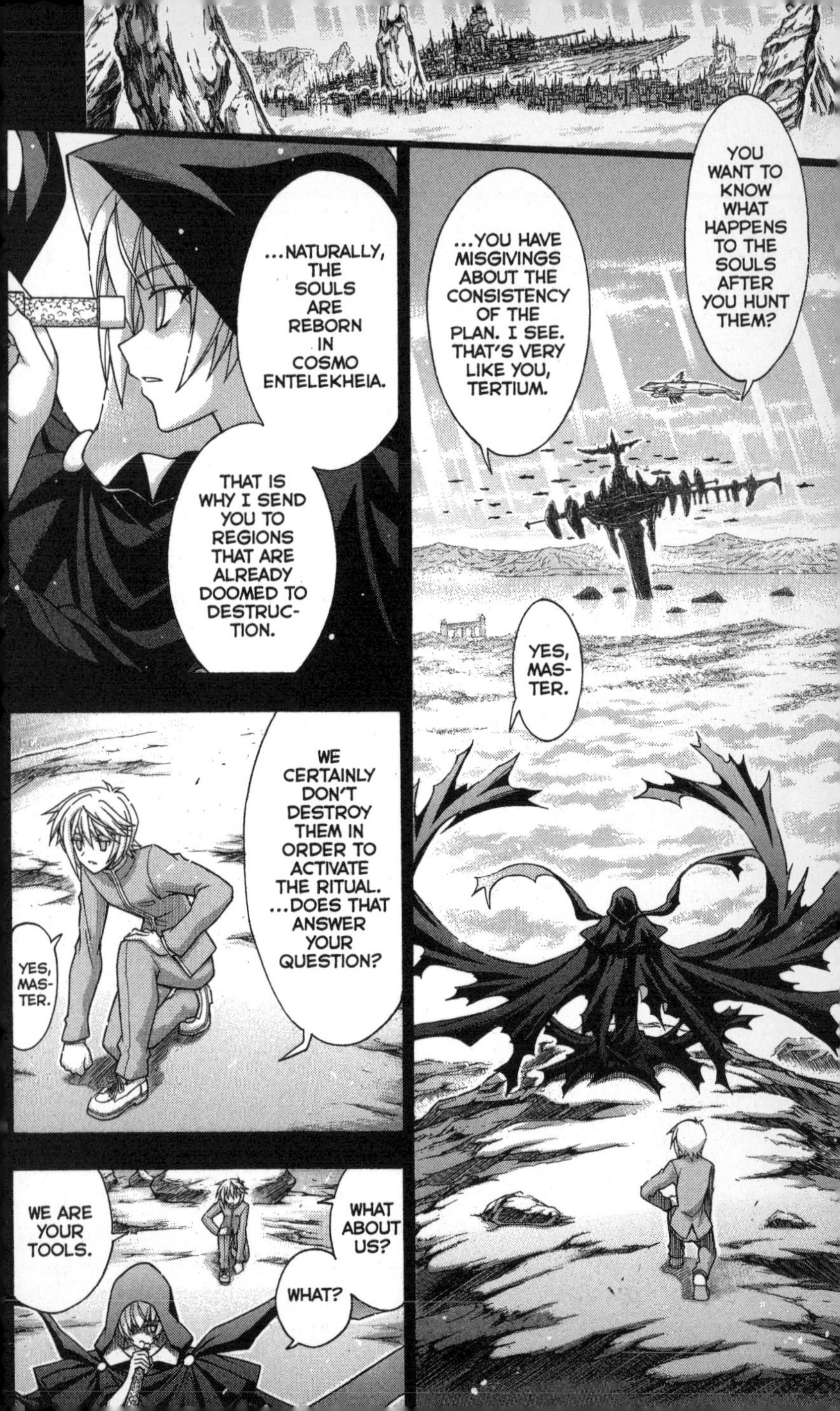
YOU WANT TO KNOW WHAT HAPPENS TO THE SOULS AFTER YOU HUNT THEM?
...YOU HAVE MISGIVINGS ABOUT THE CONSISTENCY OF THE PLAN. I SEE. THAT'S VERY LIKE YOU, TERTIUM.
YES, MASTER.
...NATURALLY, THE SOULS ARE REBORN IN COSMO ENTELEKHEIA.
THAT IS WHY I SEND YOU TO REGIONS THAT ARE ALREADY DOOMED TO DESTRUCTION.
WE CERTAINLY DON'T DESTROY THEM IN ORDER TO ACTIVATE THE RITUAL. ...DOES THAT ANSWER YOUR QUESTION?
YES, MASTER.
WHAT ABOUT US?
WHAT?
WE ARE YOUR TOOLS.

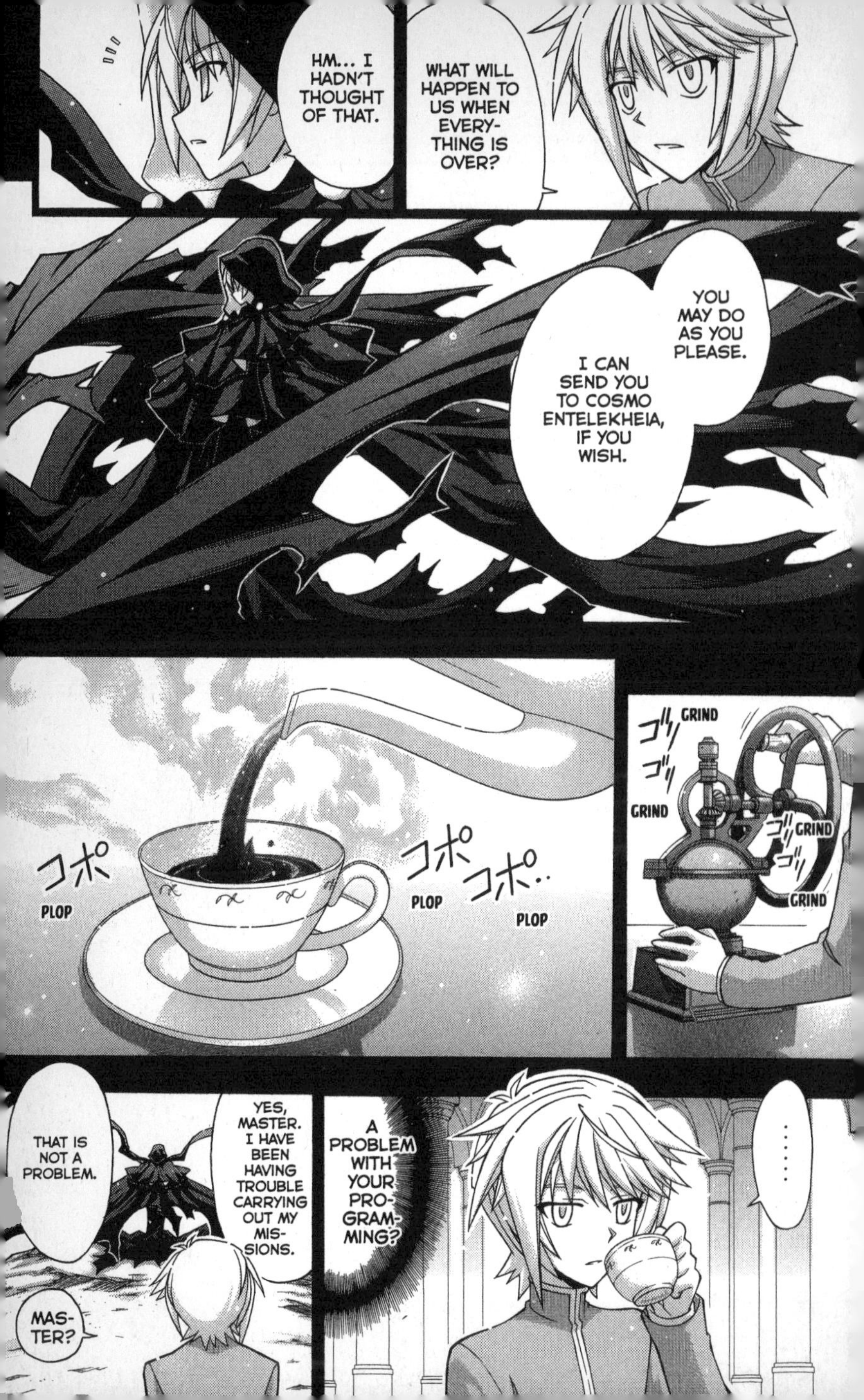

WHAT WILL HAPPEN TO US WHEN EVERYTHING IS OVER?
HM... I HADN'T THOUGHT OF THAT.
YOU MAY DO AS YOU PLEASE.
I CAN SEND YOU TO COSMO ENTELEKHEIA, IF YOU WISH.
ゴリ GRIND
ゴリ GRIND
ゴリ GRIND
ゴリ GRIND
コポ PLOP
コポ... PLOP
コポ PLOP
......
A PROBLEM WITH YOUR PROGRAMMING?
YES, MASTER. I HAVE BEEN HAVING TROUBLE CARRYING OUT MY MISSIONS.
THAT IS NOT A PROBLEM.
MASTER?

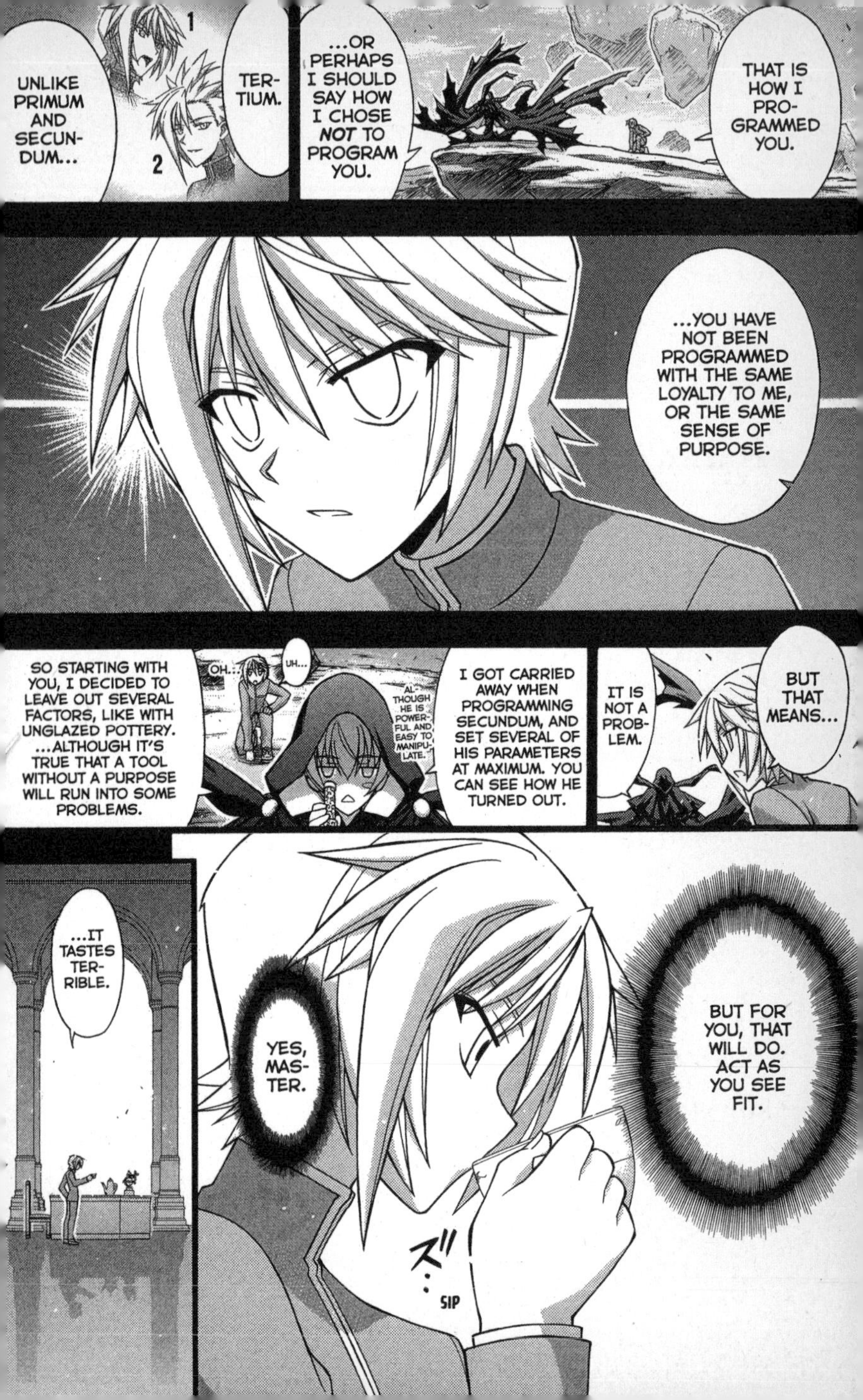
THAT IS HOW I PROGRAMMED YOU.
...OR PERHAPS I SHOULD SAY HOW I CHOSE *NOT* TO PROGRAM YOU.
1
TERTIUM.
2
UNLIKE PRIMUM AND SECUNDUM...
...YOU HAVE NOT BEEN PROGRAMMED WITH THE SAME LOYALTY TO ME, OR THE SAME SENSE OF PURPOSE.
BUT THAT MEANS...
IT IS NOT A PROBLEM.
I GOT CARRIED AWAY WHEN PROGRAMMING SECUNDUM, AND SET SEVERAL OF HIS PARAMETERS AT MAXIMUM. YOU CAN SEE HOW HE TURNED OUT.
ALTHOUGH HE IS POWERFUL AND EASY TO MANIPULATE.
UH...
OH...
SO STARTING WITH YOU, I DECIDED TO LEAVE OUT SEVERAL FACTORS, LIKE WITH UNGLAZED POTTERY. ...ALTHOUGH IT'S TRUE THAT A TOOL WITHOUT A PURPOSE WILL RUN INTO SOME PROBLEMS.
BUT FOR YOU, THAT WILL DO. ACT AS YOU SEE FIT.
YES, MASTER.
SIP
...IT TASTES TERRIBLE.

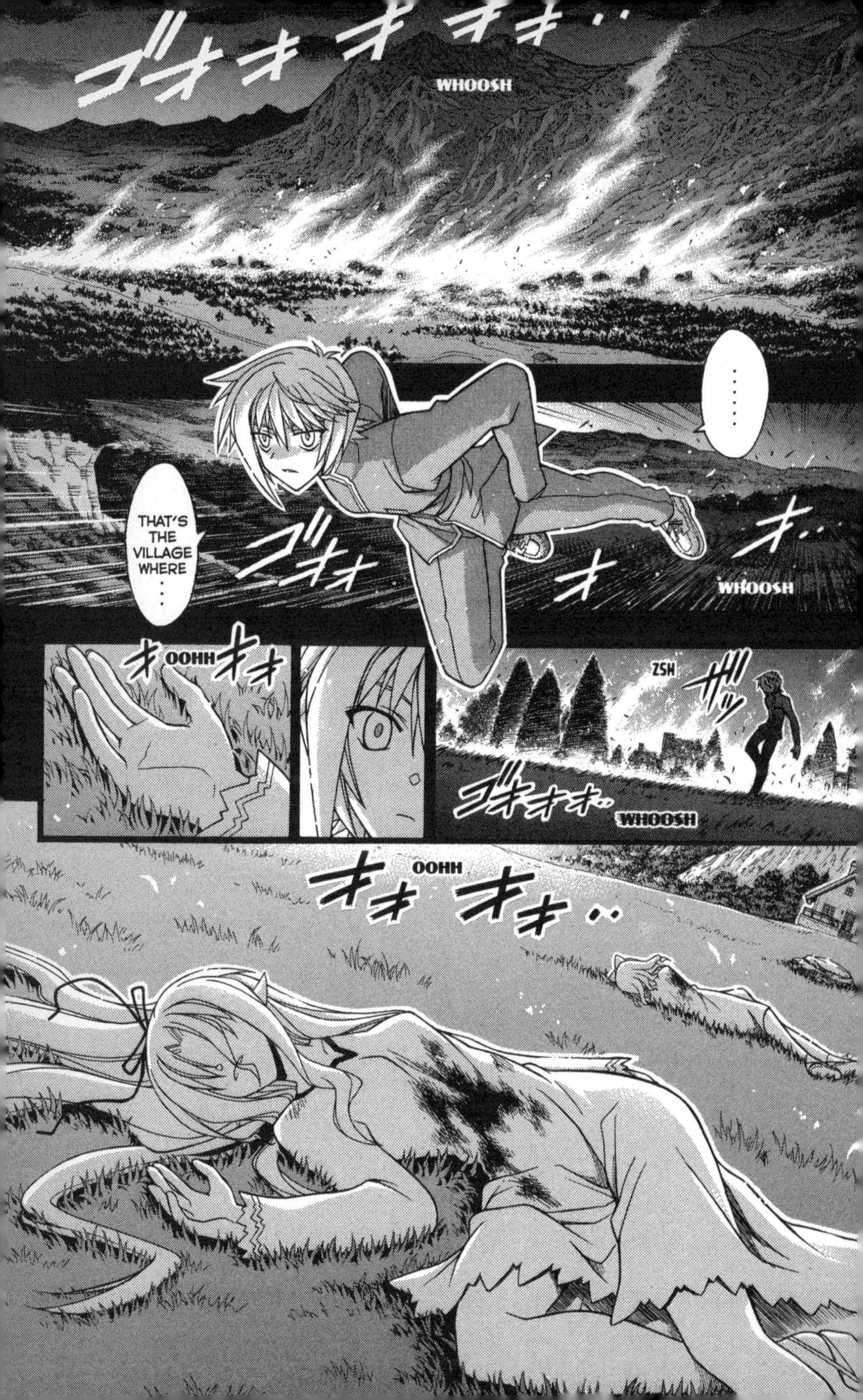
WHOOSH
......
THAT'S THE VILLAGE WHERE ...
WHOOSH
ZSH
WHOOSH
OOHH
OOHH

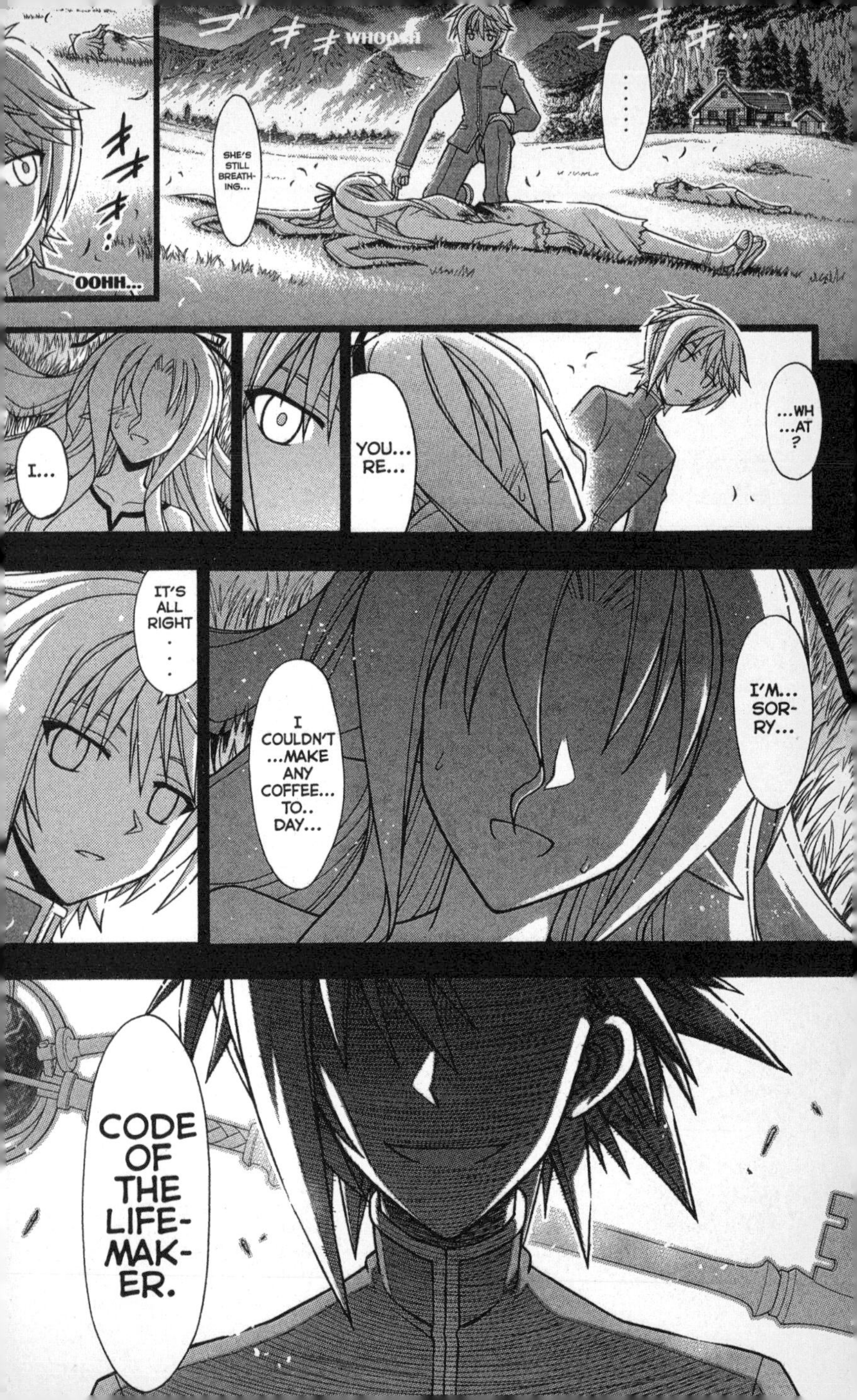
WHOOSH
......
SHE'S STILL BREATHING...
OOHH...
...WH...AT?
YOU...RE...
I...
I'M... SORRY...
I COULDN'T ...MAKE ANY COFFEE... TO.. DAY...
IT'S ALL RIGHT...
CODE OF THE LIFE-MAKER.

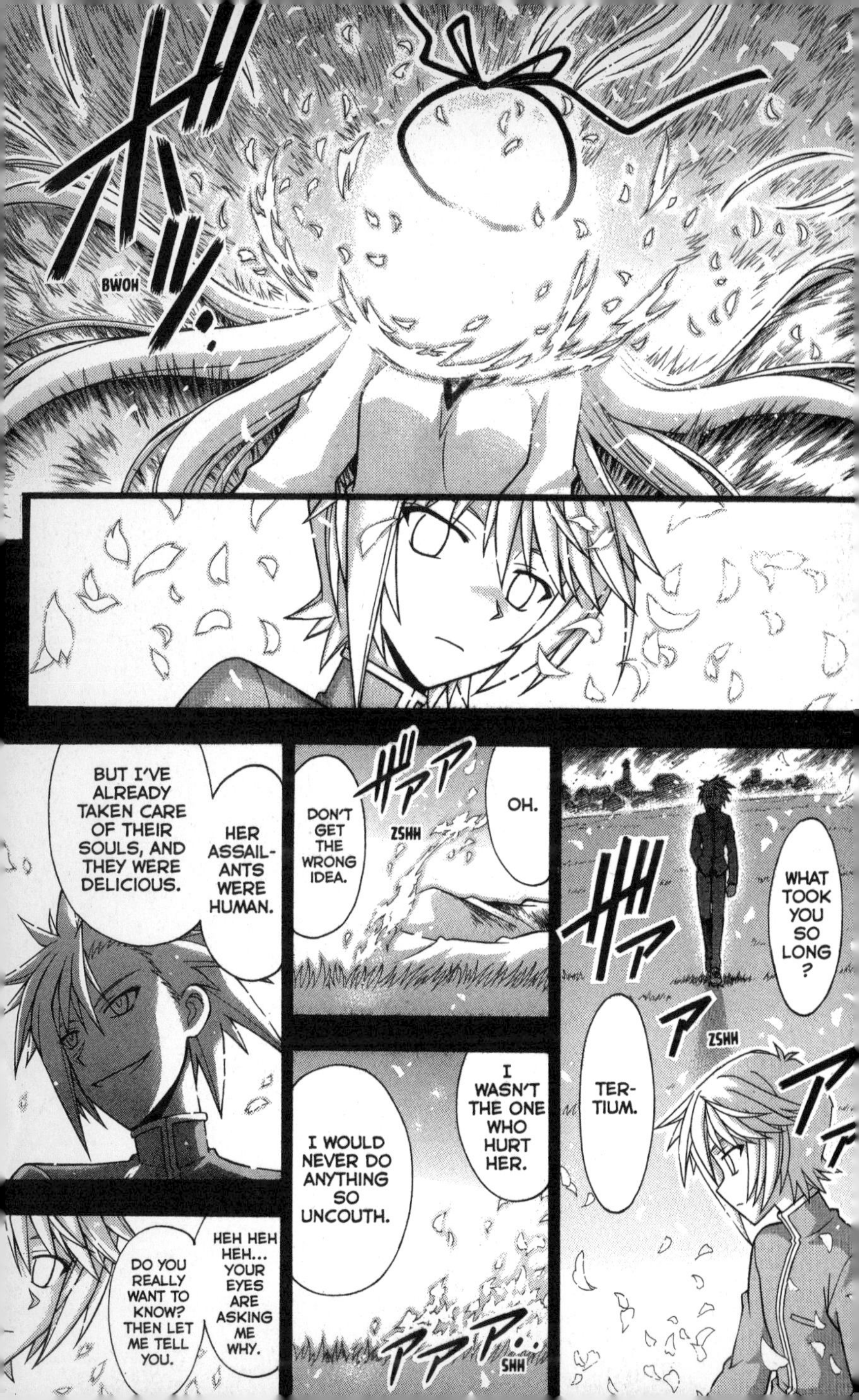
BWOH
WHAT TOOK YOU SO LONG?
ZSHH
TER-TIUM.
OH.
DON'T GET THE WRONG IDEA.
ZSHH
I WASN'T THE ONE WHO HURT HER.
I WOULD NEVER DO ANYTHING SO UNCOUTH.
SHH
HER ASSAIL-ANTS WERE HUMAN.
BUT I'VE ALREADY TAKEN CARE OF THEIR SOULS, AND THEY WERE DELICIOUS.
HEH HEH HEH... YOUR EYES ARE ASKING ME WHY.
DO YOU REALLY WANT TO KNOW? THEN LET ME TELL YOU.

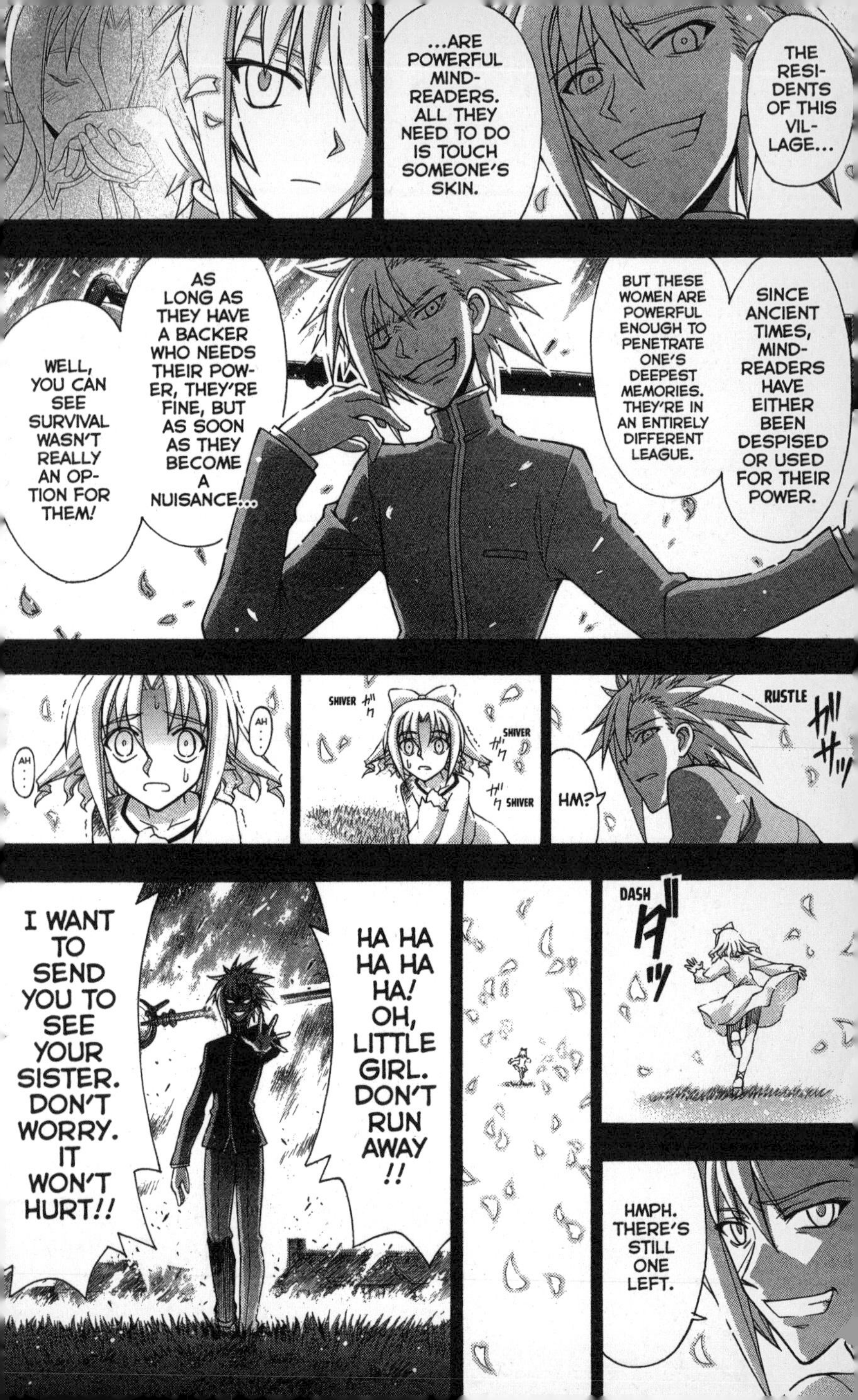
THE RESIDENTS OF THIS VILLAGE...
...ARE POWERFUL MIND-READERS. ALL THEY NEED TO DO IS TOUCH SOMEONE'S SKIN.
SINCE ANCIENT TIMES, MIND-READERS HAVE EITHER BEEN DESPISED OR USED FOR THEIR POWER.
BUT THESE WOMEN ARE POWERFUL ENOUGH TO PENETRATE ONE'S DEEPEST MEMORIES. THEY'RE IN AN ENTIRELY DIFFERENT LEAGUE.
AS LONG AS THEY HAVE A BACKER WHO NEEDS THEIR POWER, THEY'RE FINE, BUT AS SOON AS THEY BECOME A NUISANCE...
WELL, YOU CAN SEE SURVIVAL WASN'T REALLY AN OPTION FOR THEM!
RUSTLE
HM?
SHIVER
SHIVER
SHIVER
AH...
AH...
DASH
HMPH. THERE'S STILL ONE LEFT.
HA HA HA HA HA! OH, LITTLE GIRL. DON'T RUN AWAY!!
I WANT TO SEND YOU TO SEE YOUR SISTER. DON'T WORRY. IT WON'T HURT!!

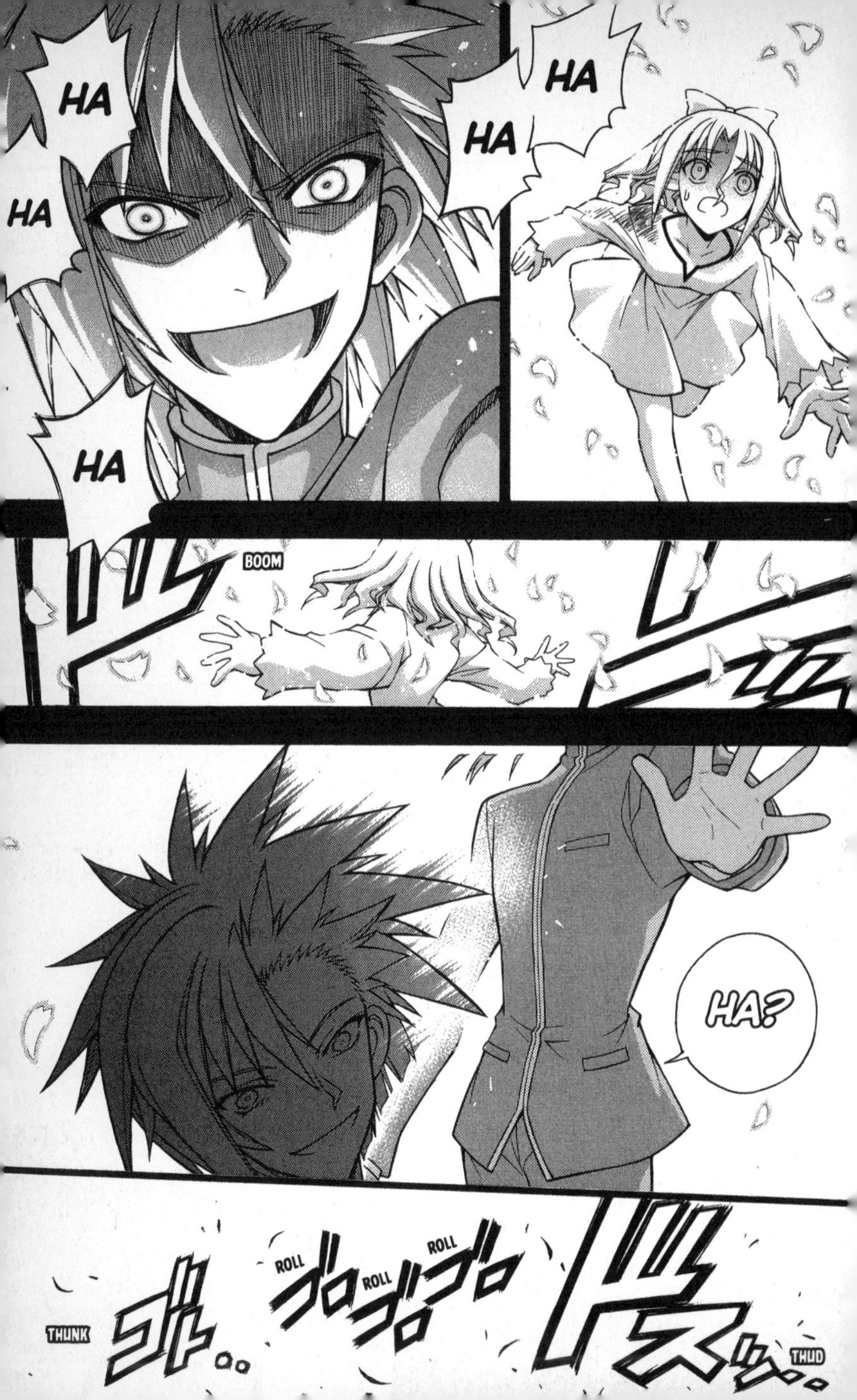
HA
HA
HA
HA
HA
BOOM
HA?
THUD
ROLL
ROLL
ROLL
THUNK

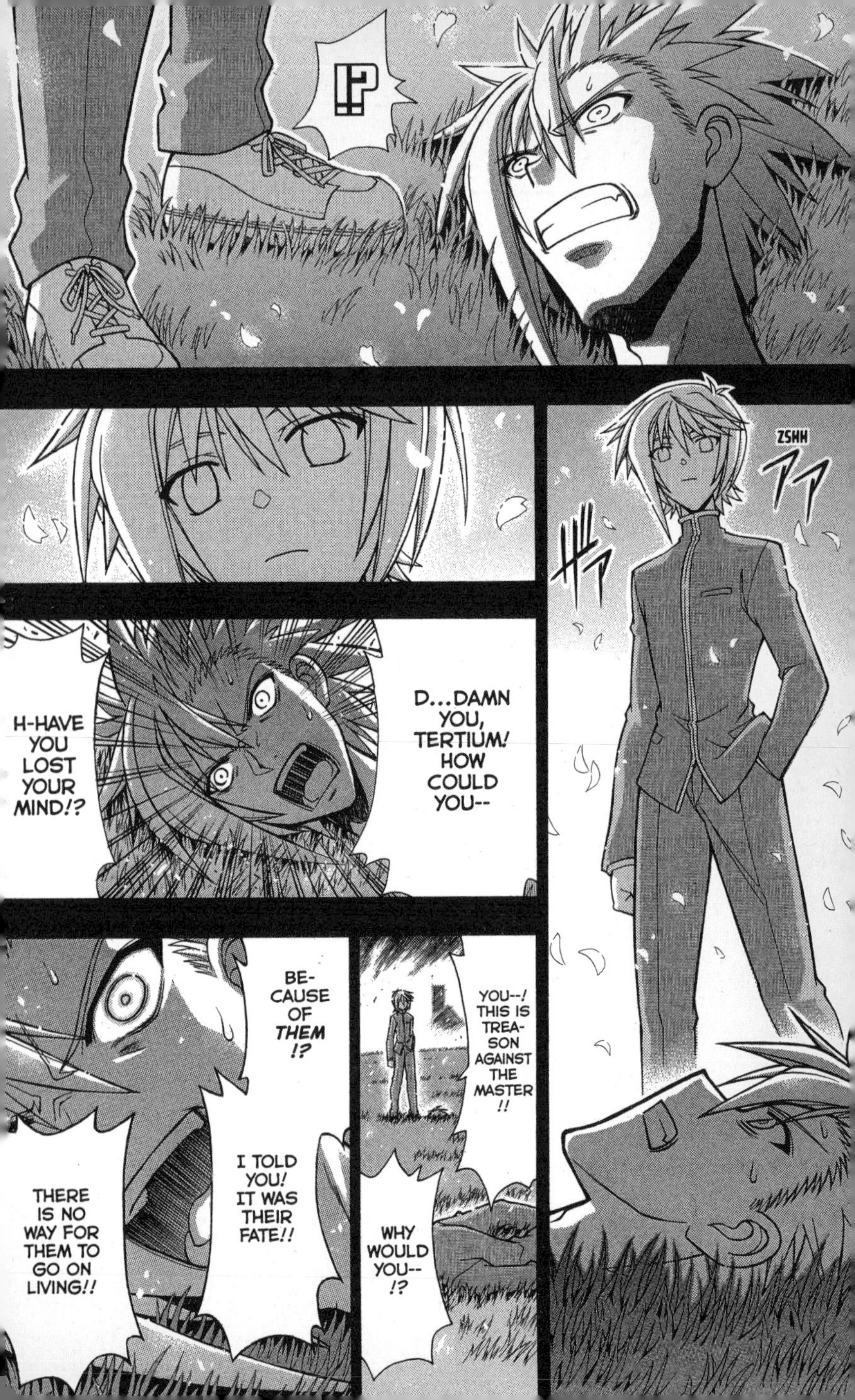
!?
ZSHH
D...DAMN YOU, TERTIUM! HOW COULD YOU--
H-HAVE YOU LOST YOUR MIND!?
YOU--! THIS IS TREASON AGAINST THE MASTER!!
WHY WOULD YOU--!?
BECAUSE OF THEM!?
I TOLD YOU! IT WAS THEIR FATE!!
THERE IS NO WAY FOR THEM TO GO ON LIVING!!

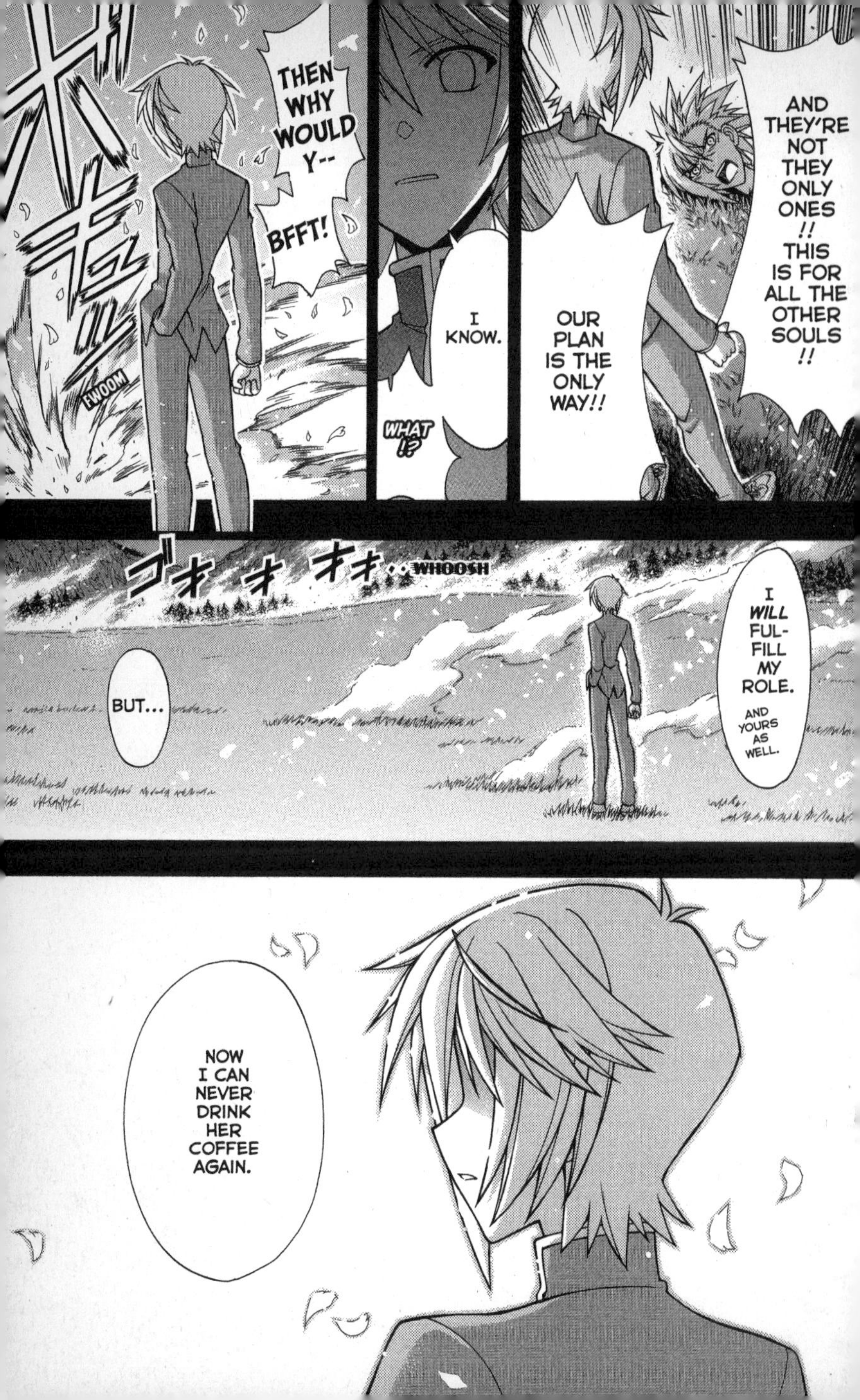
AND THEY'RE NOT THEY ONLY ONES!! THIS IS FOR ALL THE OTHER SOULS!!
OUR PLAN IS THE ONLY WAY!!
I KNOW.
WHAT!?
THEN WHY WOULD Y--
BFFT!
FWOOM
I WILL FUL-FILL MY ROLE.
AND YOURS AS WELL.
WHOOSH
BUT...
NOW I CAN NEVER DRINK HER COFFEE AGAIN.

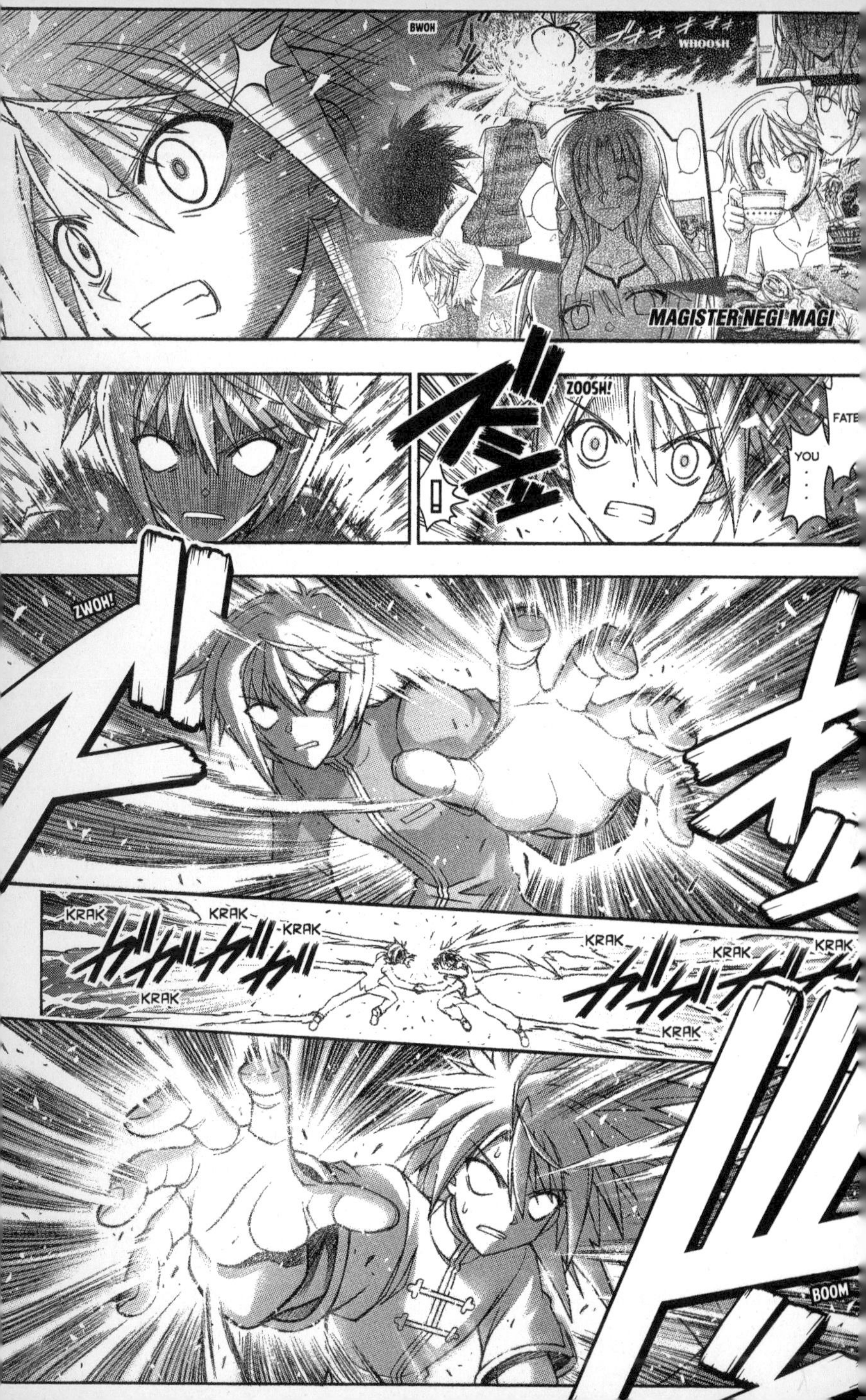
WHOOSH
BWOH
MAGISTER NEGI MAGI
FATE
YOU
. . .
ZOOSH!
!
ZWOH!
KRAK
KRAK
KRAK
KRAK
KRAK
KRAK
KRAK
KRAK
BOOM

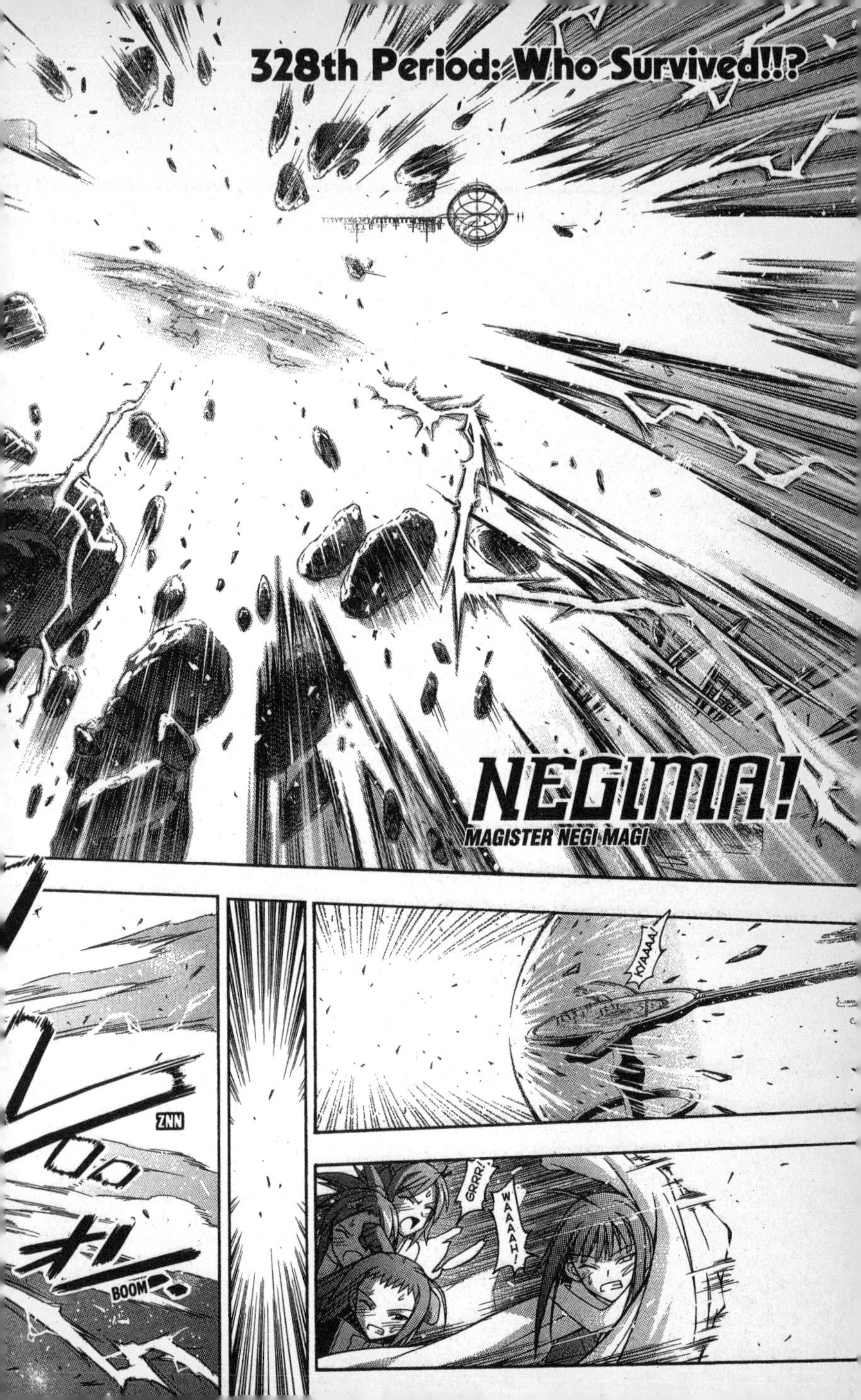
328th Period: Who Survived!!?
NEGIMA!
MAGISTER NEGI MAGI
KYAAAA!
GRRR!
WAAAAH!
ZNN
BOOM

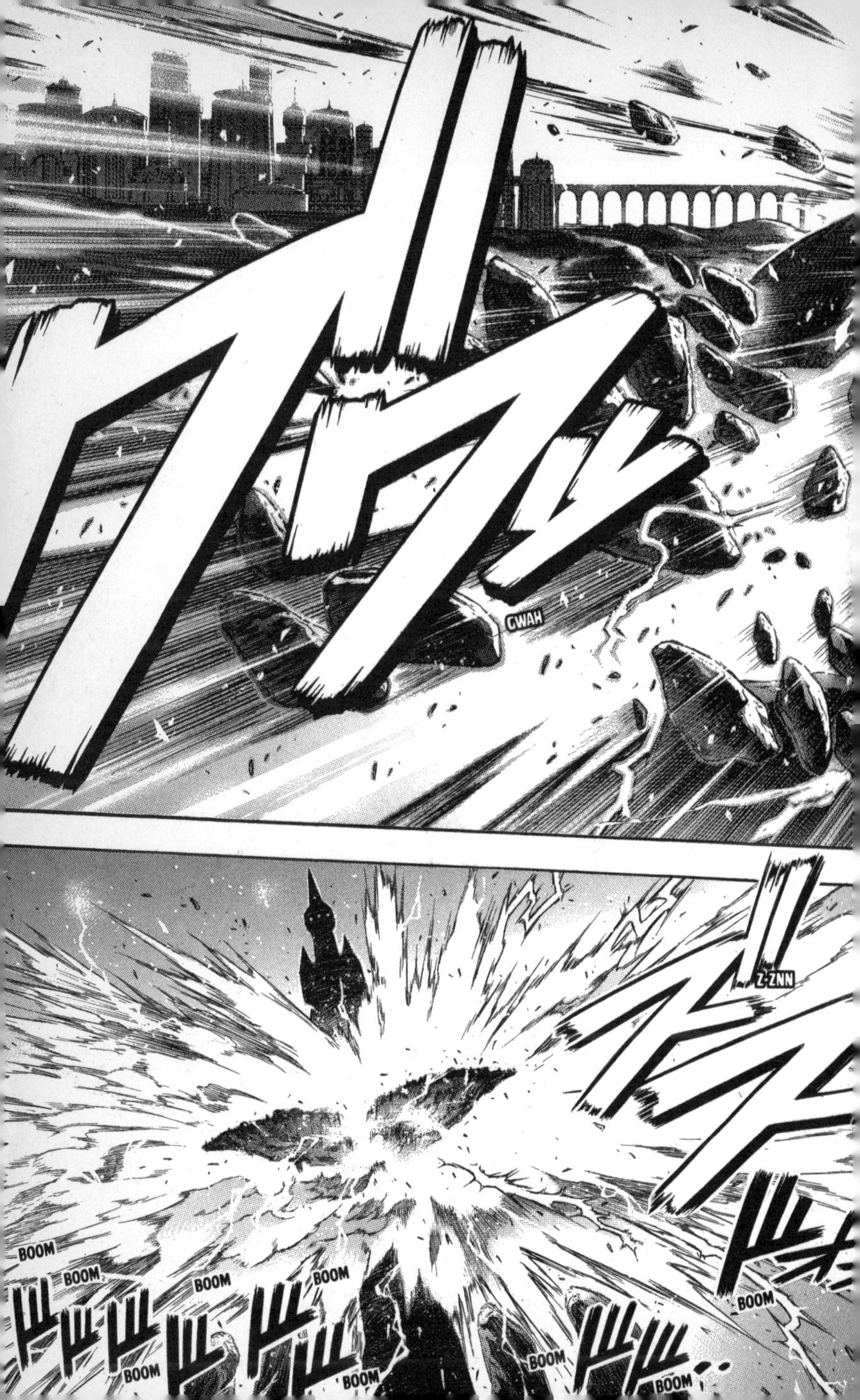
GWAH
Z-ZNN
BOOM
BOOM
BOOM
BOOM
BOOM
BOOM
BOOM
BOOM
BOOM

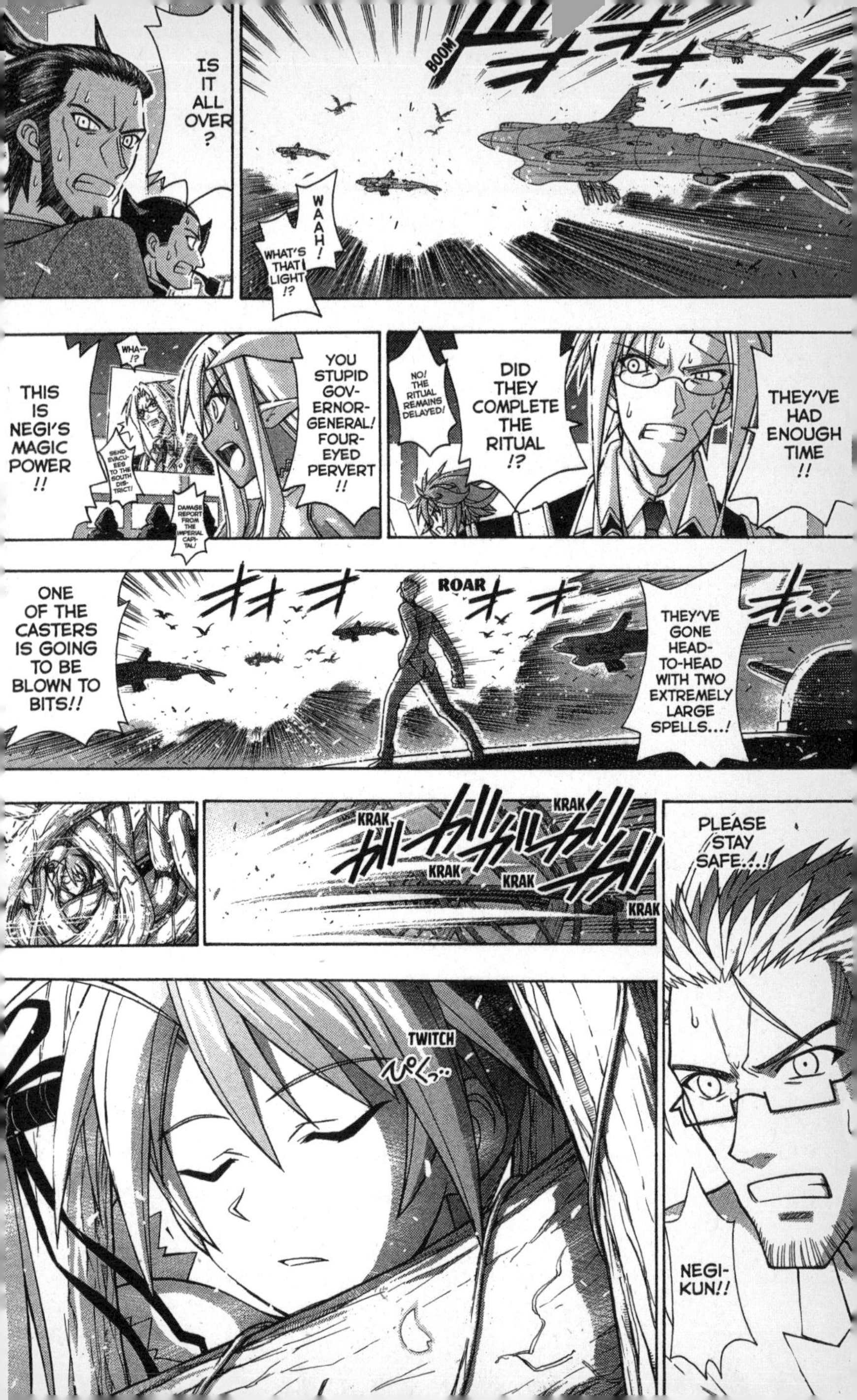
BOOM
WAAH!
WHAT'S THAT LIGHT!?
IS IT ALL OVER?
THEY'VE HAD ENOUGH TIME!!
DID THEY COMPLETE THE RITUAL!?
NO! THE RITUAL REMAINS DELAYED!
YOU STUPID GOVERNOR-GENERAL! FOUR-EYED PERVERT!!
WHA-!?
THIS IS NEGI'S MAGIC POWER!!
SEND EVACUEES TO THE SOUTH DISTRICT!
DAMAGE REPORT FROM THE IMPERIAL CAPITAL!
THEY'VE GONE HEAD-TO-HEAD WITH TWO EXTREMELY LARGE SPELLS...!
ROAR
ONE OF THE CASTERS IS GOING TO BE BLOWN TO BITS!!
PLEASE STAY SAFE...!
NEGI-KUN!!
KRAK
KRAK
KRAK
KRAK
KRAK
TWITCH

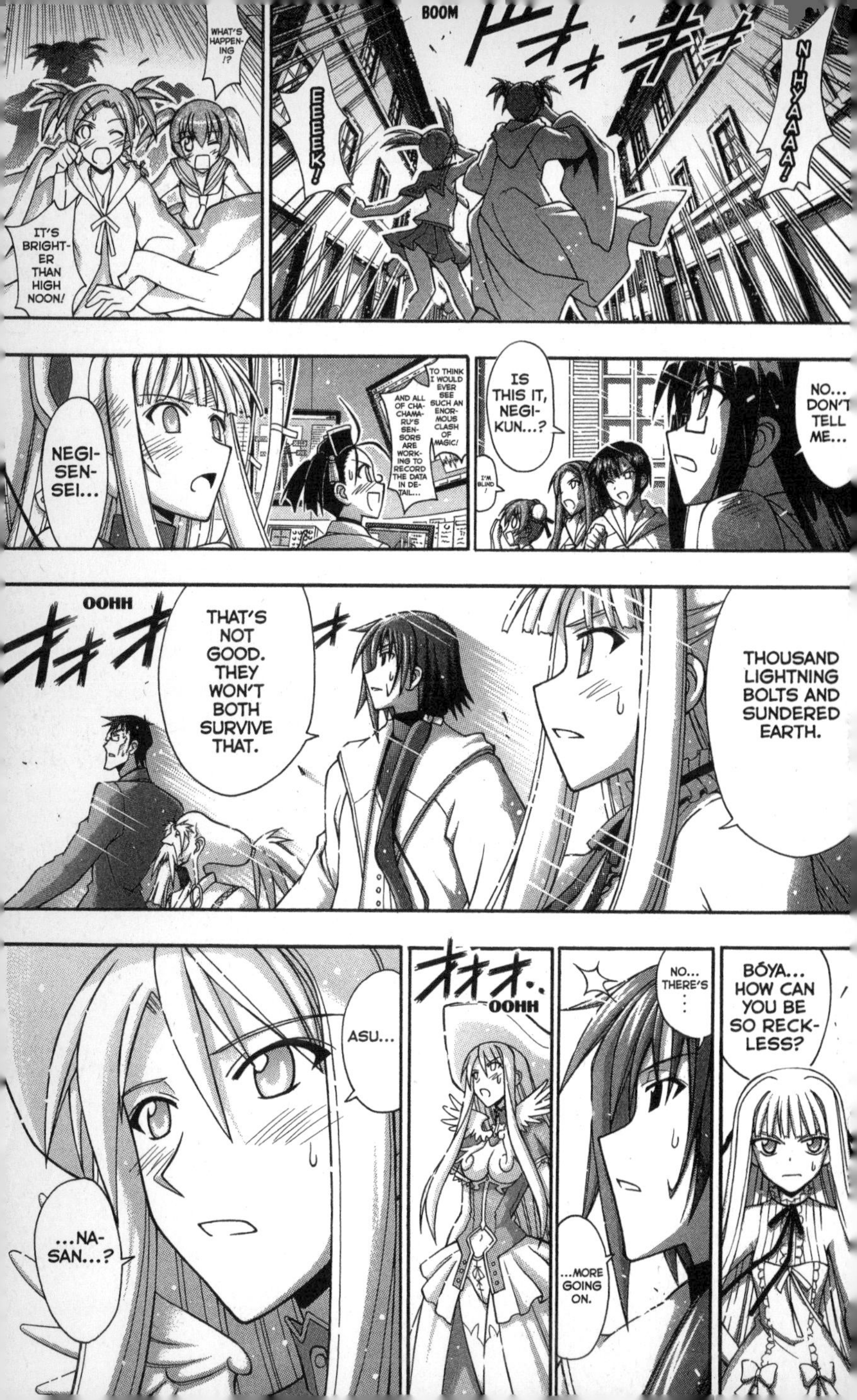
BOOM
NIHYAAAA!
EEEEEK!
WHAT'S HAPPENING!?
IT'S BRIGHTER THAN HIGH NOON!
NO... DON'T TELL ME...
IS THIS IT, NEGI-KUN...?
I'M BLIND!
TO THINK I WOULD EVER SEE SUCH AN ENORMOUS CLASH OF MAGIC!
AND ALL OF CHACHAMARU'S SENSORS ARE WORKING TO RECORD THE DATA IN DETAIL...
NEGI-SENSEI...
THOUSAND LIGHTNING BOLTS AND SUNDERED EARTH.
THAT'S NOT GOOD. THEY WON'T BOTH SURVIVE THAT.
OOHH
BŌYA... HOW CAN YOU BE SO RECKLESS?
NO... THERE'S...
...MORE GOING ON.
OOHH
ASU...
...NASAN...?

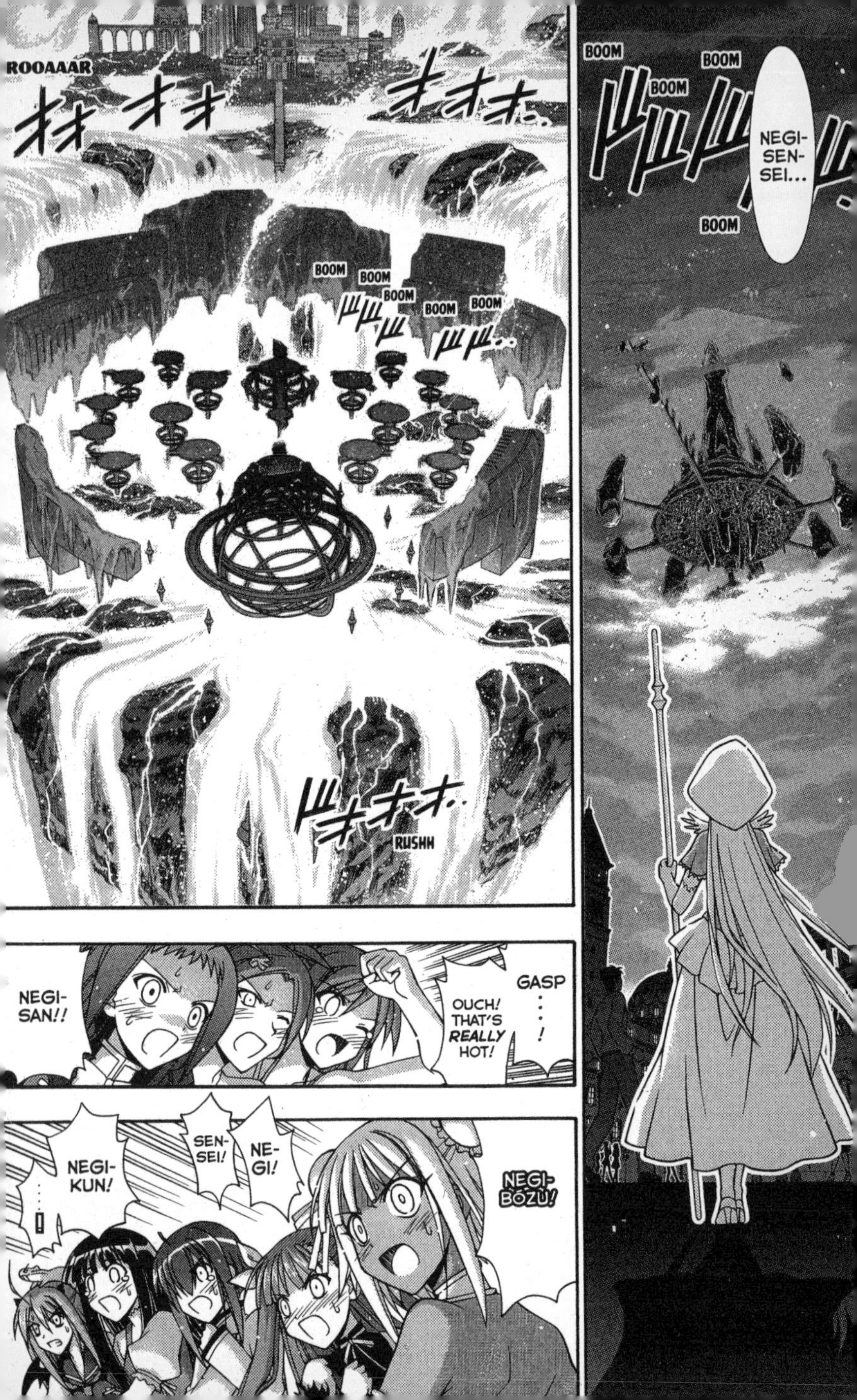
NEGI-SEN-SEI...
BOOM
BOOM
BOOM
BOOM
ROOAAAR
BOOM
BOOM
BOOM
BOOM
BOOM
RUSHH
GASP...!
OUCH! THAT'S REALLY HOT!
NEGI-SAN!!
NEGI-BŌZU!
NE-GI!
SEN-SEI!
NEGI-KUN!
......!

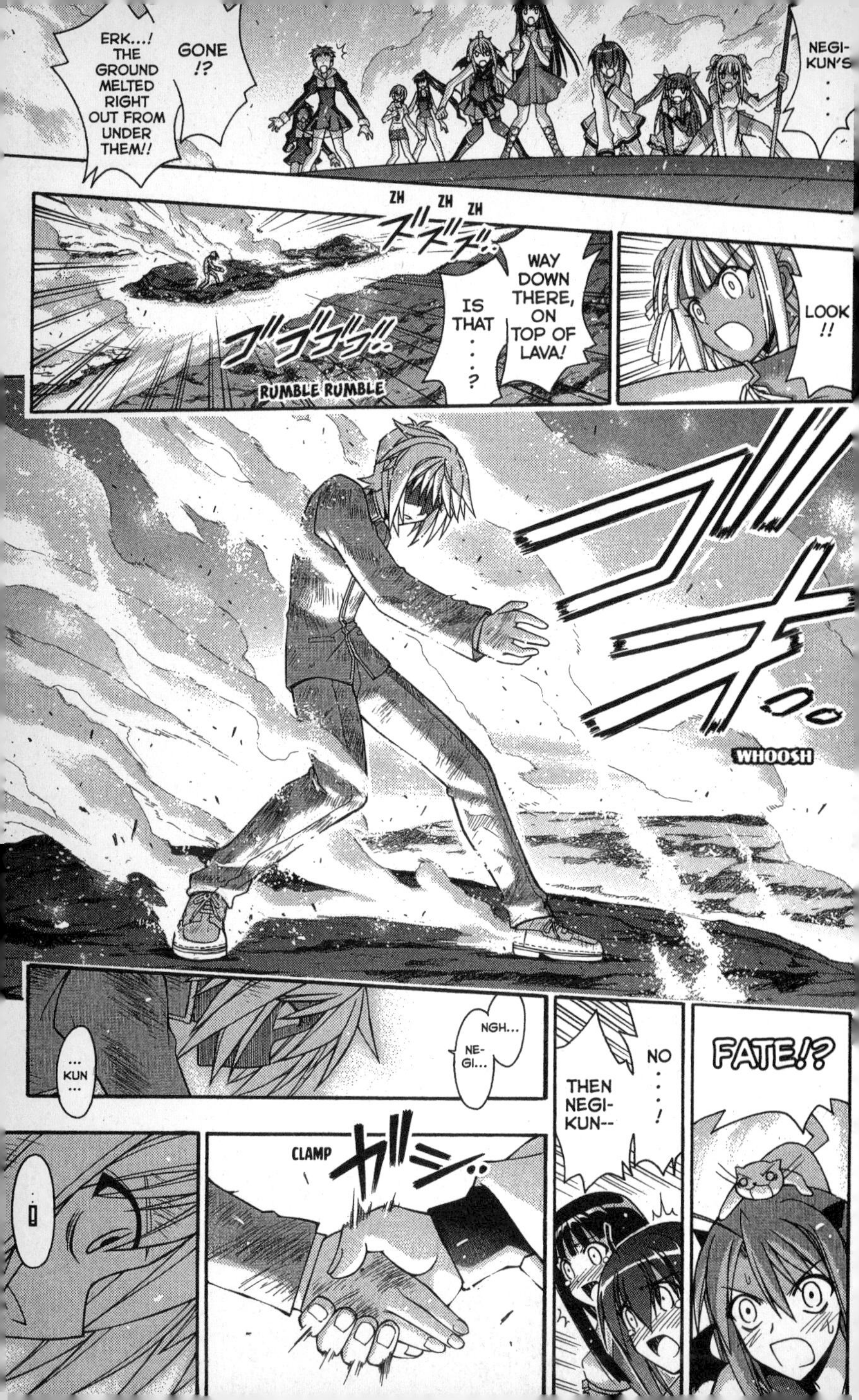
NEGI-KUN'S . . .
GONE !?
ERK...! THE GROUND MELTED RIGHT OUT FROM UNDER THEM!!
LOOK !!
WAY DOWN THERE, ON TOP OF LAVA!
IS THAT . . . ?
ZH ZH ZH
RUMBLE RUMBLE
WHOOSH
FATE!?
NO . . . !
THEN NEGI-KUN--
NGH... NE-GI...
... KUN ...
CLAMP
!

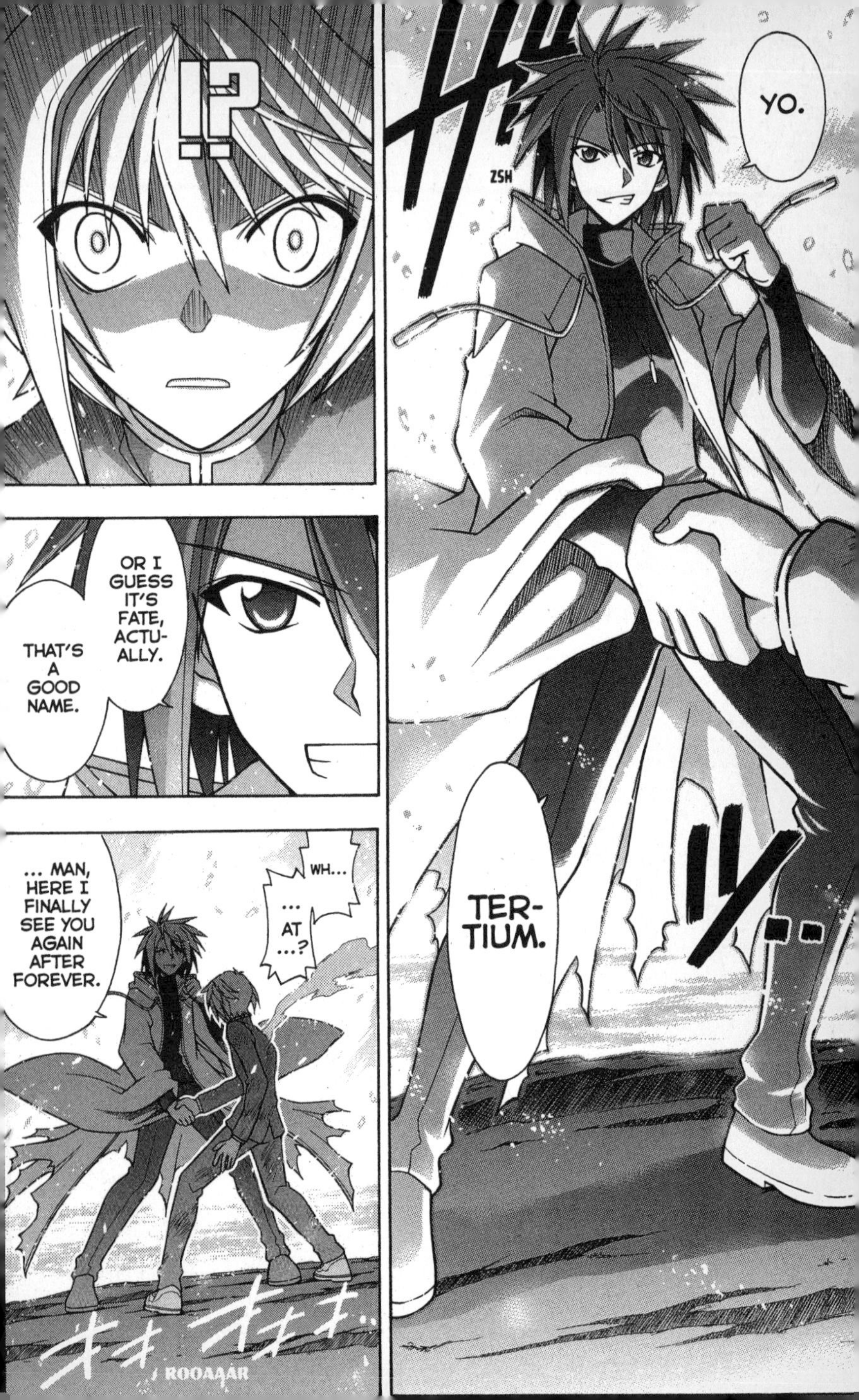
ZSH
YO.
TERTIUM.
!?
OR I GUESS IT'S FATE, ACTUALLY.
THAT'S A GOOD NAME.
WH...
... AT ...?
... MAN, HERE I FINALLY SEE YOU AGAIN AFTER FOREVER.
ROOAAAR

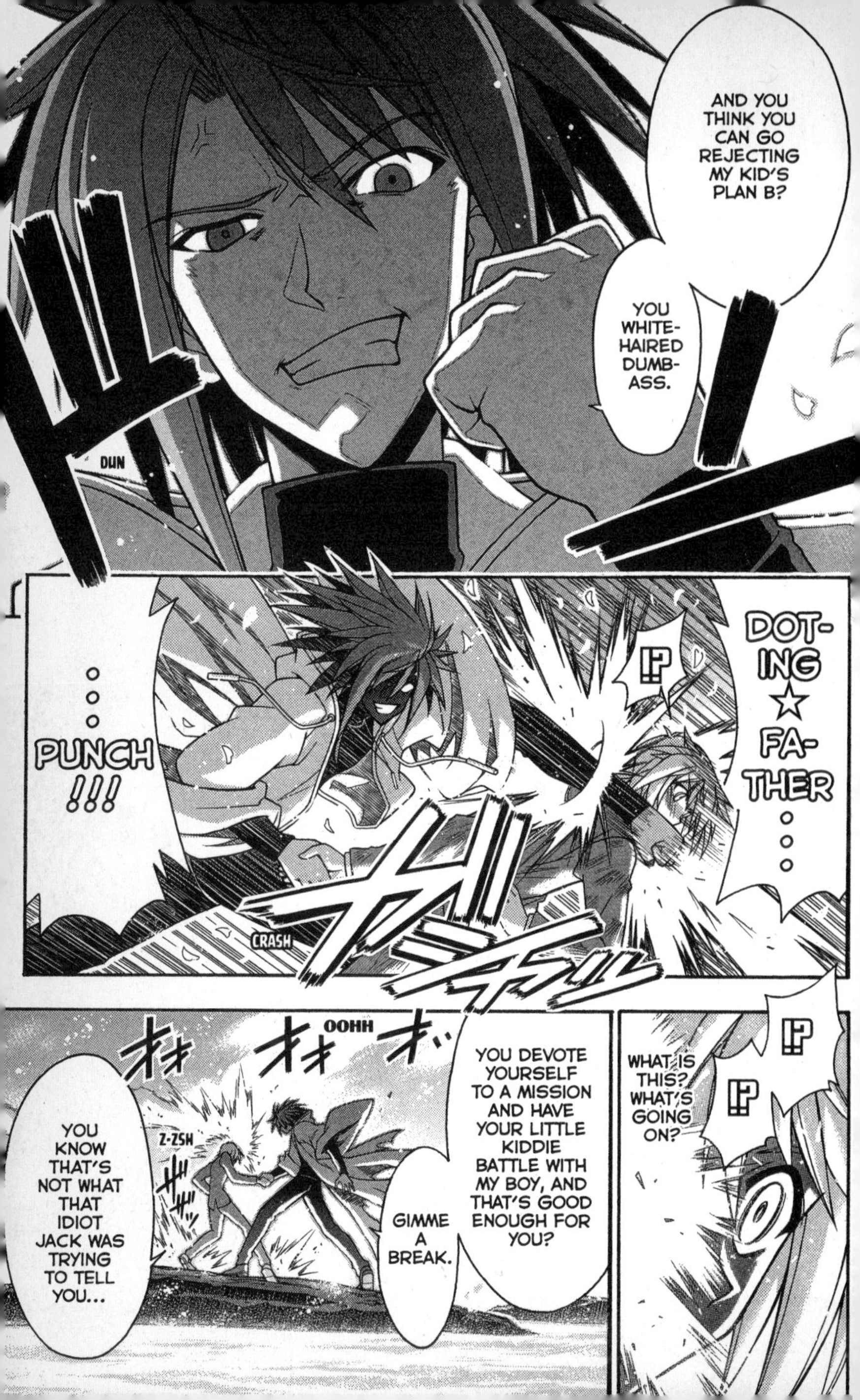
AND YOU THINK YOU CAN GO REJECTING MY KID'S PLAN B?
YOU WHITE-HAIRED DUMB-ASS.
DUN
DOTING☆FATHER...
!?
...PUNCH!!!
CRASH
!?
!?
WHAT IS THIS? WHAT'S GOING ON?
YOU DEVOTE YOURSELF TO A MISSION AND HAVE YOUR LITTLE KIDDIE BATTLE WITH MY BOY, AND THAT'S GOOD ENOUGH FOR YOU?
GIMME A BREAK.
OOHH
Z-ZSH
YOU KNOW THAT'S NOT WHAT THAT IDIOT JACK WAS TRYING TO TELL YOU...

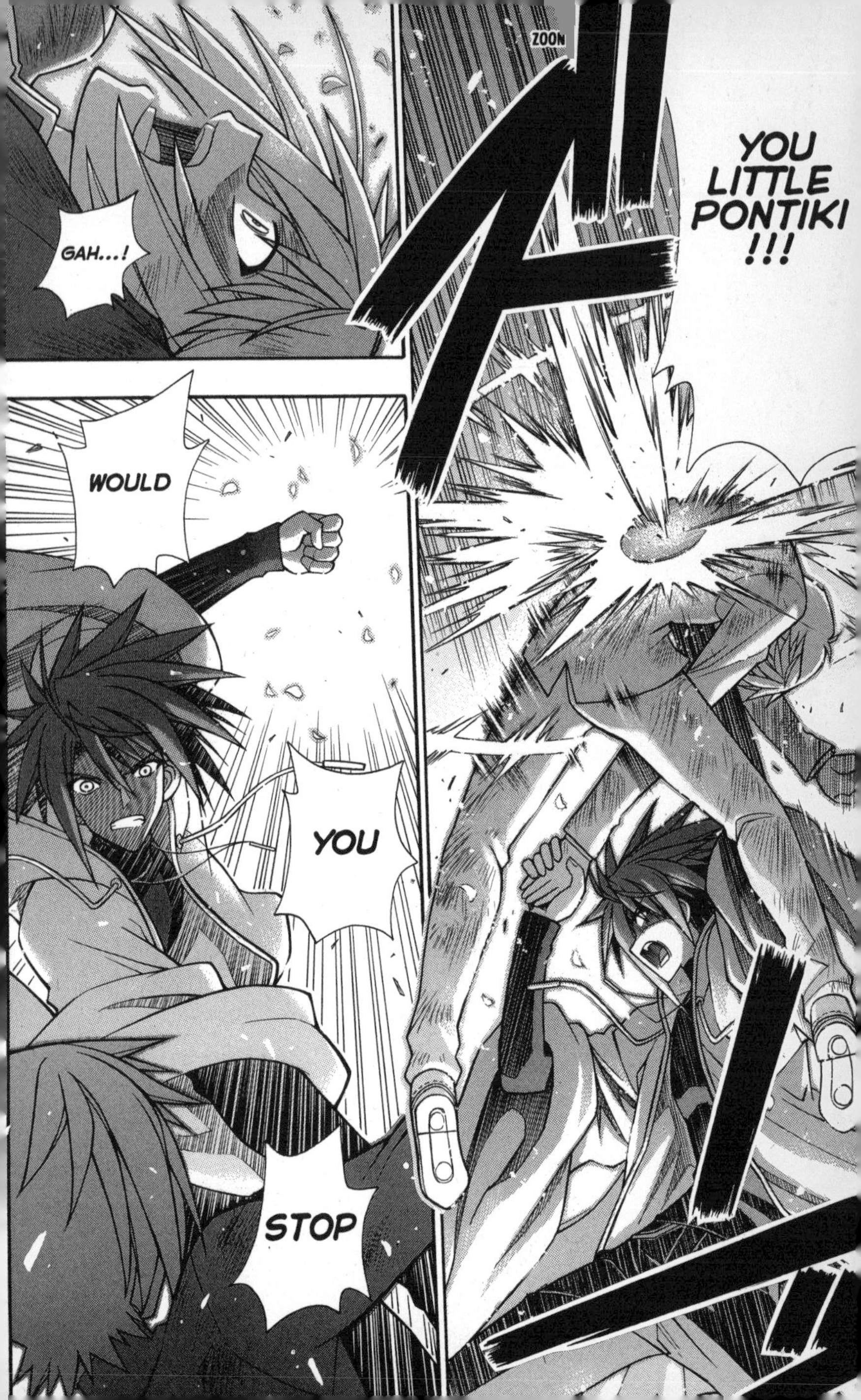
ZOON
YOU LITTLE PONTIKI !!!
GAH...!
WOULD
YOU
STOP

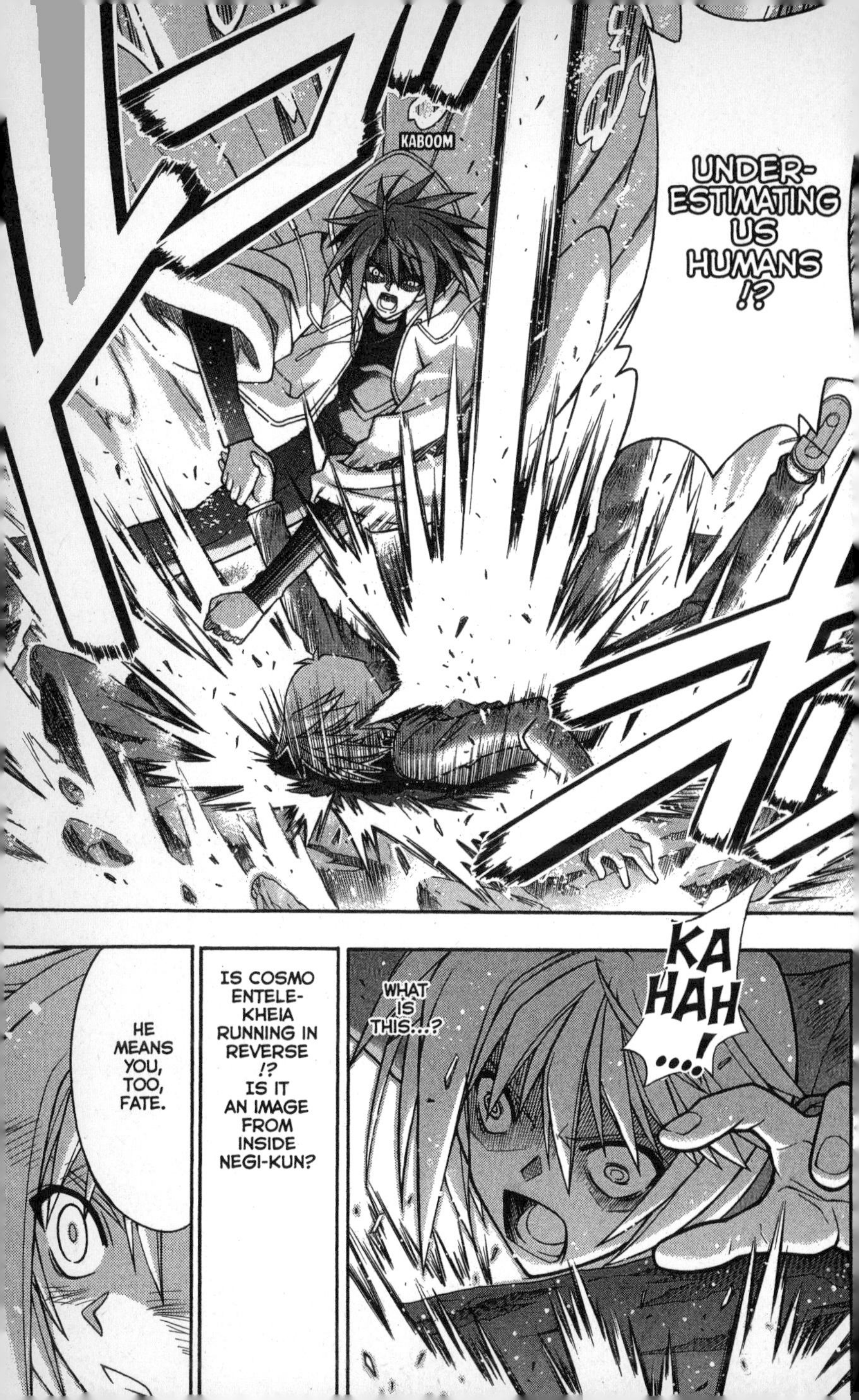

UNDER-ESTIMATING US HUMANS!?
KABOOM
KAHAH...!
WHAT IS THIS...?
IS COSMO ENTELEKHEIA RUNNING IN REVERSE!? IS IT AN IMAGE FROM INSIDE NEGI-KUN?
HE MEANS YOU, TOO, FATE.

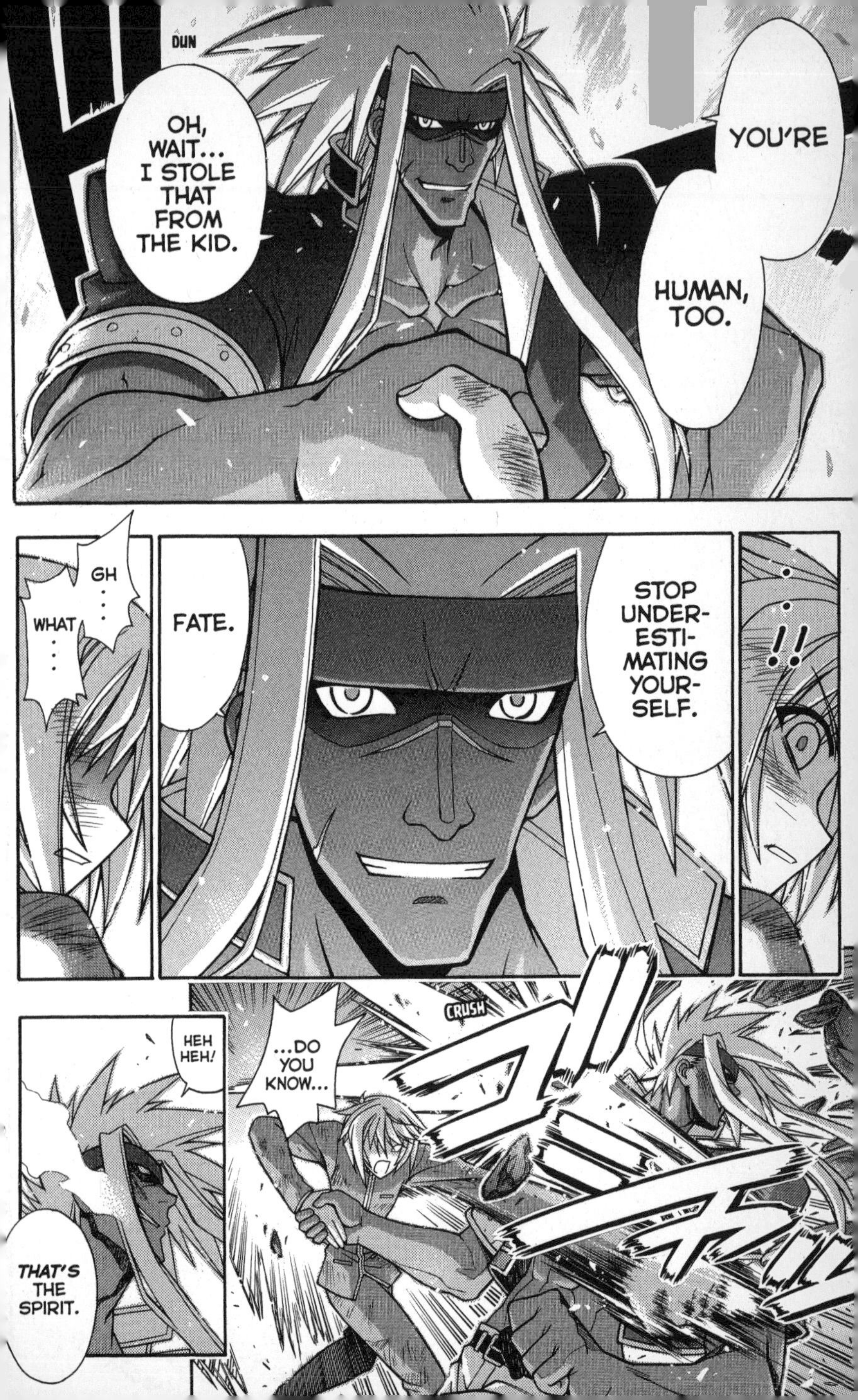
DUN
YOU'RE
HUMAN, TOO.
OH, WAIT... I STOLE THAT FROM THE KID.
...!!
STOP UNDER-ESTI-MATING YOUR-SELF.
FATE.
GH...
WHAT...
CRUSH
...DO YOU KNOW...
HEH HEH!
THAT'S THE SPIRIT.

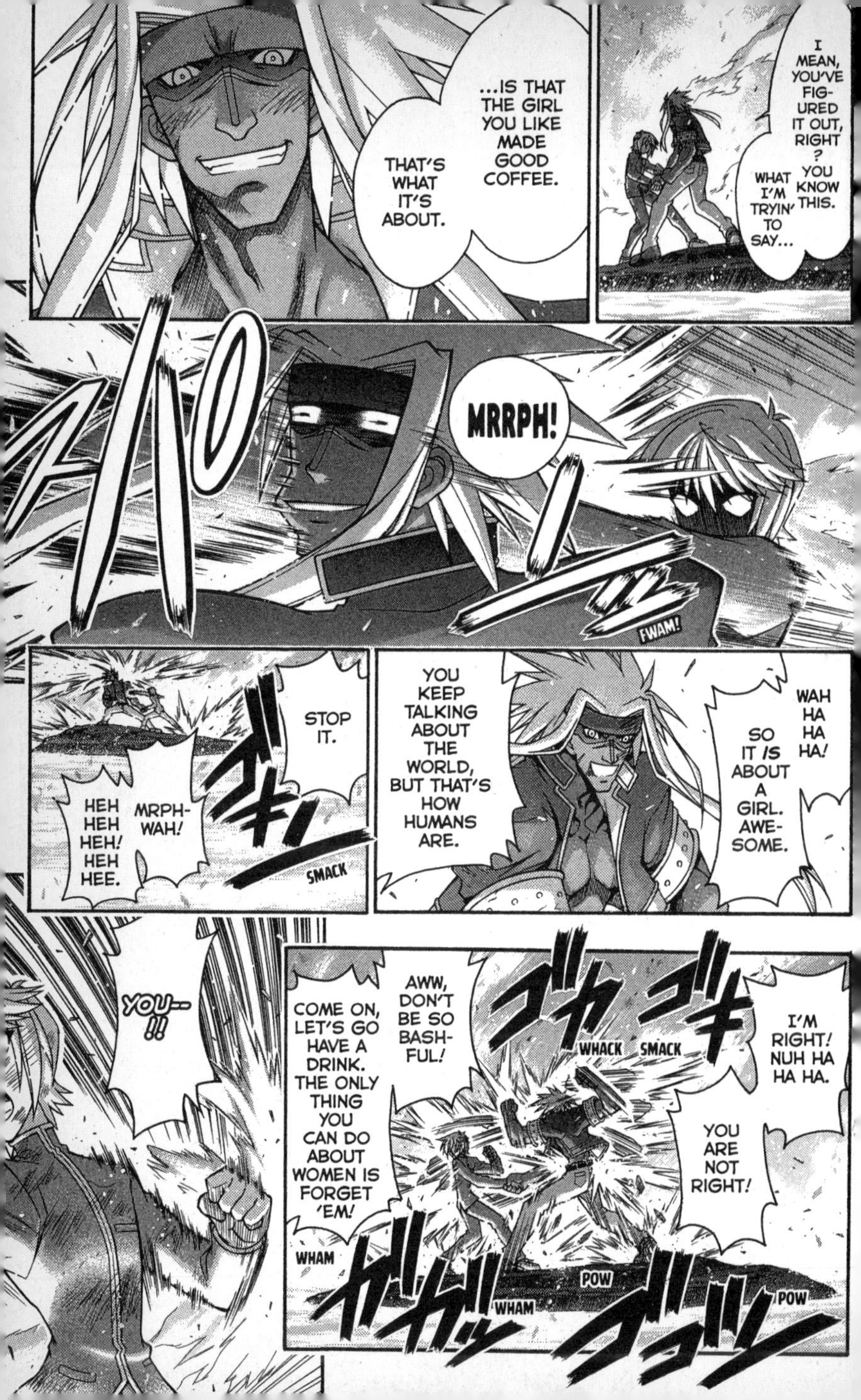
I MEAN, YOU'VE FIG-URED IT OUT, RIGHT? YOU KNOW THIS.
WHAT I'M TRYIN' TO SAY...
...IS THAT THE GIRL YOU LIKE MADE GOOD COFFEE.
THAT'S WHAT IT'S ABOUT.
MRRPH!
FWAM!
WAH HA HA HA!
SO IT IS ABOUT A GIRL. AWE-SOME.
YOU KEEP TALKING ABOUT THE WORLD, BUT THAT'S HOW HUMANS ARE.
STOP IT.
SMACK
MRPH-WAH!
HEH HEH HEH! HEH HEE.
I'M RIGHT! NUH HA HA HA.
SMACK
WHACK
AWW, DON'T BE SO BASH-FUL!
COME ON, LET'S GO HAVE A DRINK. THE ONLY THING YOU CAN DO ABOUT WOMEN IS FORGET 'EM!
YOU ARE NOT RIGHT!
POW
POW
WHAM
WHAM
YOU--!!

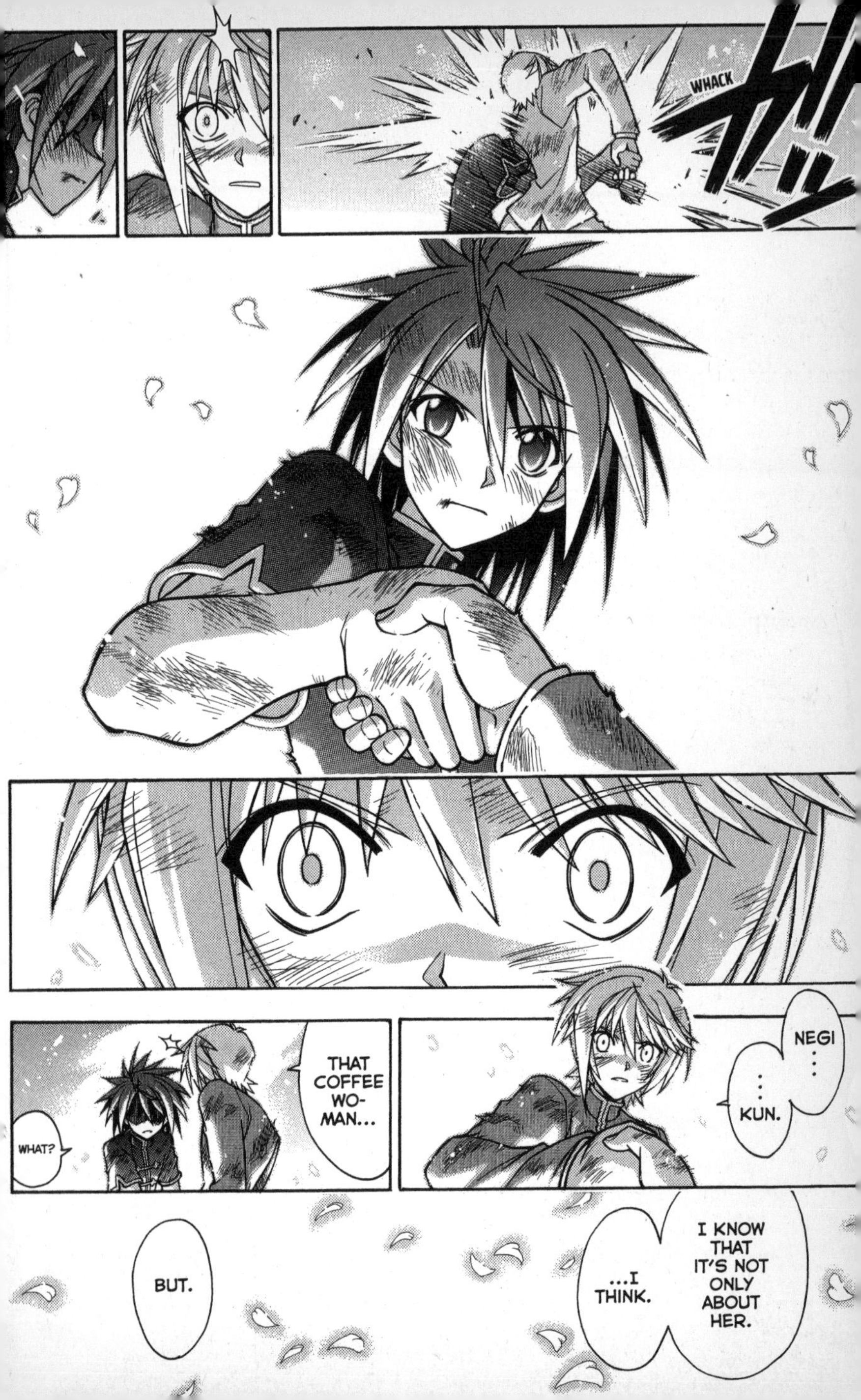
WHACK
NEGI... ...KUN.
THAT COFFEE WO-MAN...
WHAT?
I KNOW THAT IT'S NOT ONLY ABOUT HER.
...I THINK.
BUT.

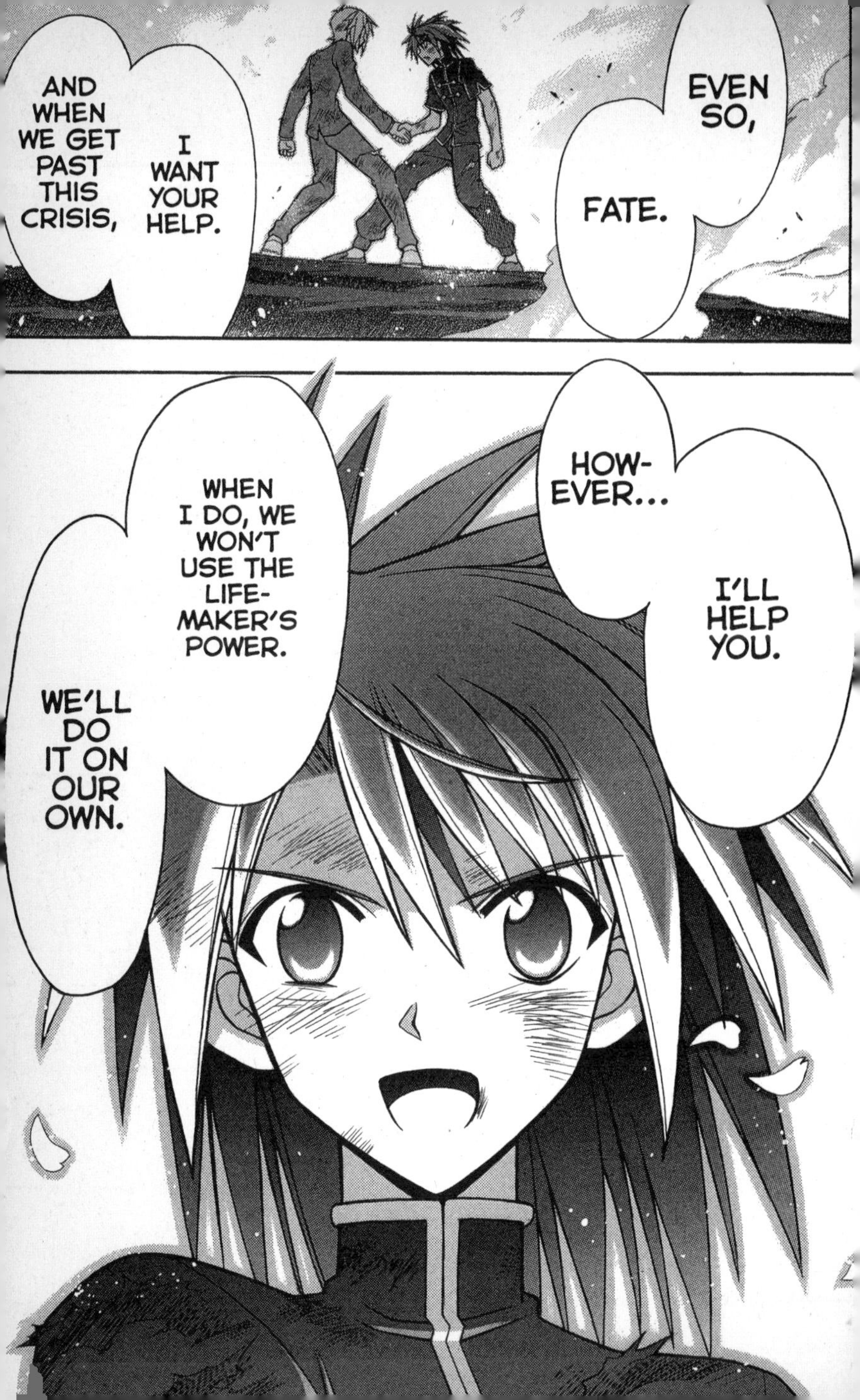
EVEN SO, FATE.
AND WHEN WE GET PAST THIS CRISIS, I WANT YOUR HELP.
HOW-EVER... I'LL HELP YOU.
WHEN I DO, WE WON'T USE THE LIFE-MAKER'S POWER. WE'LL DO IT ON OUR OWN.

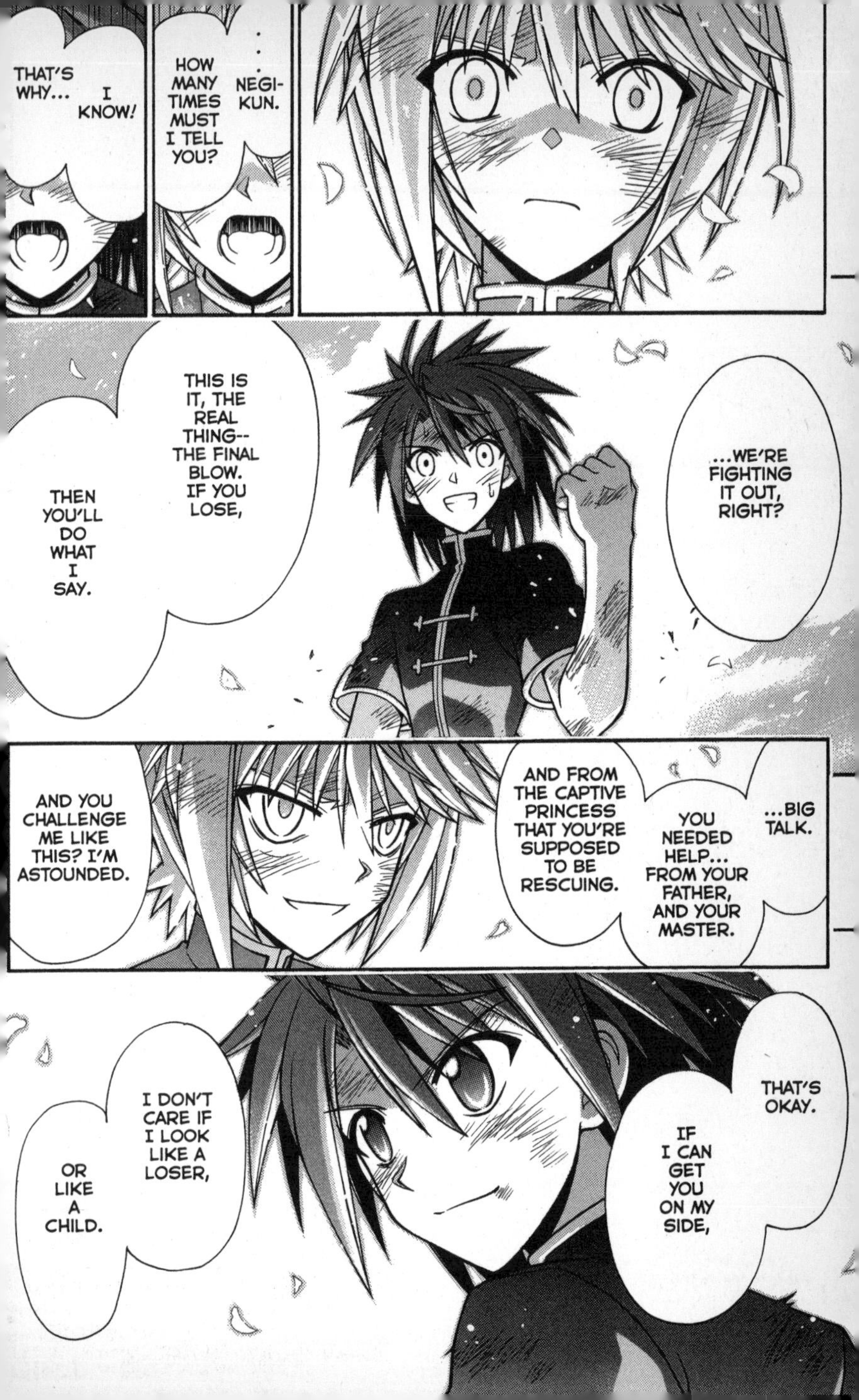
...NEGI-KUN.
HOW MANY TIMES MUST I TELL YOU?
I KNOW!
THAT'S WHY...
...WE'RE FIGHTING IT OUT, RIGHT?
THIS IS IT, THE REAL THING-- THE FINAL BLOW. IF YOU LOSE,
THEN YOU'LL DO WHAT I SAY.
...BIG TALK.
YOU NEEDED HELP... FROM YOUR FATHER, AND YOUR MASTER.
AND FROM THE CAPTIVE PRINCESS THAT YOU'RE SUPPOSED TO BE RESCUING.
AND YOU CHALLENGE ME LIKE THIS? I'M ASTOUNDED.
THAT'S OKAY.
IF I CAN GET YOU ON MY SIDE,
I DON'T CARE IF I LOOK LIKE A LOSER,
OR LIKE A CHILD.

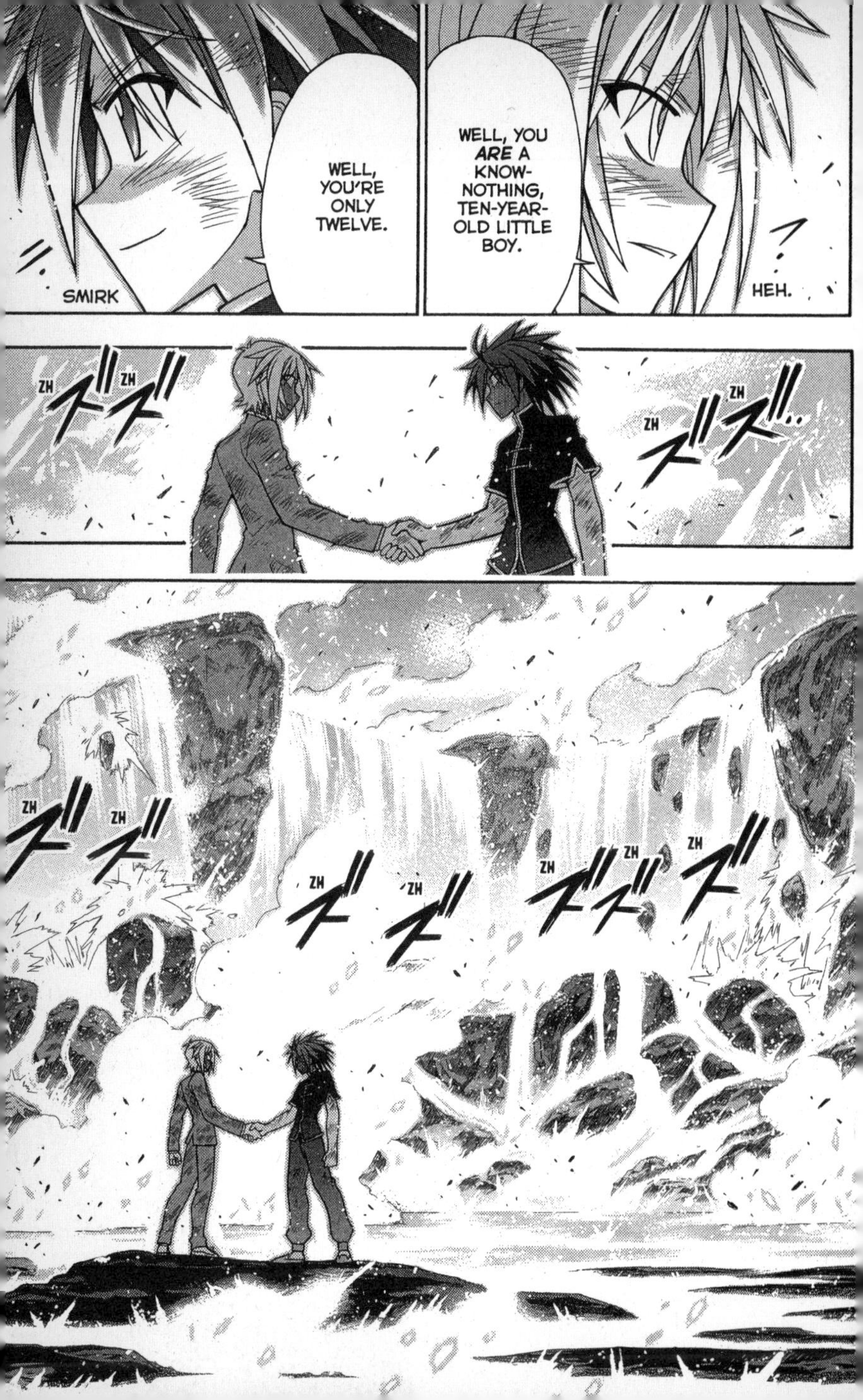

WELL, YOU *ARE* A KNOW-NOTHING, TEN-YEAR-OLD LITTLE BOY.
HEH.
WELL, YOU'RE ONLY TWELVE.
SMIRK
ZH ZH
ZH ZH
ZH ZH ZH ZH
ZH ZH ZH ZH

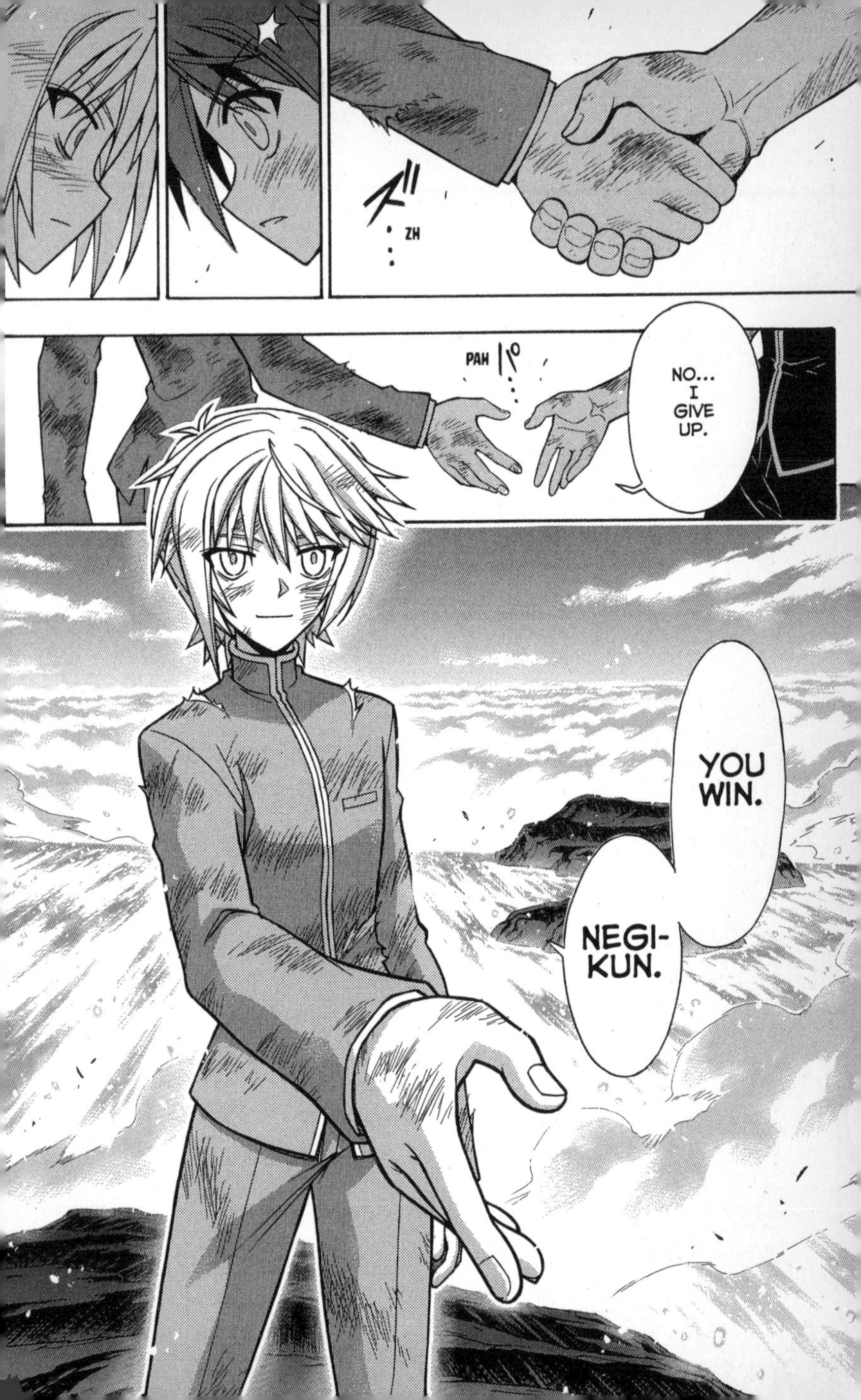
ZH
NO... I GIVE UP.
PAH
YOU WIN.
NEGI-KUN.

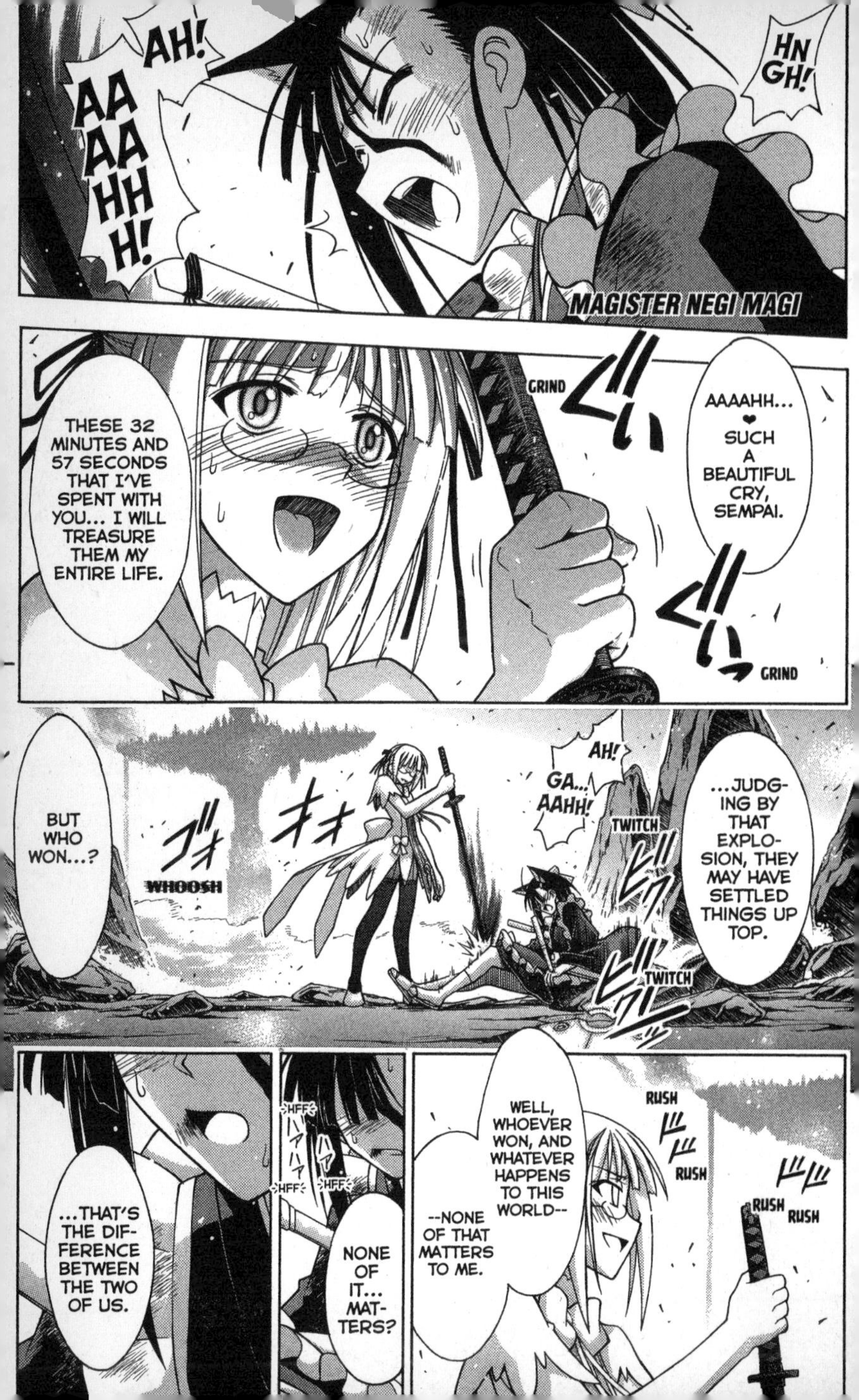
HNGH!
AH!
AAAAAHHHH!
MAGISTER NEGI MAGI
AAAAHH... ❤ SUCH A BEAUTIFUL CRY, SEMPAI.
GRIND
GRIND
THESE 32 MINUTES AND 57 SECONDS THAT I'VE SPENT WITH YOU... I WILL TREASURE THEM MY ENTIRE LIFE.
...JUDGING BY THAT EXPLOSION, THEY MAY HAVE SETTLED THINGS UP TOP.
AH! GA... AAHH!
TWITCH
TWITCH
WHOOSH
BUT WHO WON...?
RUSH
RUSH
RUSH
RUSH
WELL, WHOEVER WON, AND WHATEVER HAPPENS TO THIS WORLD--
--NONE OF THAT MATTERS TO ME.
HFF
HFF
HFF
NONE OF IT... MATTERS?
...THAT'S THE DIFFERENCE BETWEEN THE TWO OF US.

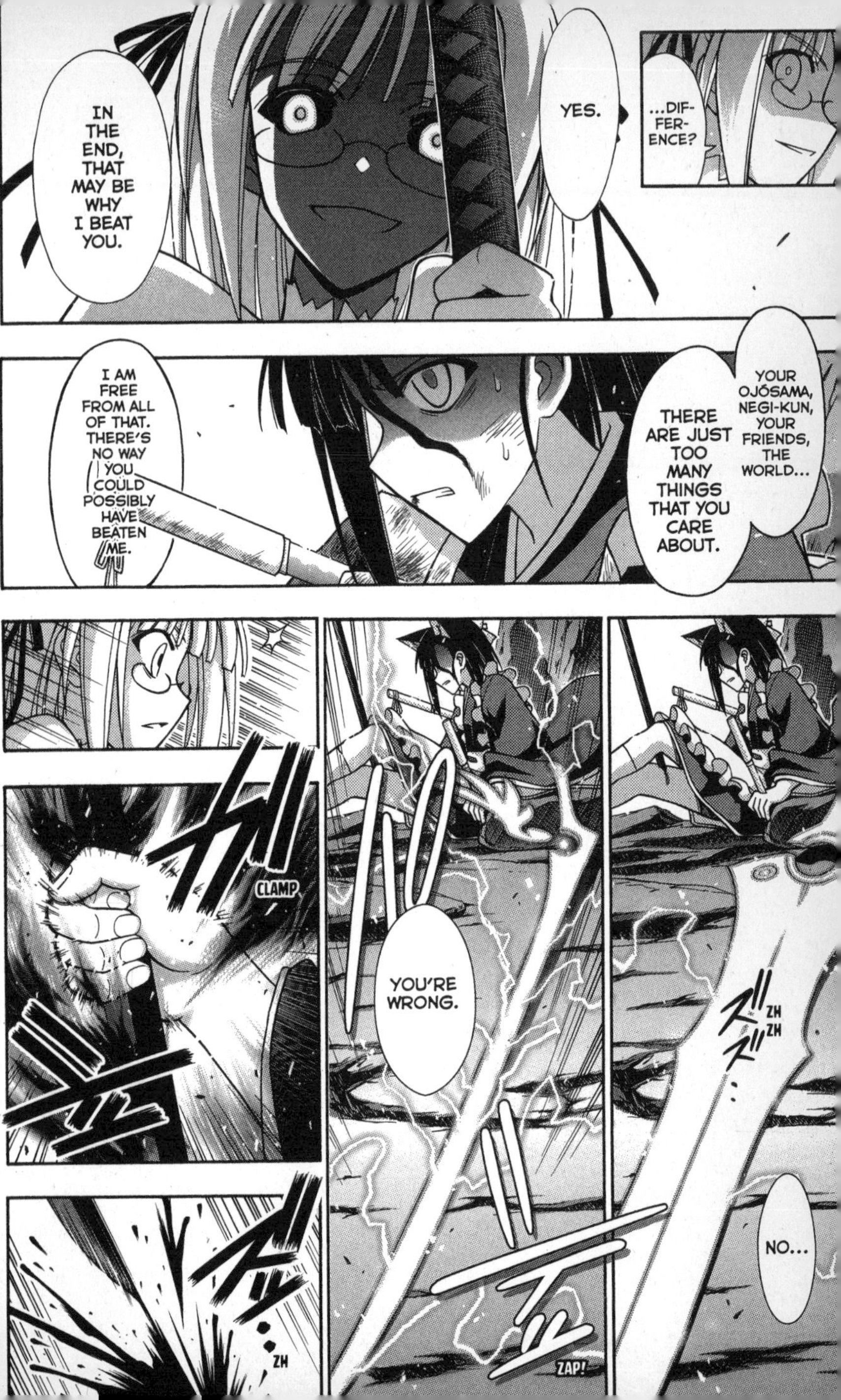

...DIF-FERENCE?
YES.
IN THE END, THAT MAY BE WHY I BEAT YOU.
YOUR OJÓSAMA, NEGI-KUN, YOUR FRIENDS, THE WORLD...
THERE ARE JUST TOO MANY THINGS THAT YOU CARE ABOUT.
I AM FREE FROM ALL OF THAT. THERE'S NO WAY YOU COULD POSSIBLY HAVE BEATEN ME.
ZH ZH
NO...
YOU'RE WRONG.
ZAP!
CLAMP
ZH

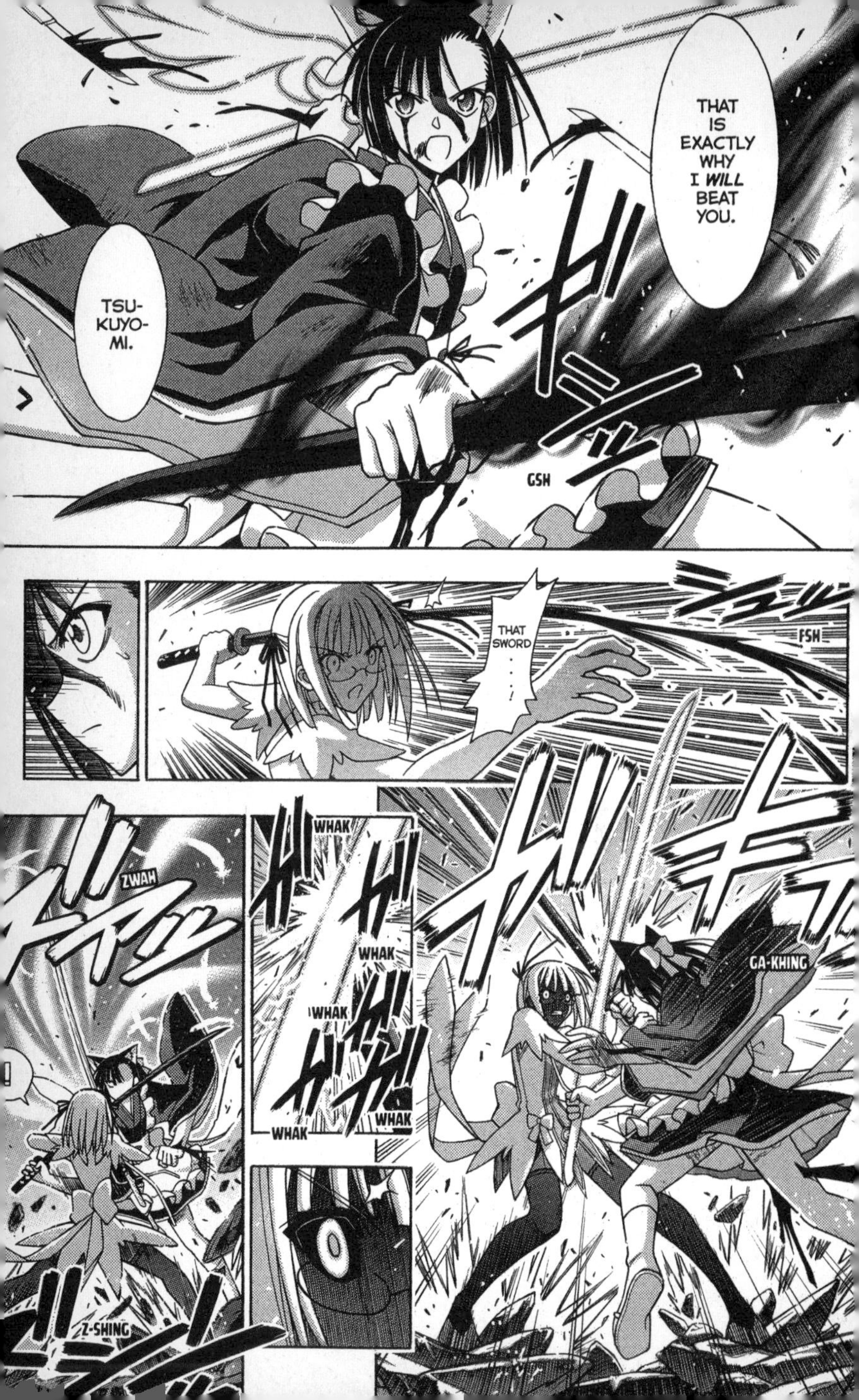
THAT IS EXACTLY WHY I WILL BEAT YOU.
TSU-KUYO-MI.
GSH
FSH
THAT SWORD
...
GA-KHING
WHAK
WHAK
WHAK
WHAK
WHAK
ZWAH
!
Z-SHING

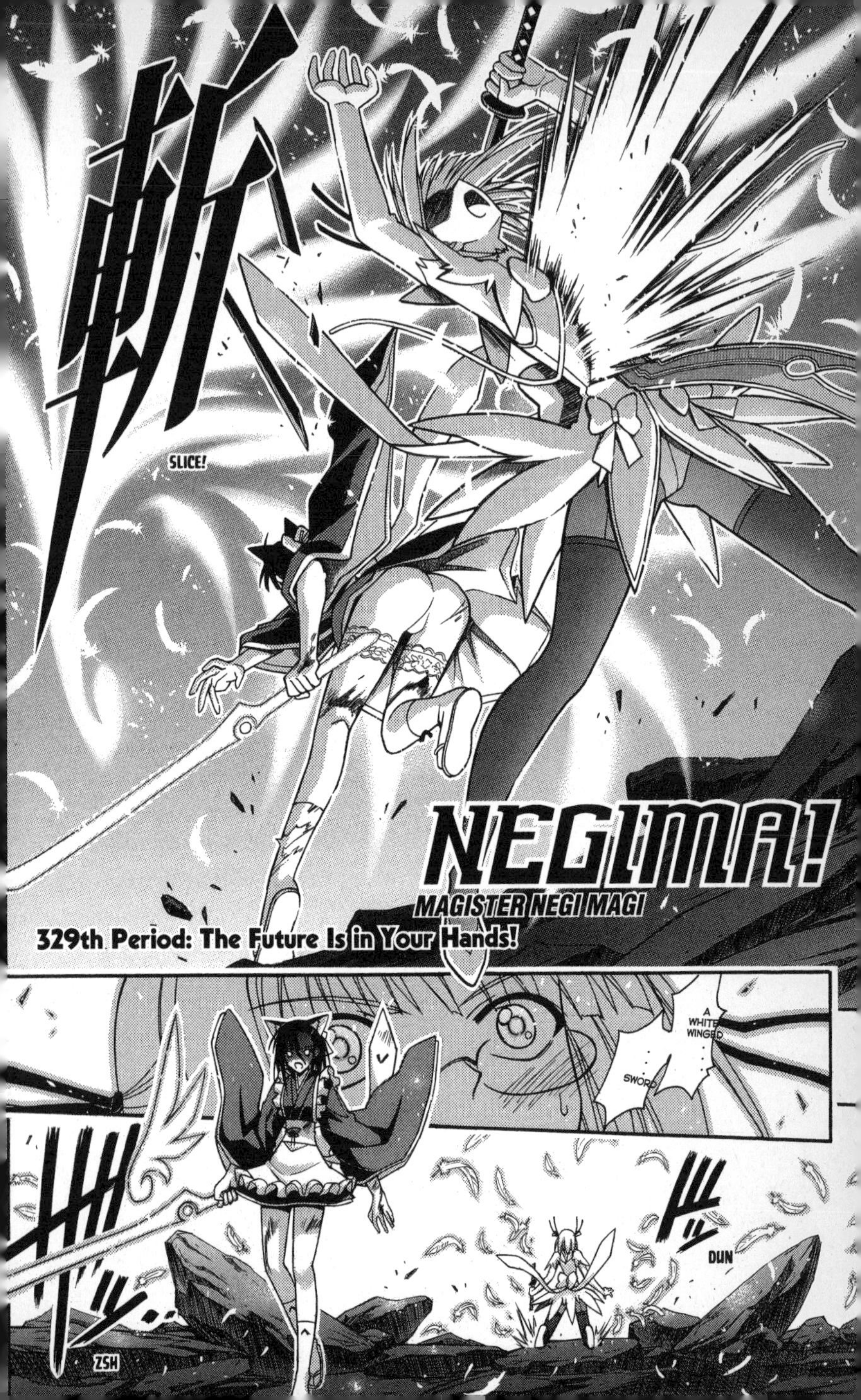
SLICE!
NEGIMA!
MAGISTER NEGI MAGI
329th Period: The Future Is in Your Hands!
A WHITE WINGED
...
SWORD
DUN
ZSH

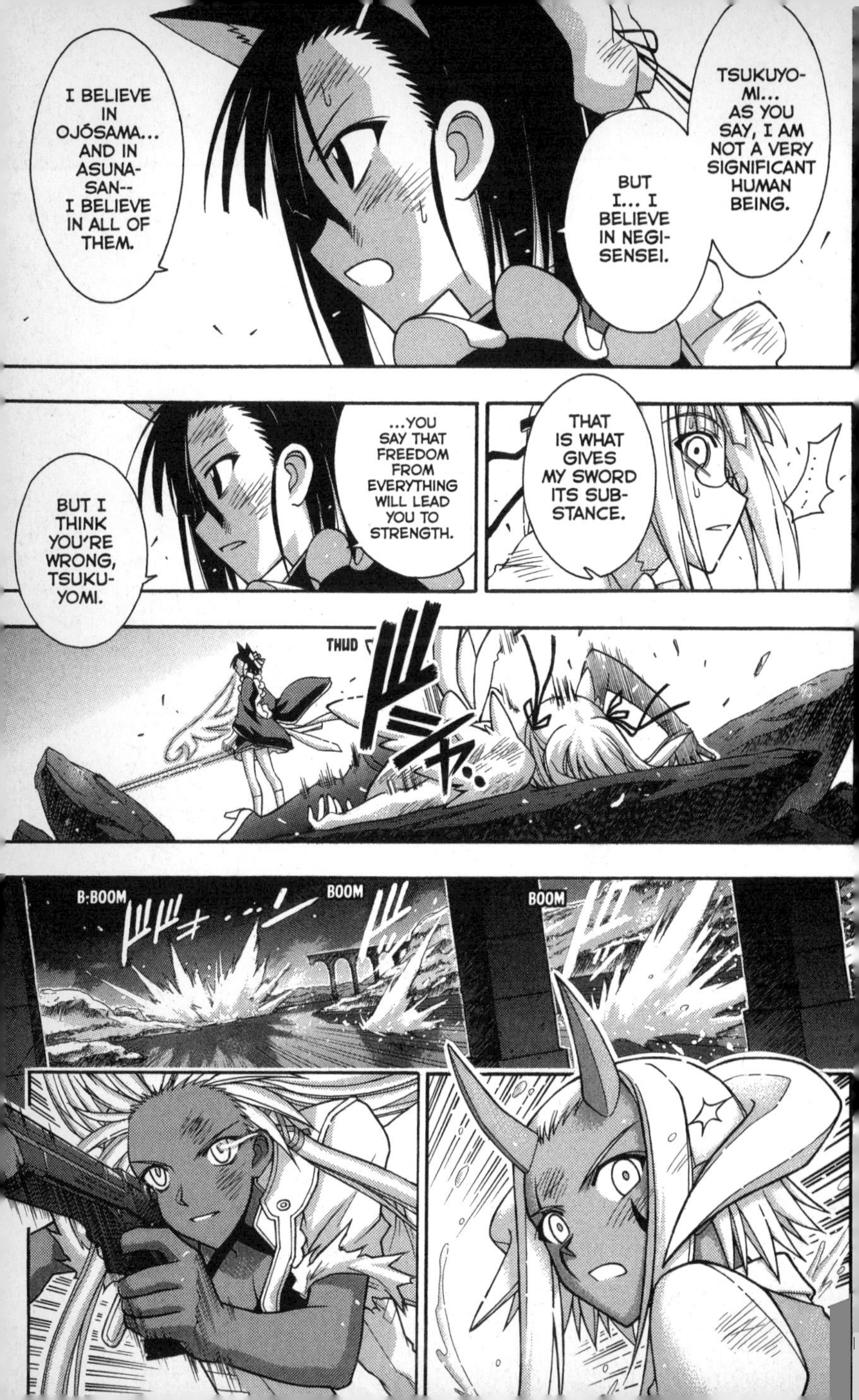
TSUKUYOMI... AS YOU SAY, I AM NOT A VERY SIGNIFICANT HUMAN BEING.
BUT I... I BELIEVE IN NEGI-SENSEI.
I BELIEVE IN OJÓSAMA... AND IN ASUNA-SAN-- I BELIEVE IN ALL OF THEM.
THAT IS WHAT GIVES MY SWORD ITS SUBSTANCE.
...YOU SAY THAT FREEDOM FROM EVERYTHING WILL LEAD YOU TO STRENGTH.
BUT I THINK YOU'RE WRONG, TSUKUYOMI.
THUD
BOOM
BOOM
B·BOOM

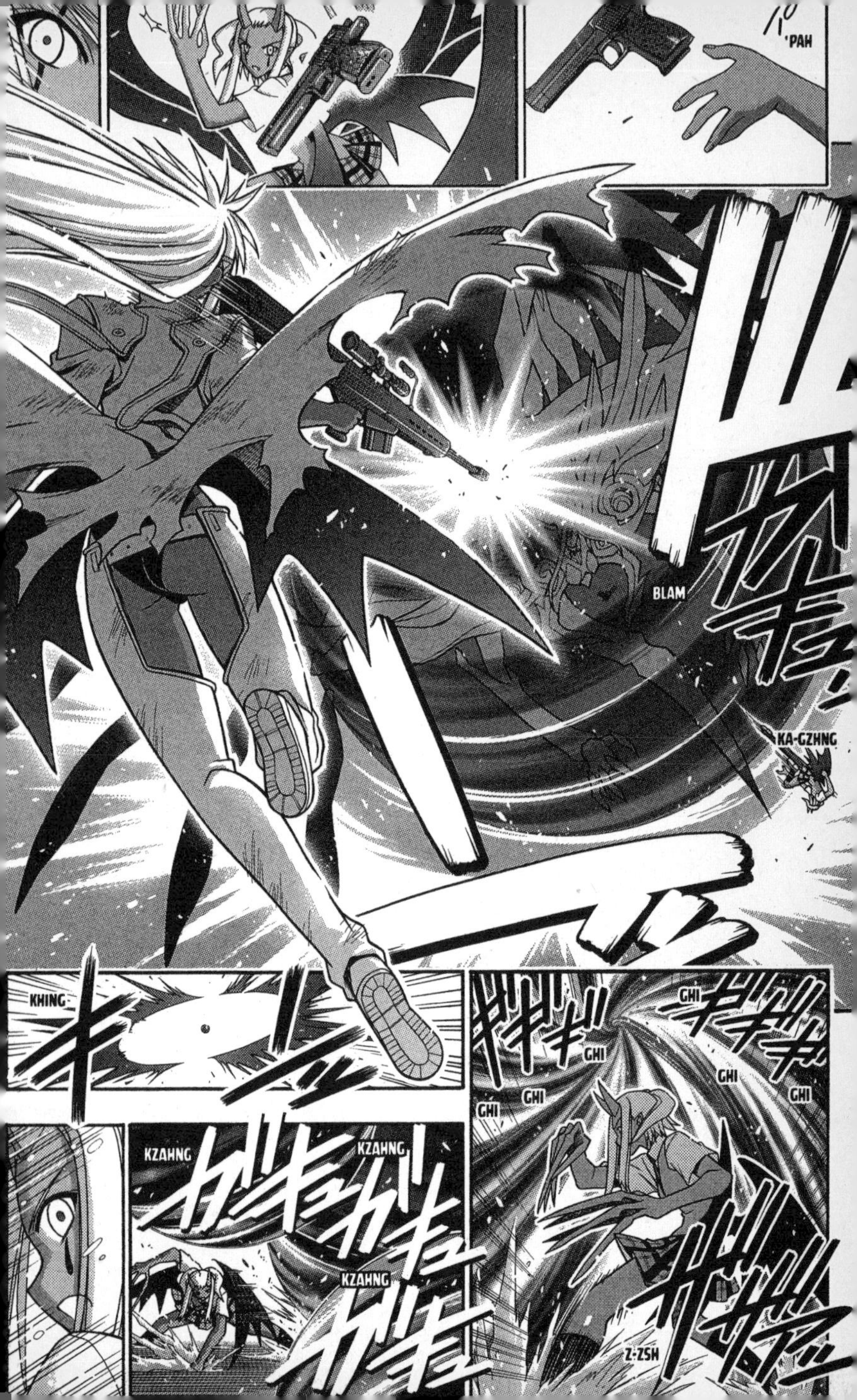
PAH
BLAM
KA-GZHNG
GHI
GHI
GHI
GHI
GHI
GHI
Z-ZSH
KHING
KZAHNG
KZAHNG
KZAHNG

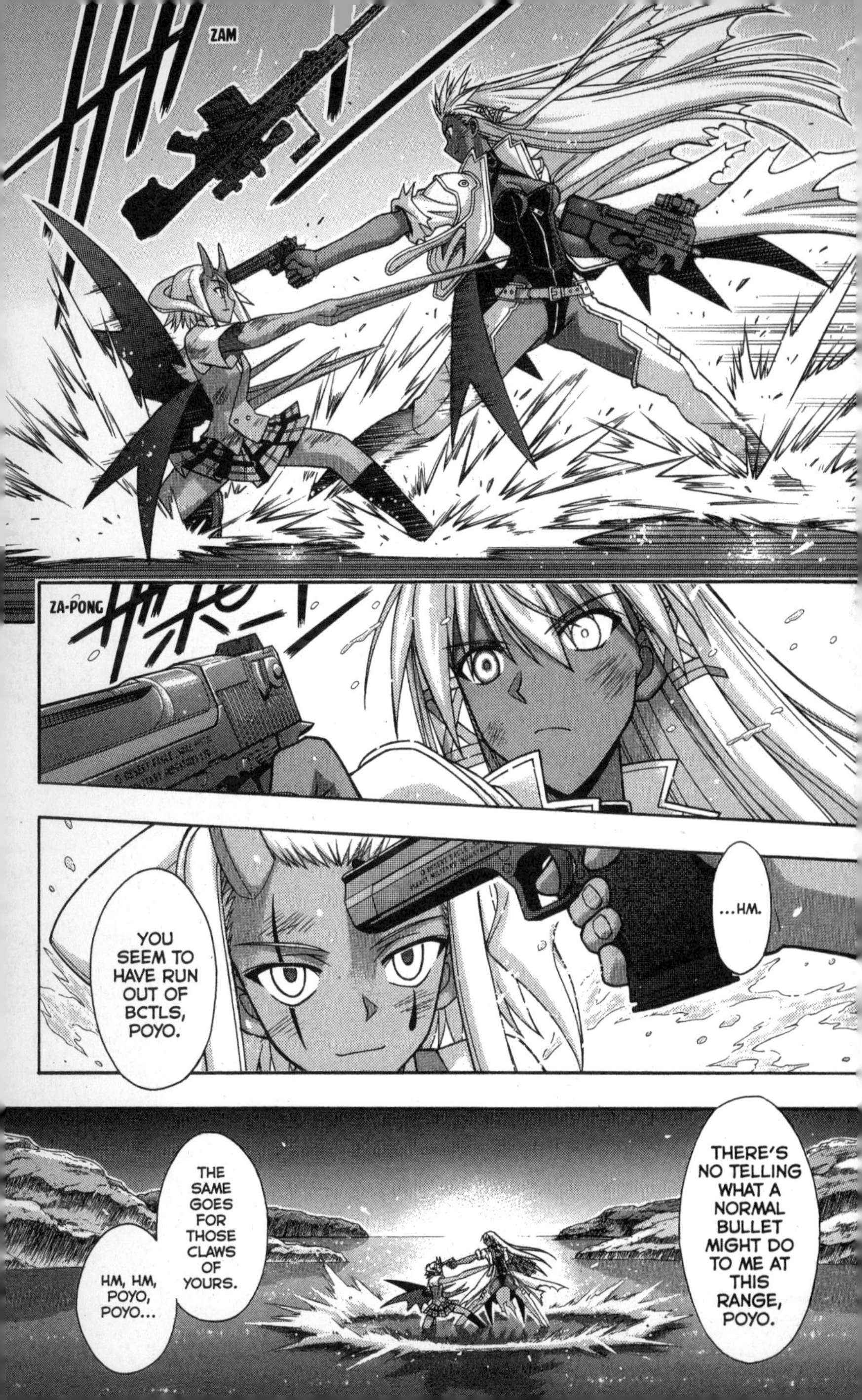
ZAM
ZA-PONG
...HM.
YOU SEEM TO HAVE RUN OUT OF BCTLS, POYO.
THERE'S NO TELLING WHAT A NORMAL BULLET MIGHT DO TO ME AT THIS RANGE, POYO.
THE SAME GOES FOR THOSE CLAWS OF YOURS.
HM, HM, POYO, POYO...

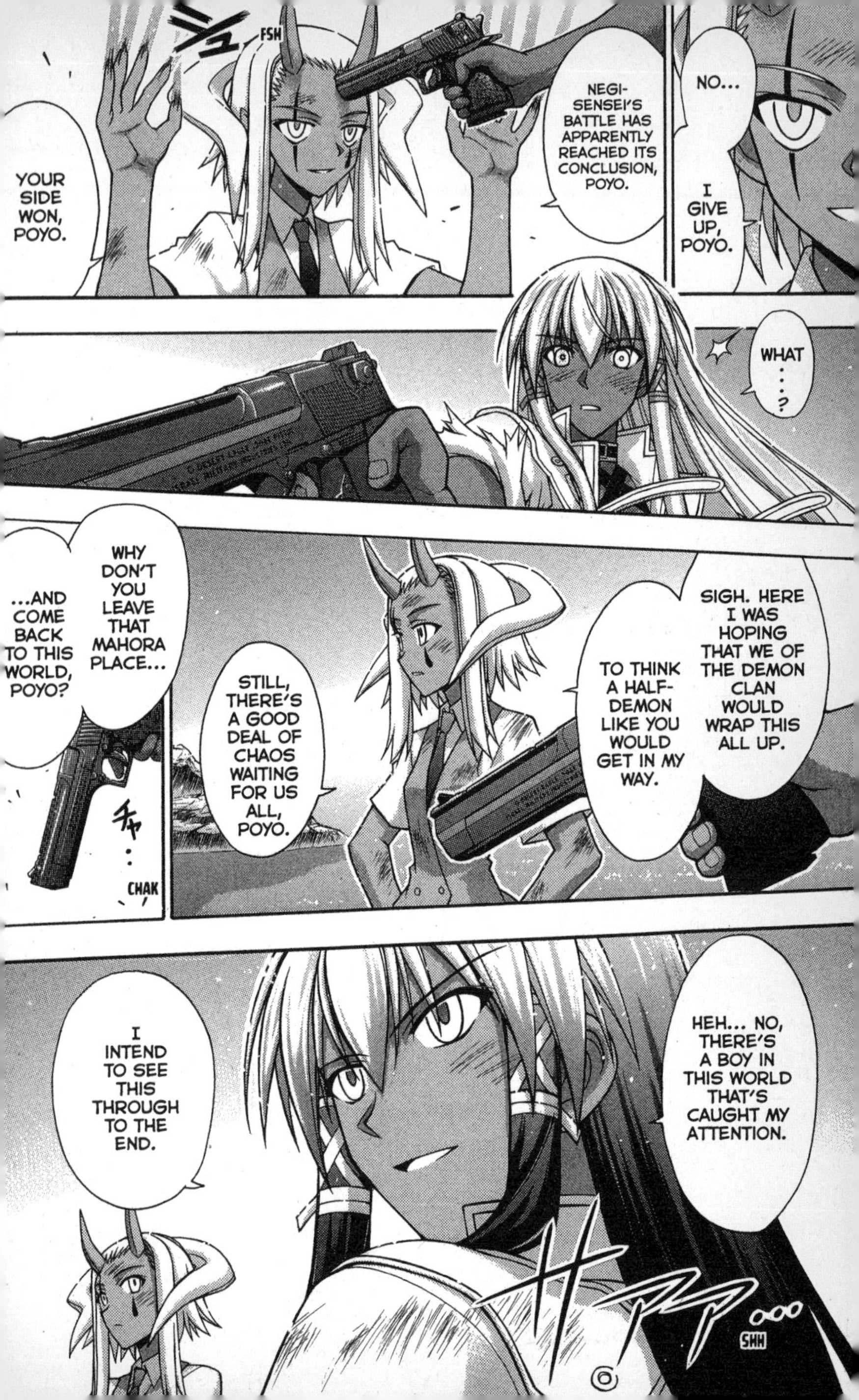
NO...
I GIVE UP, POYO.
FSH
NEGI-SENSEI'S BATTLE HAS APPARENTLY REACHED ITS CONCLUSION, POYO.
YOUR SIDE WON, POYO.
WHAT...?
SIGH. HERE I WAS HOPING THAT WE OF THE DEMON CLAN WOULD WRAP THIS ALL UP.
TO THINK A HALF-DEMON LIKE YOU WOULD GET IN MY WAY.
STILL, THERE'S A GOOD DEAL OF CHAOS WAITING FOR US ALL, POYO.
CHAK
WHY DON'T YOU LEAVE THAT MAHORA PLACE...
...AND COME BACK TO THIS WORLD, POYO?
HEH... NO, THERE'S A BOY IN THIS WORLD THAT'S CAUGHT MY ATTENTION.
I INTEND TO SEE THIS THROUGH TO THE END.
SHH

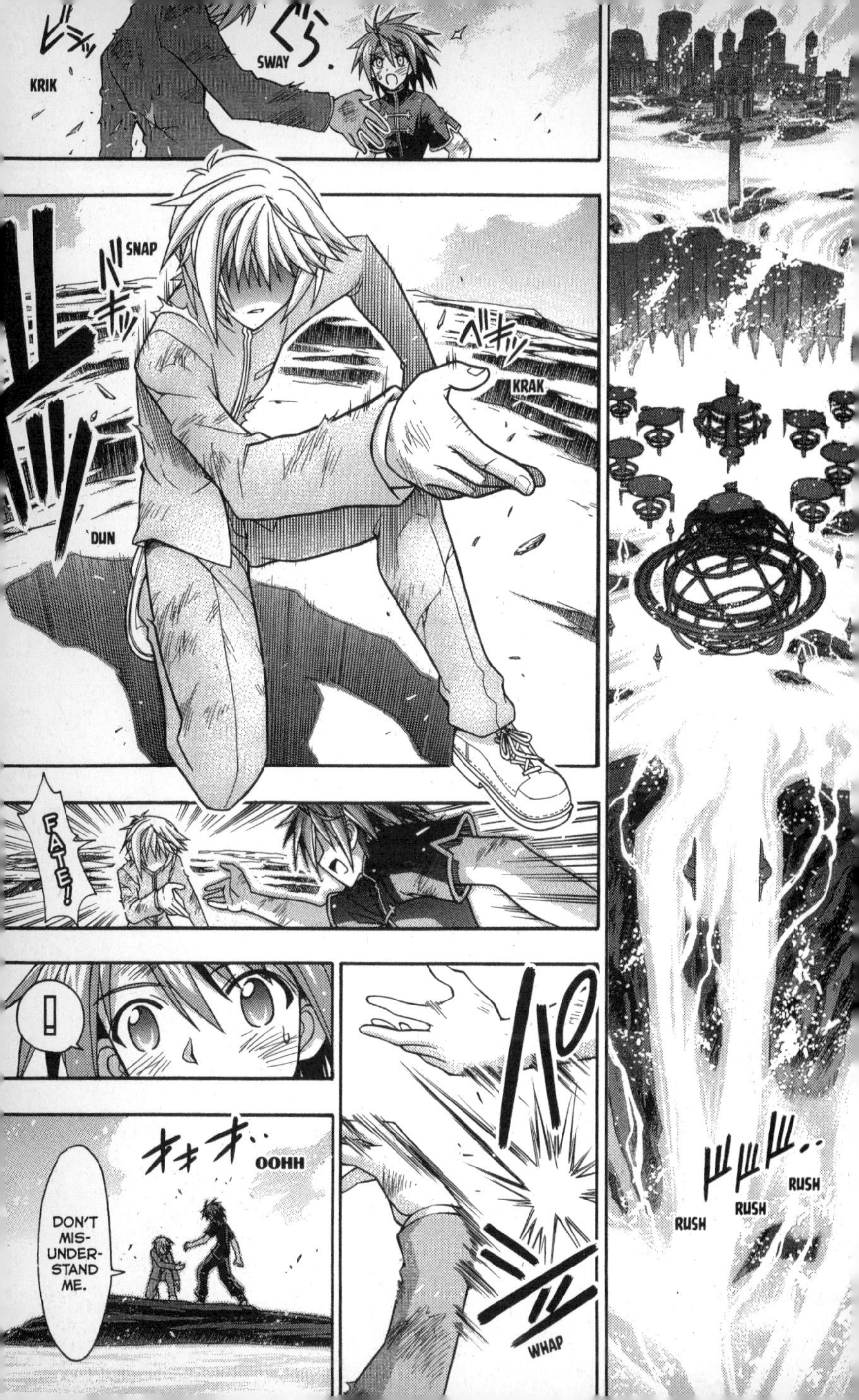
RUSH
RUSH
RUSH
KRIK
SWAY
SNAP
KRAK
DUN
FATE!
WHAP
!
OOHH
DON'T MIS-UNDER-STAND ME.

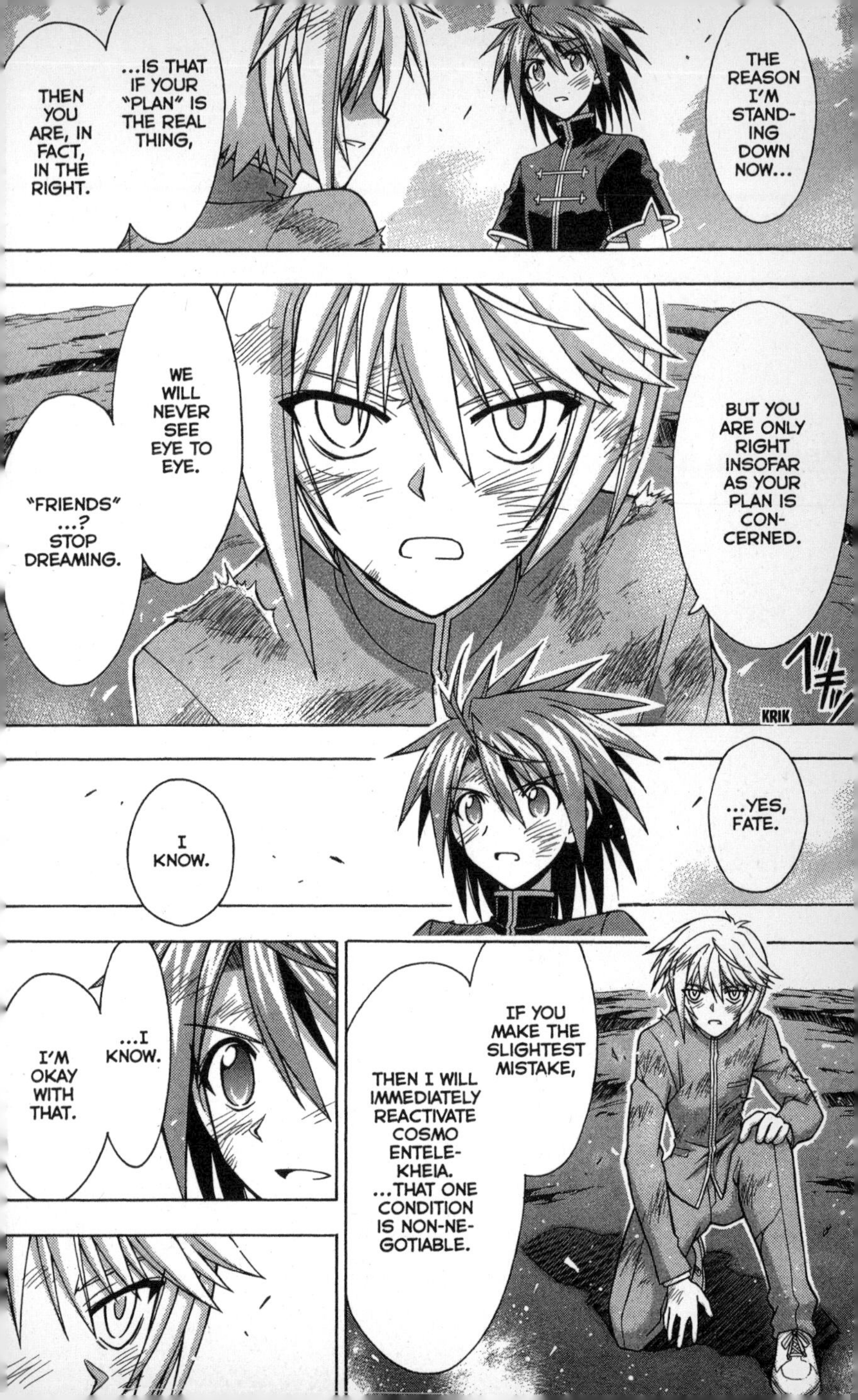
THE REASON I'M STANDING DOWN NOW...
...IS THAT IF YOUR "PLAN" IS THE REAL THING,
THEN YOU ARE, IN FACT, IN THE RIGHT.
BUT YOU ARE ONLY RIGHT INSOFAR AS YOUR PLAN IS CONCERNED.
WE WILL NEVER SEE EYE TO EYE.
"FRIENDS" ...? STOP DREAMING.
KRIK
...YES, FATE.
I KNOW.
IF YOU MAKE THE SLIGHTEST MISTAKE,
THEN I WILL IMMEDIATELY REACTIVATE COSMO ENTELEKHEIA. ...THAT ONE CONDITION IS NON-NEGOTIABLE.
...I KNOW.
I'M OKAY WITH THAT.

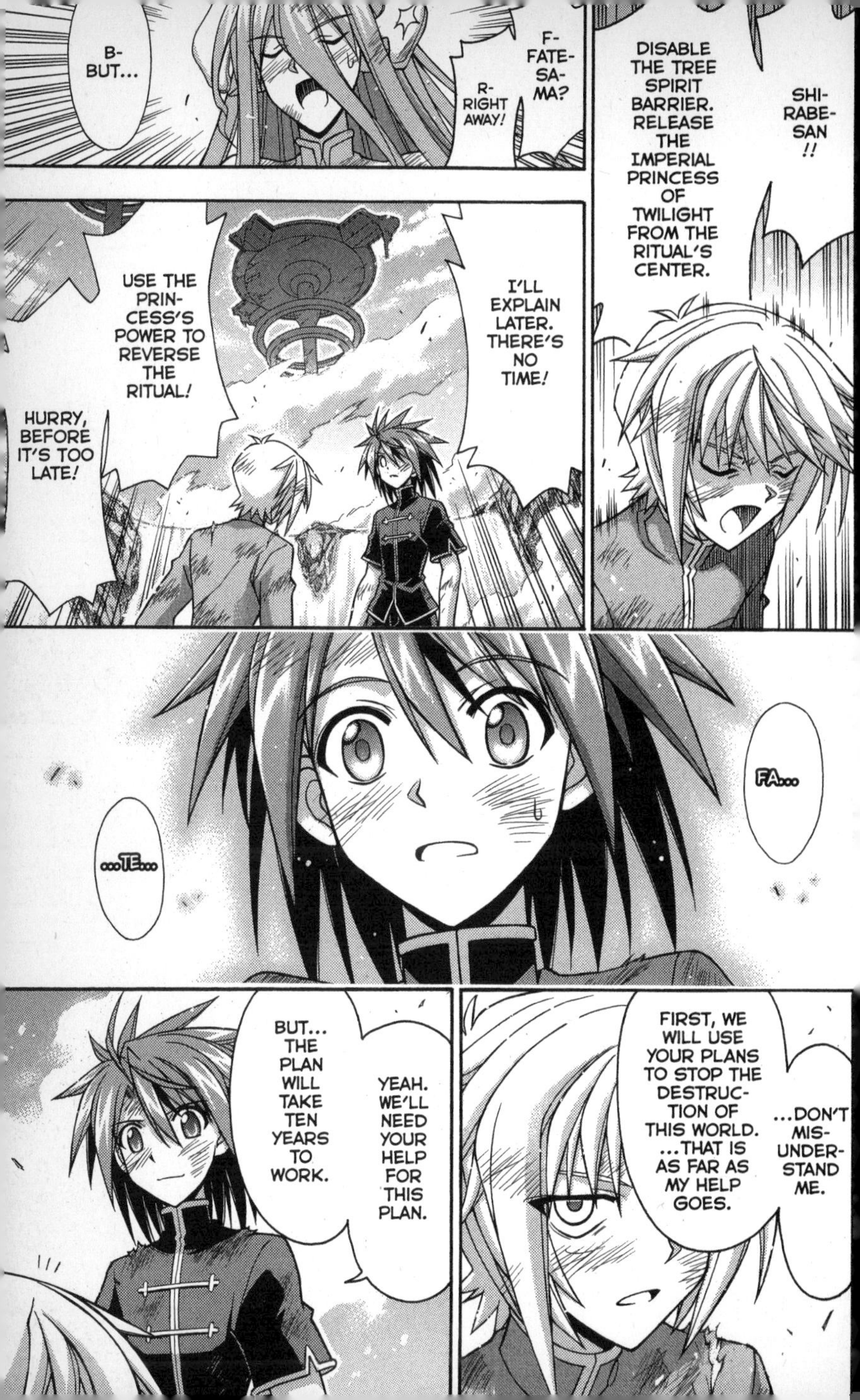
SHIRABE-SAN!!
DISABLE THE TREE SPIRIT BARRIER. RELEASE THE IMPERIAL PRINCESS OF TWILIGHT FROM THE RITUAL'S CENTER.
F-FATE-SAMA?
R-RIGHT AWAY!
B-BUT...
I'LL EXPLAIN LATER. THERE'S NO TIME!
USE THE PRINCESS'S POWER TO REVERSE THE RITUAL!
HURRY, BEFORE IT'S TOO LATE!
FA...
...TE...
...DON'T MISUNDERSTAND ME.
FIRST, WE WILL USE YOUR PLANS TO STOP THE DESTRUCTION OF THIS WORLD. ...THAT IS AS FAR AS MY HELP GOES.
YEAH. WE'LL NEED YOUR HELP FOR THIS PLAN.
BUT... THE PLAN WILL TAKE TEN YEARS TO WORK.

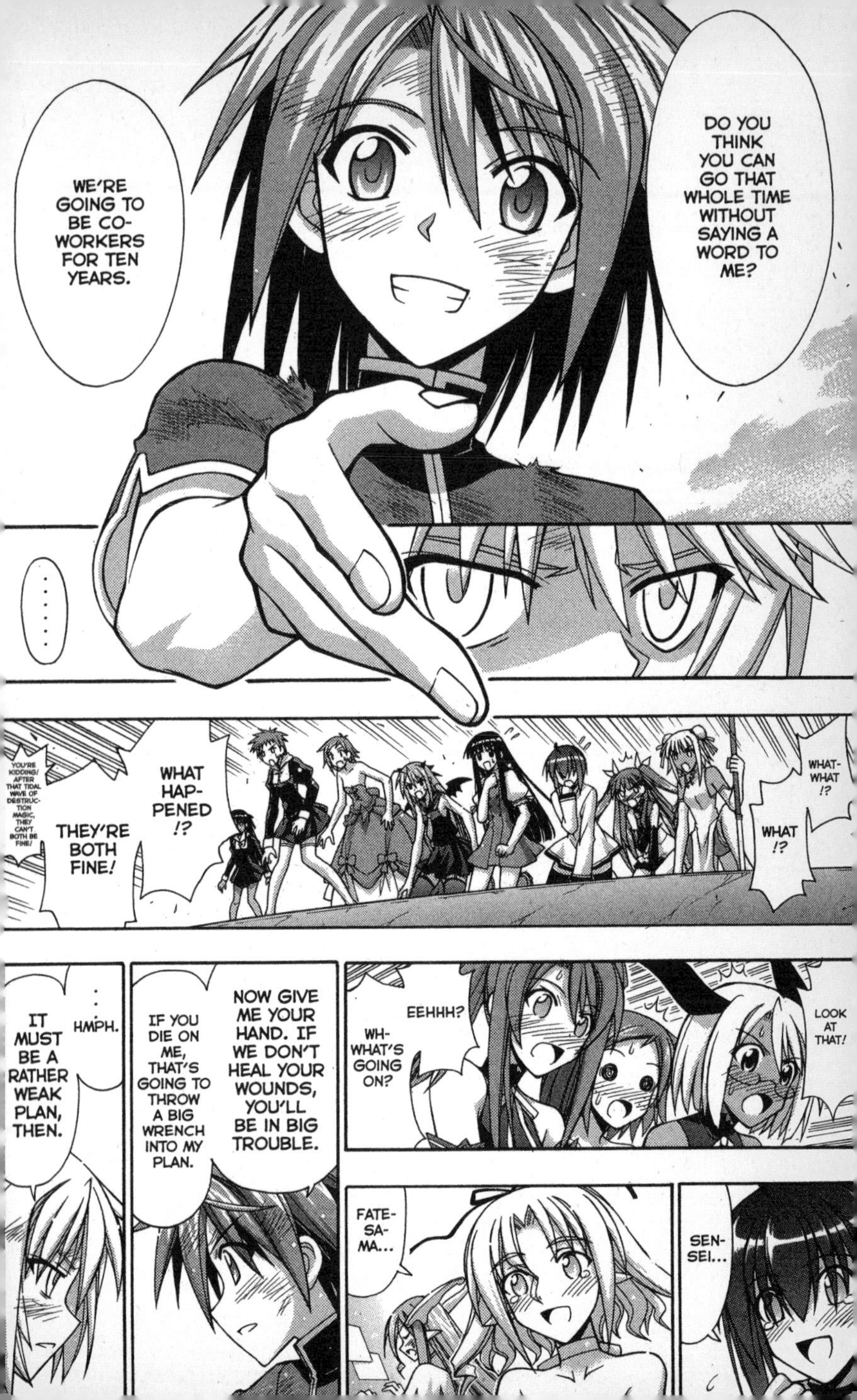
DO YOU THINK YOU CAN GO THAT WHOLE TIME WITHOUT SAYING A WORD TO ME?
WE'RE GOING TO BE CO-WORKERS FOR TEN YEARS.
......
WHAT-WHAT!?
WHAT!?
WHAT HAP-PENED!?
THEY'RE BOTH FINE!
YOU'RE KIDDING! AFTER THAT TIDAL WAVE OF DESTRUCTION MAGIC, THEY CAN'T BOTH BE FINE!
LOOK AT THAT!
EEHHH?
WH-WHAT'S GOING ON?
SEN-SEI...
FATE-SA-MA...
NOW GIVE ME YOUR HAND. IF WE DON'T HEAL YOUR WOUNDS, YOU'LL BE IN BIG TROUBLE.
IF YOU DIE ON ME, THAT'S GOING TO THROW A BIG WRENCH INTO MY PLAN.
...HMPH.
IT MUST BE A RATHER WEAK PLAN, THEN.

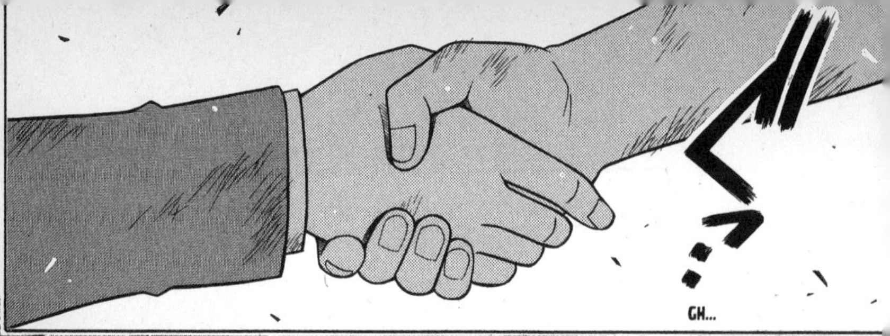
GH...
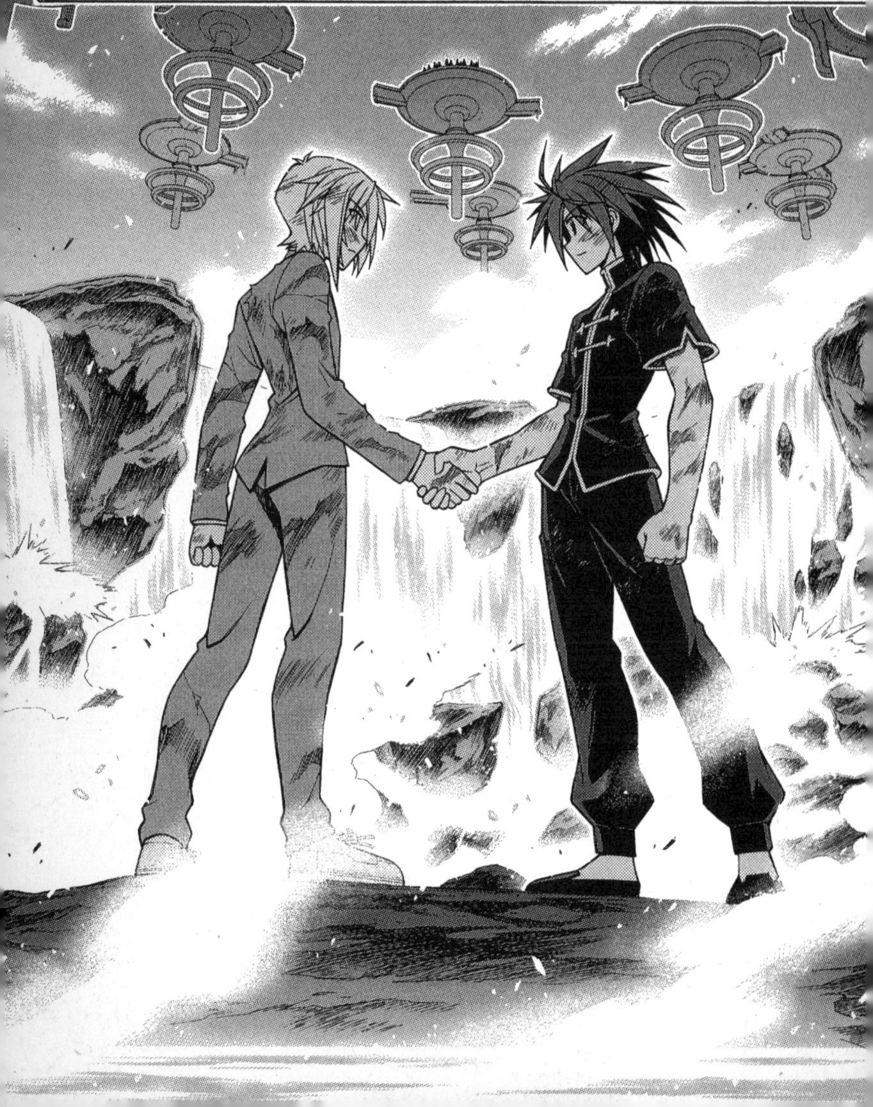

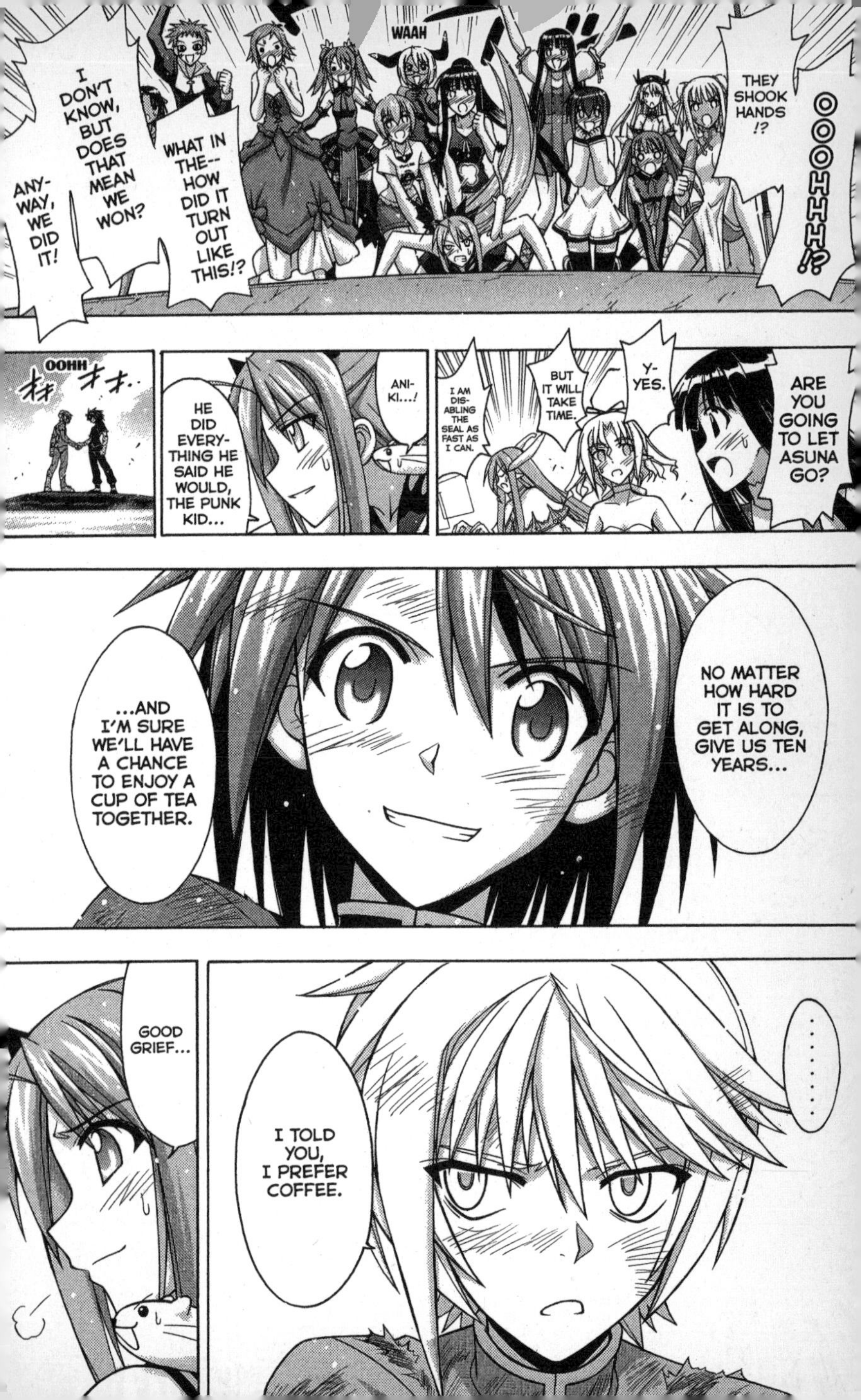
OOOHHHH!?
THEY SHOOK HANDS!?
WAAH
WHAT IN THE-- HOW DID IT TURN OUT LIKE THIS!?
I DON'T KNOW, BUT DOES THAT MEAN WE WON?
ANYWAY, WE DID IT!
ARE YOU GOING TO LET ASUNA GO?
Y-YES.
BUT IT WILL TAKE TIME.
I AM DISABLING THE SEAL AS FAST AS I CAN.
ANIKI...!
HE DID EVERYTHING HE SAID HE WOULD, THE PUNK KID...
OOHH
NO MATTER HOW HARD IT IS TO GET ALONG, GIVE US TEN YEARS...
...AND I'M SURE WE'LL HAVE A CHANCE TO ENJOY A CUP OF TEA TOGETHER.
....
I TOLD YOU, I PREFER COFFEE.
GOOD GRIEF...

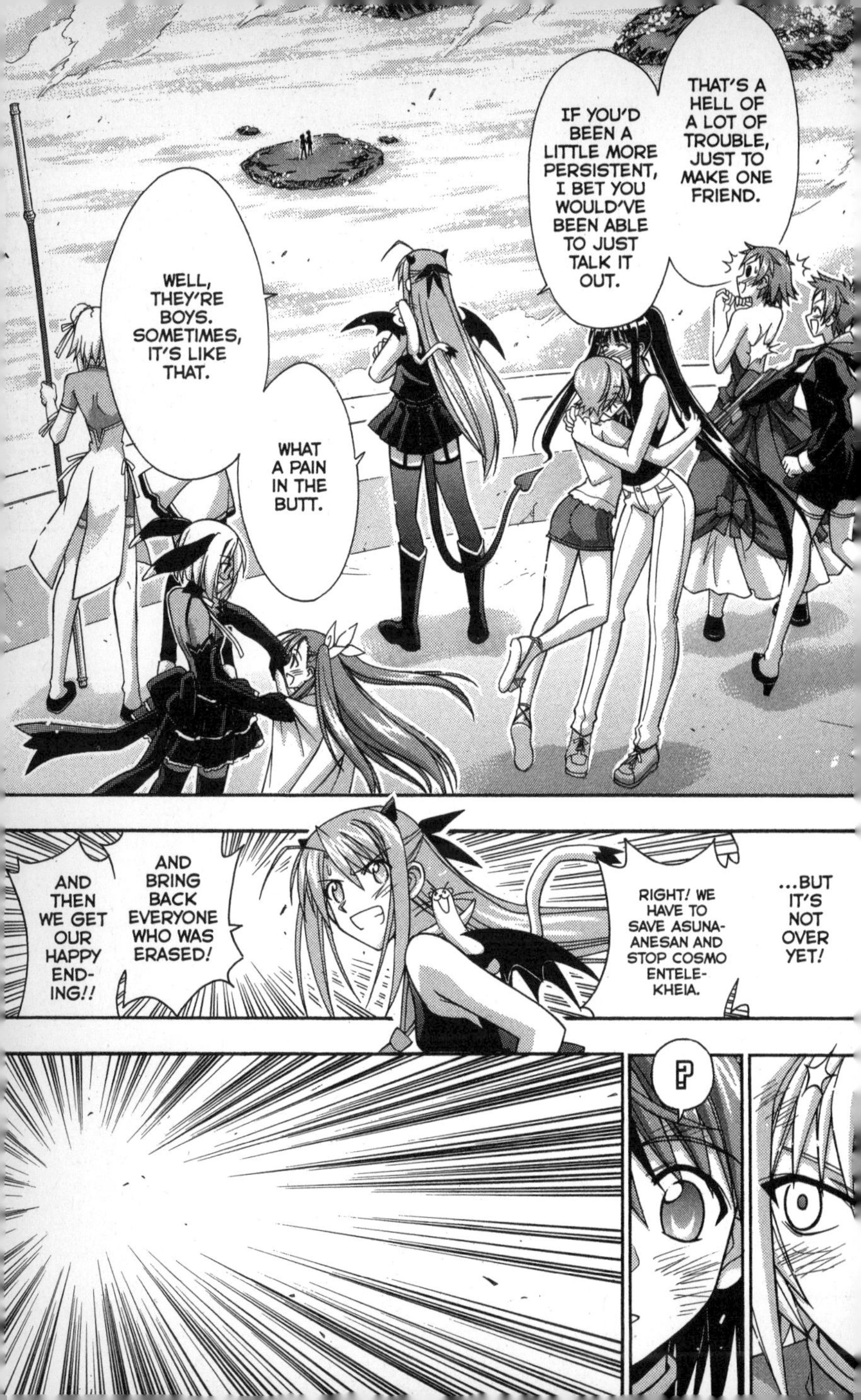
THAT'S A HELL OF A LOT OF TROUBLE, JUST TO MAKE ONE FRIEND.
IF YOU'D BEEN A LITTLE MORE PERSISTENT, I BET YOU WOULD'VE BEEN ABLE TO JUST TALK IT OUT.
WELL, THEY'RE BOYS. SOMETIMES, IT'S LIKE THAT.
WHAT A PAIN IN THE BUTT.
...BUT IT'S NOT OVER YET!
RIGHT! WE HAVE TO SAVE ASUNA-ANESAN AND STOP COSMO ENTELE-KHEIA.
AND BRING BACK EVERYONE WHO WAS ERASED!
AND THEN WE GET OUR HAPPY END-ING!!
?

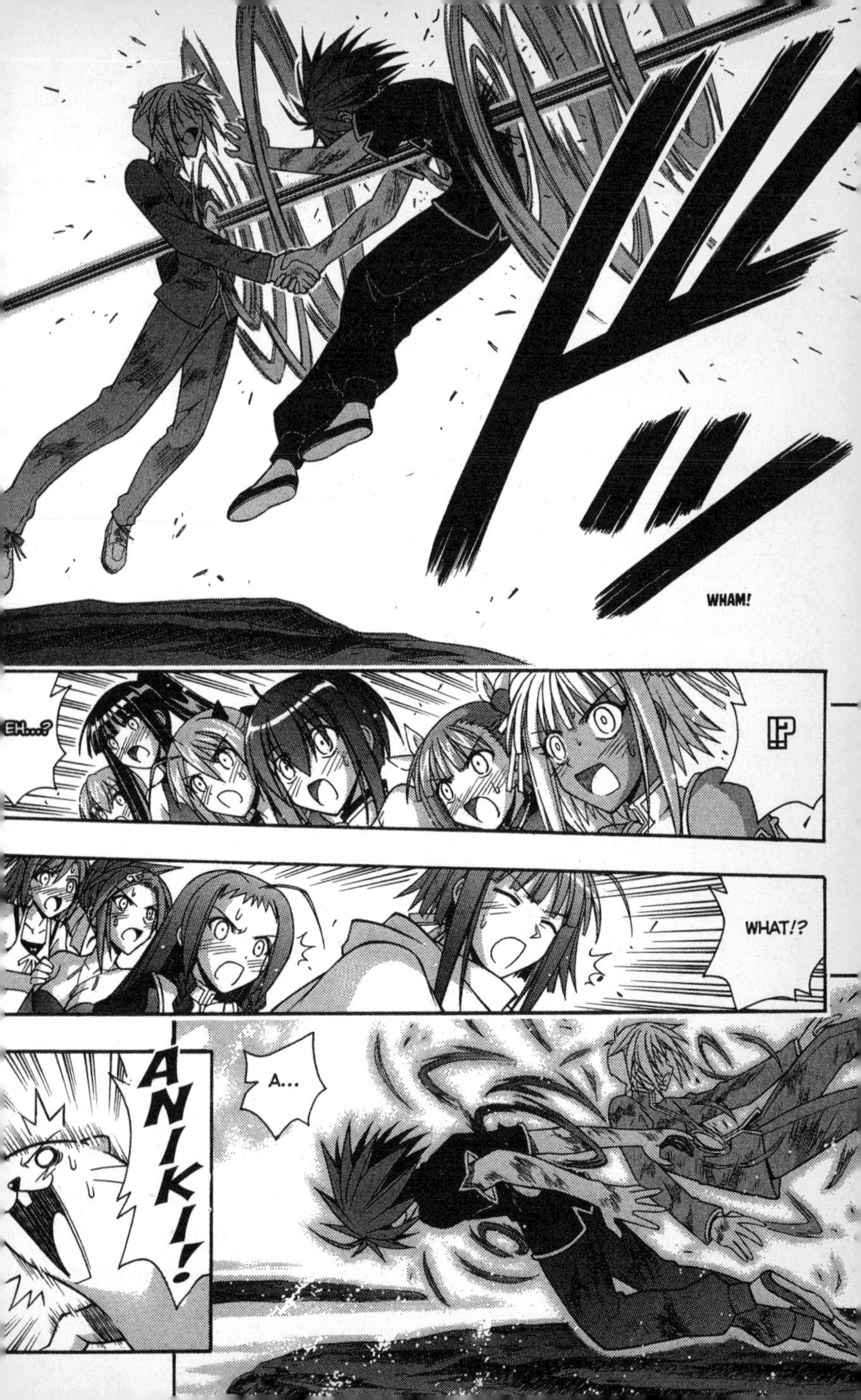
WHAM!
!?
EH...?
WHAT!?
A...
ANIKI!

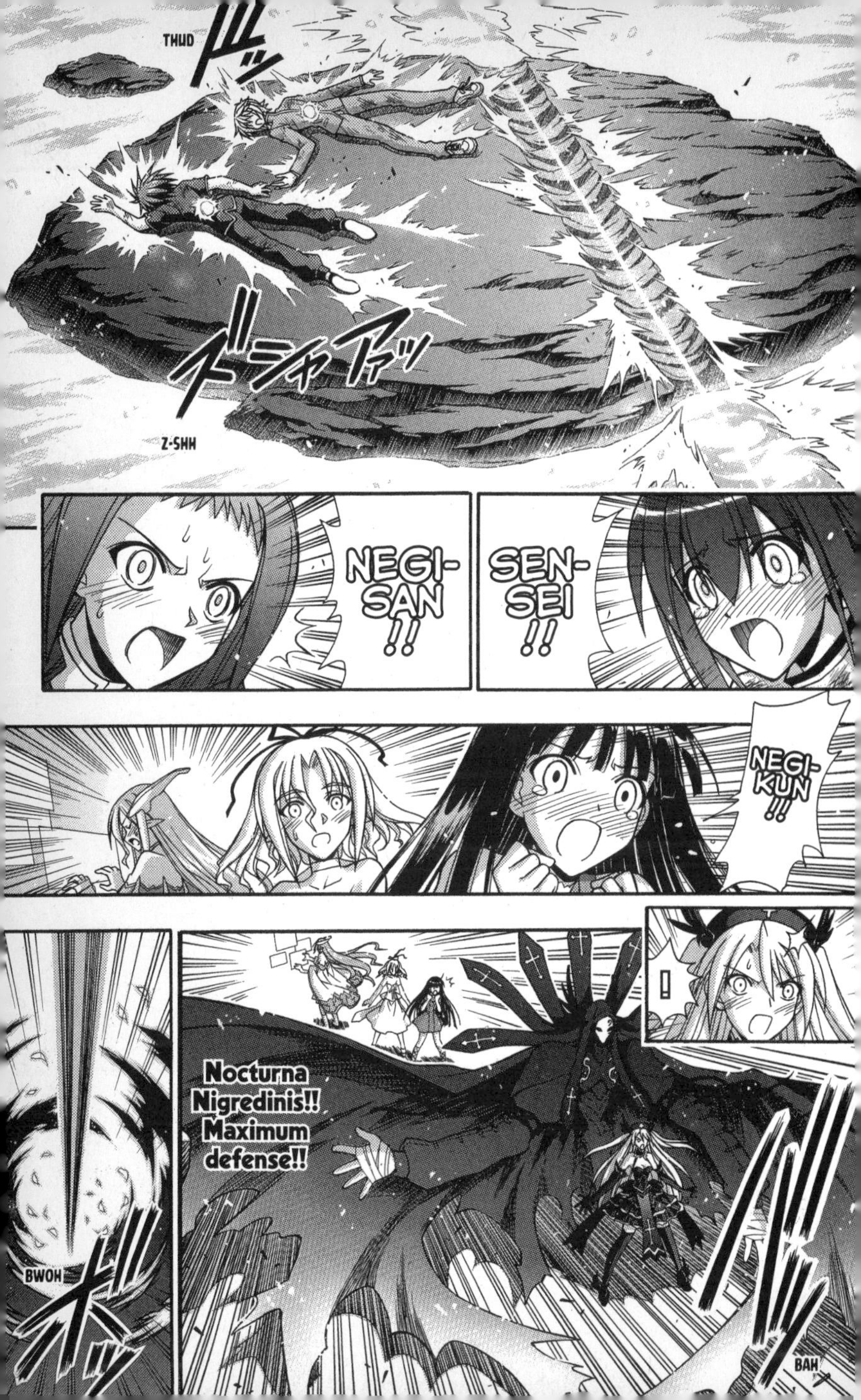
THUD
Z-SHH
SEN-SEI!!
NEGI-SAN!!
NEGI-KUN!!
!
Nocturna Nigredinis!! Maximum defense!!
BAH
BWOH

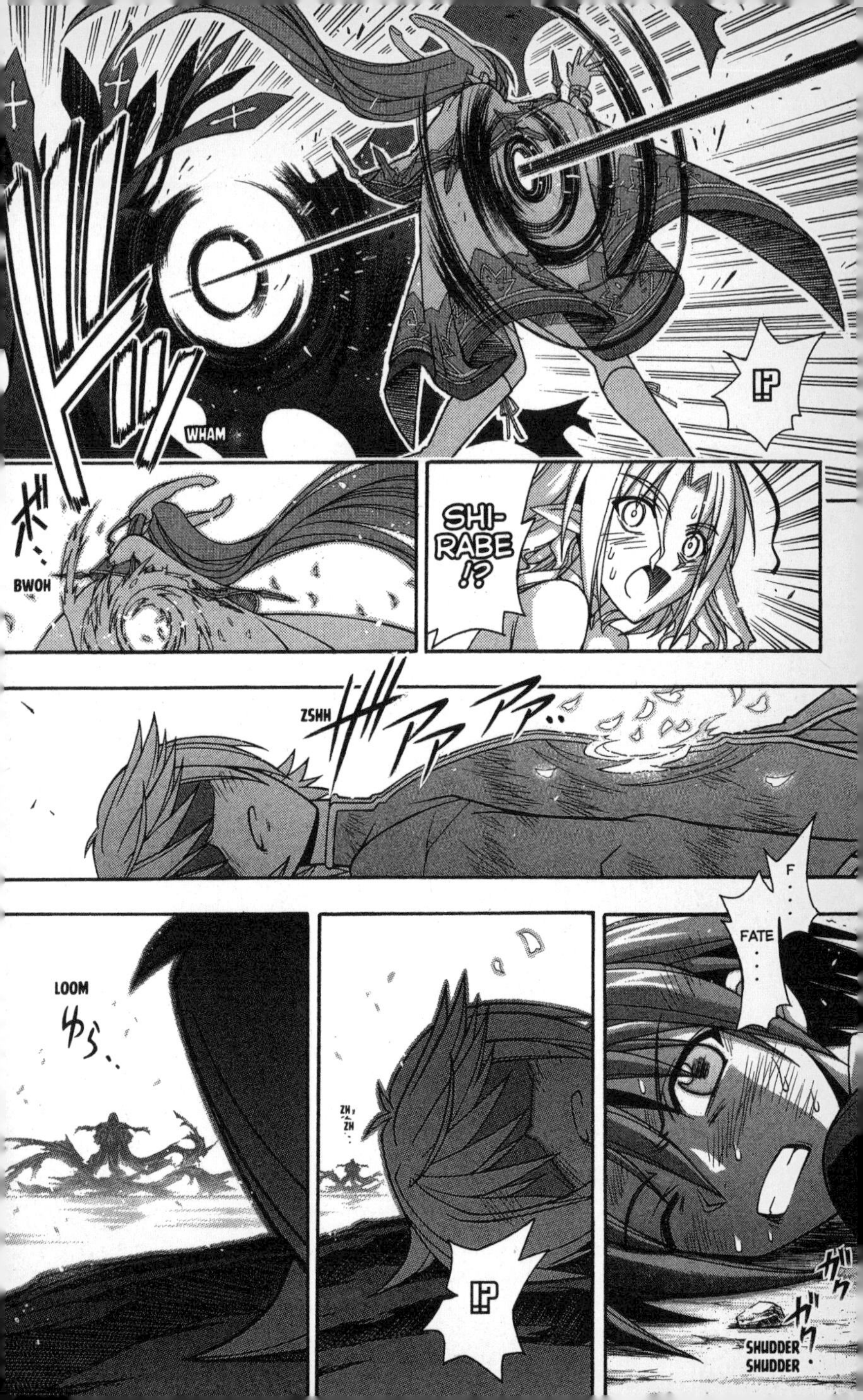

!?
WHAM
SHI-RABE!?
BWOH
ZSHH
F... FATE...
SHUDDER SHUDDER
!?
ZH ZH
LOOM
ゆら...

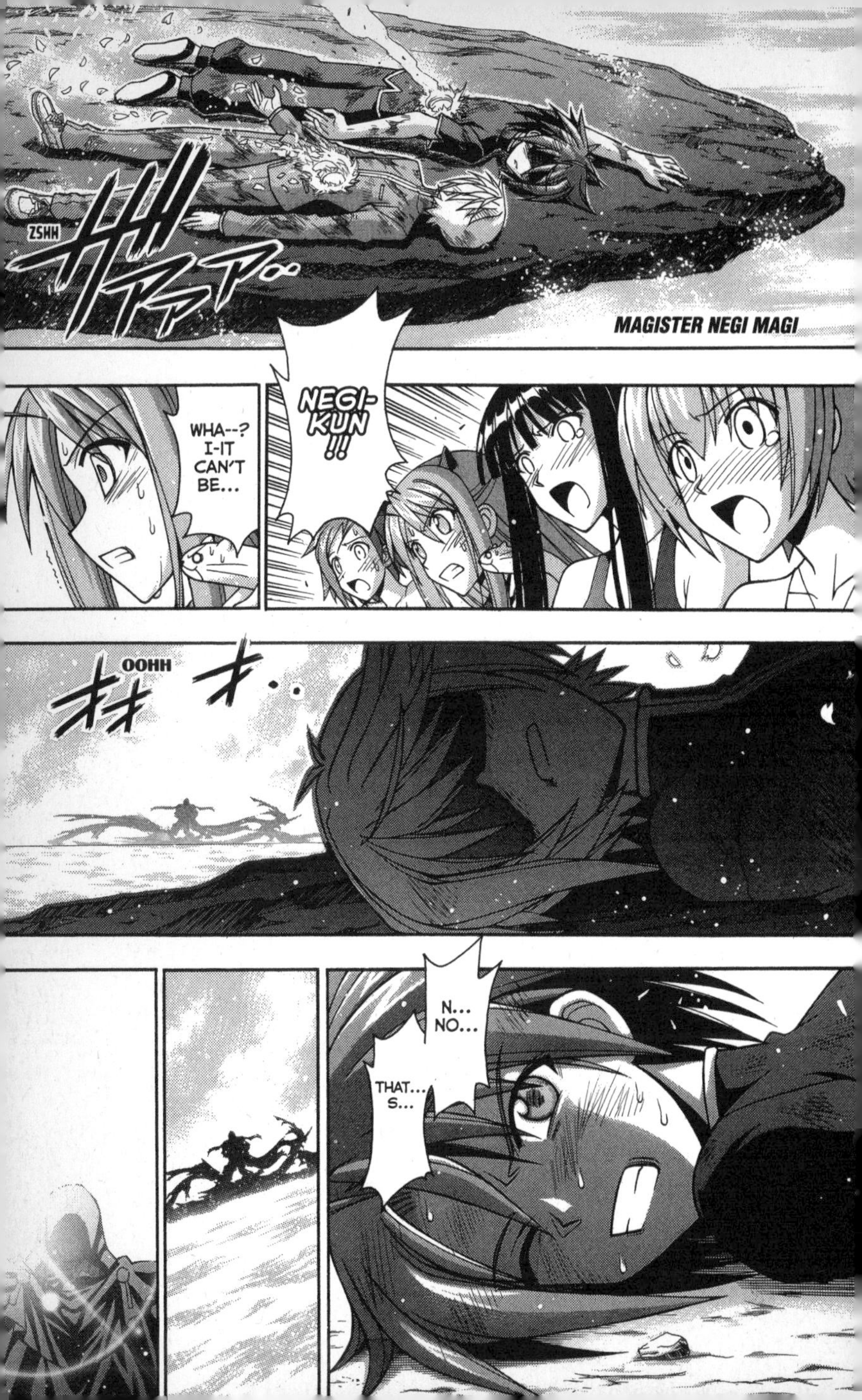
ZSHH
MAGISTER NEGI MAGI
NEGI-KUN!!
WHA--? I-IT CAN'T BE...
OOHH
N... NO...
THAT... S...

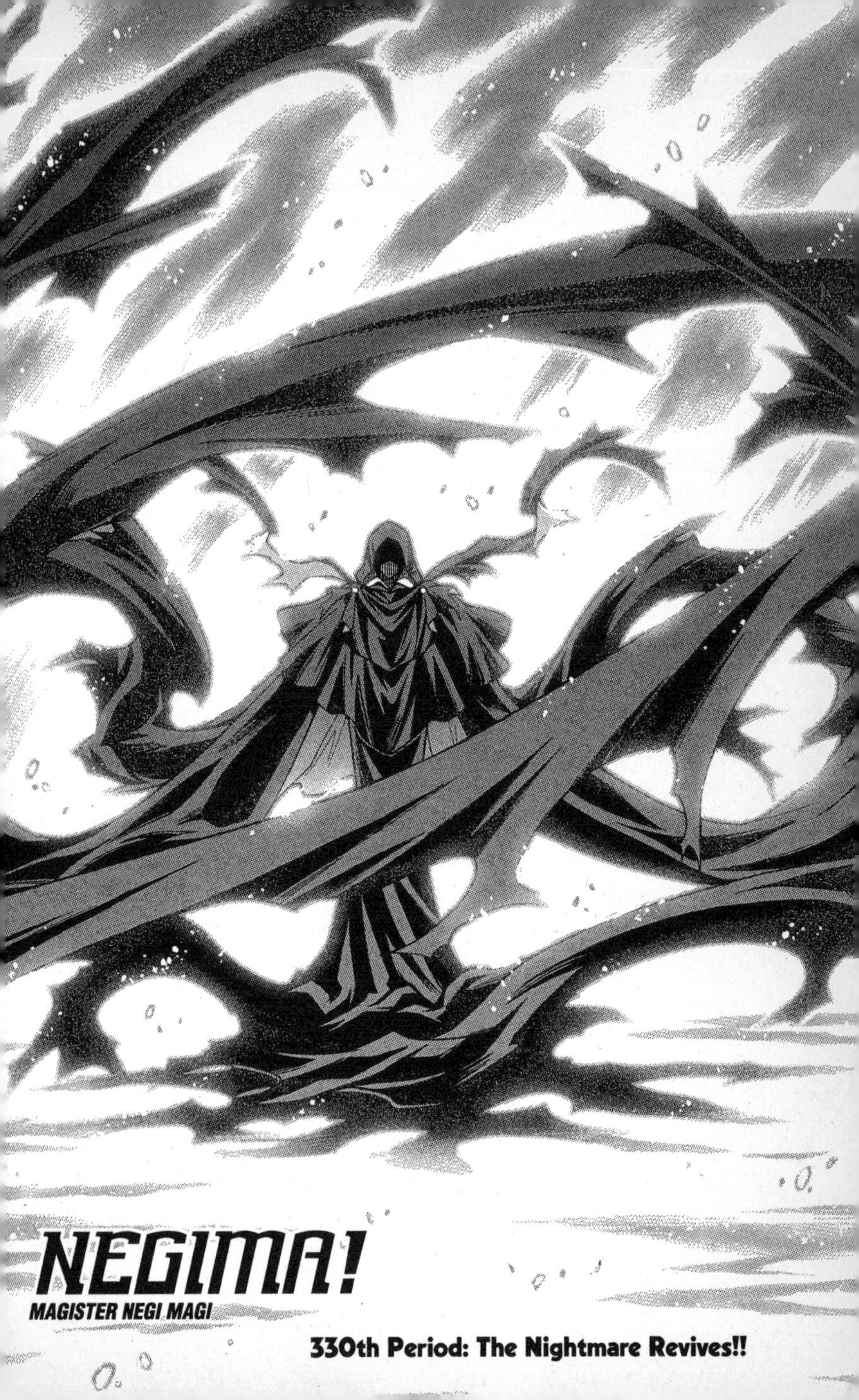
NEGIMA!
MAGISTER NEGI MAGI
330th Period: The Nightmare Revives!!

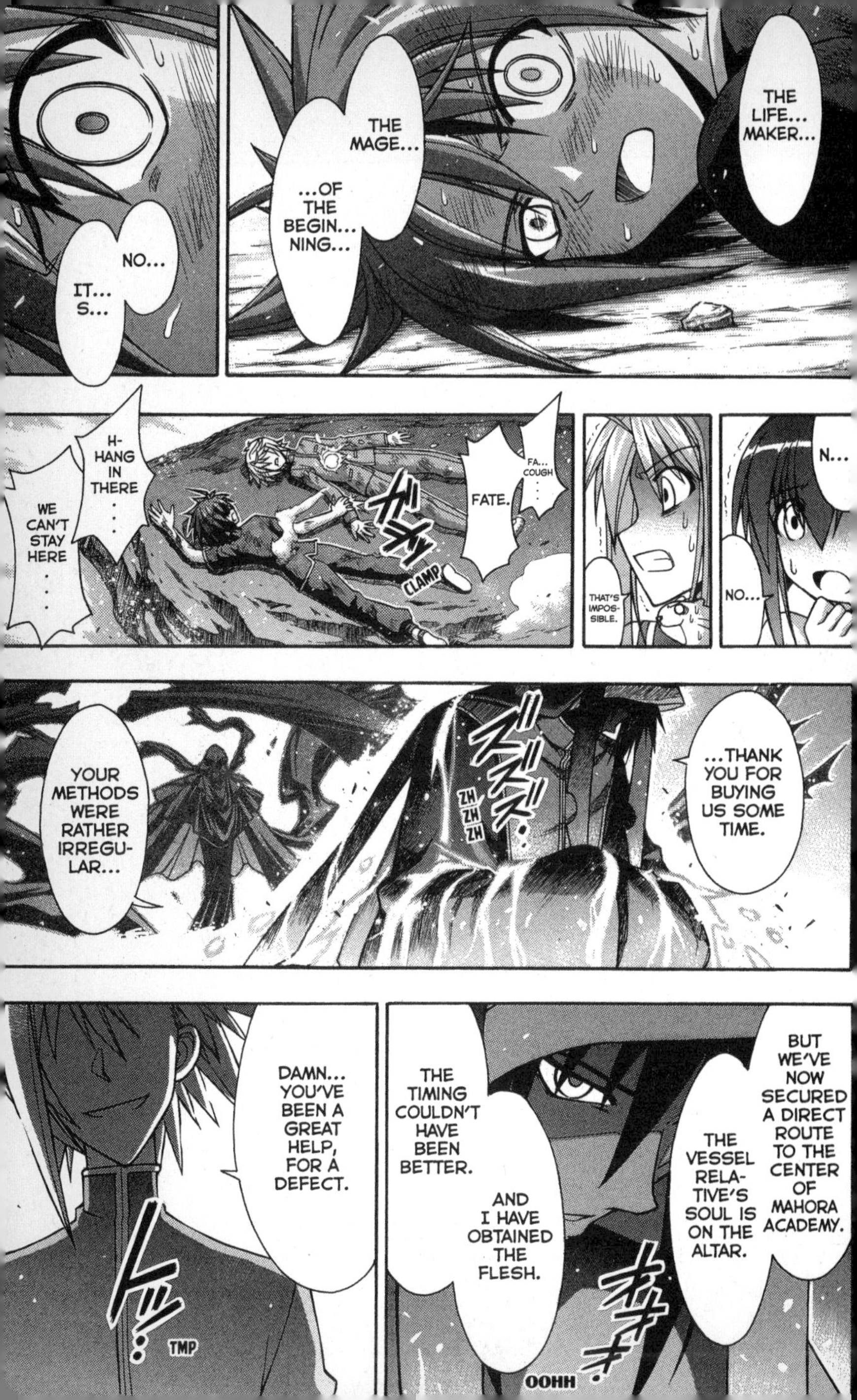
THE LIFE... MAKER...
THE MAGE...
...OF THE BEGIN... NING...
NO...
IT... S...
N...
NO...
THAT'S IMPOSSIBLE.
FATE.
FA... COUGH...
CLAMP
H-HANG IN THERE...
WE CAN'T STAY HERE...
...THANK YOU FOR BUYING US SOME TIME.
ZH ZH ZH
YOUR METHODS WERE RATHER IRREGULAR...
BUT WE'VE NOW SECURED A DIRECT ROUTE TO THE CENTER OF MAHORA ACADEMY.
THE VESSEL RELATIVE'S SOUL IS ON THE ALTAR.
AND I HAVE OBTAINED THE FLESH.
THE TIMING COULDN'T HAVE BEEN BETTER.
OOHH
DAMN... YOU'VE BEEN A GREAT HELP, FOR A DEFECT.
TMP

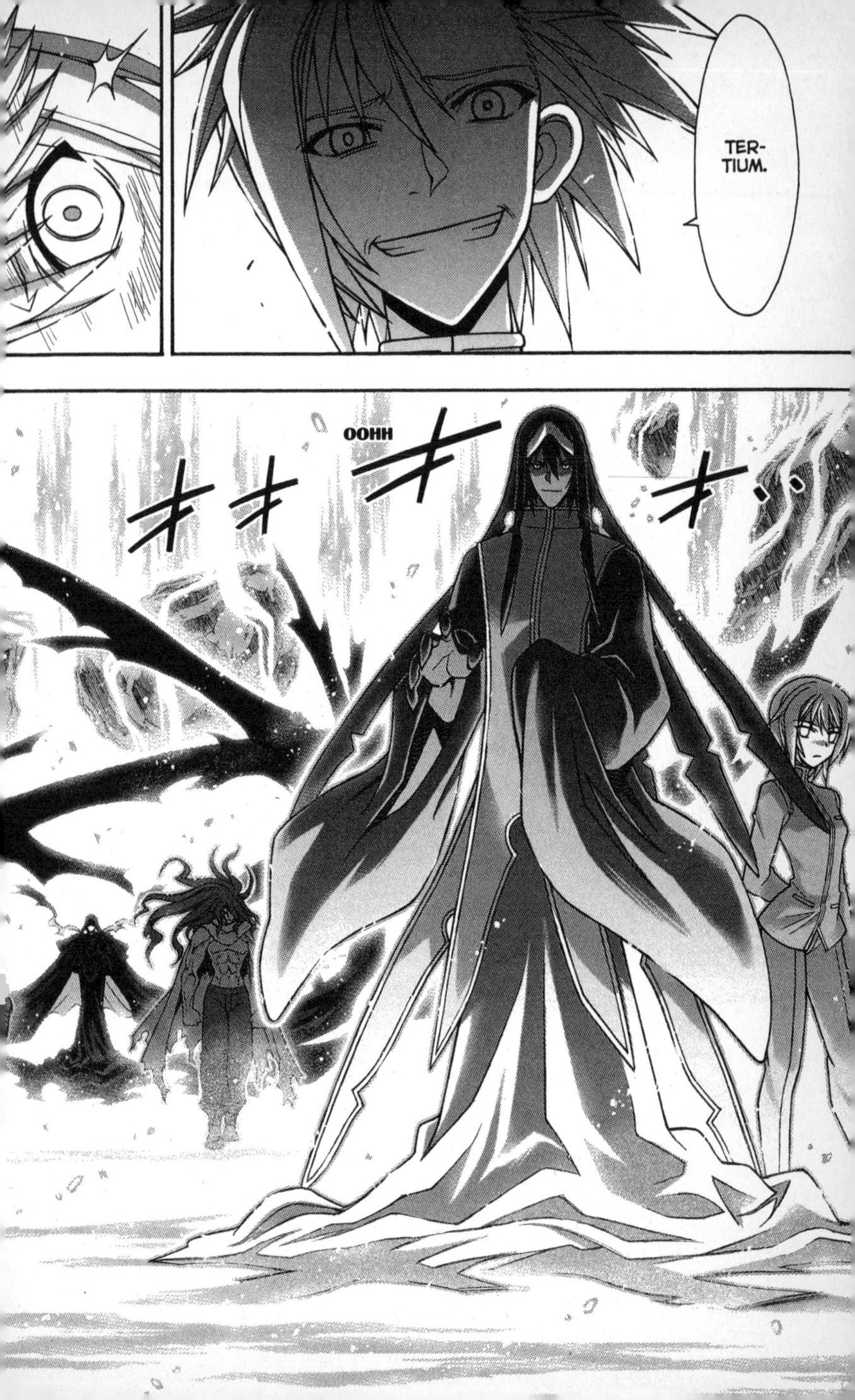
TER-
TIUM.
OOHH

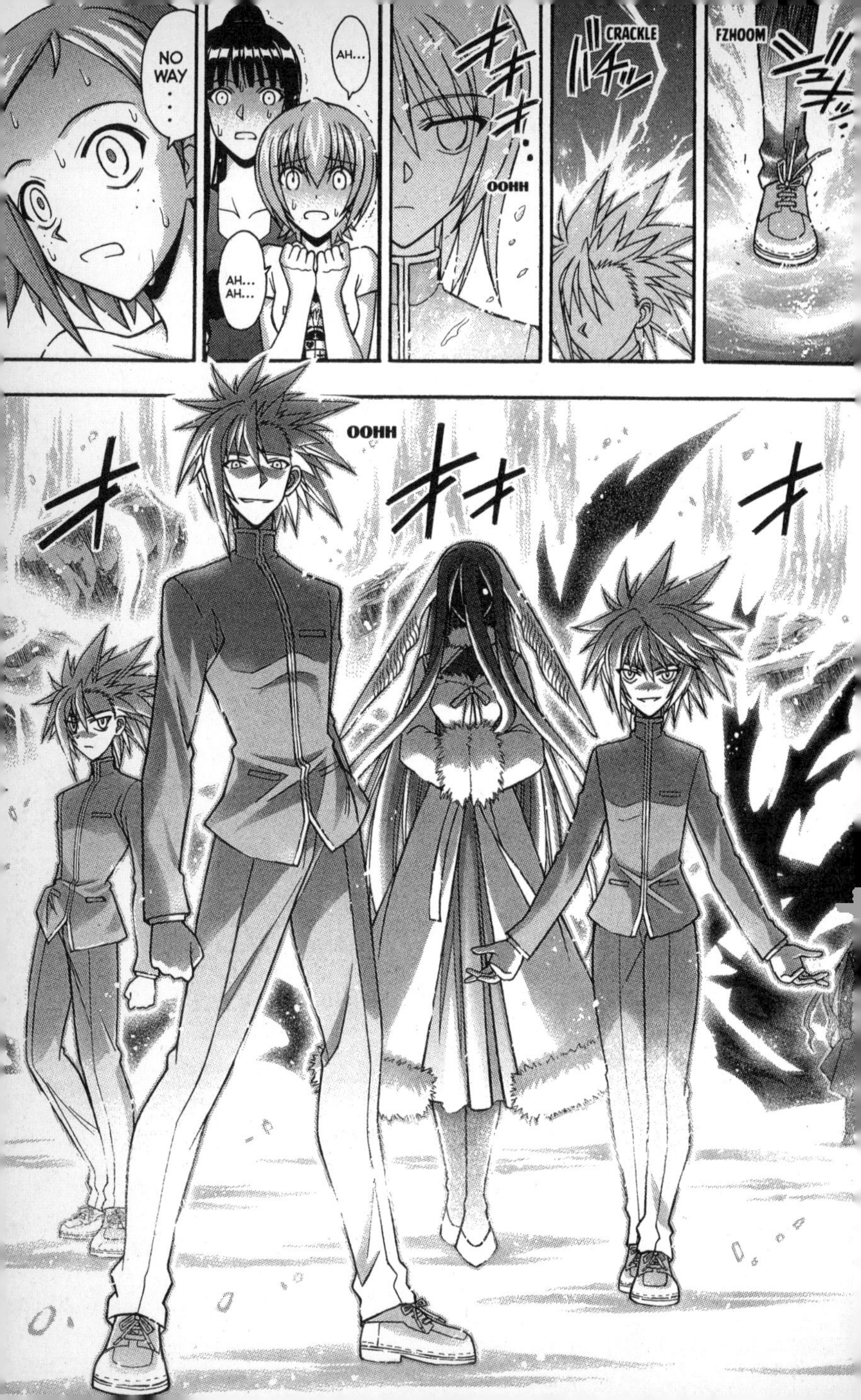
FZHOOM
CRACKLE
OOHH
AH...
AH... AH...
NO WAY
...
OOHH

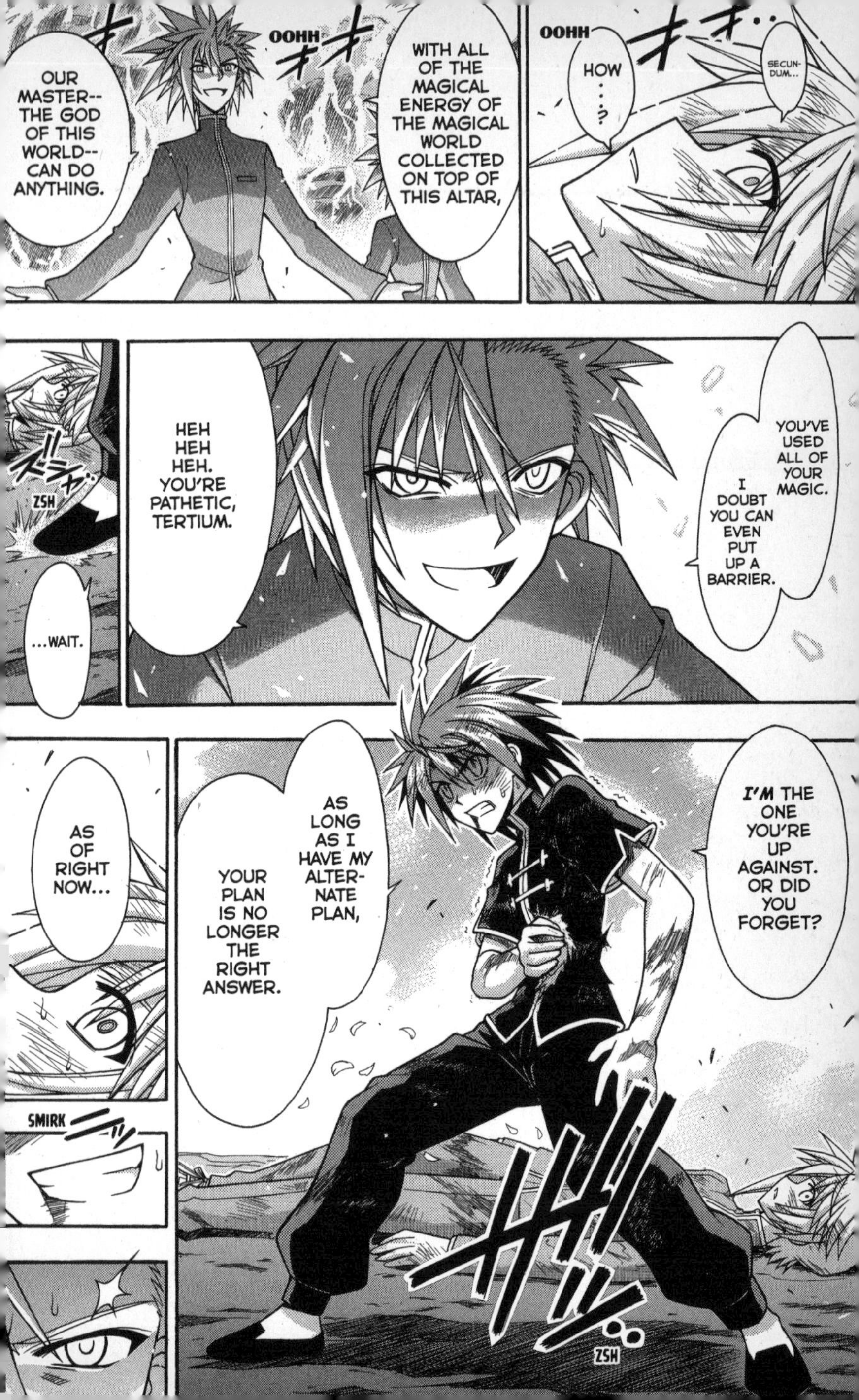
SECUNDUM...
HOW...?
OOHH
WITH ALL OF THE MAGICAL ENERGY OF THE MAGICAL WORLD COLLECTED ON TOP OF THIS ALTAR,
OOHH
OUR MASTER--THE GOD OF THIS WORLD--CAN DO ANYTHING.
YOU'VE USED ALL OF YOUR MAGIC.
I DOUBT YOU CAN EVEN PUT UP A BARRIER.
HEH HEH HEH. YOU'RE PATHETIC, TERTIUM.
ZSH
...WAIT.
I'M THE ONE YOU'RE UP AGAINST. OR DID YOU FORGET?
AS LONG AS I HAVE MY ALTERNATE PLAN,
YOUR PLAN IS NO LONGER THE RIGHT ANSWER.
ZSH
AS OF RIGHT NOW...
SMIRK

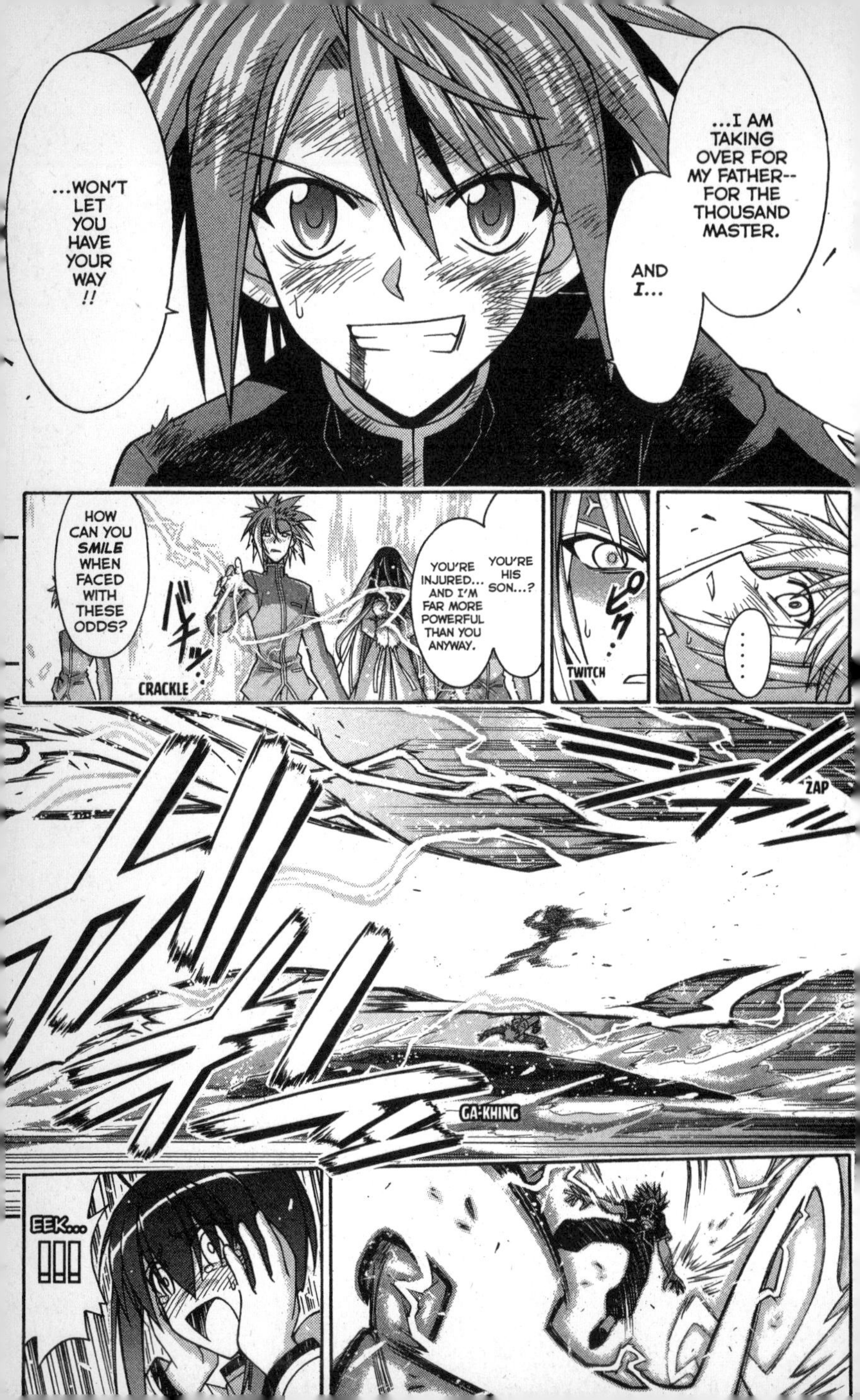
...I AM TAKING OVER FOR MY FATHER-- FOR THE THOUSAND MASTER.
AND *I*...
...WON'T LET YOU HAVE YOUR WAY !!
......
TWITCH
YOU'RE HIS SON...?
YOU'RE INJURED... AND I'M FAR MORE POWERFUL THAN YOU ANYWAY.
HOW CAN YOU **SMILE** WHEN FACED WITH THESE ODDS?
CRACKLE
ZAP
GA-KHING
EEK... !!!

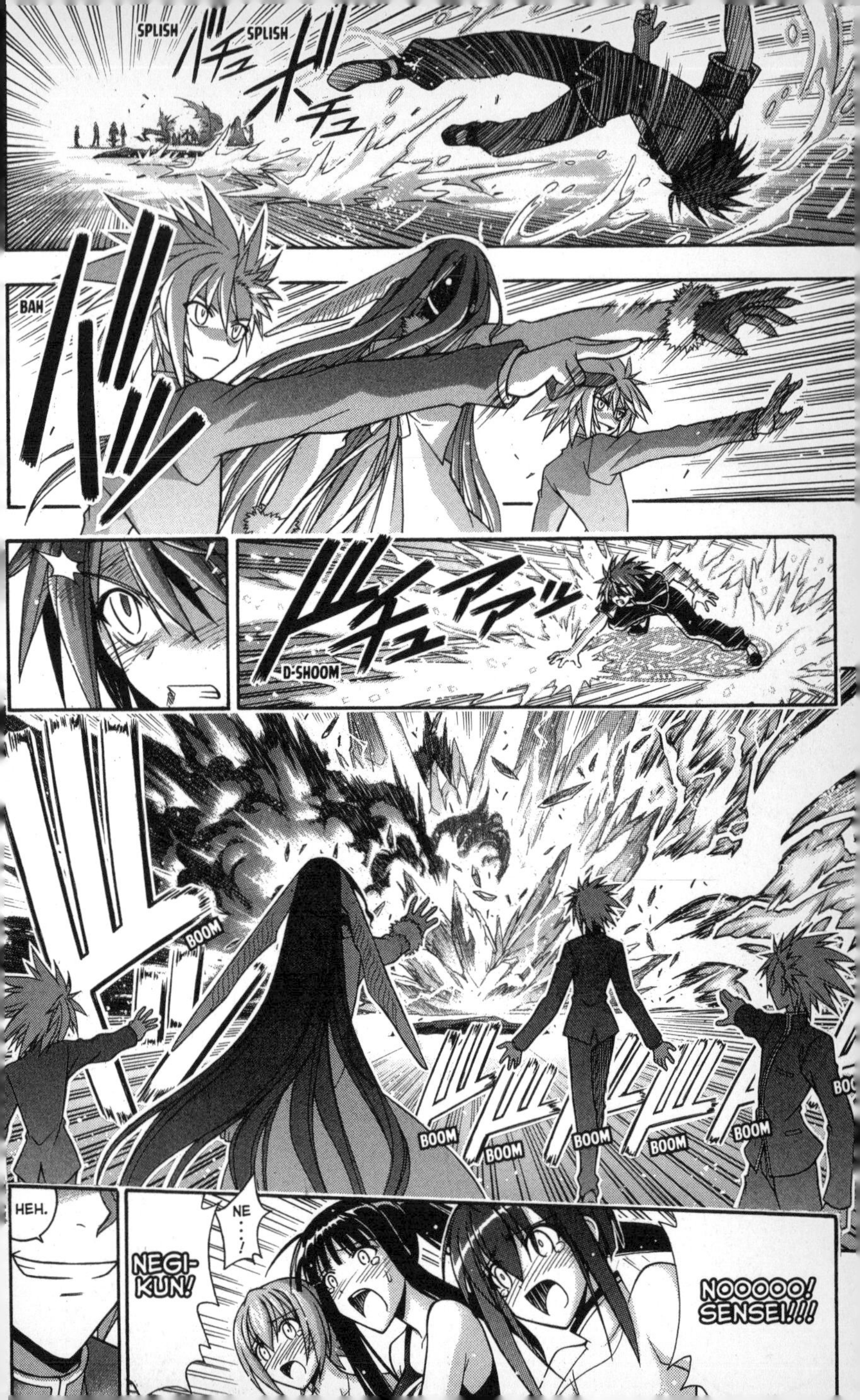
SPLISH
SPLISH
ボチュ
バチュ
BAH
D-SHOOM
ドチュアアッ
BOOM
BOO
BOOM
BOOM
BOOM
BOOM
BOOM
NOOOOO! SENSEI!!!
NE.....!
NEGI-KUN!
HEH.

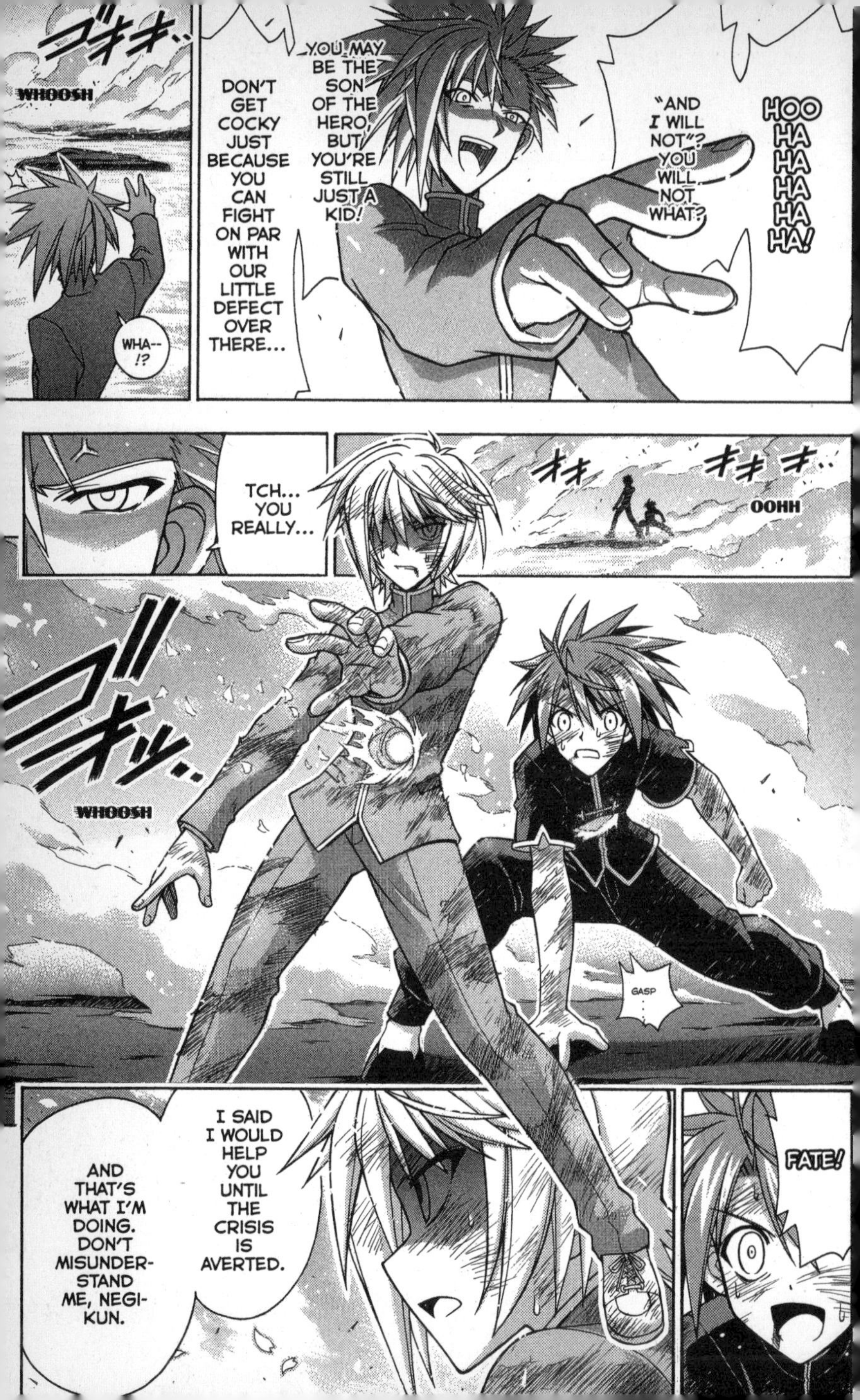
HOO HA HA HA HA HA HA!
"AND I WILL NOT"? YOU WILL NOT WHAT?
YOU MAY BE THE SON OF THE HERO, BUT YOU'RE STILL JUST A KID!
DON'T GET COCKY JUST BECAUSE YOU CAN FIGHT ON PAR WITH OUR LITTLE DEFECT OVER THERE...
WHOOSH
WHA-- !?
OOHH
TCH... YOU REALLY...
WHOOSH
GASP
FATE!
I SAID I WOULD HELP YOU UNTIL THE CRISIS IS AVERTED.
AND THAT'S WHAT I'M DOING. DON'T MISUNDER-STAND ME, NEGI-KUN.

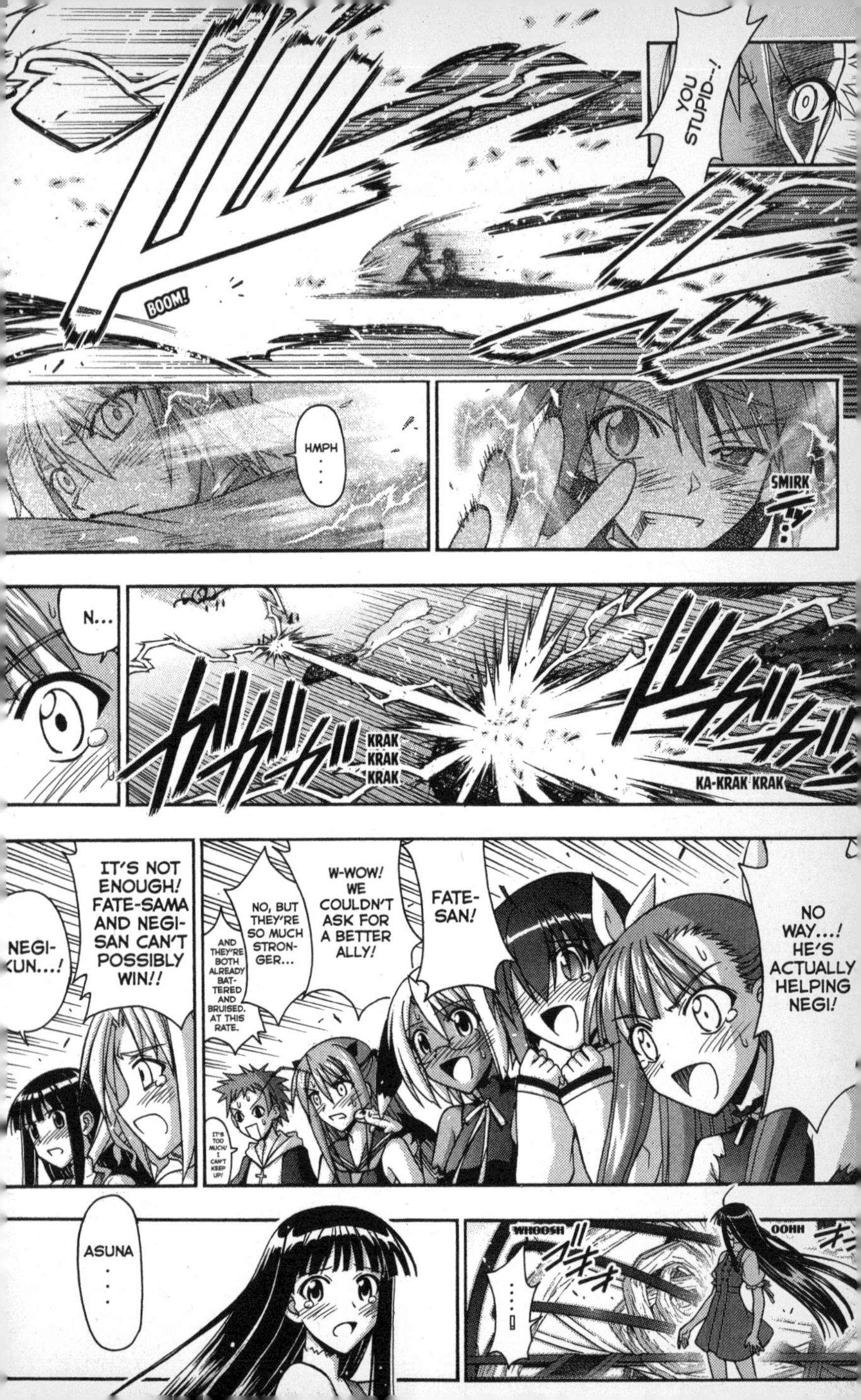
YOU STUPID--!
BOOM!
SMIRK
HMPH . . .
KA-KRAK KRAK
KRAK KRAK KRAK
N...
NO WAY...! HE'S ACTUALLY HELPING NEGI!
FATE-SAN!
W-WOW! WE COULDN'T ASK FOR A BETTER ALLY!
NO, BUT THEY'RE SO MUCH STRONGER...
AND THEY'RE BOTH ALREADY BATTERED AND BRUISED. AT THIS RATE.
IT'S TOO MUCH! I CAN'T KEEP UP!
IT'S NOT ENOUGH! FATE-SAMA AND NEGI-SAN CAN'T POSSIBLY WIN!!
NEGI-KUN...!
OOHH
WHOOSH
...!
ASUNA . . . . .

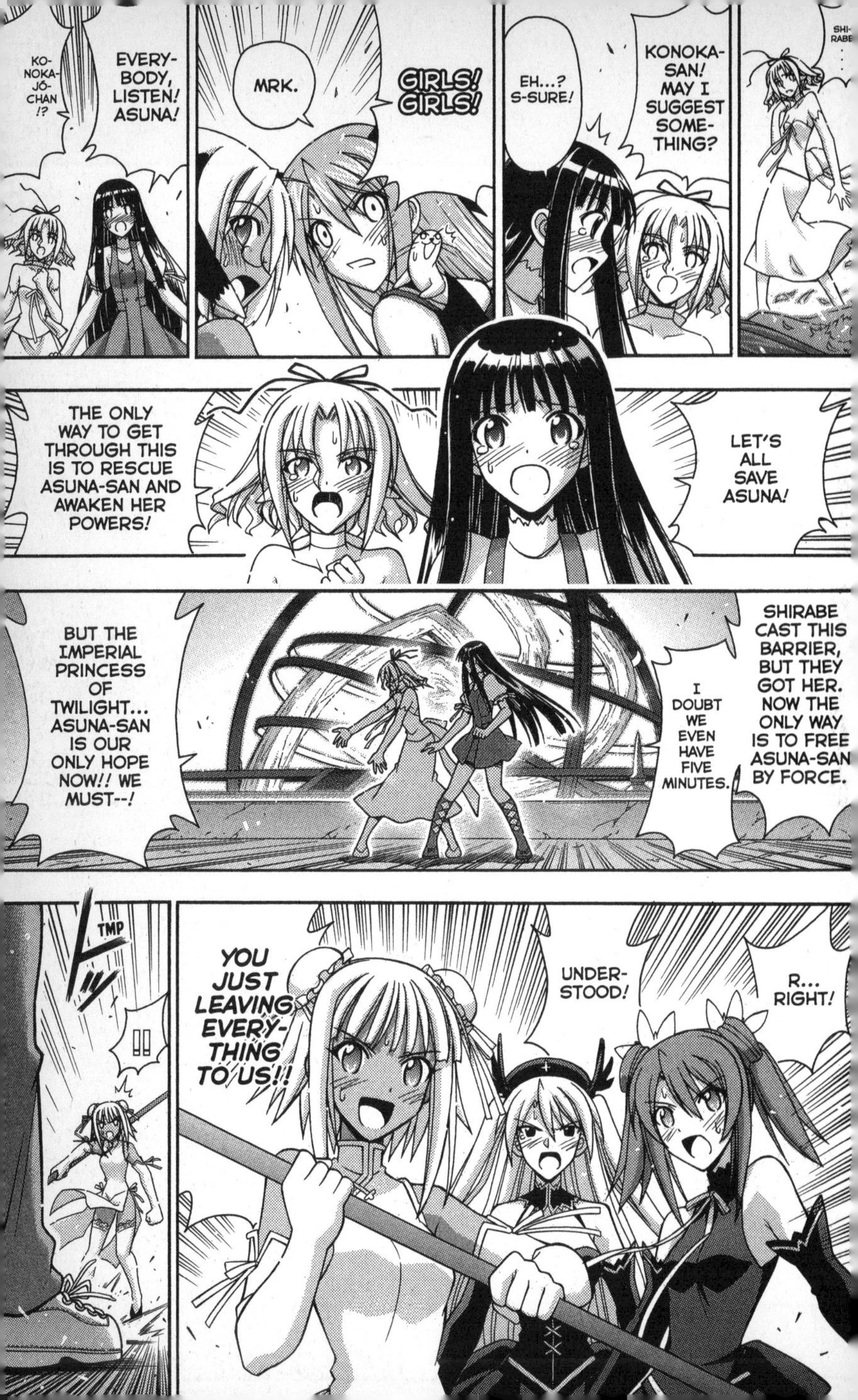
SHIRABE...
KONOKA-SAN! MAY I SUGGEST SOMETHING?
EH...? S-SURE!
GIRLS! GIRLS!
MRK.
EVERYBODY, LISTEN! ASUNA!
KONOKA-JŌCHAN!?
LET'S ALL SAVE ASUNA!
THE ONLY WAY TO GET THROUGH THIS IS TO RESCUE ASUNA-SAN AND AWAKEN HER POWERS!
SHIRABE CAST THIS BARRIER, BUT THEY GOT HER. NOW THE ONLY WAY IS TO FREE ASUNA-SAN BY FORCE.
I DOUBT WE EVEN HAVE FIVE MINUTES.
BUT THE IMPERIAL PRINCESS OF TWILIGHT... ASUNA-SAN IS OUR ONLY HOPE NOW!! WE MUST--!
R... RIGHT!
UNDERSTOOD!
YOU JUST LEAVING EVERYTHING TO US!!
TMP
!!

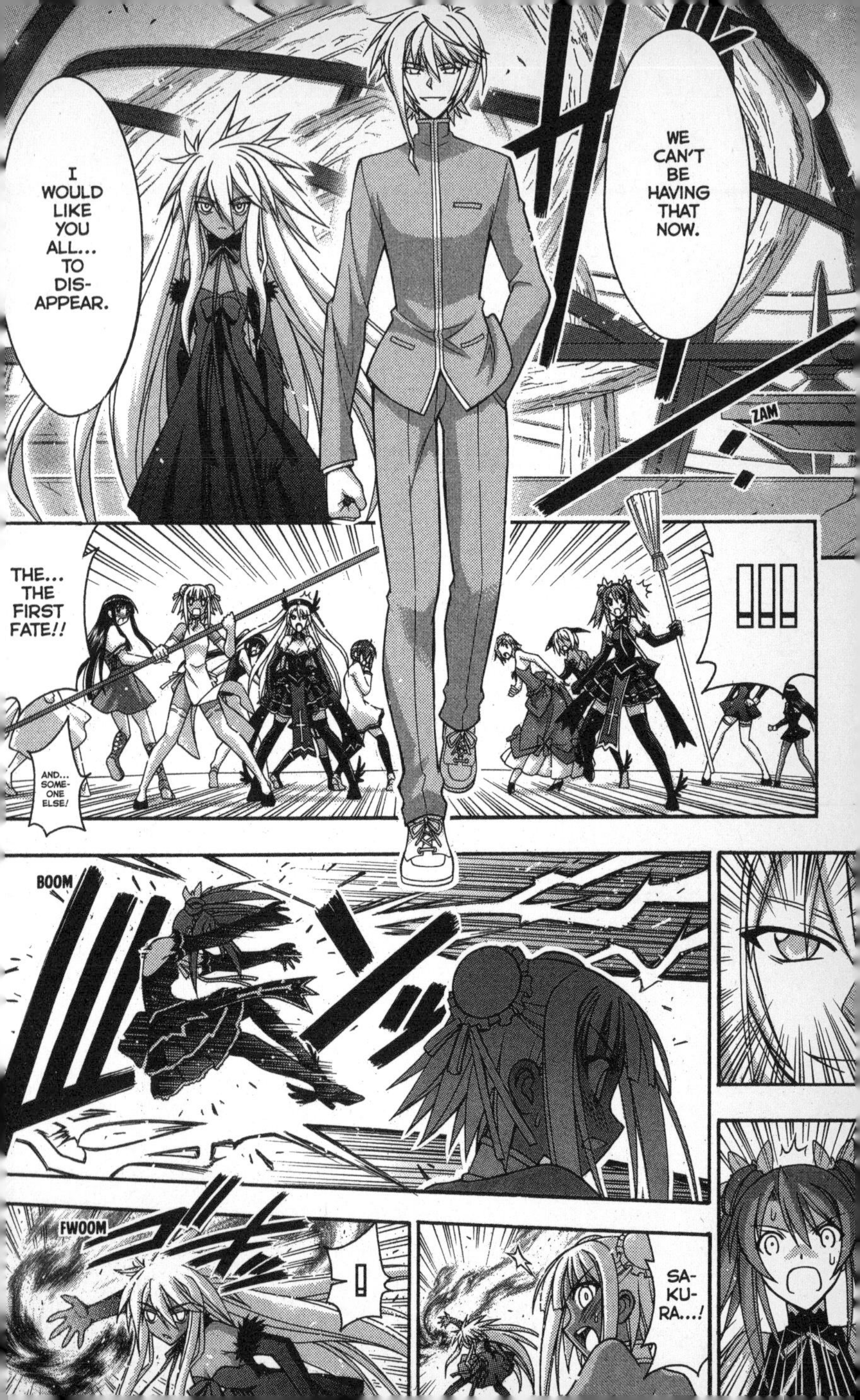
WE CAN'T BE HAVING THAT NOW.
I WOULD LIKE YOU ALL... TO DIS-APPEAR.
ZAM
!!!
THE... THE FIRST FATE!!
AND... SOME-ONE ELSE!
BOOM
SA-KU-RA...!
!
FWOOM

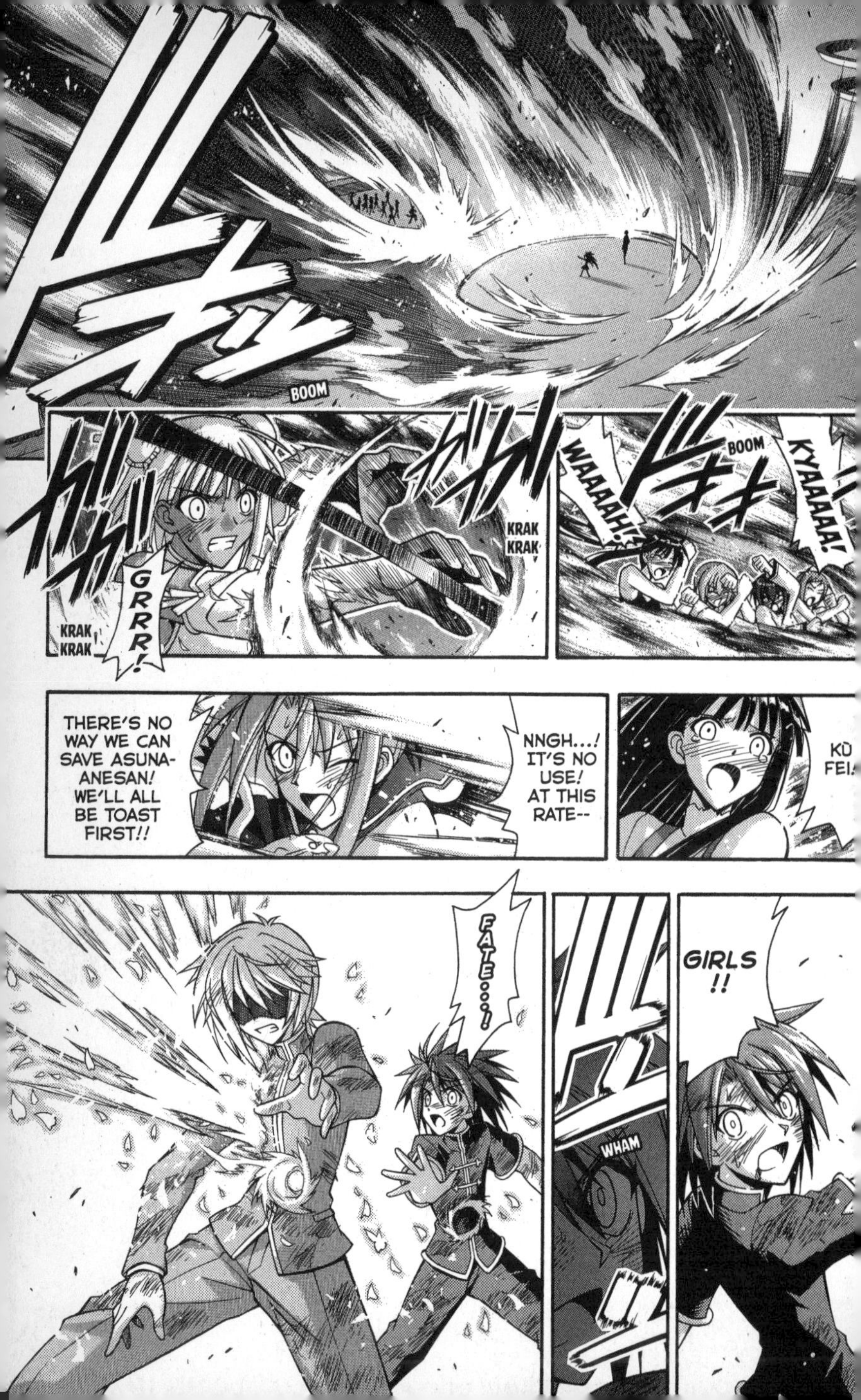
BOOM
BOOM
KYAAAAA!
WAAAAH!!
KRAK KRAK
GRRR!
KRAK KRAK
KŪ FEI!
NNGH...! IT'S NO USE! AT THIS RATE--
THERE'S NO WAY WE CAN SAVE ASUNA-ANESAN! WE'LL ALL BE TOAST FIRST!!
GIRLS!!
WHAM
FATE...!

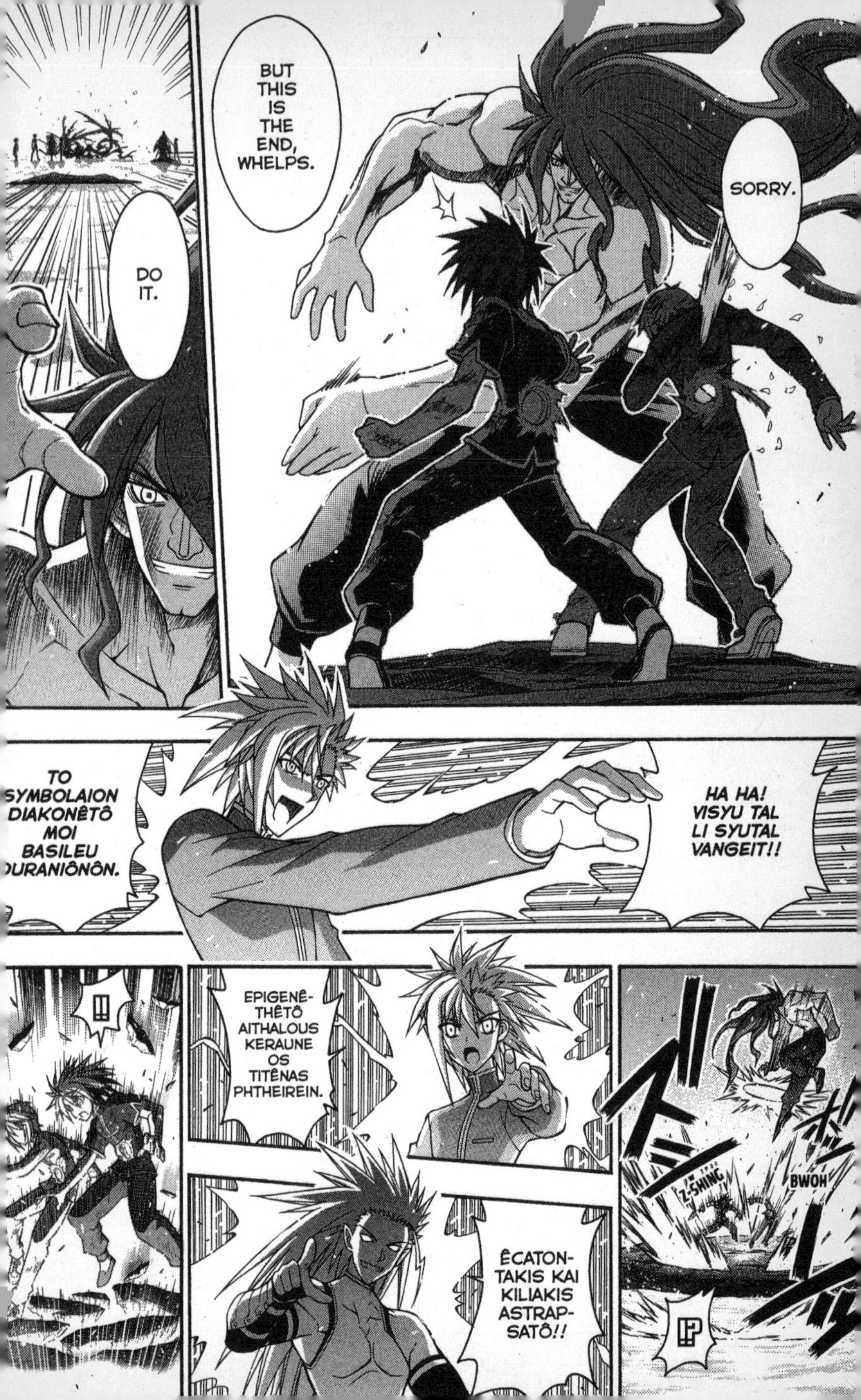
BUT THIS IS THE END, WHELPS.
SORRY.
DO IT.
HA HA! VISYU TAL LI SYUTAL VANGEIT!!
TO SYMBOLAION DIAKONÊTÔ MOI BASILEU OURANIÔNÔN.
Z-SHING
BWOH
!?
EPIGENÊ-THÊTÔ AITHALOUS KERAUNE OS TITÊNAS PHTHEIREIN.
ÊCATON-TAKIS KAI KILIAKIS ASTRAP-SATÔ!!
!!

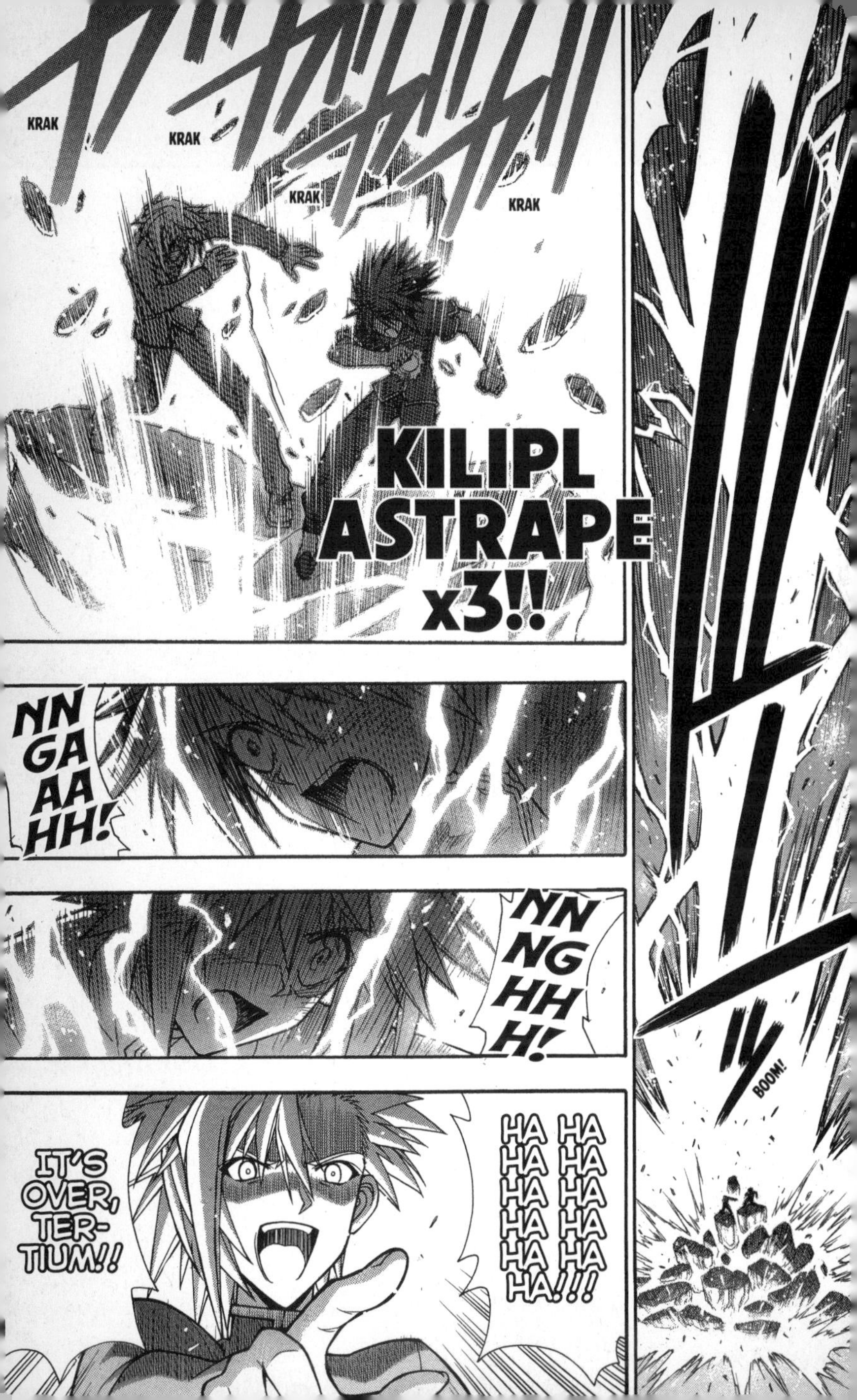
BOOM!
KRAK
KRAK
KRAK
KRAK
KILIPL ASTRAPE x3!!
NNGAAAHH!
NNNGHHHH!
HA HA HA HA HA HA HA HA HA HA HA!!!
IT'S OVER, TER-TIUM!!

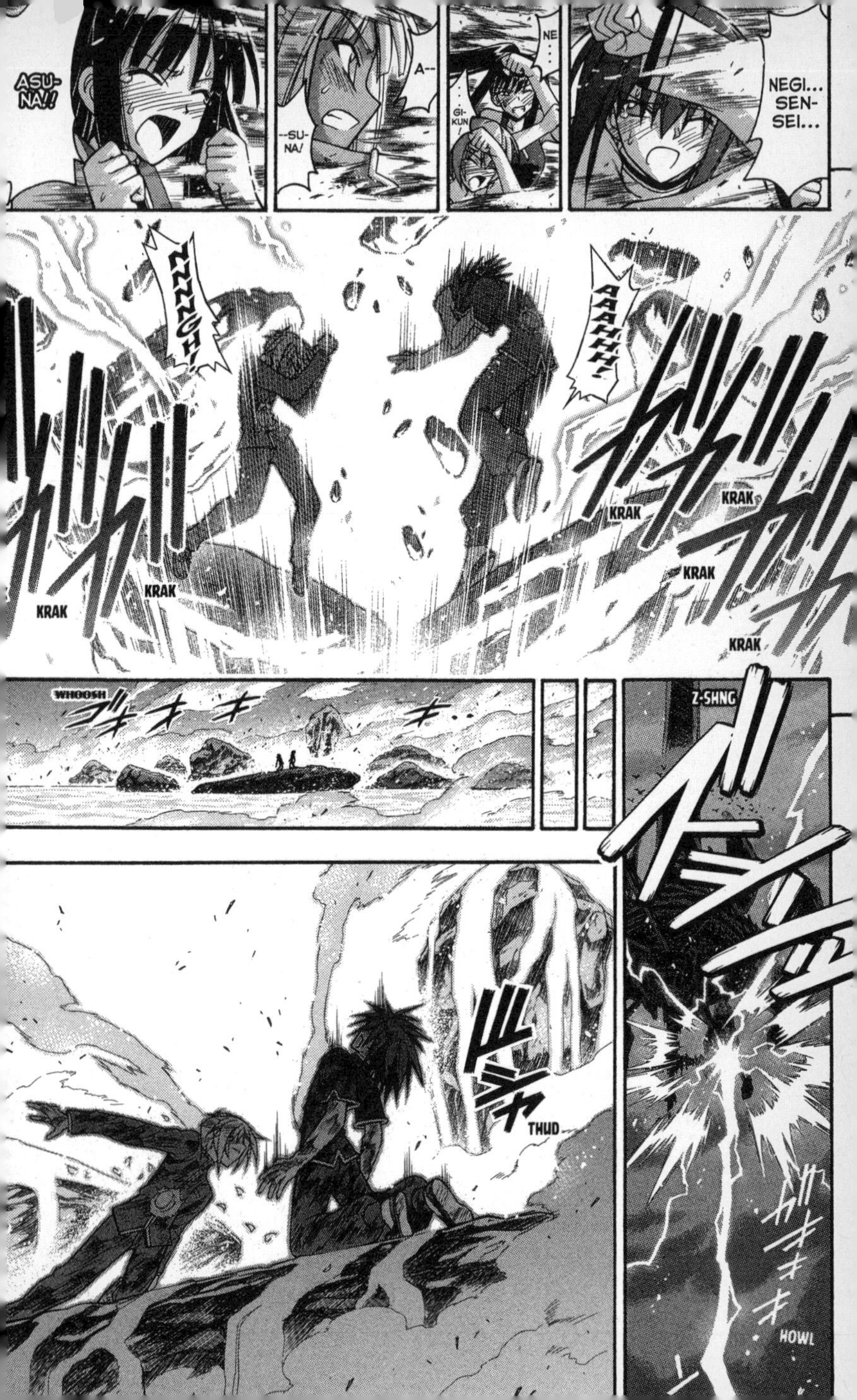
NEGI... SEN-SEI...
NE...
...GI-KUN!
A--
--SUNA!
ASU-NA!!
AAAAHHH!
NNNNGH!
KRAK
KRAK
KRAK
KRAK
KRAK
KRAK
Z-SHNG
HOWL
WHOOSH
THUD

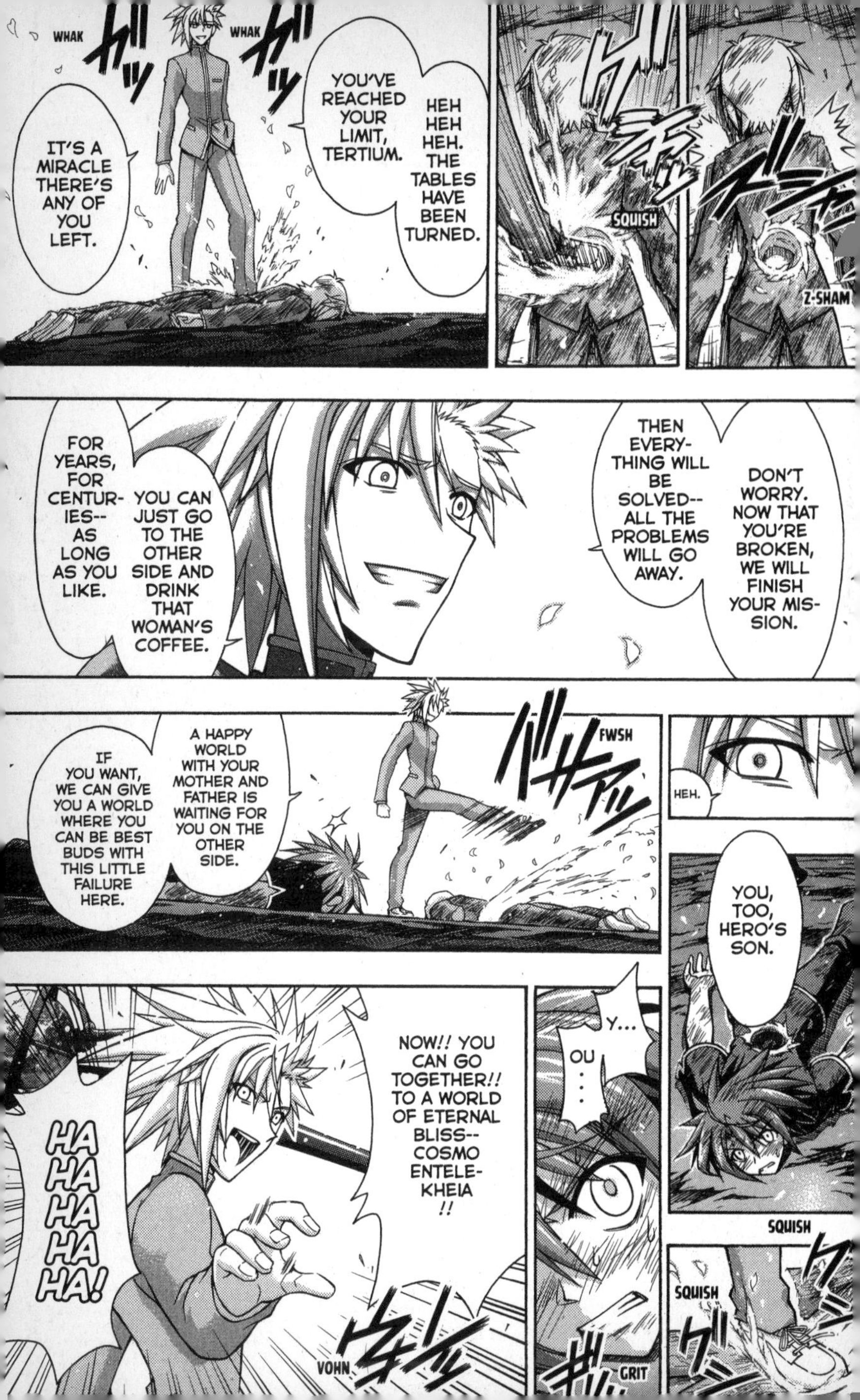
Z-SHAM
SQUISH
HEH HEH HEH. THE TABLES HAVE BEEN TURNED.
YOU'VE REACHED YOUR LIMIT, TERTIUM.
WHAK
WHAK
IT'S A MIRACLE THERE'S ANY OF YOU LEFT.
DON'T WORRY. NOW THAT YOU'RE BROKEN, WE WILL FINISH YOUR MISSION.
THEN EVERYTHING WILL BE SOLVED-- ALL THE PROBLEMS WILL GO AWAY.
YOU CAN JUST GO TO THE OTHER SIDE AND DRINK THAT WOMAN'S COFFEE.
FOR YEARS, FOR CENTURIES-- AS LONG AS YOU LIKE.
HEH.
FWSH
A HAPPY WORLD WITH YOUR MOTHER AND FATHER IS WAITING FOR YOU ON THE OTHER SIDE.
IF YOU WANT, WE CAN GIVE YOU A WORLD WHERE YOU CAN BE BEST BUDS WITH THIS LITTLE FAILURE HERE.
YOU, TOO, HERO'S SON.
SQUISH
SQUISH
Y...
OU...
GRIT
NOW!! YOU CAN GO TOGETHER!! TO A WORLD OF ETERNAL BLISS-- COSMO ENTELEKHEIA!!
HA HA HA HA HA HA!
VOHN

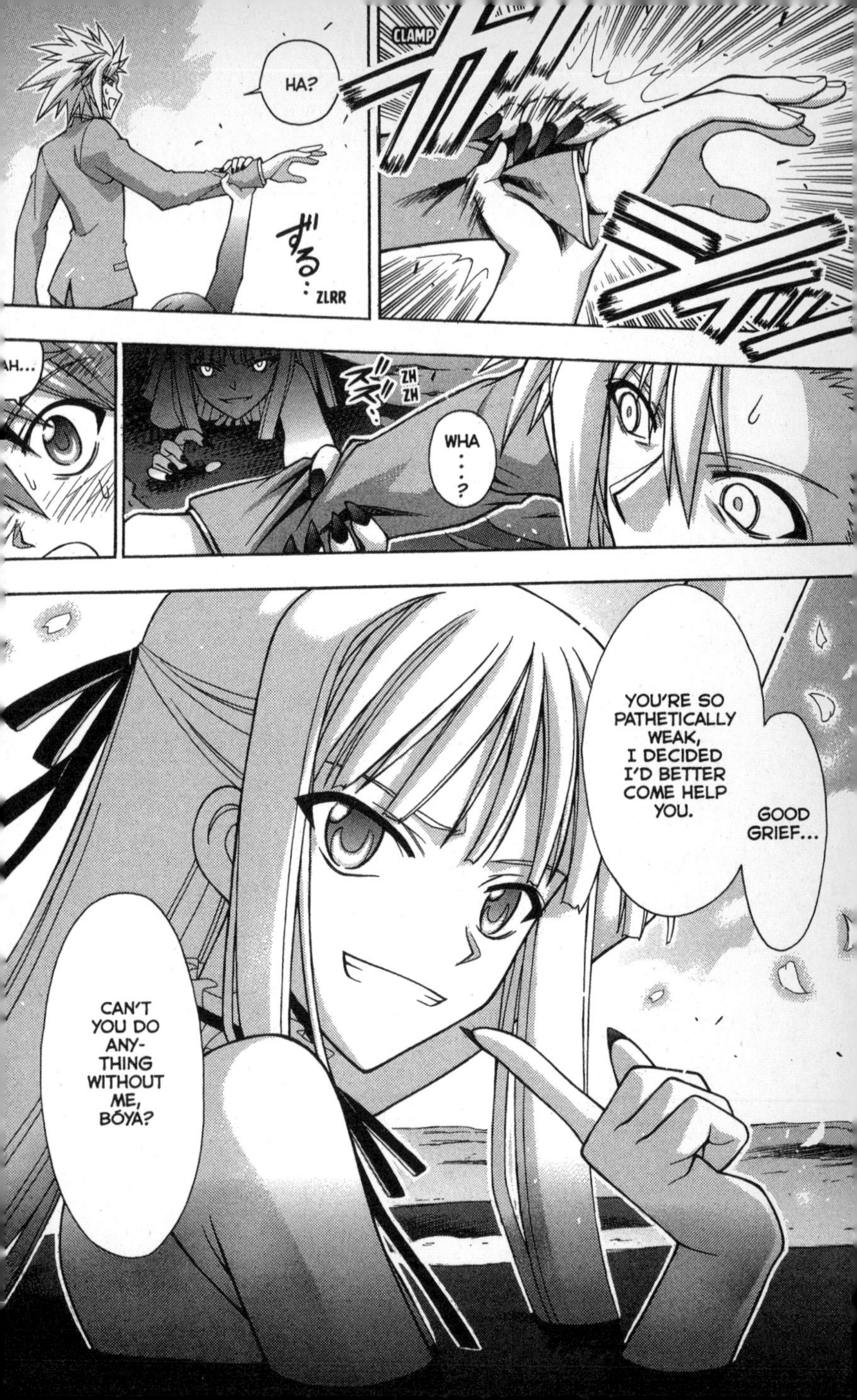
CLAMP
HA?
ずる..
ZLRR
WHA...?
ZH ZH
AH...
GOOD GRIEF...
YOU'RE SO PATHETICALLY WEAK, I DECIDED I'D BETTER COME HELP YOU.
CAN'T YOU DO ANY-THING WITHOUT ME, BŌYA?

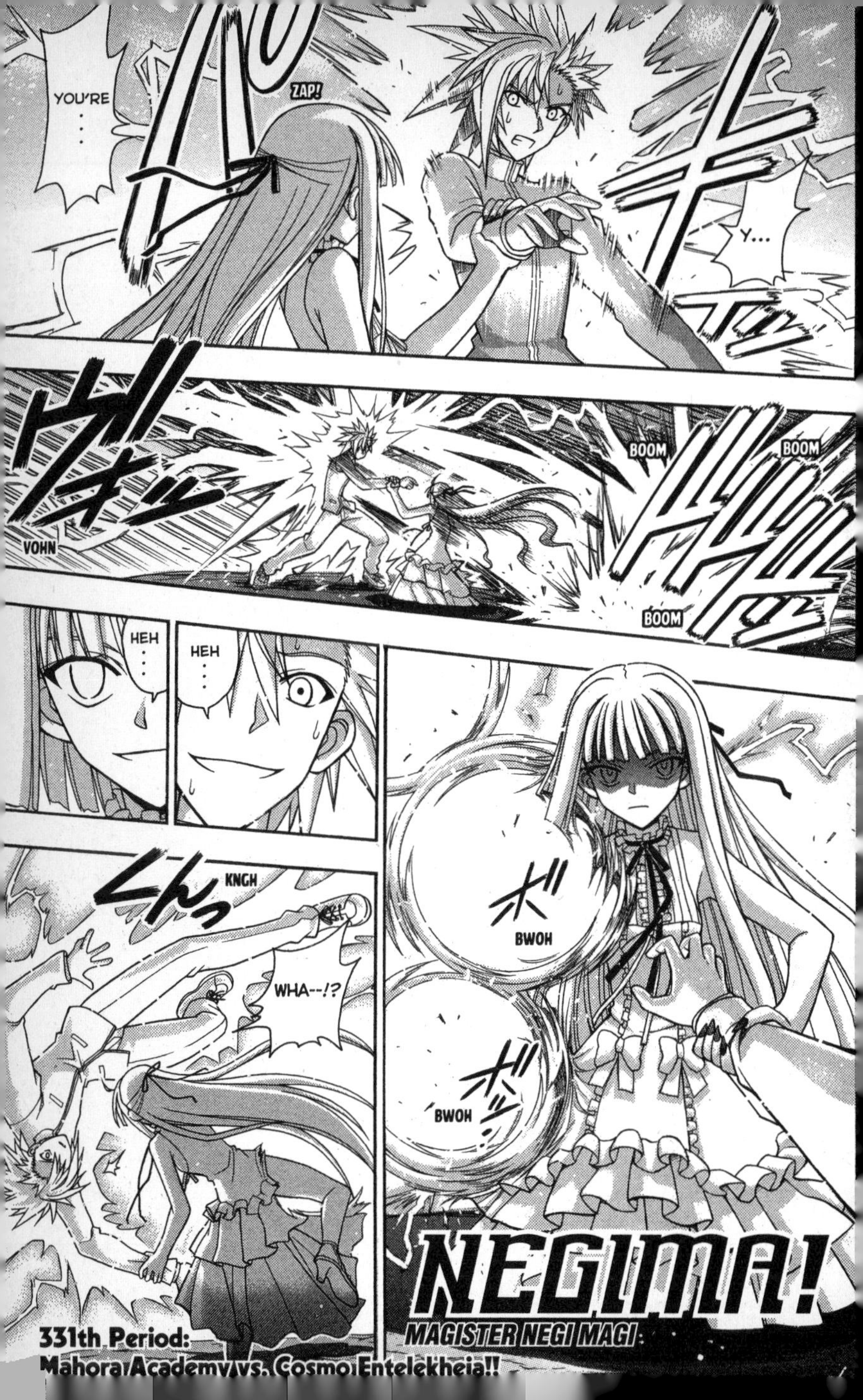

Y...
ZAP!
YOU'RE . . .
BOOM
BOOM
BOOM
VOHN
HEH . . .
HEH . . .
KNGH
WHA--!?
BWOH
BWOH
NEGIMA!
MAGISTER NEGI MAGI
331th Period:
Mahora Academy vs. Cosmo Entelekheia!!

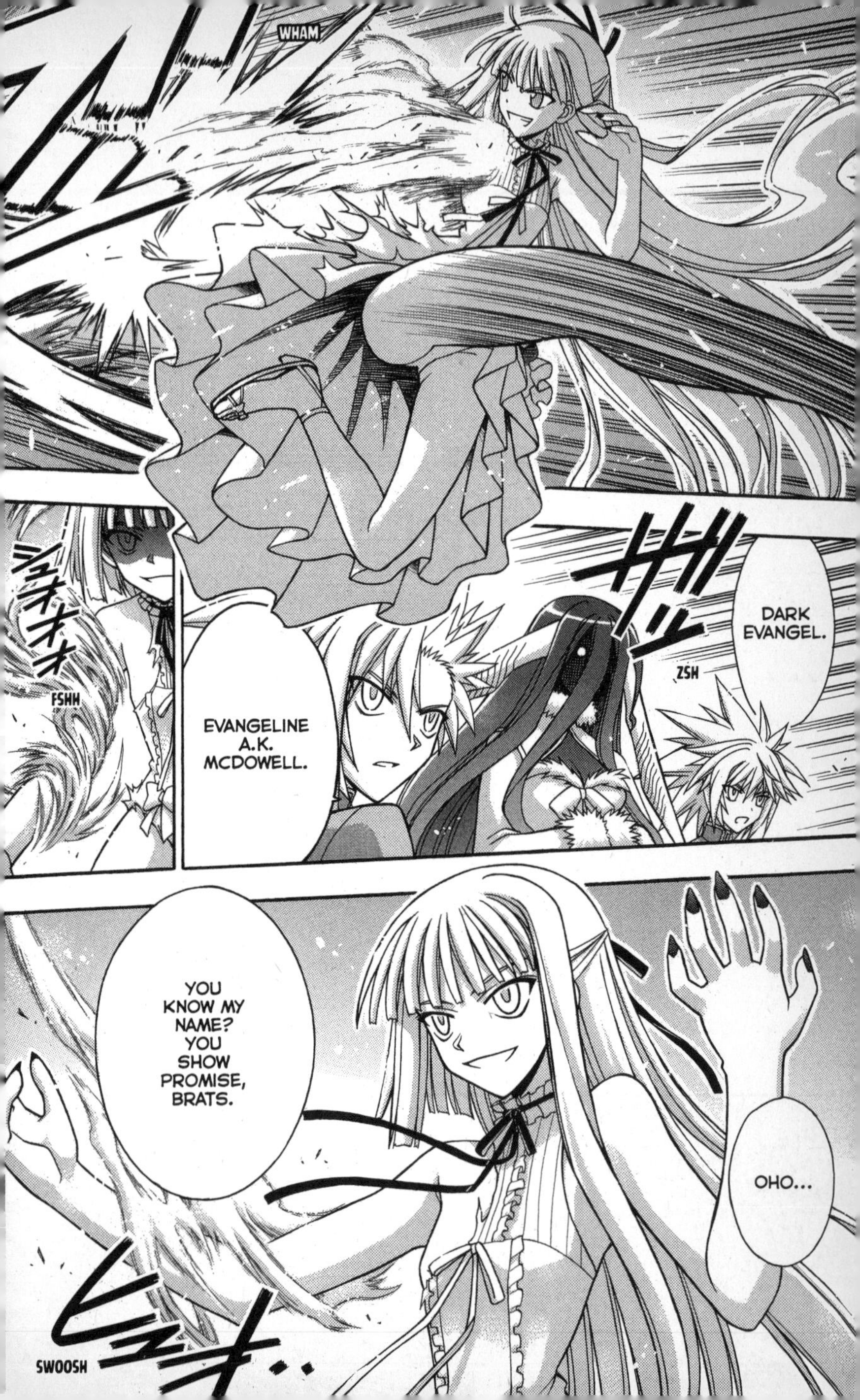
WHAM
DARK EVANGEL.
ZSH
EVANGELINE A.K. MCDOWELL.
FSHH
OHO...
YOU KNOW MY NAME? YOU SHOW PROMISE, BRATS.
SWOOSH

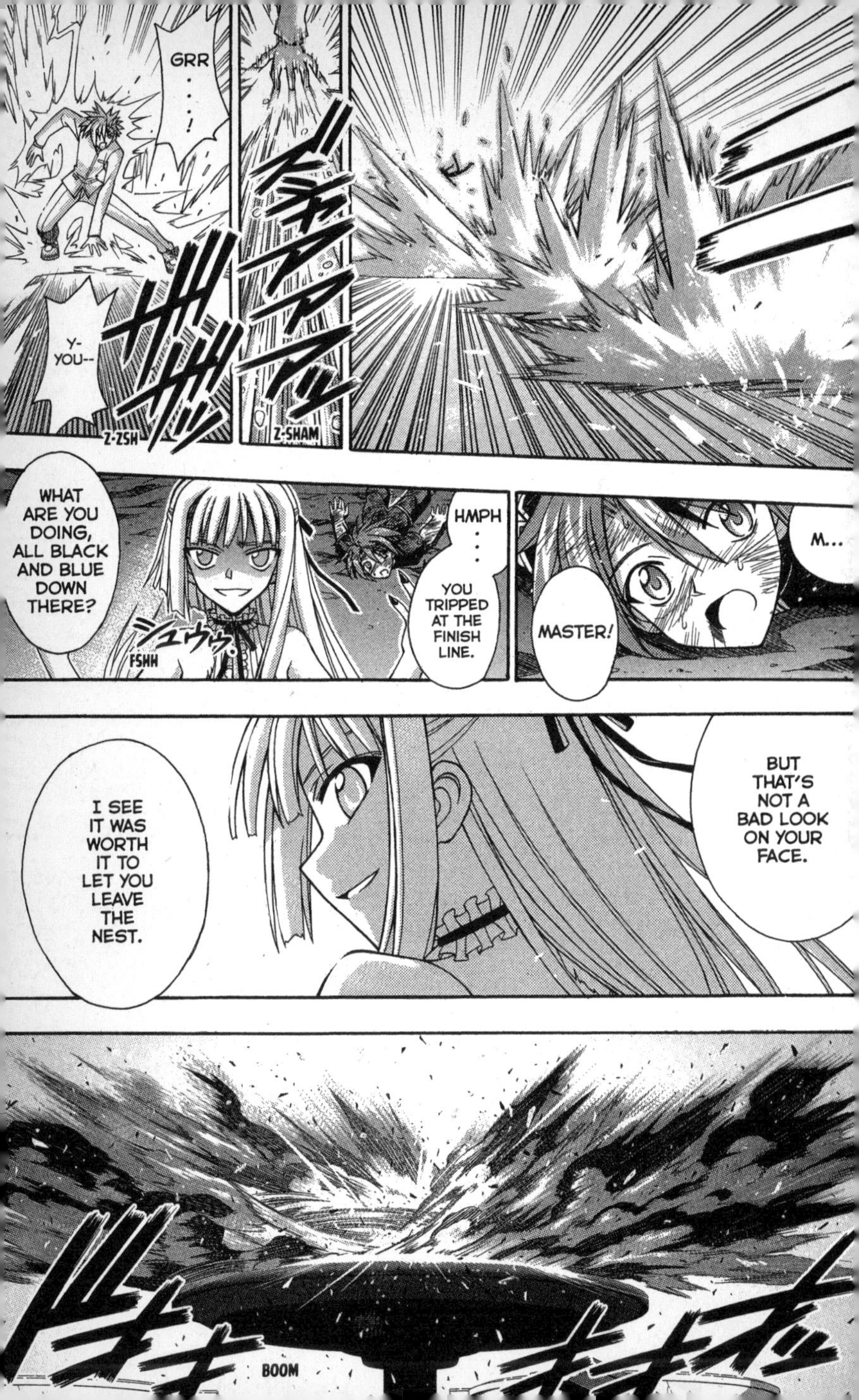
Z-SHAM
GRR . . . !
Y-YOU--
Z-ZSH
M...
MASTER!
HMPH . . .
YOU TRIPPED AT THE FINISH LINE.
WHAT ARE YOU DOING, ALL BLACK AND BLUE DOWN THERE?
FSHH
BUT THAT'S NOT A BAD LOOK ON YOUR FACE.
I SEE IT WAS WORTH IT TO LET YOU LEAVE THE NEST.
BOOM

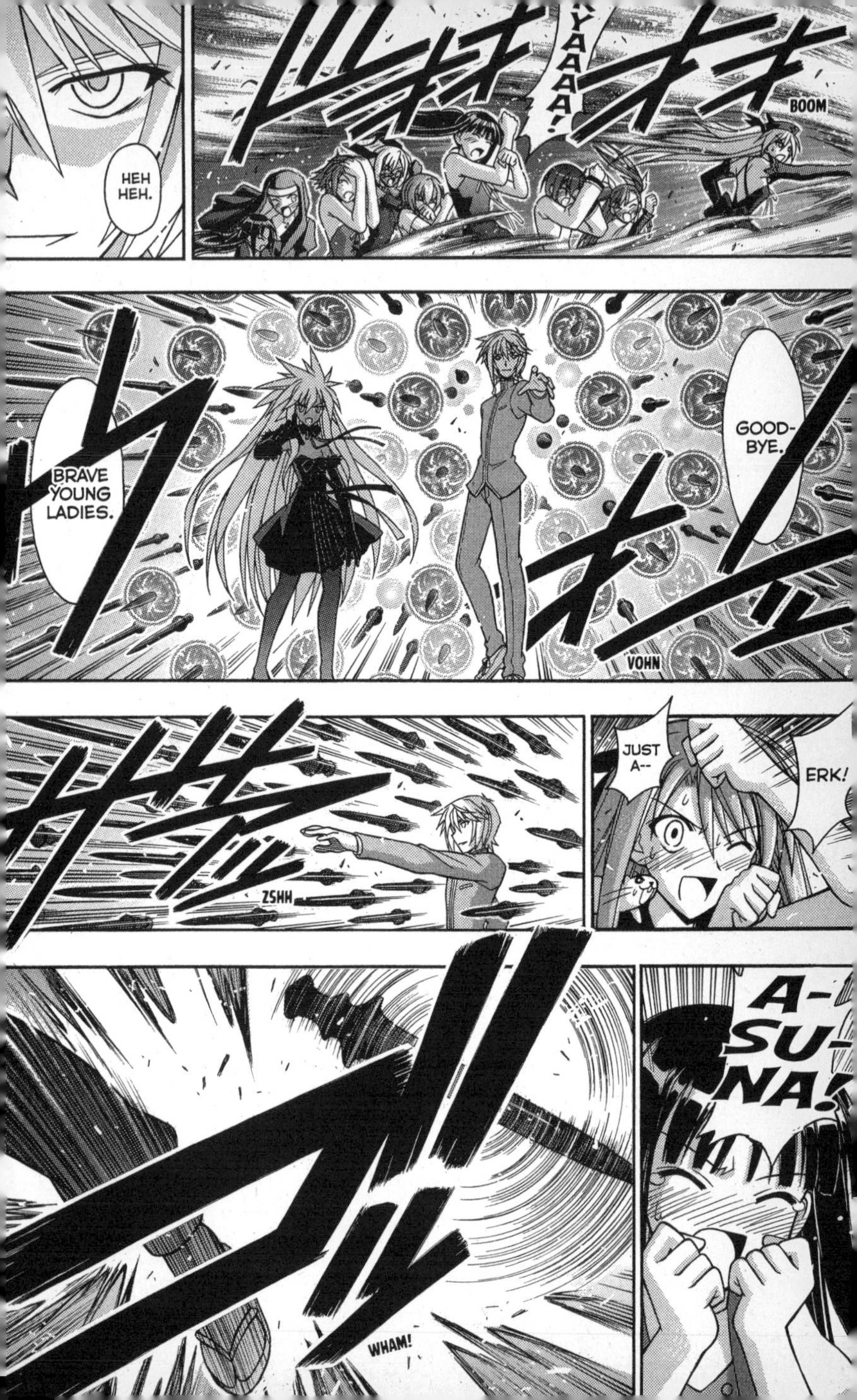
BOOM
YAAAAA!
HEH HEH.
GOOD-BYE.
VOHN
BRAVE YOUNG LADIES.
ERK!
JUST A--
ZSHH
A-SU-NA!
WHAM!

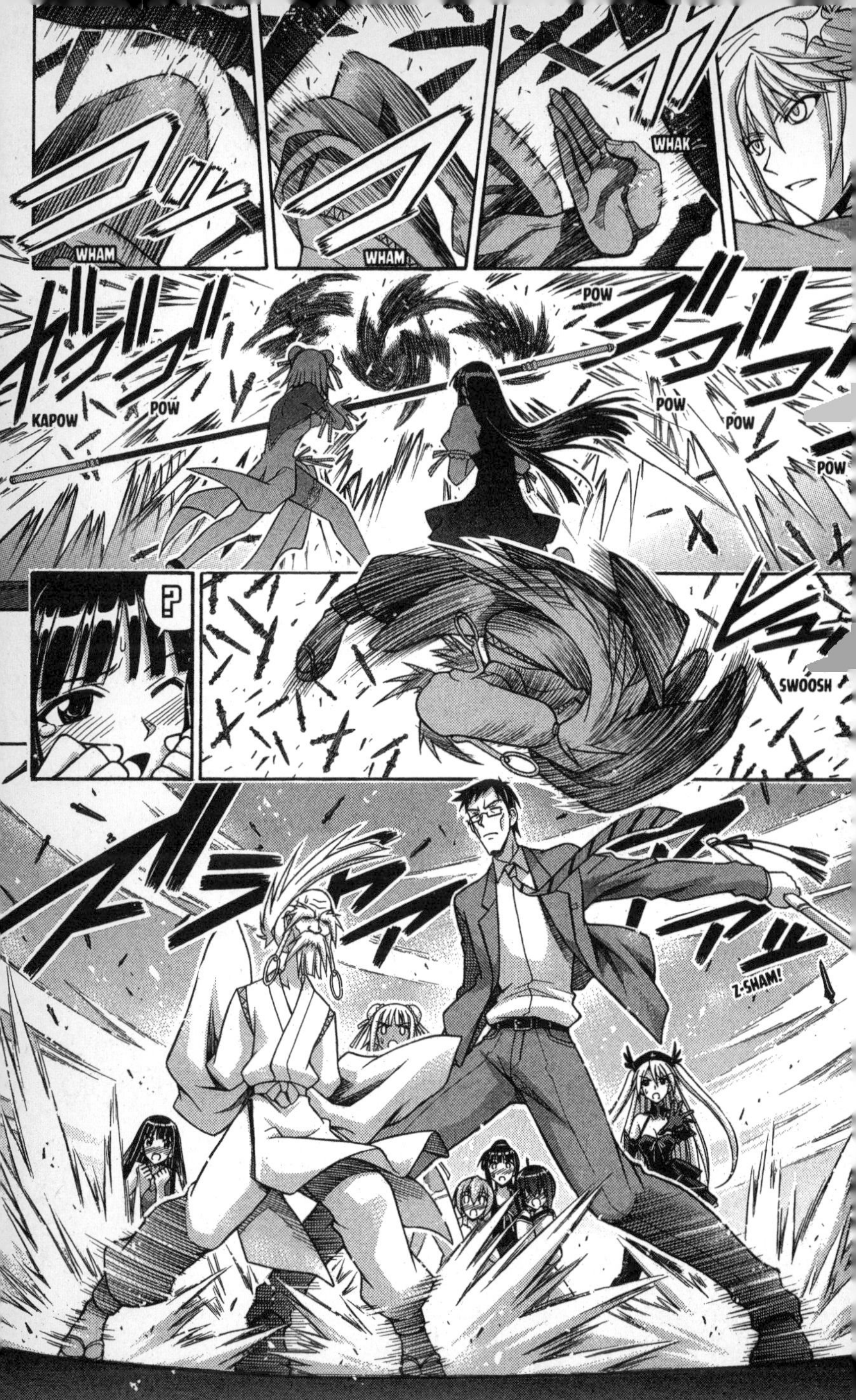
WHAK
WHAM
WHAM
POW
POW
POW
POW
POW
KAPOW
SWOOSH
?
Z-SHAM!

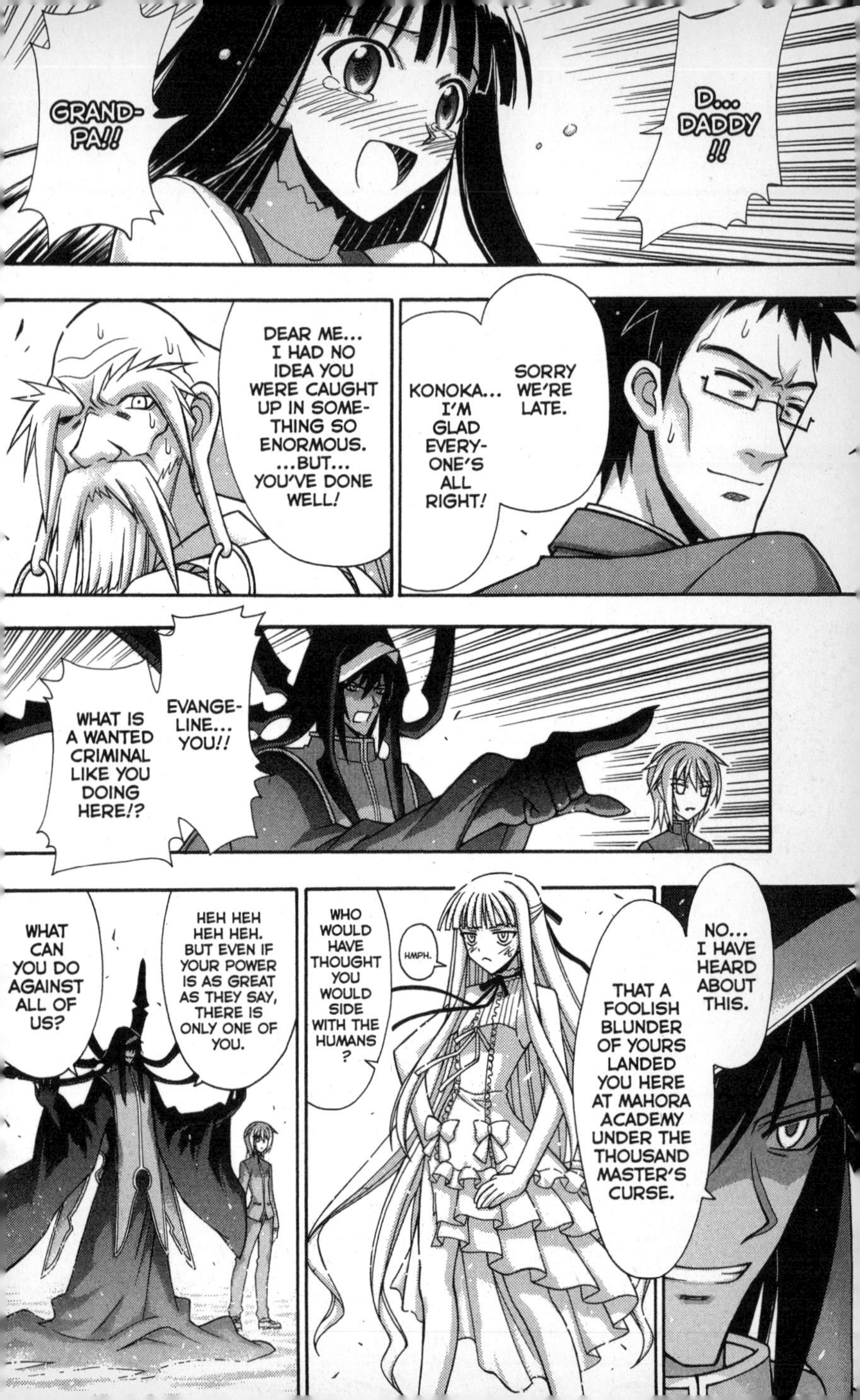
D... DADDY!!
GRAND-PA!!
KONOKA... I'M GLAD EVERY-ONE'S ALL RIGHT!
SORRY WE'RE LATE.
DEAR ME... I HAD NO IDEA YOU WERE CAUGHT UP IN SOME-THING SO ENORMOUS. ...BUT... YOU'VE DONE WELL!
EVANGE-LINE... YOU!!
WHAT IS A WANTED CRIMINAL LIKE YOU DOING HERE!?
NO... I HAVE HEARD ABOUT THIS.
THAT A FOOLISH BLUNDER OF YOURS LANDED YOU HERE AT MAHORA ACADEMY UNDER THE THOUSAND MASTER'S CURSE.
HMPH.
WHO WOULD HAVE THOUGHT YOU WOULD SIDE WITH THE HUMANS?
HEH HEH HEH HEH. BUT EVEN IF YOUR POWER IS AS GREAT AS THEY SAY, THERE IS ONLY ONE OF YOU.
WHAT CAN YOU DO AGAINST ALL OF US?

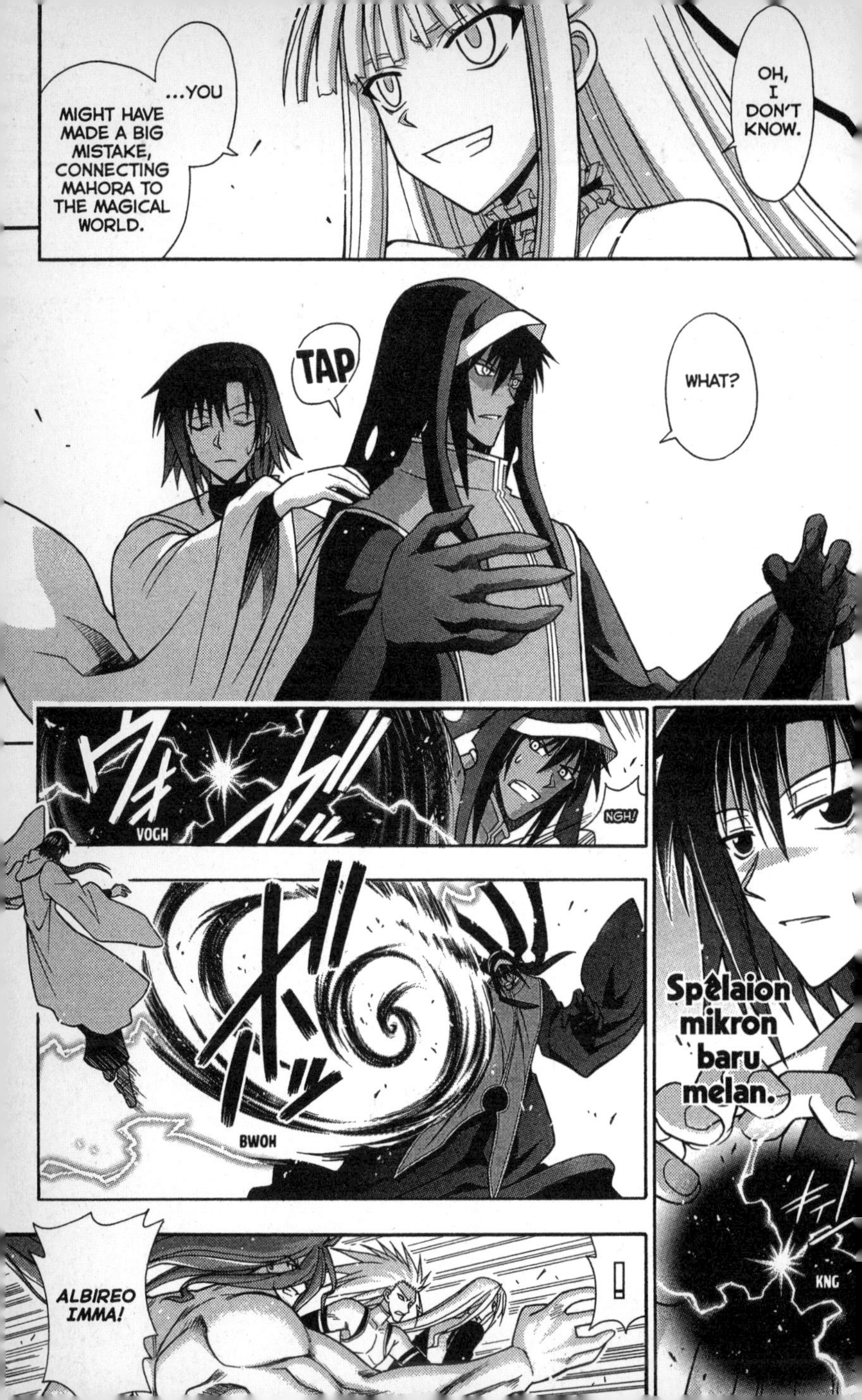
OH, I DON'T KNOW.
...YOU MIGHT HAVE MADE A BIG MISTAKE, CONNECTING MAHORA TO THE MAGICAL WORLD.
WHAT?
TAP
Spêlaion mikron baru melan.
KNG
NGH!
VOGH
BWOH
!
ALBIREO IMMA!

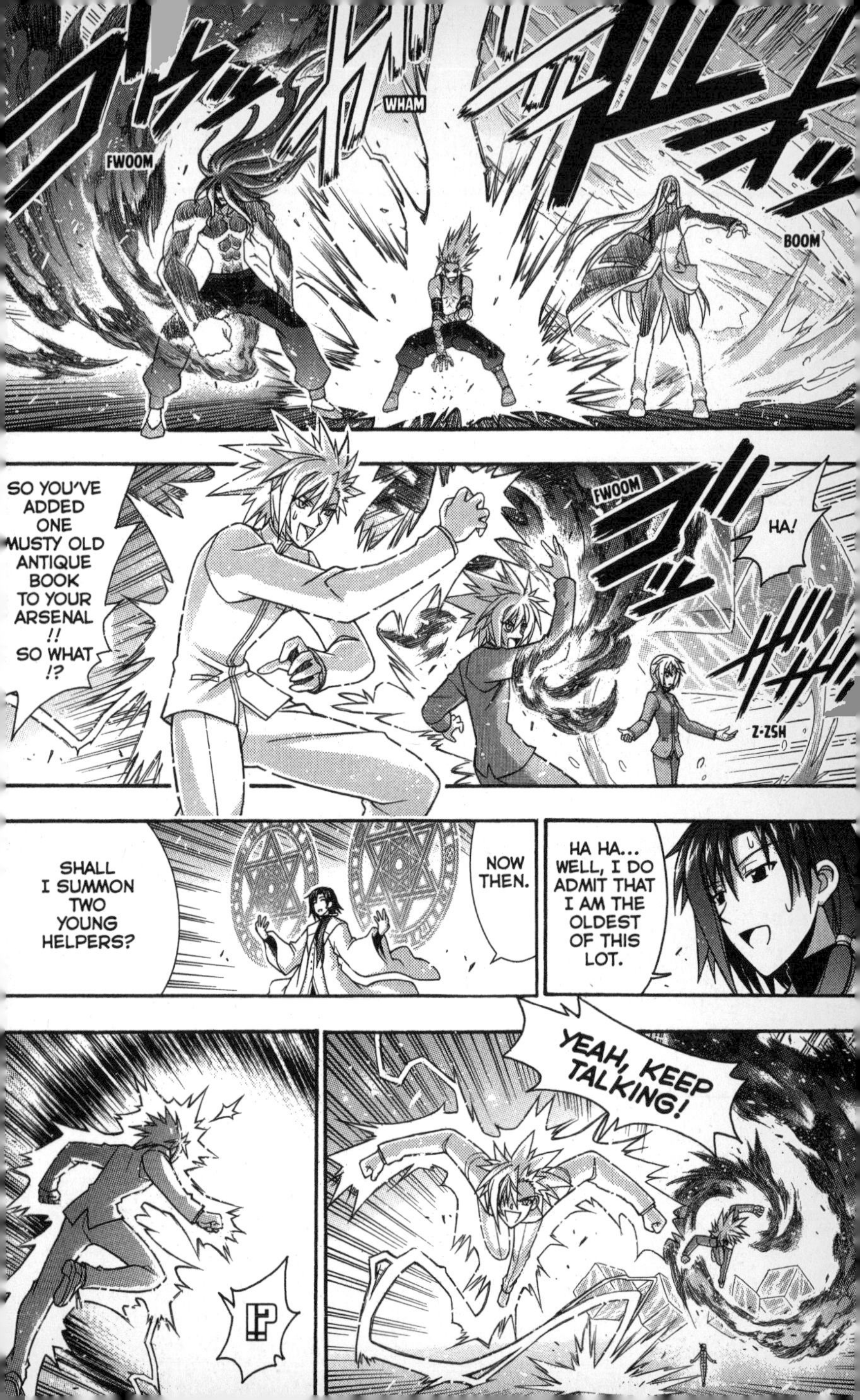
BOOM
WHAM
FWOOM
HA!
FWOOM
Z-ZSH
SO YOU'VE ADDED ONE MUSTY OLD ANTIQUE BOOK TO YOUR ARSENAL!! SO WHAT!?
HA HA... WELL, I DO ADMIT THAT I AM THE OLDEST OF THIS LOT.
NOW THEN.
SHALL I SUMMON TWO YOUNG HELPERS?
YEAH, KEEP TALKING!
!?

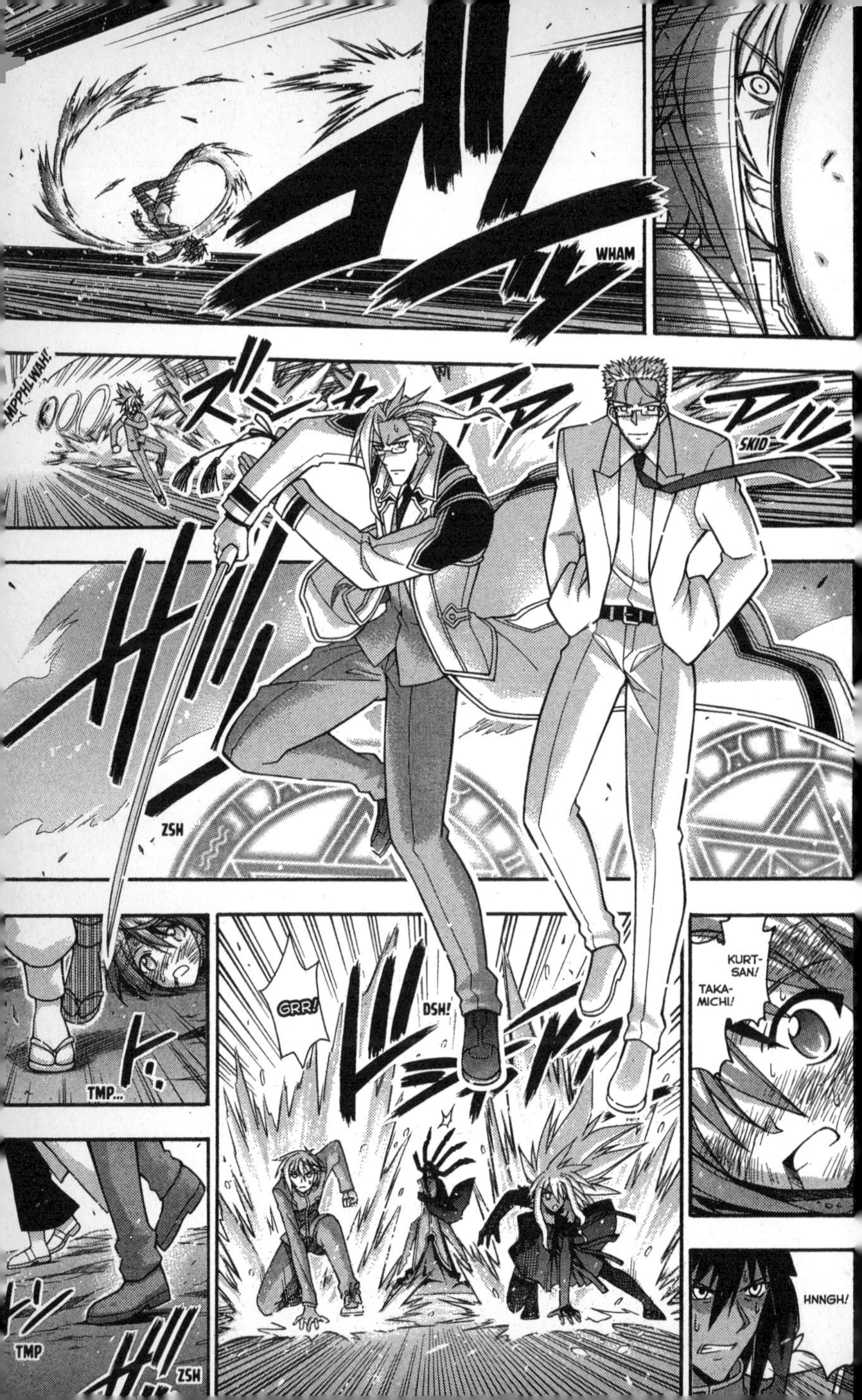
WHAM
SKID
MPPH! WAH!
ZSH
KURT-SAN!
TAKA-MICHI!
HNNGH!
GRR!
DSH!
TMP...
TMP
ZSH

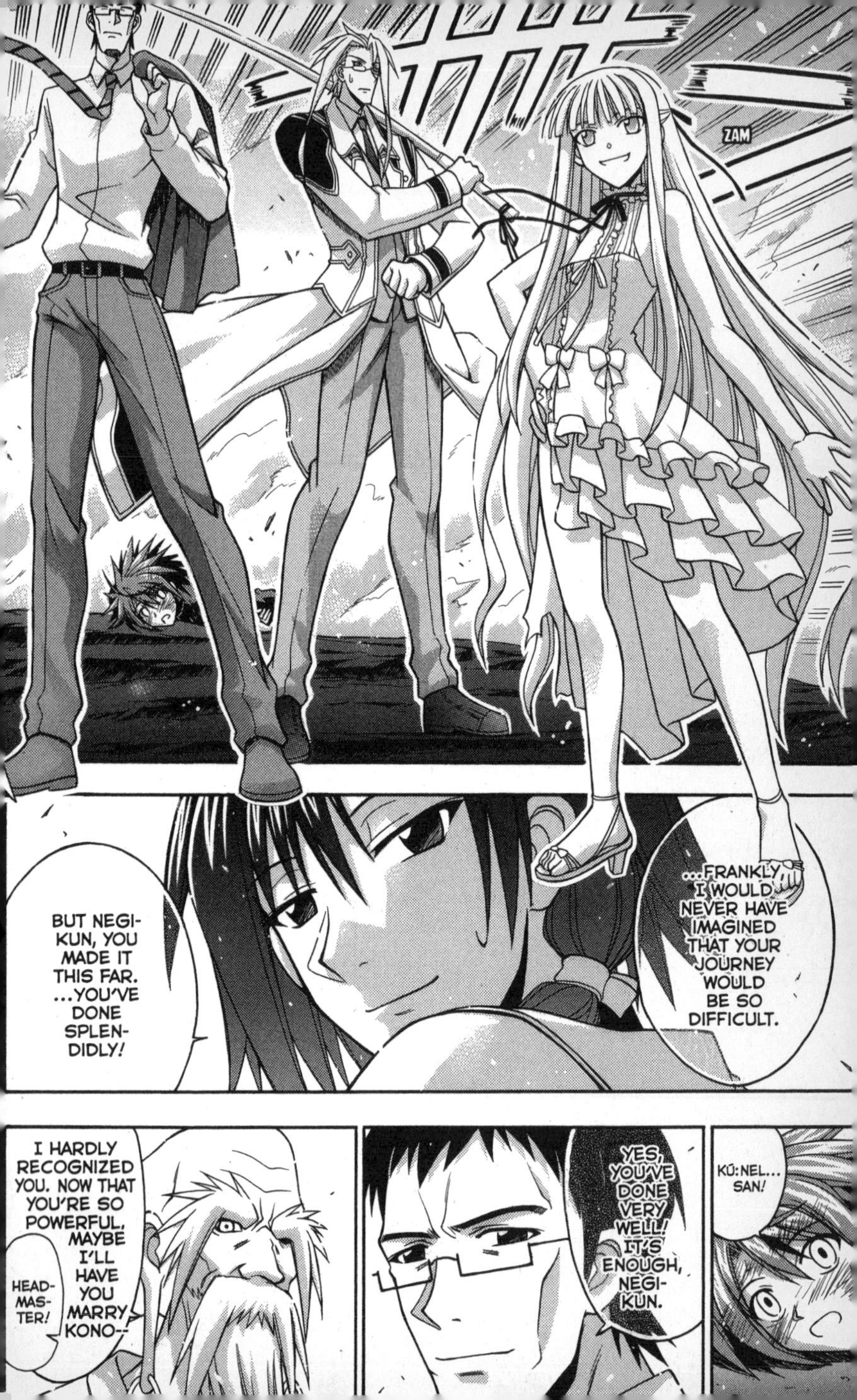
ZAM
...FRANKLY I WOULD NEVER HAVE IMAGINED THAT YOUR JOURNEY WOULD BE SO DIFFICULT.
BUT NEGI-KUN, YOU MADE IT THIS FAR. ...YOU'VE DONE SPLEN-DIDLY!
KŪ:NEL... SAN!
YES, YOU'VE DONE VERY WELL! IT'S ENOUGH, NEGI-KUN.
I HARDLY RECOGNIZED YOU. NOW THAT YOU'RE SO POWERFUL, MAYBE I'LL HAVE YOU MARRY KONO--
HEAD-MAS-TER!

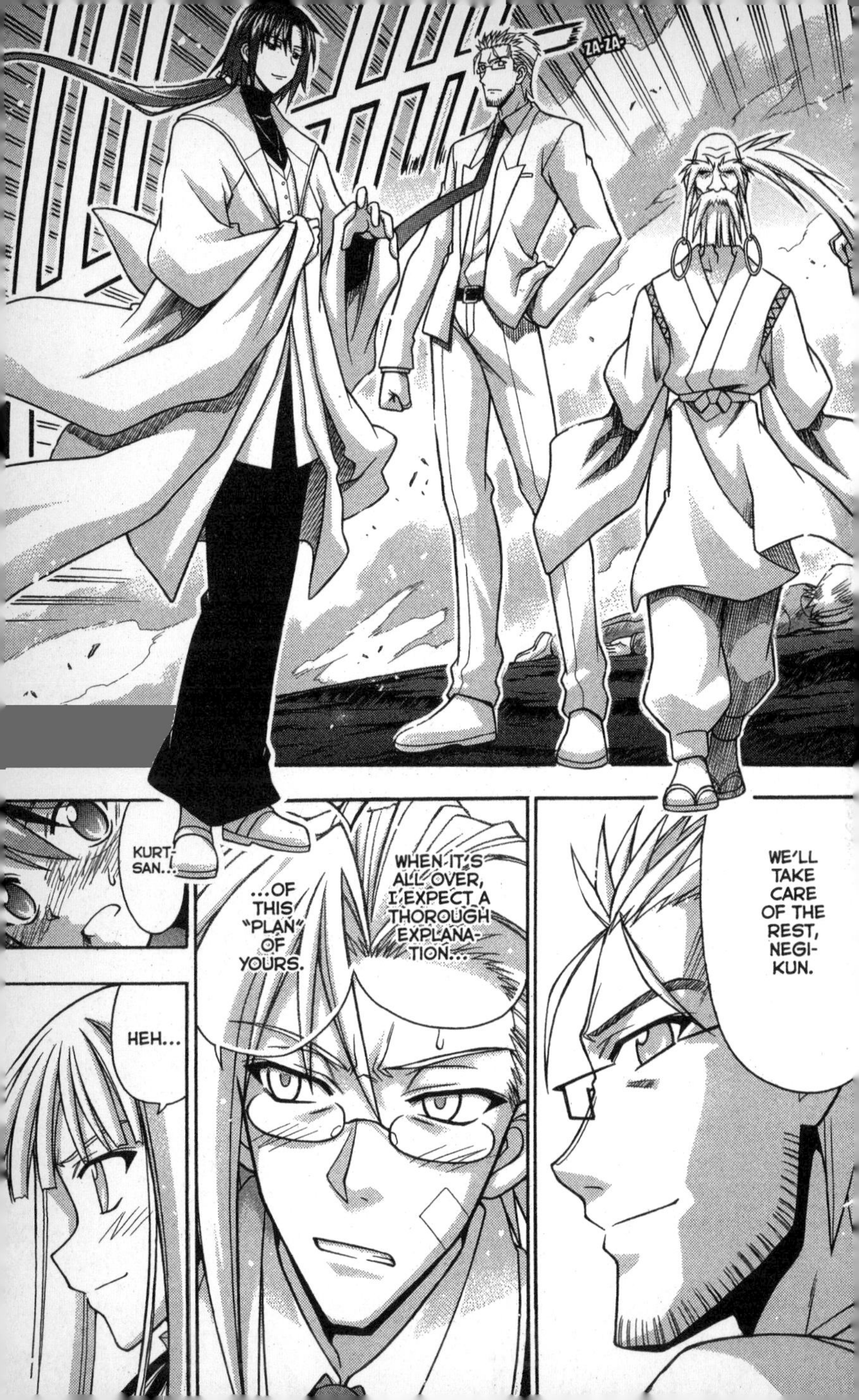
ZA-ZA
WE'LL TAKE CARE OF THE REST, NEGI-KUN.
WHEN IT'S ALL OVER, I EXPECT A THOROUGH EXPLANA-TION...
...OF THIS "PLAN" OF YOURS.
KURT-SAN...
HEH...

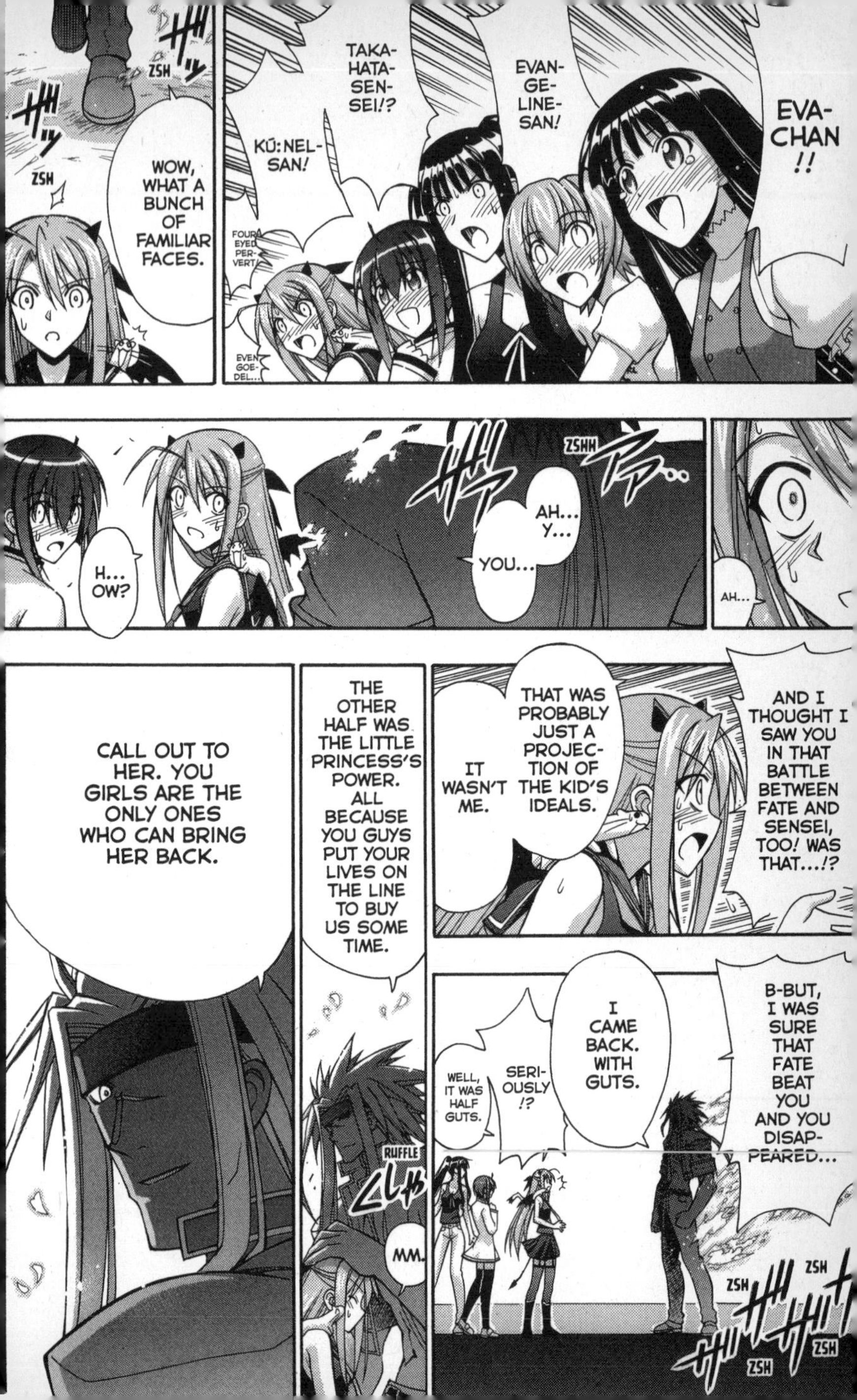
EVA-CHAN!!
EVAN-GE-LINE-SAN!
TAKA-HATA-SEN-SEI!?
KŪ:NEL-SAN!
FOUR EYED PER-VERT!
EVEN GOE-DEL...
ZSH
WOW, WHAT A BUNCH OF FAMILIAR FACES.
ZSH
AH...
ZSHH
AH... Y...
YOU...
H... OW?
AND I THOUGHT I SAW YOU IN THAT BATTLE BETWEEN FATE AND SENSEI, TOO! WAS THAT...!?
THAT WAS PROBABLY JUST A PROJEC-TION OF THE KID'S IDEALS.
IT WASN'T ME.
B-BUT, I WAS SURE THAT FATE BEAT YOU AND YOU DISAP-PEARED...
I CAME BACK. WITH GUTS.
SERI-OUSLY!?
WELL, IT WAS HALF GUTS.
ZSH
ZSH
ZSH
ZSH
THE OTHER HALF WAS THE LITTLE PRINCESS'S POWER. ALL BECAUSE YOU GUYS PUT YOUR LIVES ON THE LINE TO BUY US SOME TIME.
RUFFLE
MM.
CALL OUT TO HER. YOU GIRLS ARE THE ONLY ONES WHO CAN BRING HER BACK.

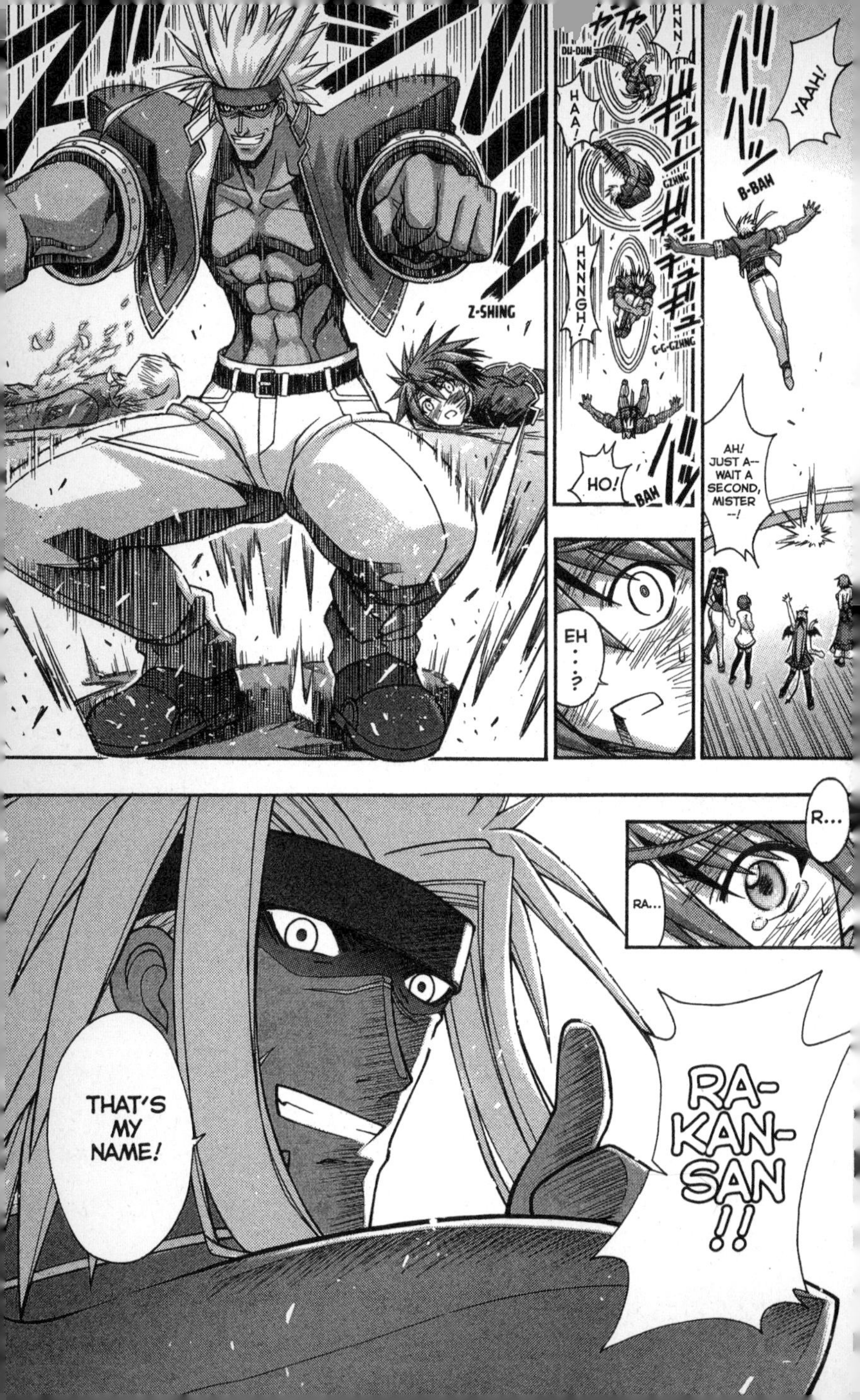
YAAH!
B-BAH
AH! JUST A-- WAIT A SECOND, MISTER --!
HNN!
DU-DUN
HAA!
GZHNG
HNNNGH!
G-G-GZHNG
HO!
BAH
EH...?
Z-SHING
R...
RA...
RA-KAN-SAN!!
THAT'S MY NAME!

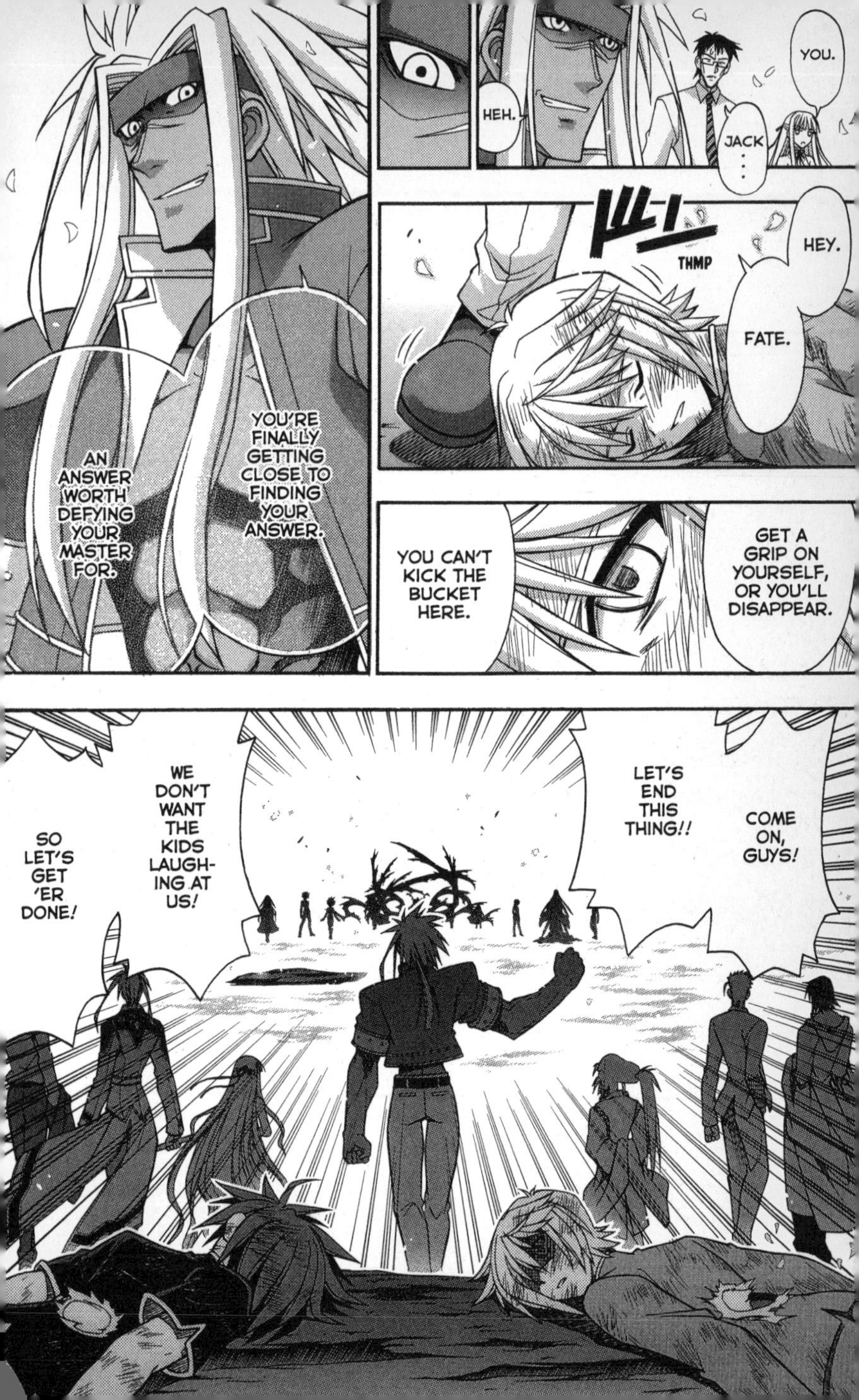
YOU.
JACK...
HEH.
HEY.
FATE.
THMP
GET A GRIP ON YOURSELF, OR YOU'LL DISAPPEAR.
YOU CAN'T KICK THE BUCKET HERE.
YOU'RE FINALLY GETTING CLOSE TO FINDING YOUR ANSWER.
AN ANSWER WORTH DEFYING YOUR MASTER FOR.
COME ON, GUYS!
LET'S END THIS THING!!
WE DON'T WANT THE KIDS LAUGHING AT US!
SO LET'S GET 'ER DONE!

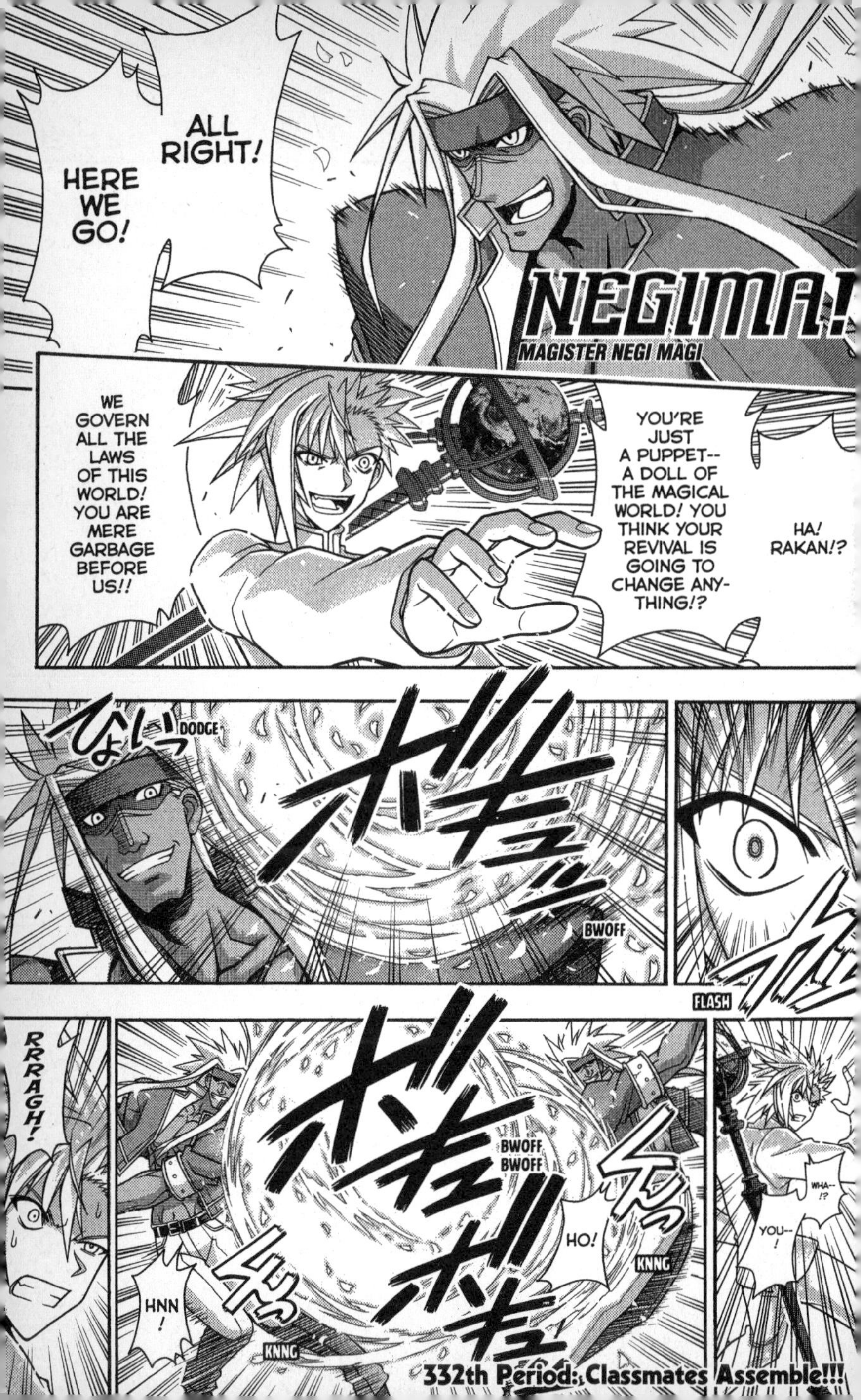
ALL RIGHT!
HERE WE GO!
NEGIMA!
MAGISTER NEGI MAGI
HA! RAKAN!?
YOU'RE JUST A PUPPET-- A DOLL OF THE MAGICAL WORLD! YOU THINK YOUR REVIVAL IS GOING TO CHANGE ANY-THING!?
WE GOVERN ALL THE LAWS OF THIS WORLD! YOU ARE MERE GARBAGE BEFORE US!!
FLASH
DODGE
BWOFF
WHA-- !?
YOU--
HO!
KNNG
BWOFF BWOFF
HNN !
KNNG
RRRAGH!
332th Period: Classmates Assemble!!!

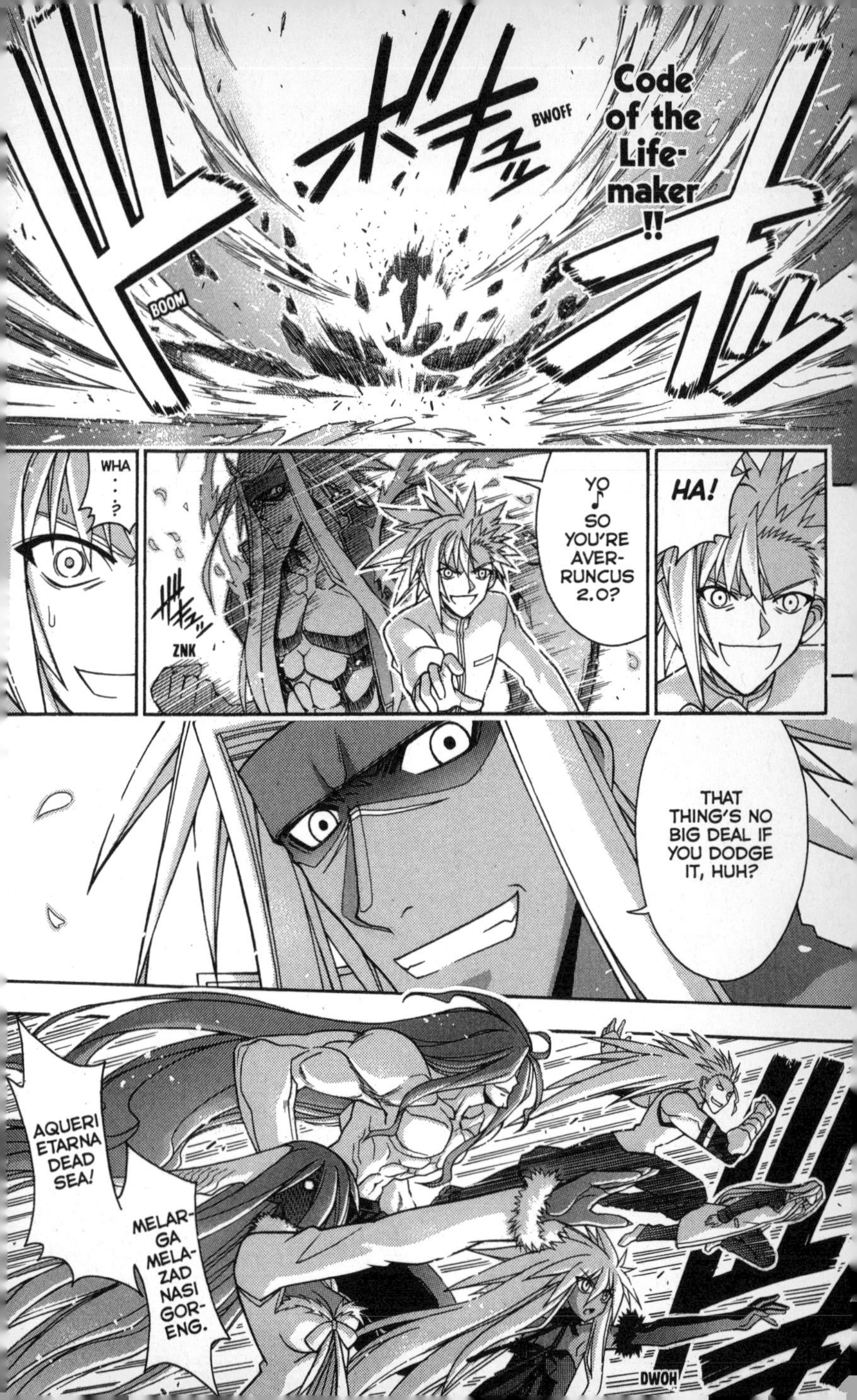
Code of the Life-maker!!
BWOFF
BOOM
HA!
YO ♪ SO YOU'RE AVERRUNCUS 2.0?
ZNK
WHA . . . ?
THAT THING'S NO BIG DEAL IF YOU DODGE IT, HUH?
MELARGA MELAZAD NASI GORENG.
AQUERI ETARNA DEAD SEA!
DWOH

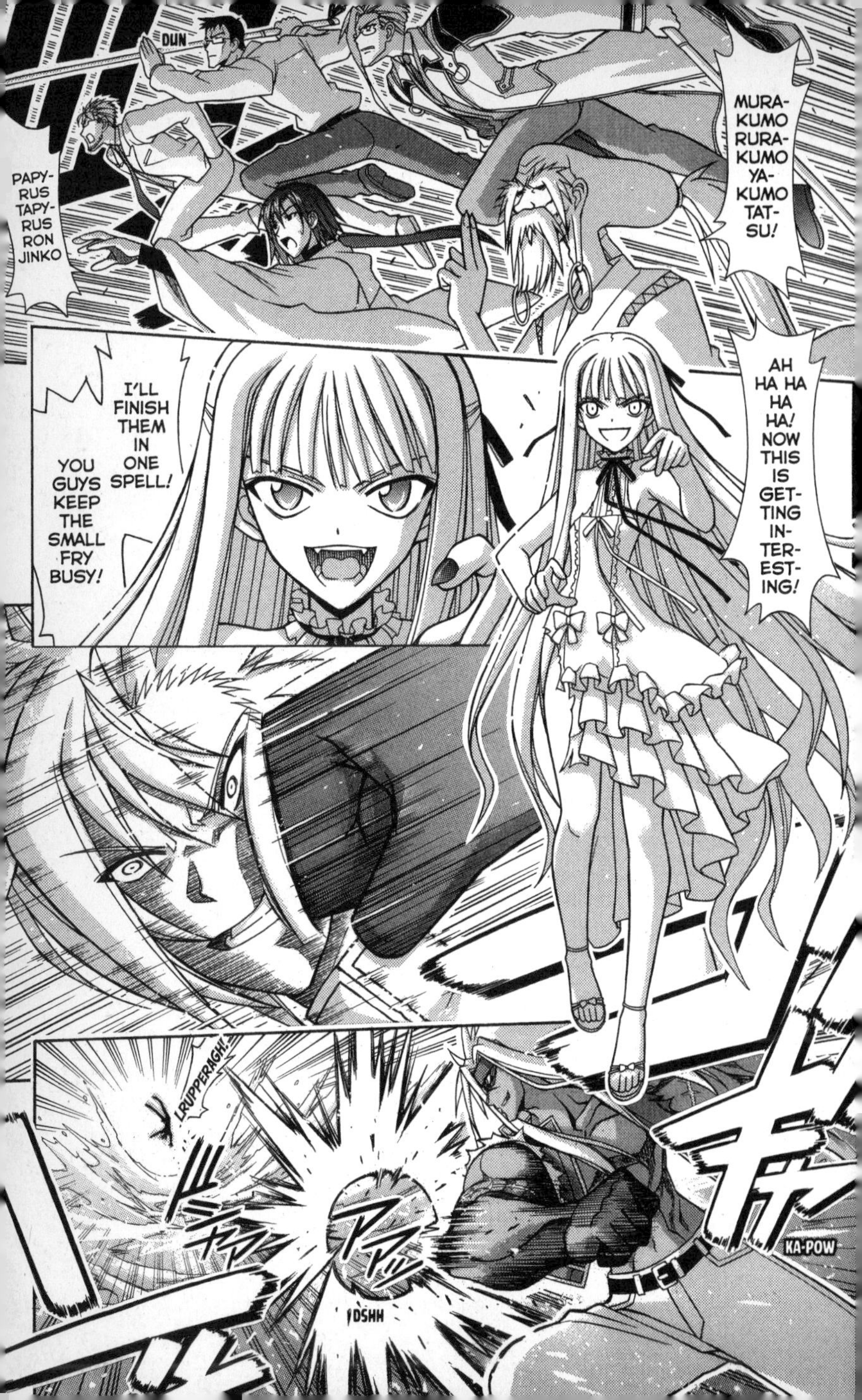
MURA-KUMO RURA-KUMO YA-KUMO TAT-SU!
DUN
PAPY-RUS TAPY-RUS RON JINKO
AH HA HA HA HA! NOW THIS IS GET-TING IN-TER-EST-ING!
I'LL FINISH THEM IN ONE SPELL!
YOU GUYS KEEP THE SMALL FRY BUSY!
KA-POW
LRUPPERAGH!!
DSHH

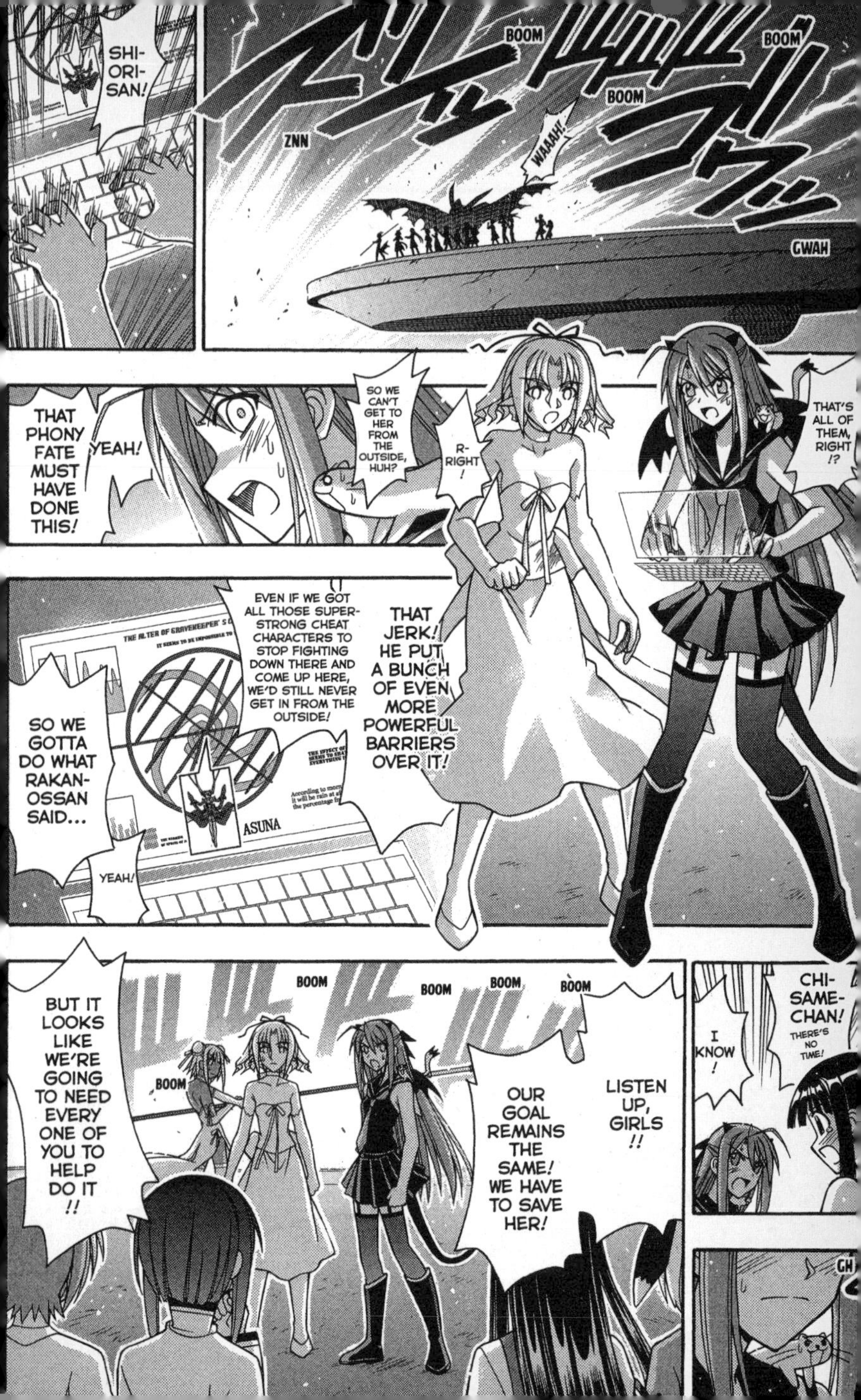
BOOM
BOOM
BOOM
ZNN
WAAAH!
GWAH
SHI-ORI-SAN!
THAT'S ALL OF THEM, RIGHT!?
R-RIGHT!
SO WE CAN'T GET TO HER FROM THE OUTSIDE, HUH?
YEAH!
THAT PHONY FATE MUST HAVE DONE THIS!
THAT JERK! HE PUT A BUNCH OF EVEN MORE POWERFUL BARRIERS OVER IT!
EVEN IF WE GOT ALL THOSE SUPER-STRONG CHEAT CHARACTERS TO STOP FIGHTING DOWN THERE AND COME UP HERE, WE'D STILL NEVER GET IN FROM THE OUTSIDE!
ASUNA
SO WE GOTTA DO WHAT RAKAN-OSSAN SAID...
YEAH!
CHI-SAME-CHAN! THERE'S NO TIME!
I KNOW!
GH
BOOM
BOOM
BOOM
BOOM
BOOM
LISTEN UP, GIRLS!!
OUR GOAL REMAINS THE SAME! WE HAVE TO SAVE HER!
BUT IT LOOKS LIKE WE'RE GOING TO NEED EVERY ONE OF YOU TO HELP DO IT!!

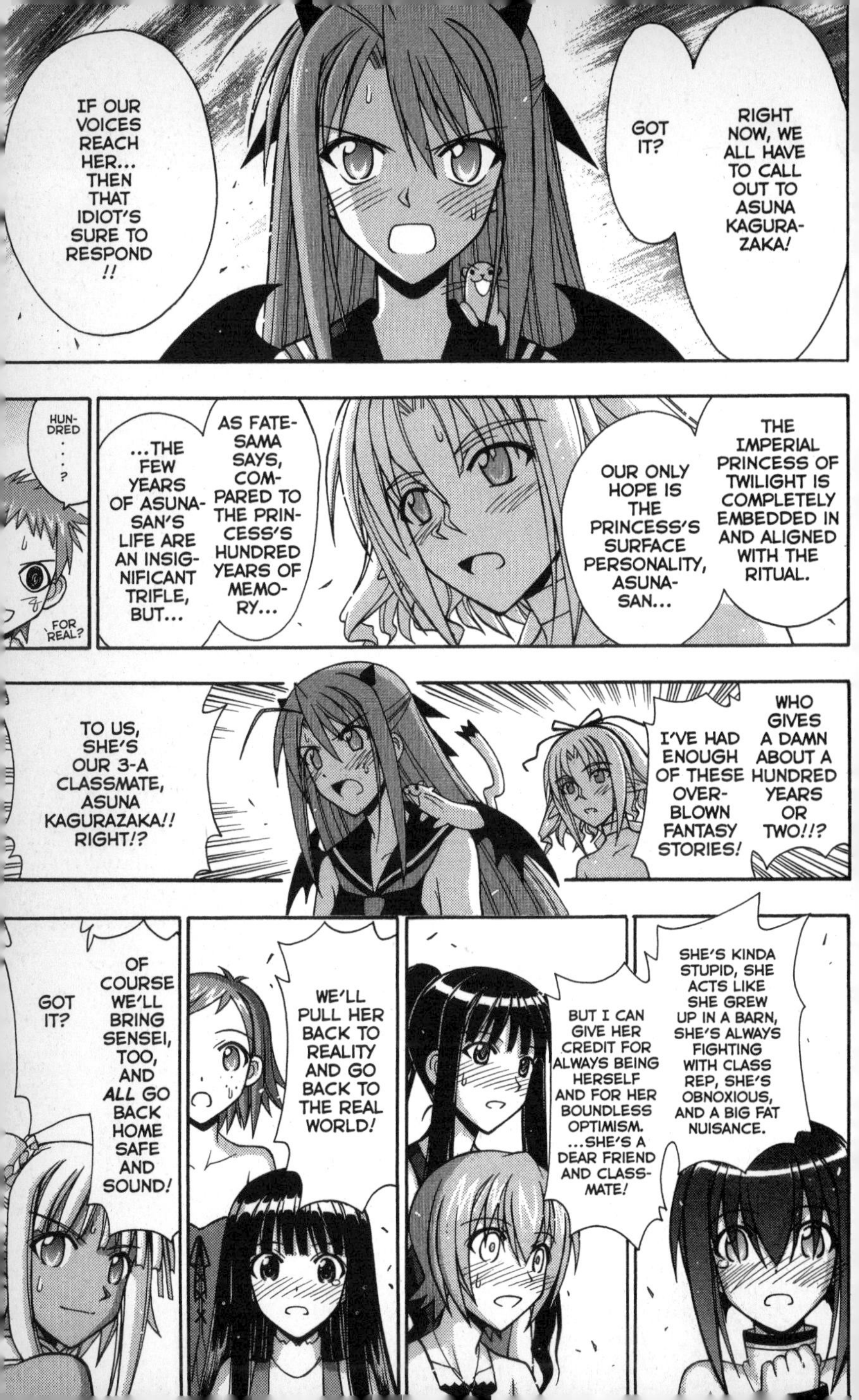
RIGHT NOW, WE ALL HAVE TO CALL OUT TO ASUNA KAGURAZAKA!
GOT IT?
IF OUR VOICES REACH HER... THEN THAT IDIOT'S SURE TO RESPOND!!
THE IMPERIAL PRINCESS OF TWILIGHT IS COMPLETELY EMBEDDED IN AND ALIGNED WITH THE RITUAL.
OUR ONLY HOPE IS THE PRINCESS'S SURFACE PERSONALITY, ASUNA-SAN...
AS FATE-SAMA SAYS, COMPARED TO THE PRINCESS'S HUNDRED YEARS OF MEMORY...
...THE FEW YEARS OF ASUNA-SAN'S LIFE ARE AN INSIGNIFICANT TRIFLE, BUT...
HUNDRED...?
FOR REAL?
WHO GIVES A DAMN ABOUT A HUNDRED YEARS OR TWO!!?
I'VE HAD ENOUGH OF THESE OVERBLOWN FANTASY STORIES!
TO US, SHE'S OUR 3-A CLASSMATE, ASUNA KAGURAZAKA!! RIGHT!?
SHE'S KINDA STUPID, SHE ACTS LIKE SHE GREW UP IN A BARN, SHE'S ALWAYS FIGHTING WITH CLASS REP, SHE'S OBNOXIOUS, AND A BIG FAT NUISANCE.
BUT I CAN GIVE HER CREDIT FOR ALWAYS BEING HERSELF AND FOR HER BOUNDLESS OPTIMISM. ...SHE'S A DEAR FRIEND AND CLASSMATE!
WE'LL PULL HER BACK TO REALITY AND GO BACK TO THE REAL WORLD!
OF COURSE WE'LL BRING SENSEI, TOO, AND ALL GO BACK HOME SAFE AND SOUND!
GOT IT?

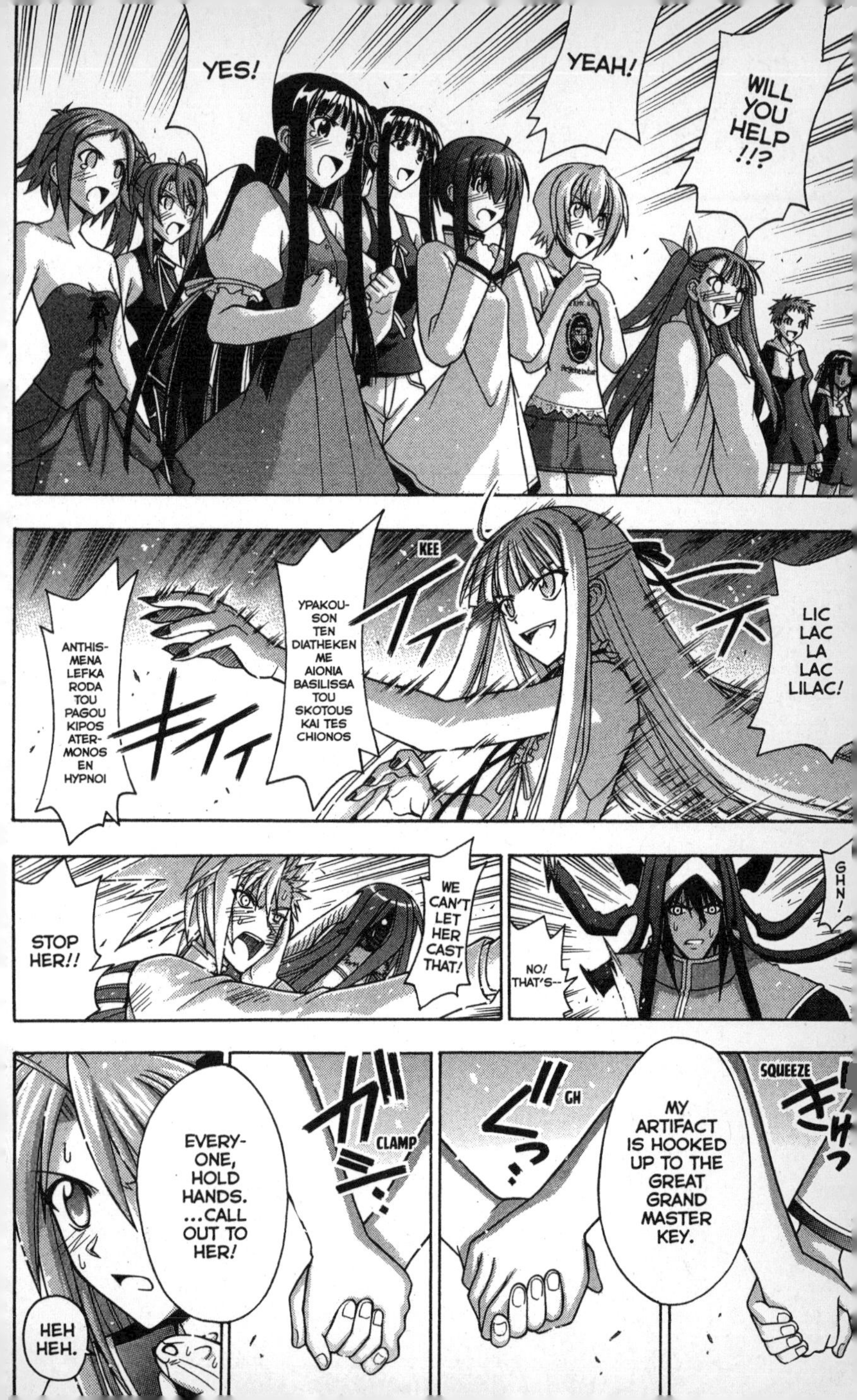
WILL YOU HELP!!?
YEAH!
YES!
LIC LAC LA LAC LILAC!
KEE
YPAKOUSON TEN DIATHEKEN ME AIONIA BASILISSA TOU SKOTOUS KAI TES CHIONOS
ANTHISMENA LEFKA RODA TOU PAGOU KIPOS ATERMONOS EN HYPNOI
GHN!
NO! THAT'S--
WE CAN'T LET HER CAST THAT!
STOP HER!!
SQUEEZE
MY ARTIFACT IS HOOKED UP TO THE GREAT GRAND MASTER KEY.
GH
CLAMP
EVERYONE, HOLD HANDS. ...CALL OUT TO HER!
HEH HEH.

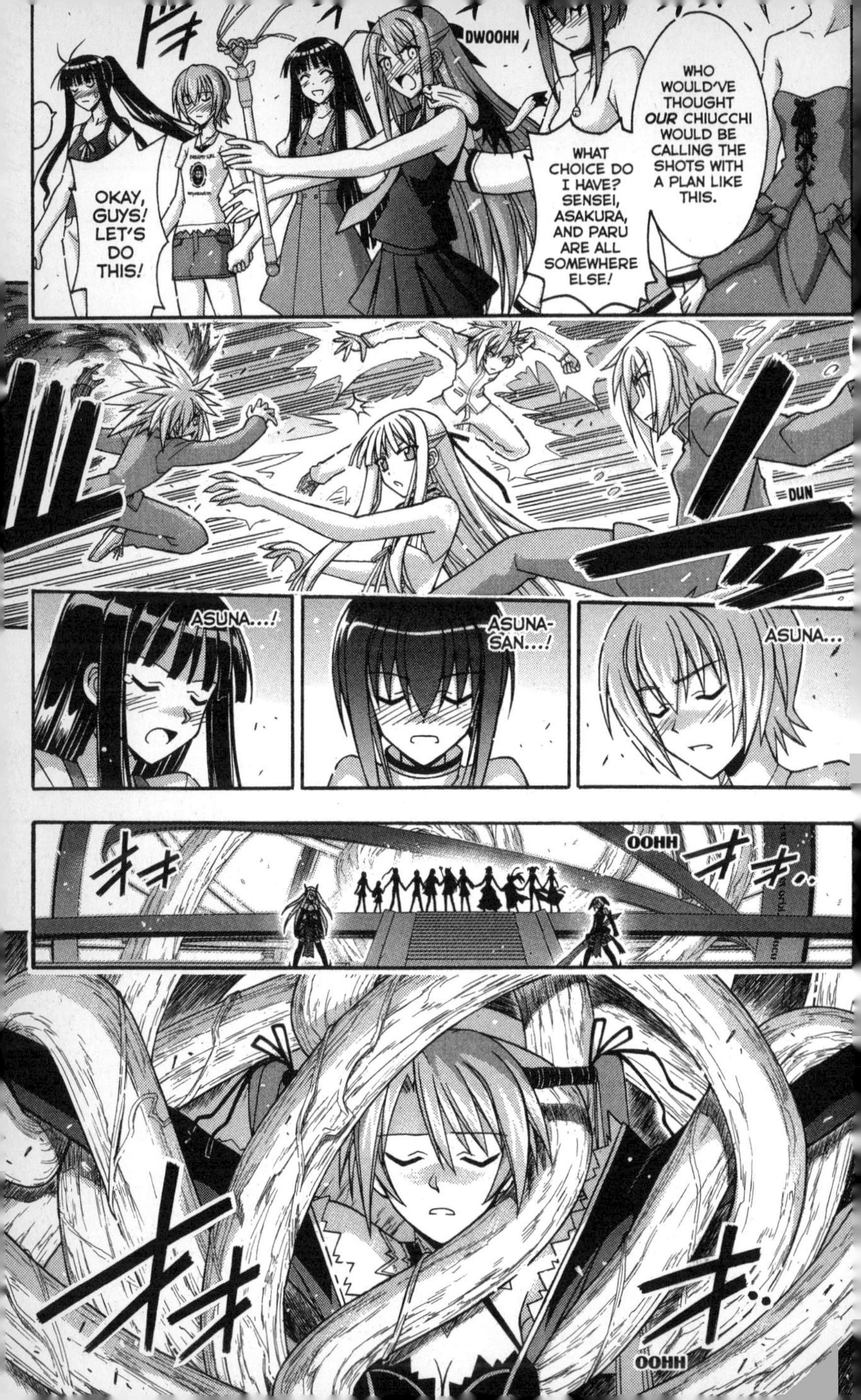
DWOOHH
WHO WOULD'VE THOUGHT OUR CHIUCCHI WOULD BE CALLING THE SHOTS WITH A PLAN LIKE THIS.
WHAT CHOICE DO I HAVE? SENSEI, ASAKURA, AND PARU ARE ALL SOMEWHERE ELSE!
OKAY, GUYS! LET'S DO THIS!
DUN
ASUNA...
ASUNA-SAN...!
ASUNA...!
OOHH
OOHH

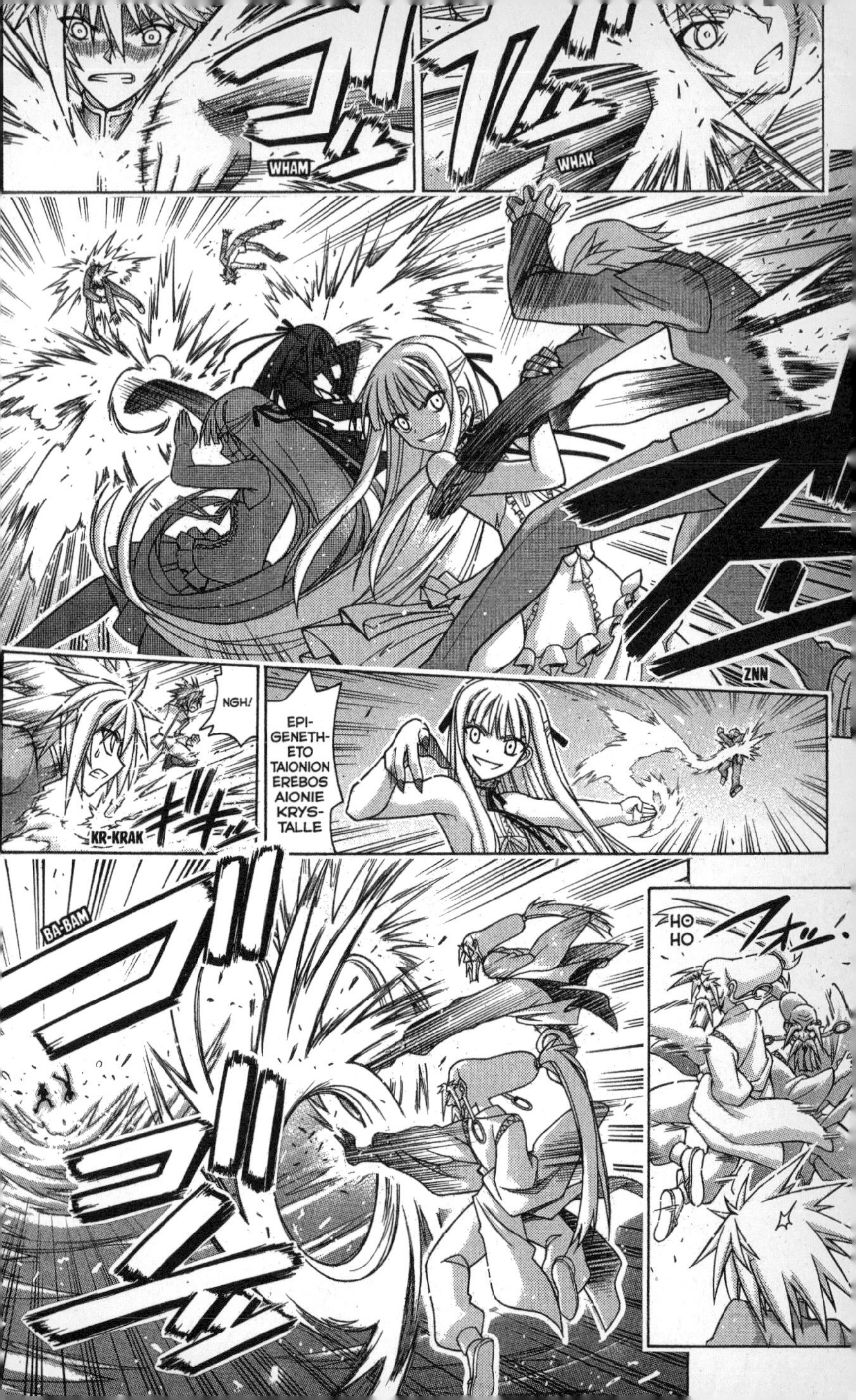
WHAK
WHAM
ZNN
EPIGENETHETO TAIONION EREBOS AIONIE KRYSTALLE
NGH!
KR-KRAK
HO HO
BA-BAM

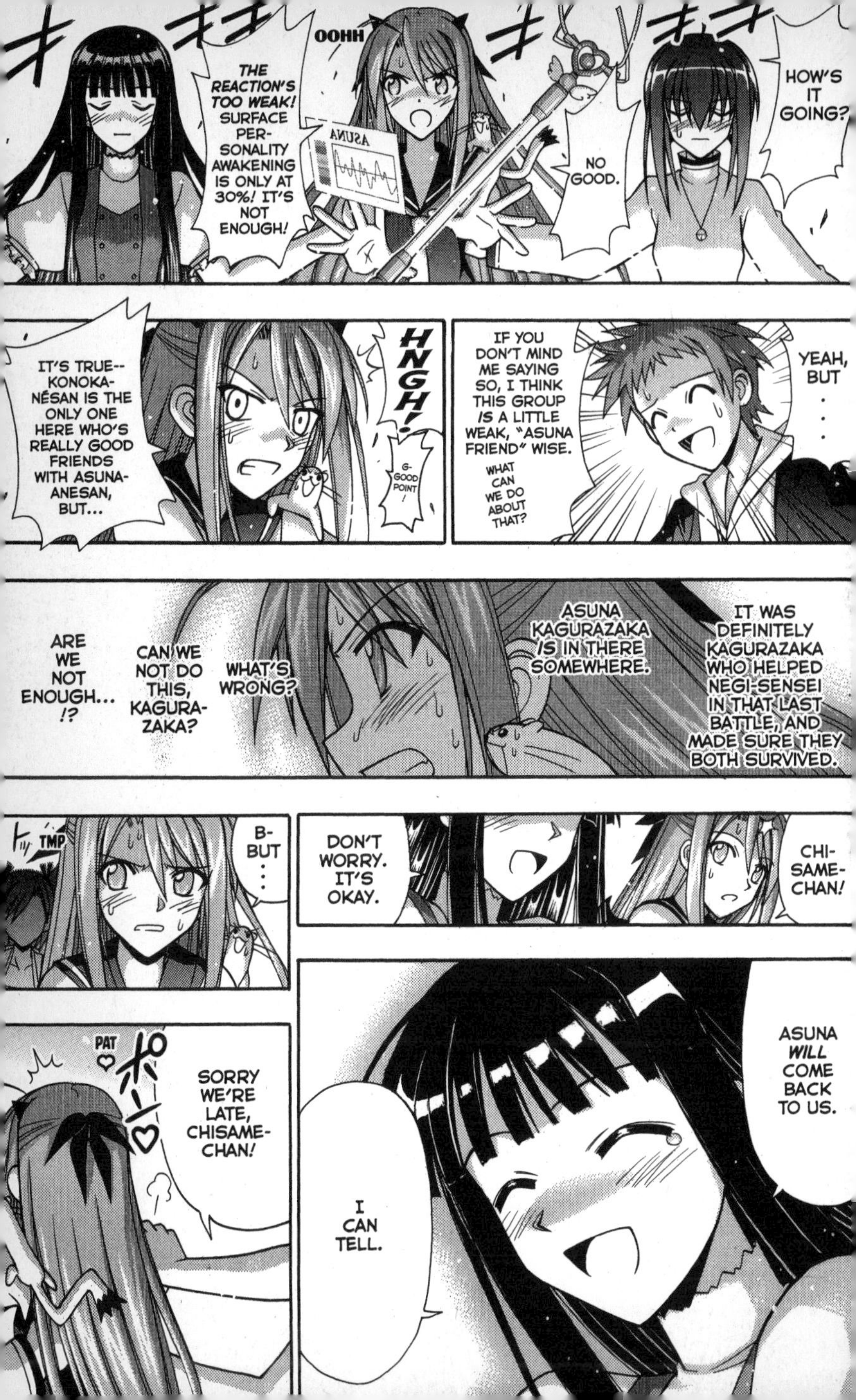
HOW'S IT GOING?
NO GOOD.
OOHH
THE REACTION'S TOO WEAK! SURFACE PER-SONALITY AWAKENING IS ONLY AT 30%! IT'S NOT ENOUGH!
YEAH, BUT . . .
IF YOU DON'T MIND ME SAYING SO, I THINK THIS GROUP IS A LITTLE WEAK, "ASUNA FRIEND" WISE.
WHAT CAN WE DO ABOUT THAT?
HNGH!
G-GOOD POINT!
IT'S TRUE--KONOKA-NÉSAN IS THE ONLY ONE HERE WHO'S REALLY GOOD FRIENDS WITH ASUNA-ANESAN, BUT...
IT WAS DEFINITELY KAGURAZAKA WHO HELPED NEGI-SENSEI IN THAT LAST BATTLE, AND MADE SURE THEY BOTH SURVIVED.
ASUNA KAGURAZAKA IS IN THERE SOMEWHERE.
WHAT'S WRONG?
CAN WE NOT DO THIS, KAGURA-ZAKA?
ARE WE NOT ENOUGH... !?
CHI-SAME-CHAN!
DON'T WORRY. IT'S OKAY.
B-BUT . . .
TMP
ASUNA WILL COME BACK TO US.
I CAN TELL.
PAT
SORRY WE'RE LATE, CHISAME-CHAN!

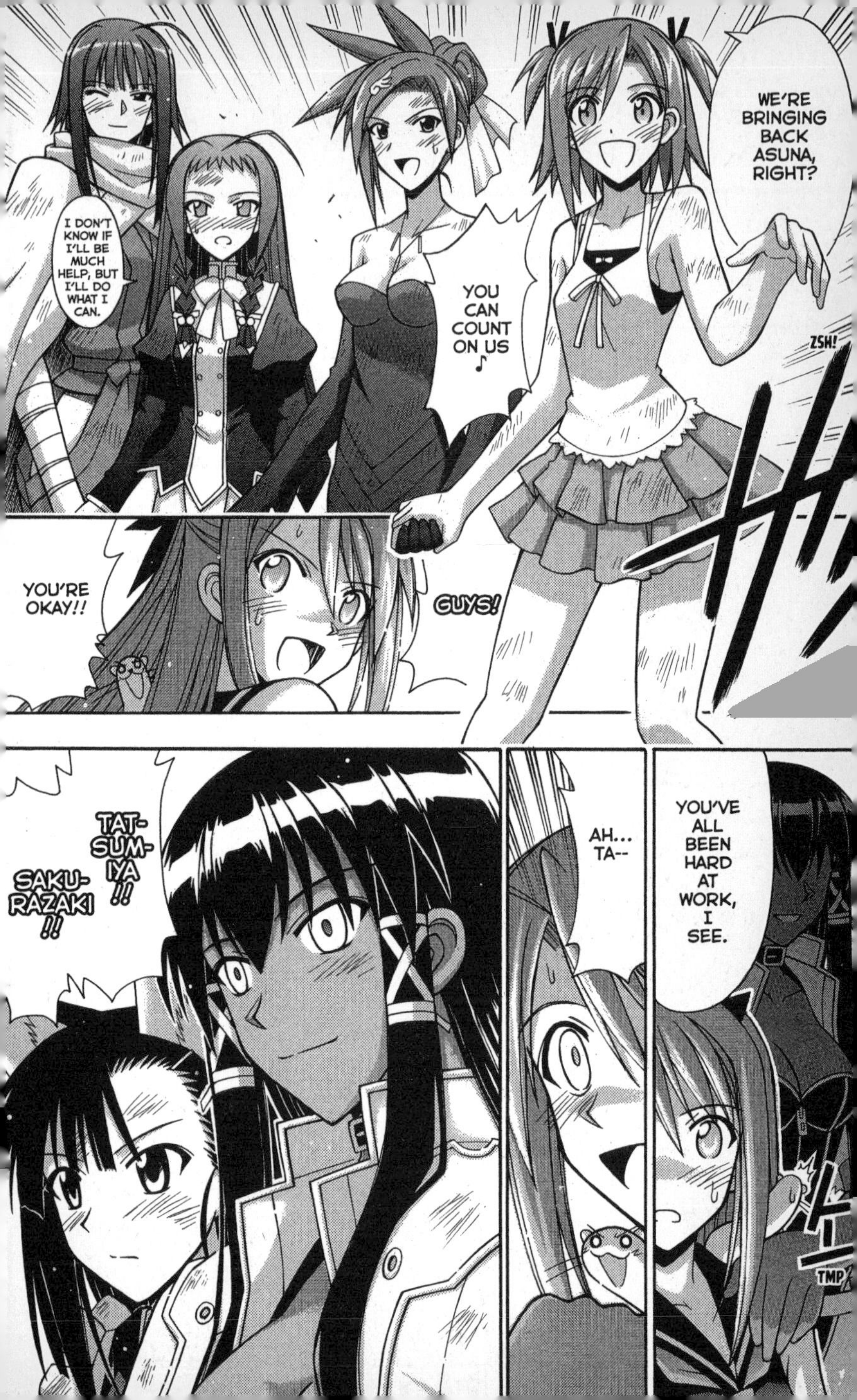
WE'RE BRINGING BACK ASUNA, RIGHT?
ZSH!
YOU CAN COUNT ON US ♪
I DON'T KNOW IF I'LL BE MUCH HELP, BUT I'LL DO WHAT I CAN.
GUYS!
YOU'RE OKAY!!
YOU'VE ALL BEEN HARD AT WORK, I SEE.
TMP
AH... TA--
TAT-SUM-IYA!!
SAKU-RAZAKI!!

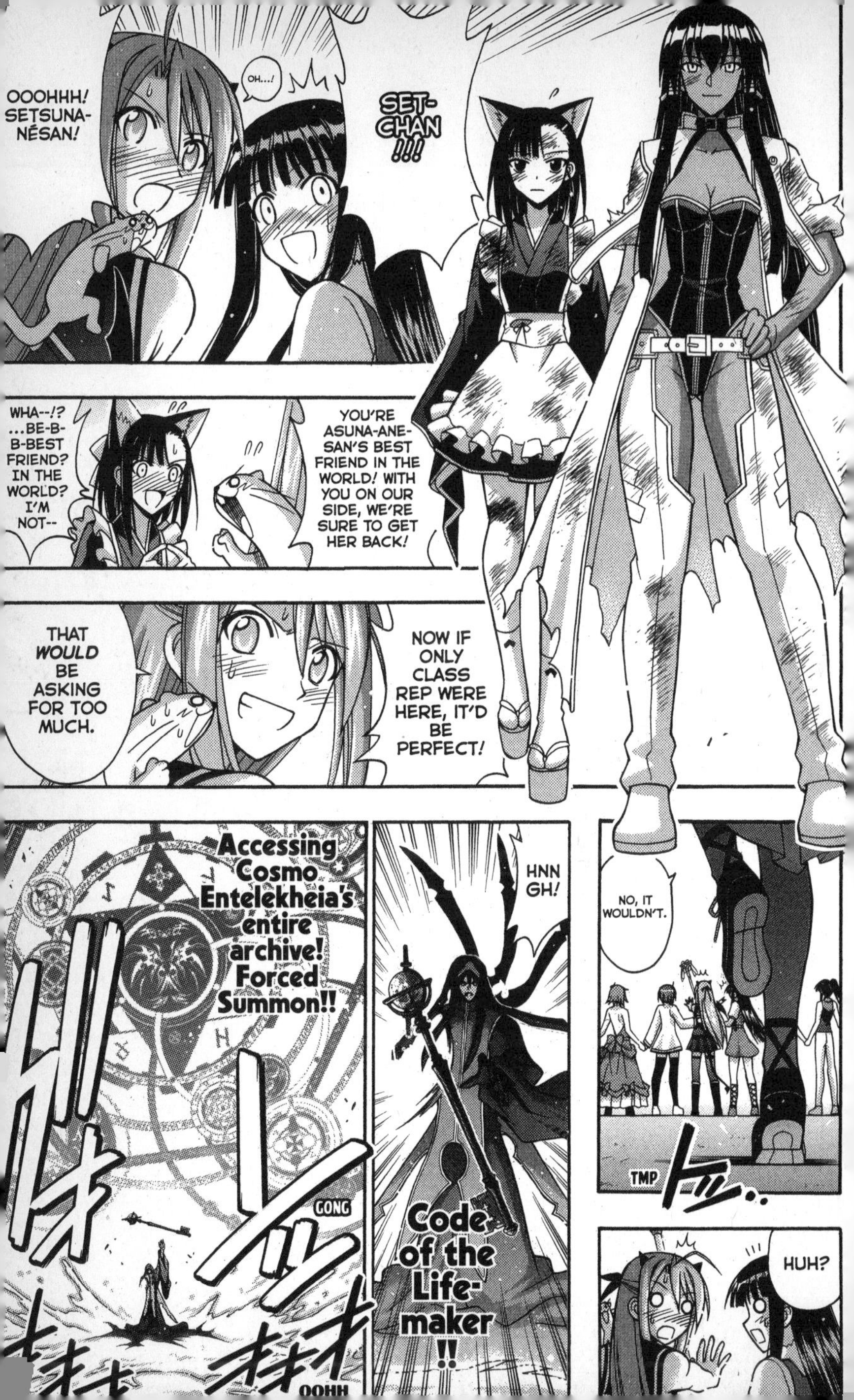
SET-CHAN!!!
OH...!
OOOHHH! SETSUNA-NÉSAN!
YOU'RE ASUNA-ANE-SAN'S BEST FRIEND IN THE WORLD! WITH YOU ON OUR SIDE, WE'RE SURE TO GET HER BACK!
WHA--!? ...BE-B-B-BEST FRIEND? IN THE WORLD? I'M NOT--
NOW IF ONLY CLASS REP WERE HERE, IT'D BE PERFECT!
THAT *WOULD* BE ASKING FOR TOO MUCH.
NO, IT WOULDN'T.
TMP
HUH?
HNN GH!
Code of the Life-maker!!
Accessing Cosmo Entelekheia's entire archive! Forced Summon!!
GONG
OOOHH

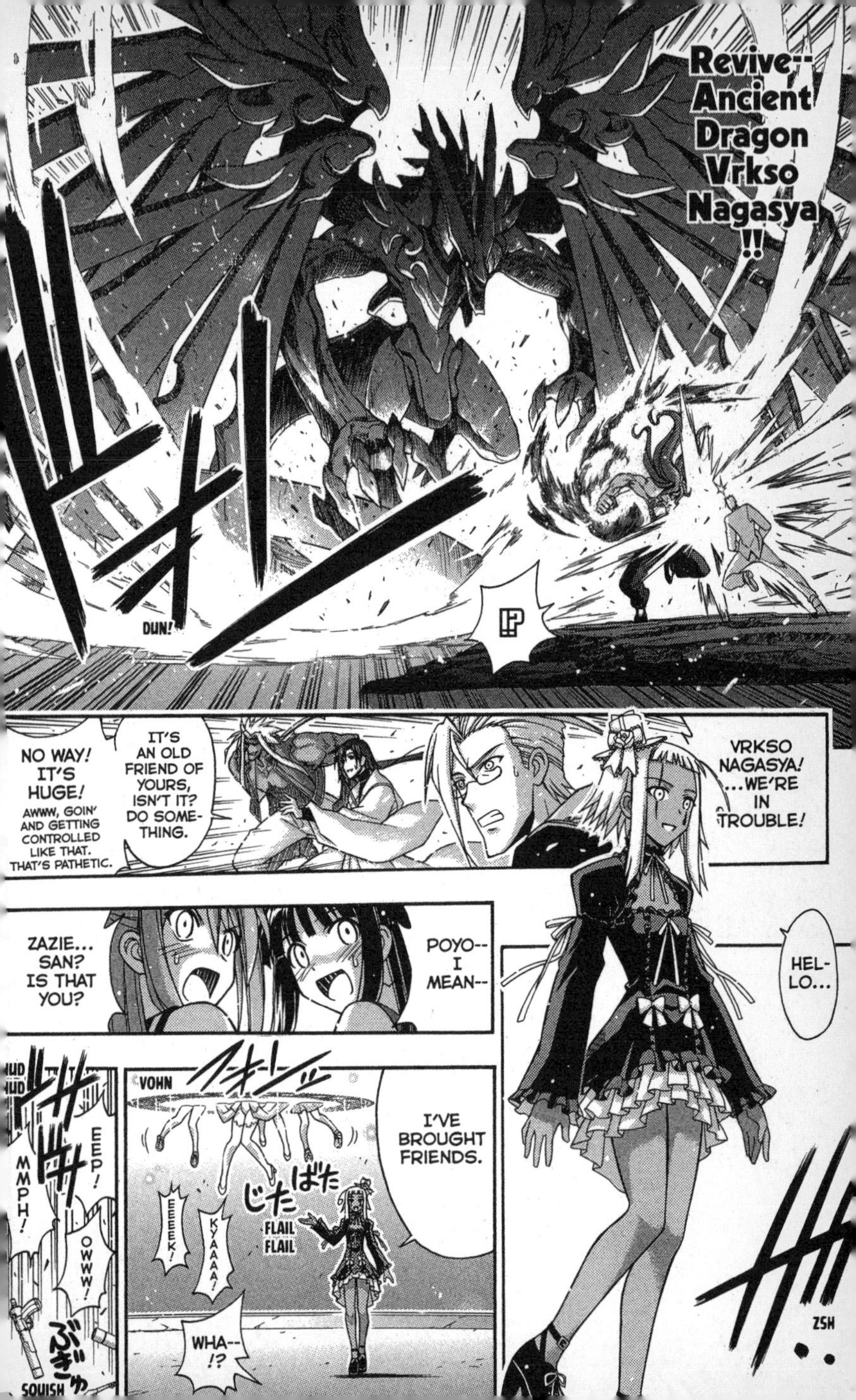
Revive-- Ancient Dragon Vrkso Nagasya!!
DUN!
!?
VRKSO NAGASYA! ...WE'RE IN TROUBLE!
IT'S AN OLD FRIEND OF YOURS, ISN'T IT? DO SOME-THING.
NO WAY! IT'S HUGE!
AWWW, GOIN' AND GETTING CONTROLLED LIKE THAT. THAT'S PATHETIC.
HEL-LO...
ZSH
POYO-- I MEAN--
ZAZIE... SAN? IS THAT YOU?
I'VE BROUGHT FRIENDS.
VOHN
FLAIL FLAIL
KYAAAA!
EEEEK!
WHA--!?
EEP!
OWWW!
MMPH!
THUD THUD
SQUISH

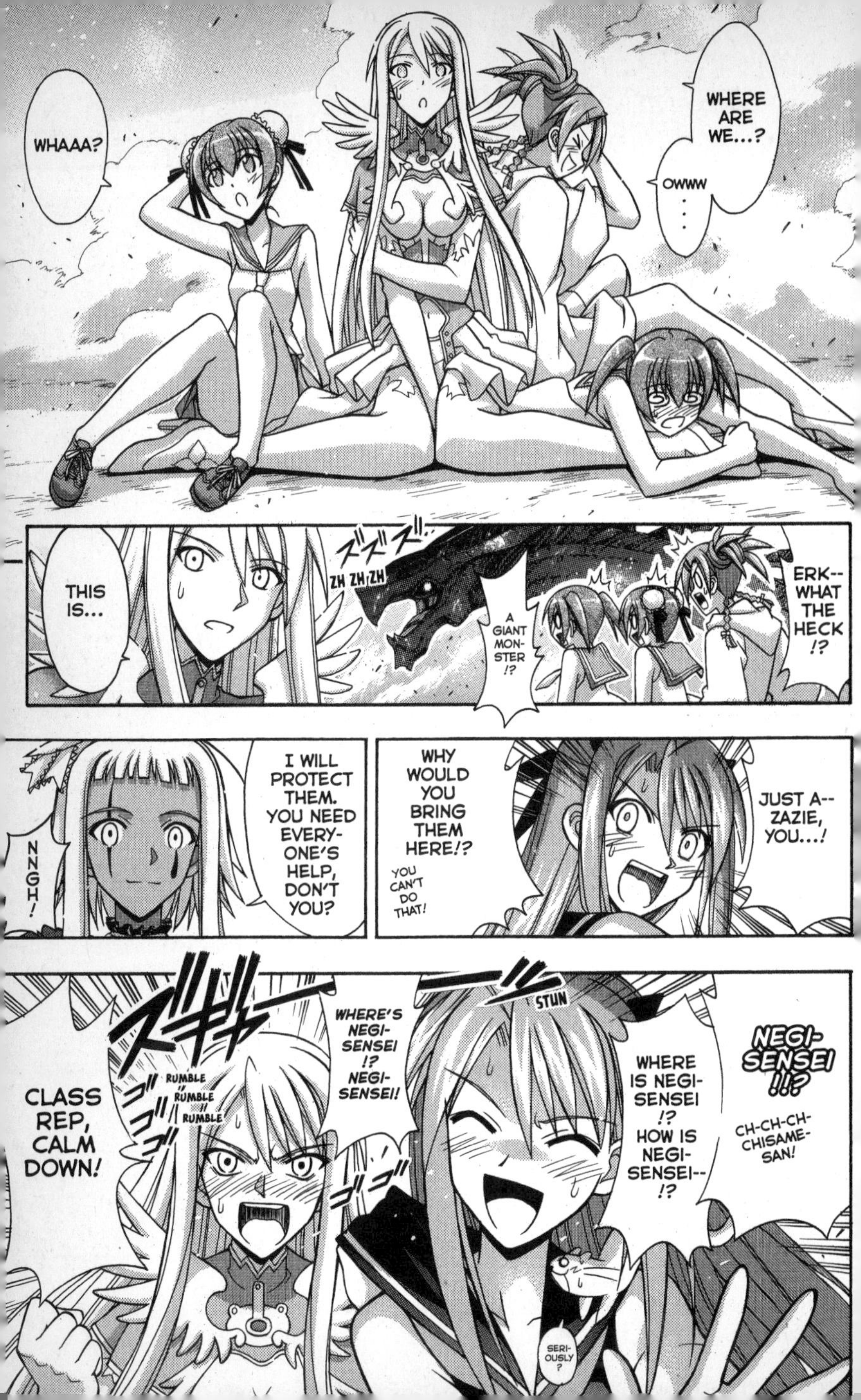
WHERE ARE WE...?
OWWW...
WHAAA?
ERK--WHAT THE HECK!?
A GIANT MONSTER!?
ZH ZH ZH
THIS IS...
JUST A-- ZAZIE, YOU...!
WHY WOULD YOU BRING THEM HERE!?
YOU CAN'T DO THAT!
I WILL PROTECT THEM. YOU NEED EVERYONE'S HELP, DON'T YOU?
NNGH!
NEGI-SENSEI!!?
CH-CH-CH-CHISAME-SAN!
WHERE IS NEGI-SENSEI!? HOW IS NEGI-SENSEI--!?
STUN
SERIOUSLY?
WHERE'S NEGI-SENSEI!? NEGI-SENSEI!
RUMBLE RUMBLE RUMBLE
CLASS REP, CALM DOWN!

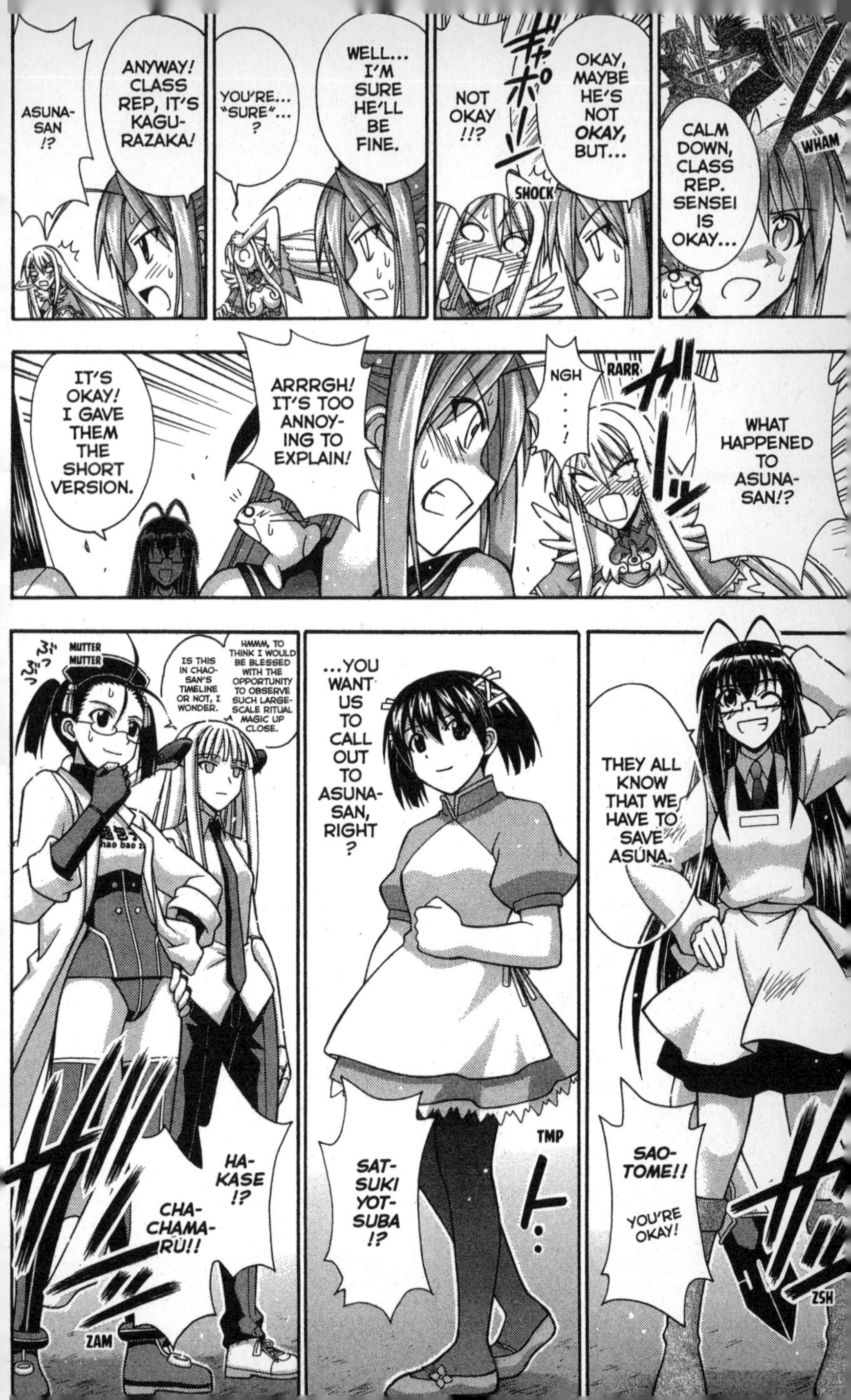
CALM DOWN, CLASS REP. SENSEI IS OKAY...
WHAM
OKAY, MAYBE HE'S NOT OKAY, BUT...
NOT OKAY !!?
SHOCK
WELL... I'M SURE HE'LL BE FINE.
YOU'RE... "SURE"...?
ANYWAY! CLASS REP, IT'S KAGURAZAKA!
ASUNA-SAN !?
WHAT HAPPENED TO ASUNA-SAN!?
RARR
NGH...!
ARRRGH! IT'S TOO ANNOYING TO EXPLAIN!
IT'S OKAY! I GAVE THEM THE SHORT VERSION.
THEY ALL KNOW THAT WE HAVE TO SAVE ASUNA.
SAOTOME!!
YOU'RE OKAY!
ZSH
...YOU WANT US TO CALL OUT TO ASUNA-SAN, RIGHT?
TMP
SATSUKI YOTSUBA !?
HMMM, TO THINK I WOULD BE BLESSED WITH THE OPPORTUNITY TO OBSERVE SUCH LARGE-SCALE RITUAL MAGIC UP CLOSE.
IS THIS IN CHAO-SAN'S TIMELINE OR NOT, I WONDER.
MUTTER MUTTER
HAKASE !?
CHACHAMARU!!
ZAM

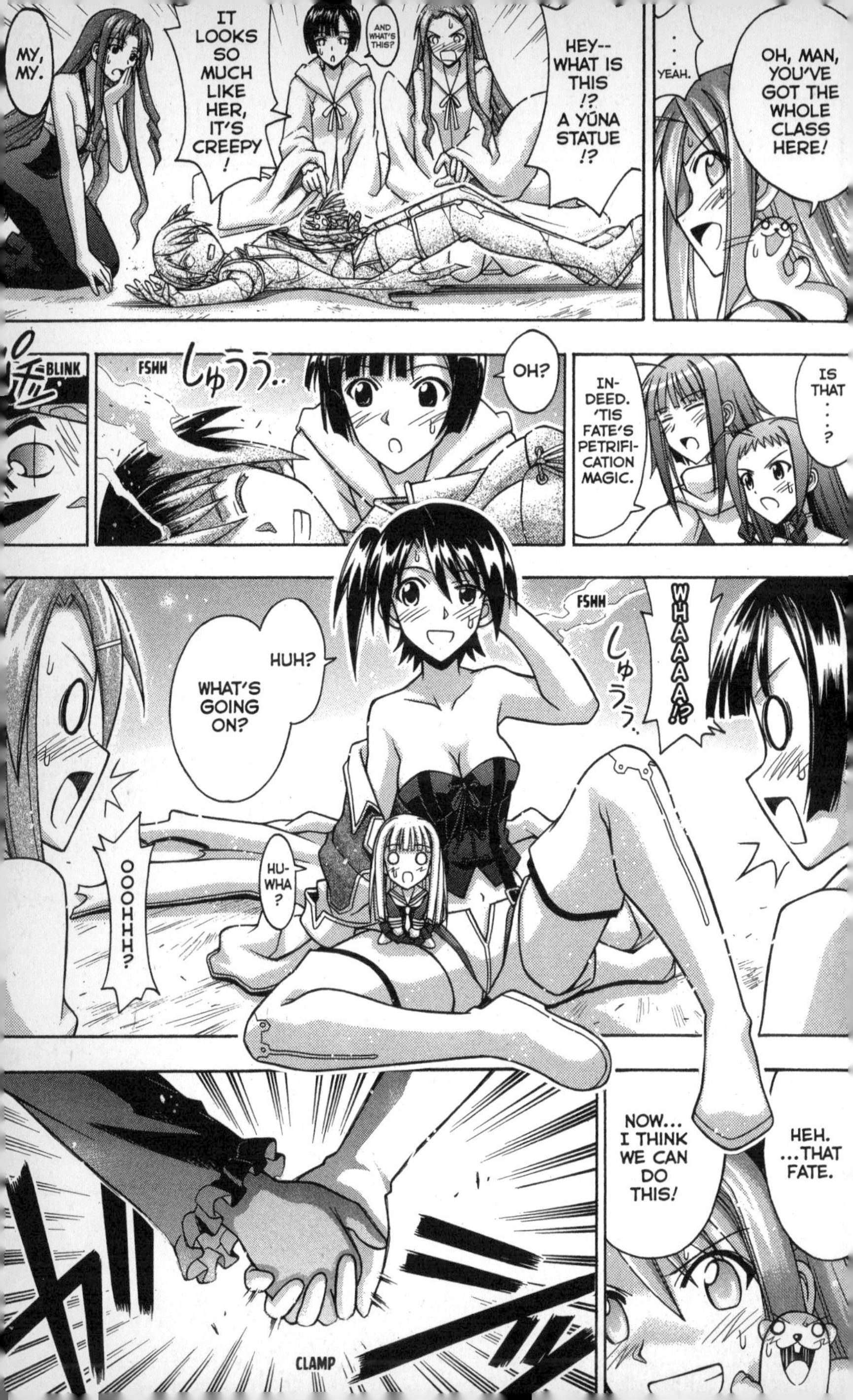
OH, MAN, YOU'VE GOT THE WHOLE CLASS HERE!
...YEAH.
HEY-- WHAT IS THIS!? A YŪNA STATUE!?
AND WHAT'S THIS?
IT LOOKS SO MUCH LIKE HER, IT'S CREEPY!
MY, MY.
IS THAT...?
INDEED. 'TIS FATE'S PETRIFICATION MAGIC.
OH?
FSHH
しゅううう..
BLINK
WHAAAAA!?
FSHH
しゅうう..
HUH?
WHAT'S GOING ON?
HU-WHA?
OOOHHH?
HEH. ...THAT FATE.
NOW... I THINK WE CAN DO THIS!
CLAMP

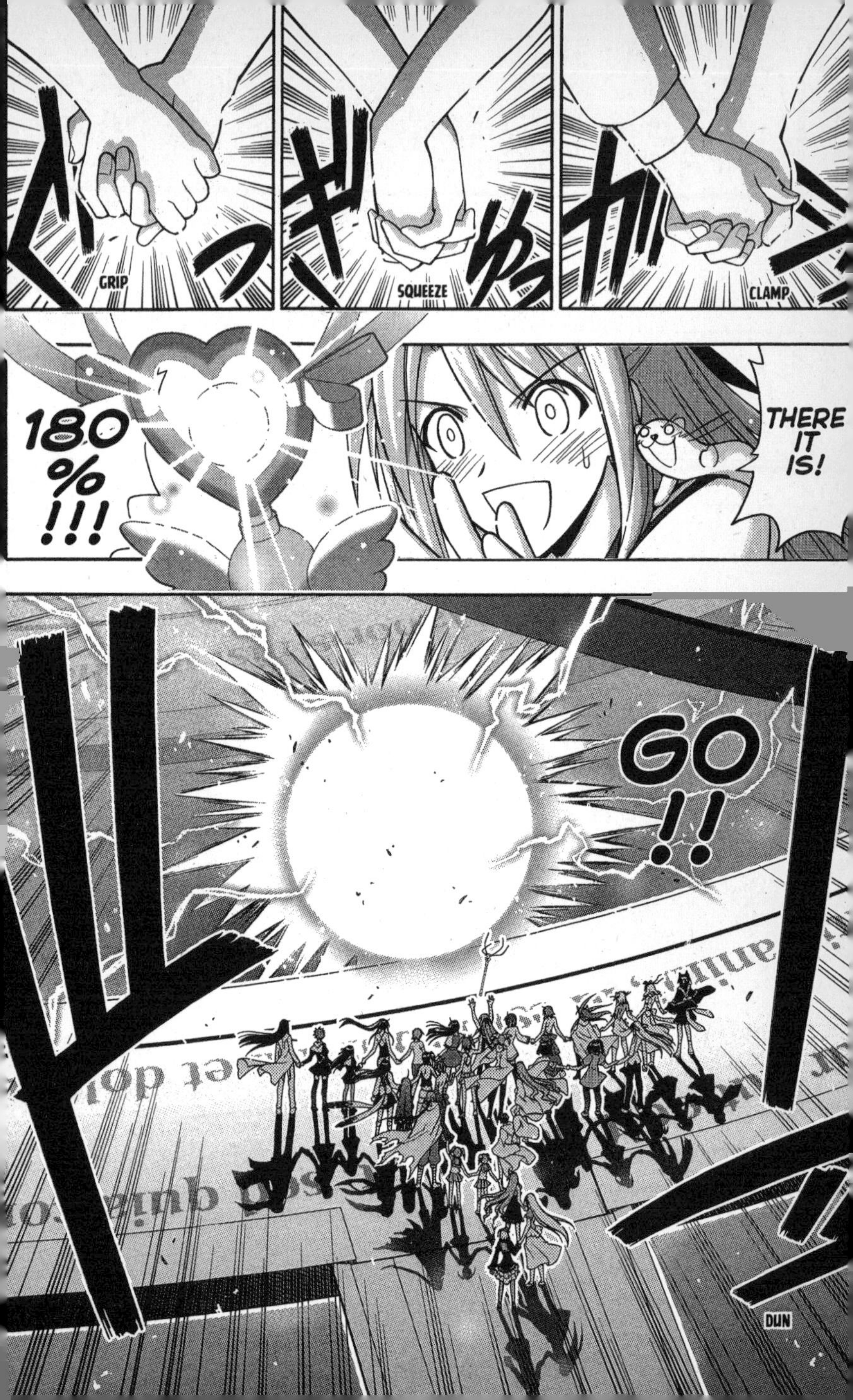
CLAMP
SQUEEZE
GRIP
THERE IT IS!
180%!!!
GO!!
DUN

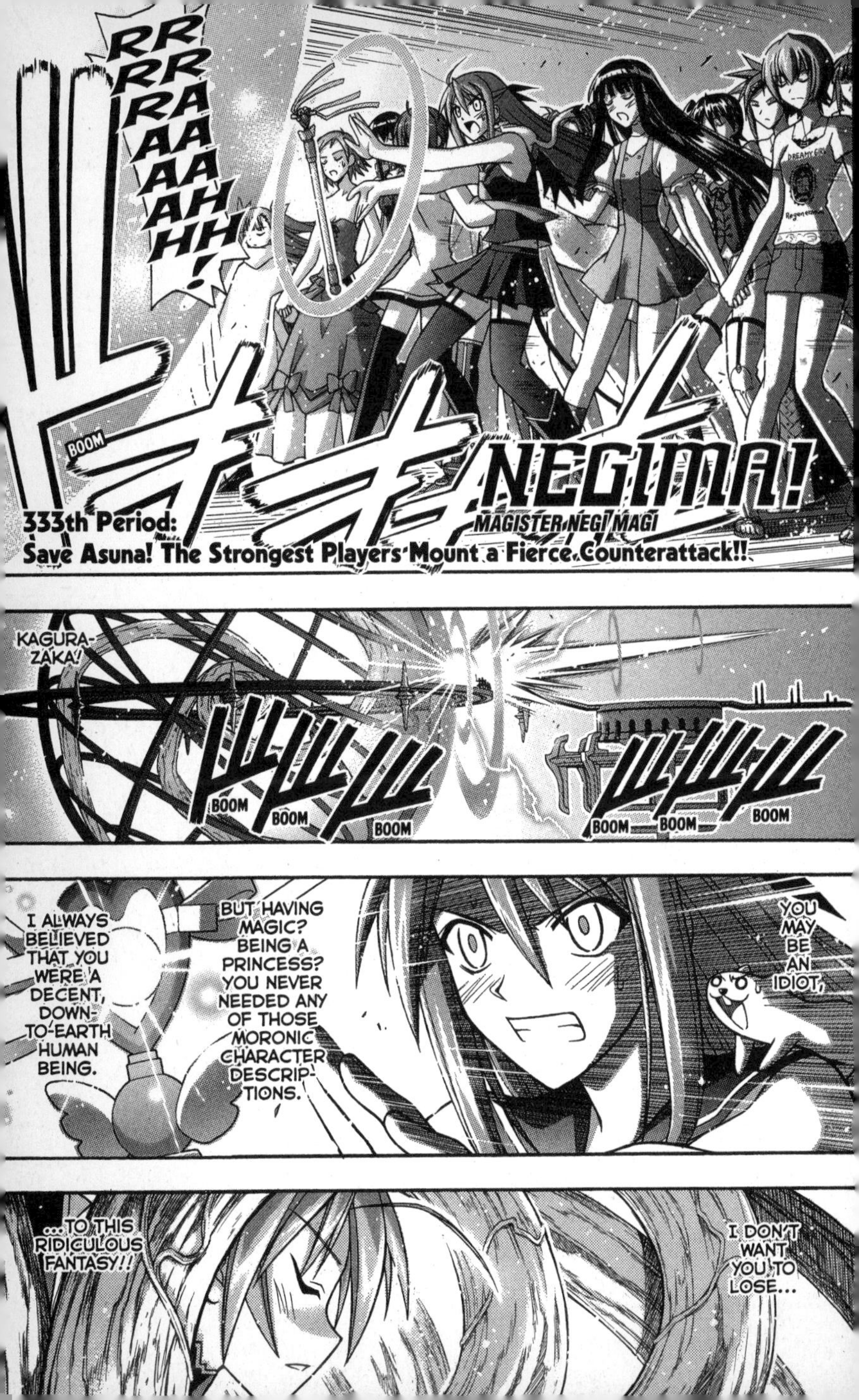
RRRRRAAAAAHH!
BOOM
NEGIMA!
MAGISTER NEGI MAGI
333th Period:
Save Asuna! The Strongest Players Mount a Fierce Counterattack!!
KAGURA-ZAKA!
BOOM
BOOM
BOOM
BOOM
BOOM
BOOM
YOU MAY BE AN IDIOT,
BUT HAVING MAGIC? BEING A PRINCESS? YOU NEVER NEEDED ANY OF THOSE MORONIC CHARACTER DESCRIPTIONS.
I ALWAYS BELIEVED THAT YOU WERE A DECENT, DOWN-TO-EARTH HUMAN BEING.
I DON'T WANT YOU TO LOSE...
...TO THIS RIDICULOUS FANTASY!!

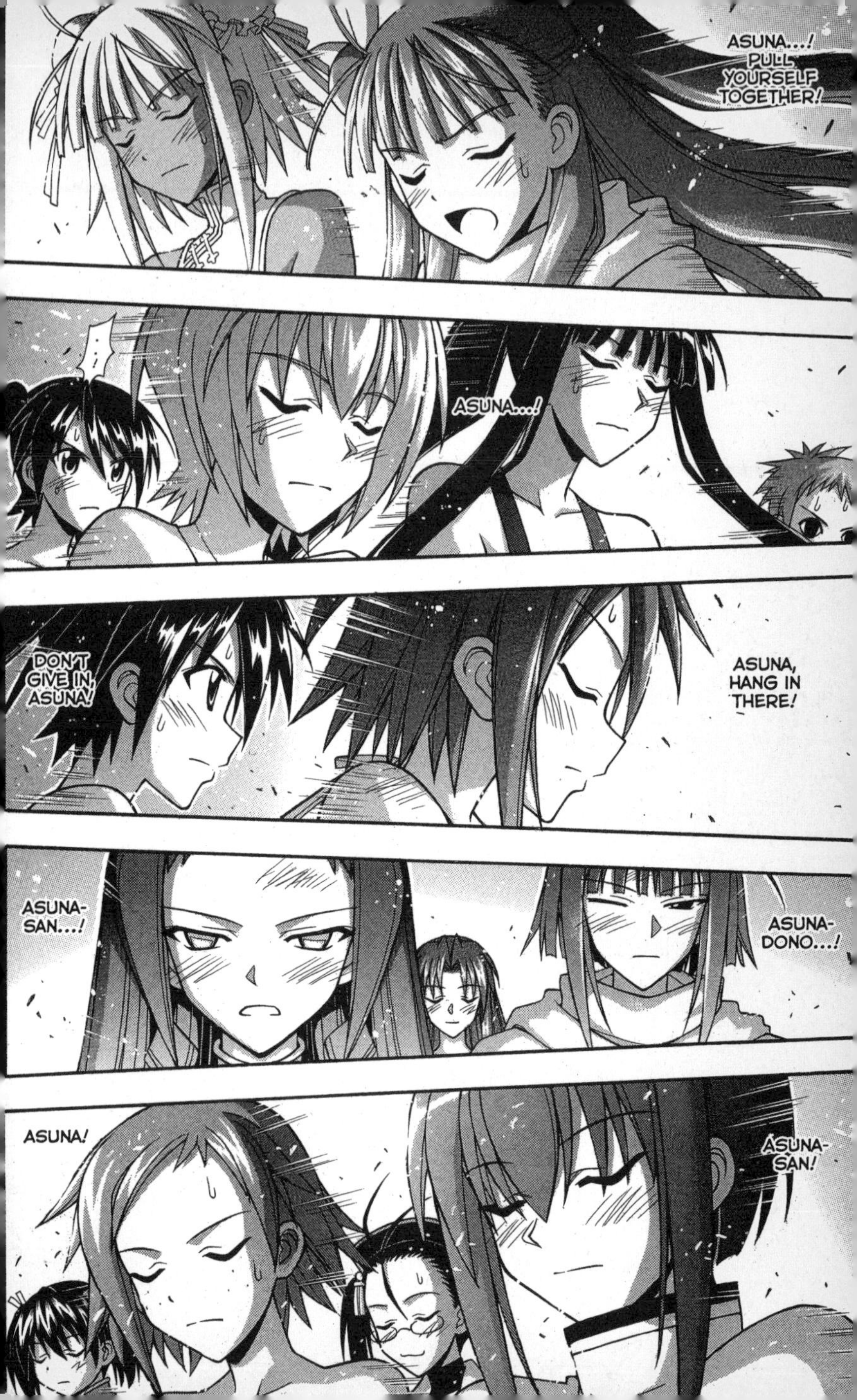
ASUNA...! PULL YOURSELF TOGETHER!
ASUNA...!
ASUNA, HANG IN THERE!
DON'T GIVE IN, ASUNA!
ASUNA-DONO...!
ASUNA-SAN...!
ASUNA-SAN!
ASUNA!

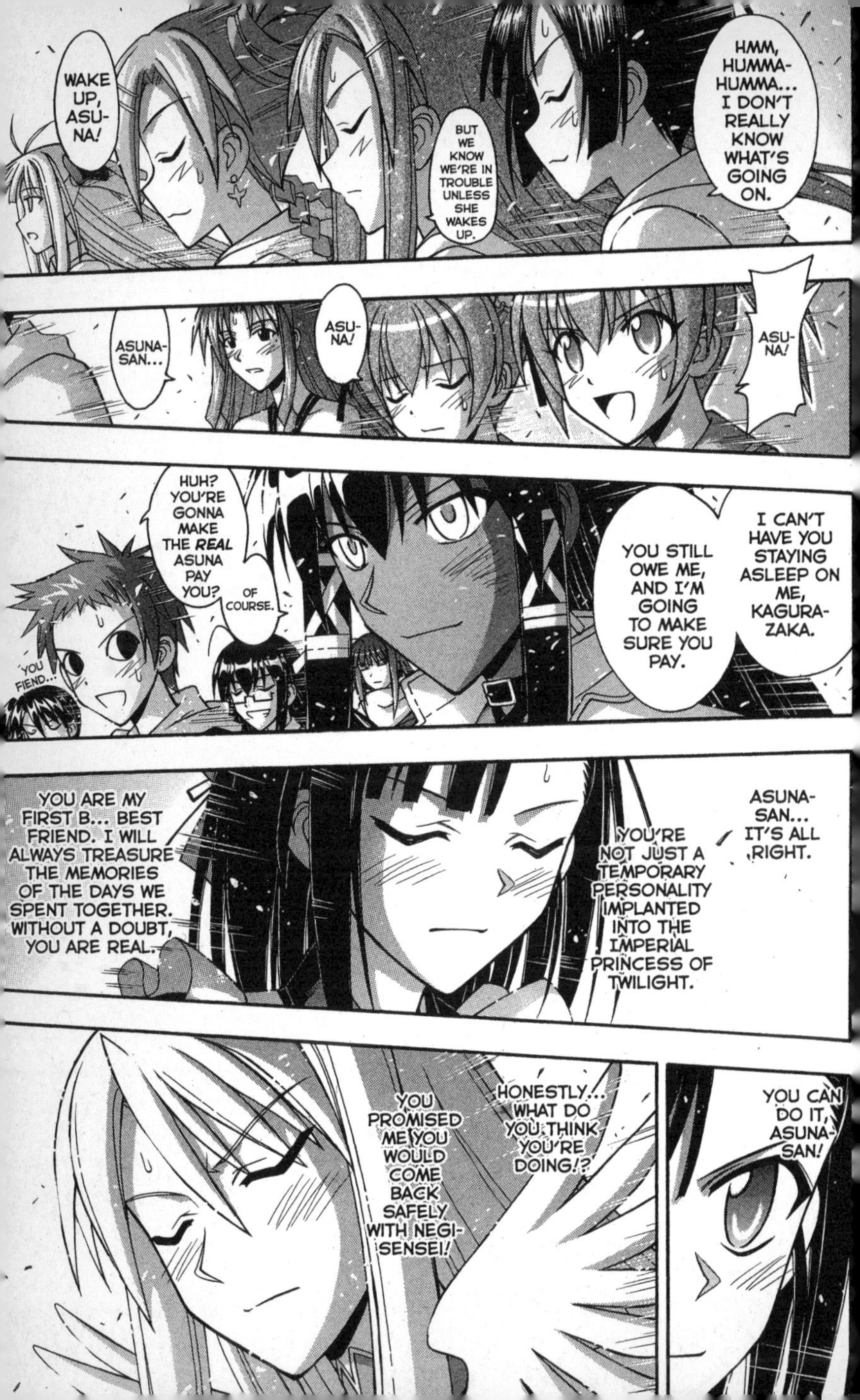
HMM, HUMMA-HUMMA... I DON'T REALLY KNOW WHAT'S GOING ON.
BUT WE KNOW WE'RE IN TROUBLE UNLESS SHE WAKES UP.
WAKE UP, ASUNA!
ASUNA!
ASUNA!
ASUNA-SAN...
I CAN'T HAVE YOU STAYING ASLEEP ON ME, KAGURAZAKA.
YOU STILL OWE ME, AND I'M GOING TO MAKE SURE YOU PAY.
HUH? YOU'RE GONNA MAKE THE *REAL* ASUNA PAY YOU?
OF COURSE.
YOU FIEND...
ASUNA-SAN... IT'S ALL RIGHT.
YOU'RE NOT JUST A TEMPORARY PERSONALITY IMPLANTED INTO THE IMPERIAL PRINCESS OF TWILIGHT.
YOU ARE MY FIRST B... BEST FRIEND. I WILL ALWAYS TREASURE THE MEMORIES OF THE DAYS WE SPENT TOGETHER. WITHOUT A DOUBT, YOU ARE REAL.
YOU CAN DO IT, ASUNA-SAN!
HONESTLY... WHAT DO YOU THINK YOU'RE DOING!?
YOU PROMISED ME YOU WOULD COME BACK SAFELY WITH NEGI-SENSEI!

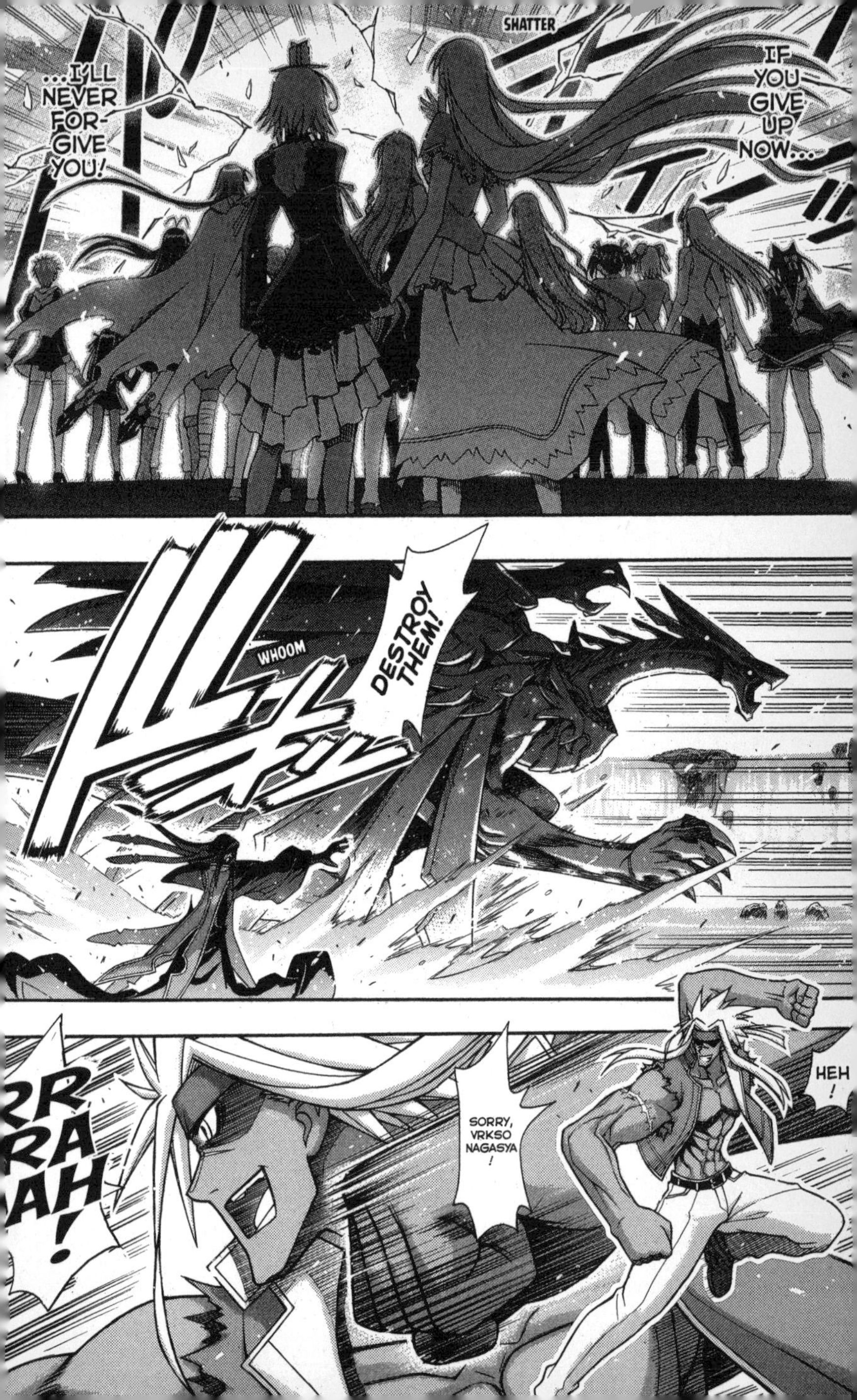
IF YOU GIVE UP NOW...
SHATTER
...I'LL NEVER FOR-GIVE YOU!
DESTROY THEM!
WHOOM
HEH!
SORRY, VRKSO NAGASYA!
RR RA AH!

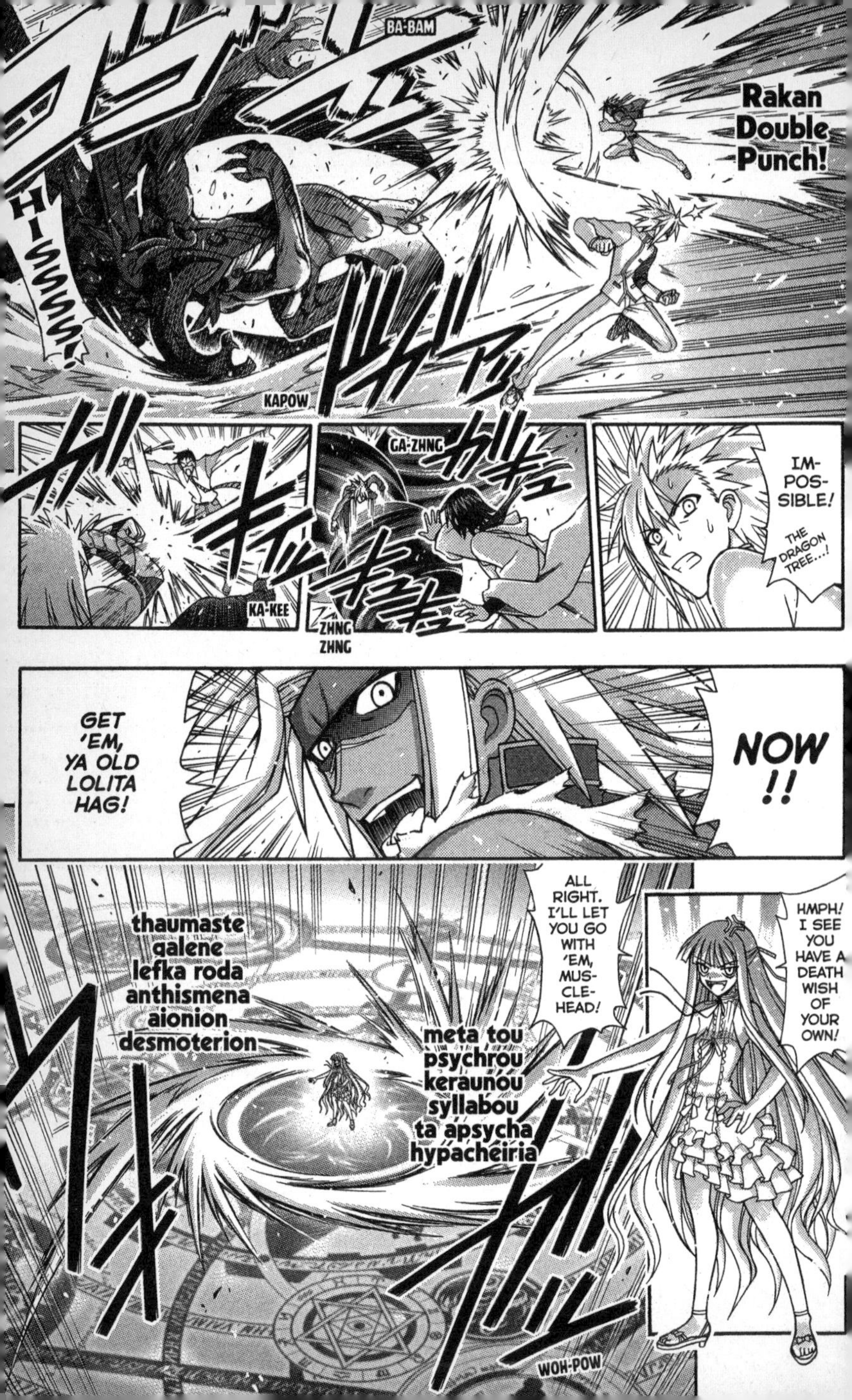
BA-BAM
Rakan Double Punch!
HISSSSSS!
KAPOW
IM-POS-SIBLE!
THE DRAGON TREE...!
GA-ZHNG
ZHNG ZHNG
KA-KEE
NOW!!
GET 'EM, YA OLD LOLITA HAG!
HMPH! I SEE YOU HAVE A DEATH WISH OF YOUR OWN!
ALL RIGHT. I'LL LET YOU GO WITH 'EM, MUS-CLE-HEAD!
thaumaste qalene lefka roda anthismena aionion desmoterion
meta tou psychrou keraunou syllabou ta apsycha hypacheiria
WOH-POW

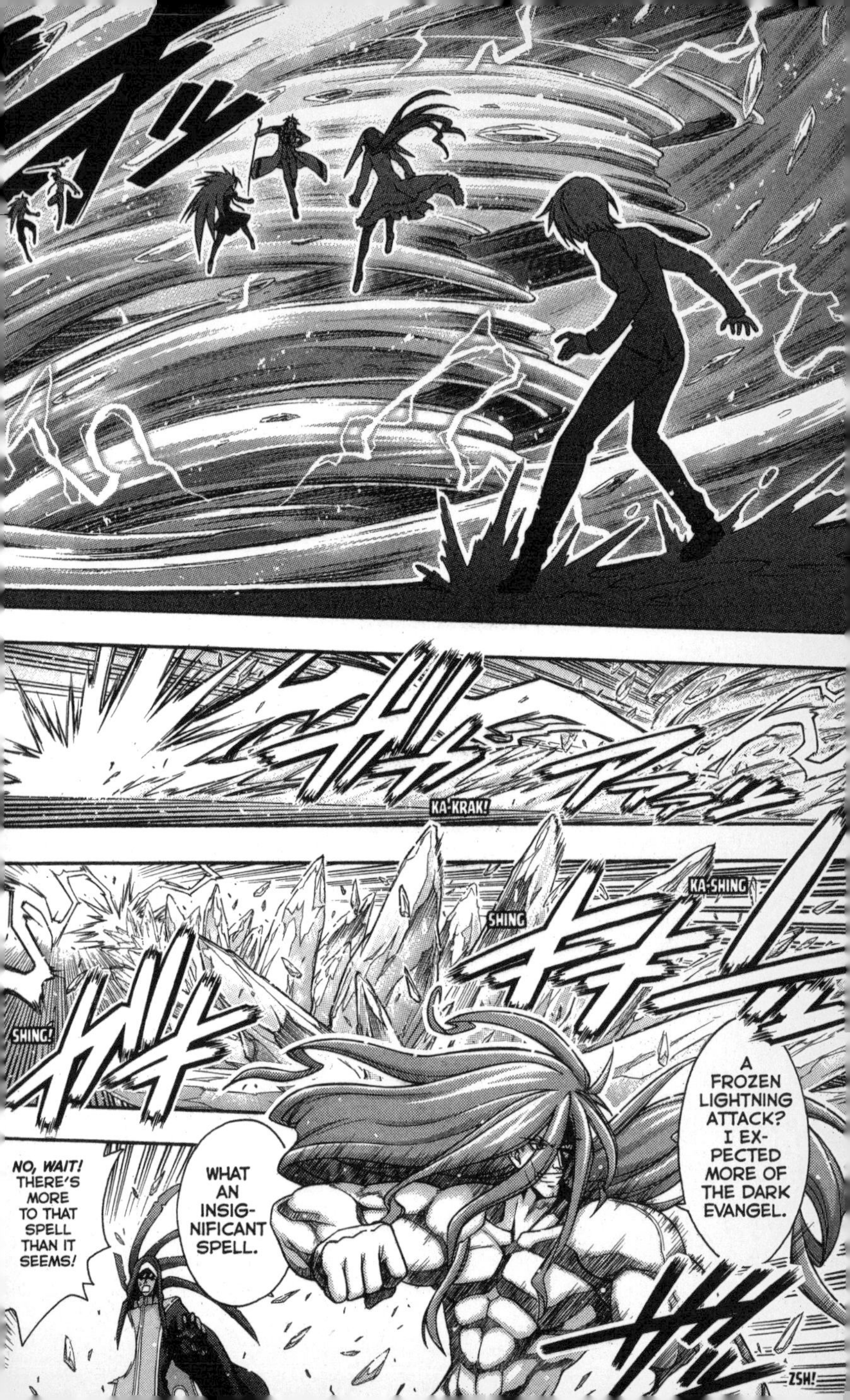
KA-KRAK!
KA-SHING
SHING
SHING!
A FROZEN LIGHTNING ATTACK? I EXPECTED MORE OF THE DARK EVANGEL.
WHAT AN INSIGNIFICANT SPELL.
NO, WAIT! THERE'S MORE TO THAT SPELL THAN IT SEEMS!
ZSH!

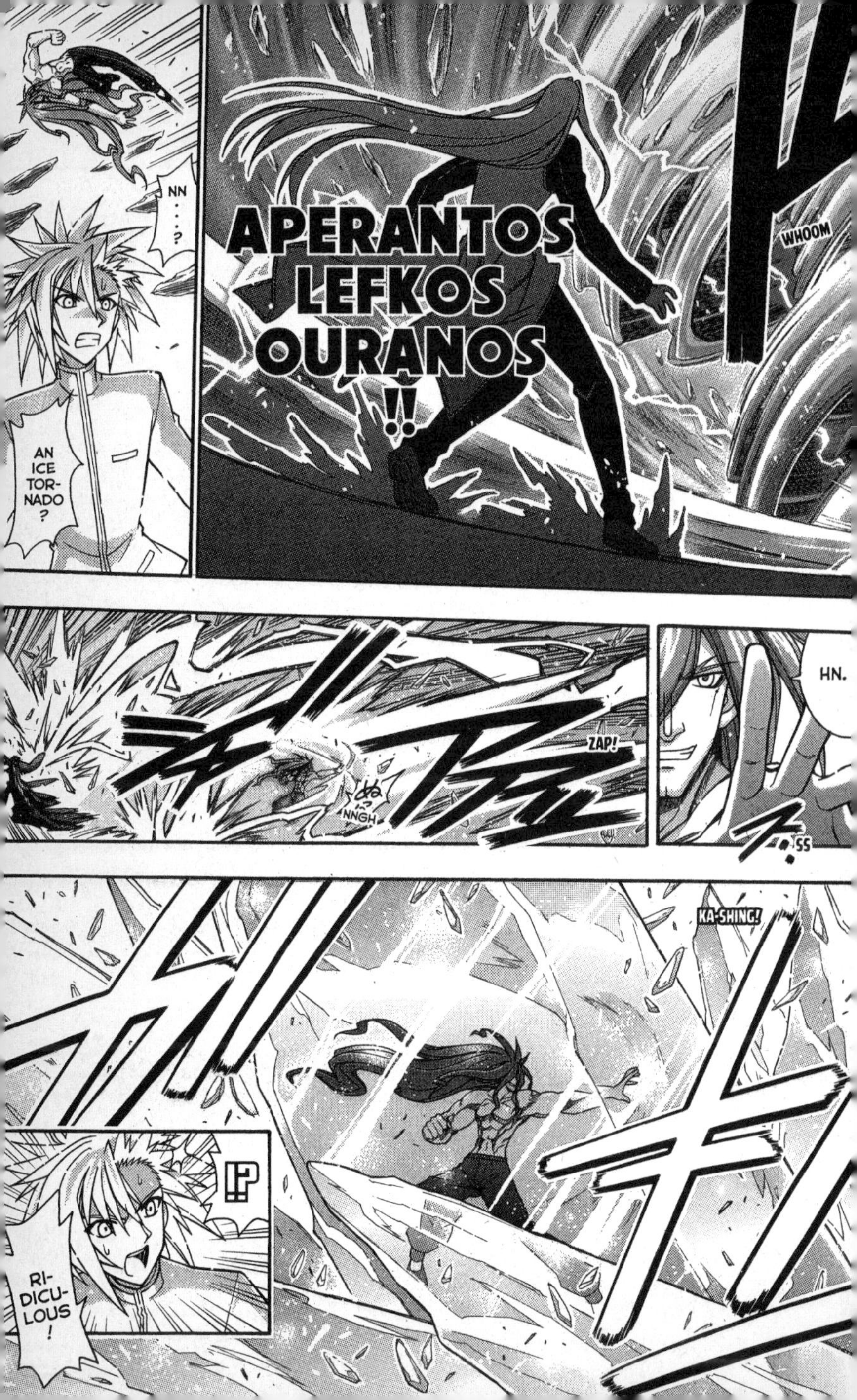
WHOOM
APERANTOS LEFKOS OURANOS!!
NN . . . ?
AN ICE TOR-NADO?
HN.
SS
ZAP!
NNGH
KA-SHING!
!?
RI-DICU-LOUS!

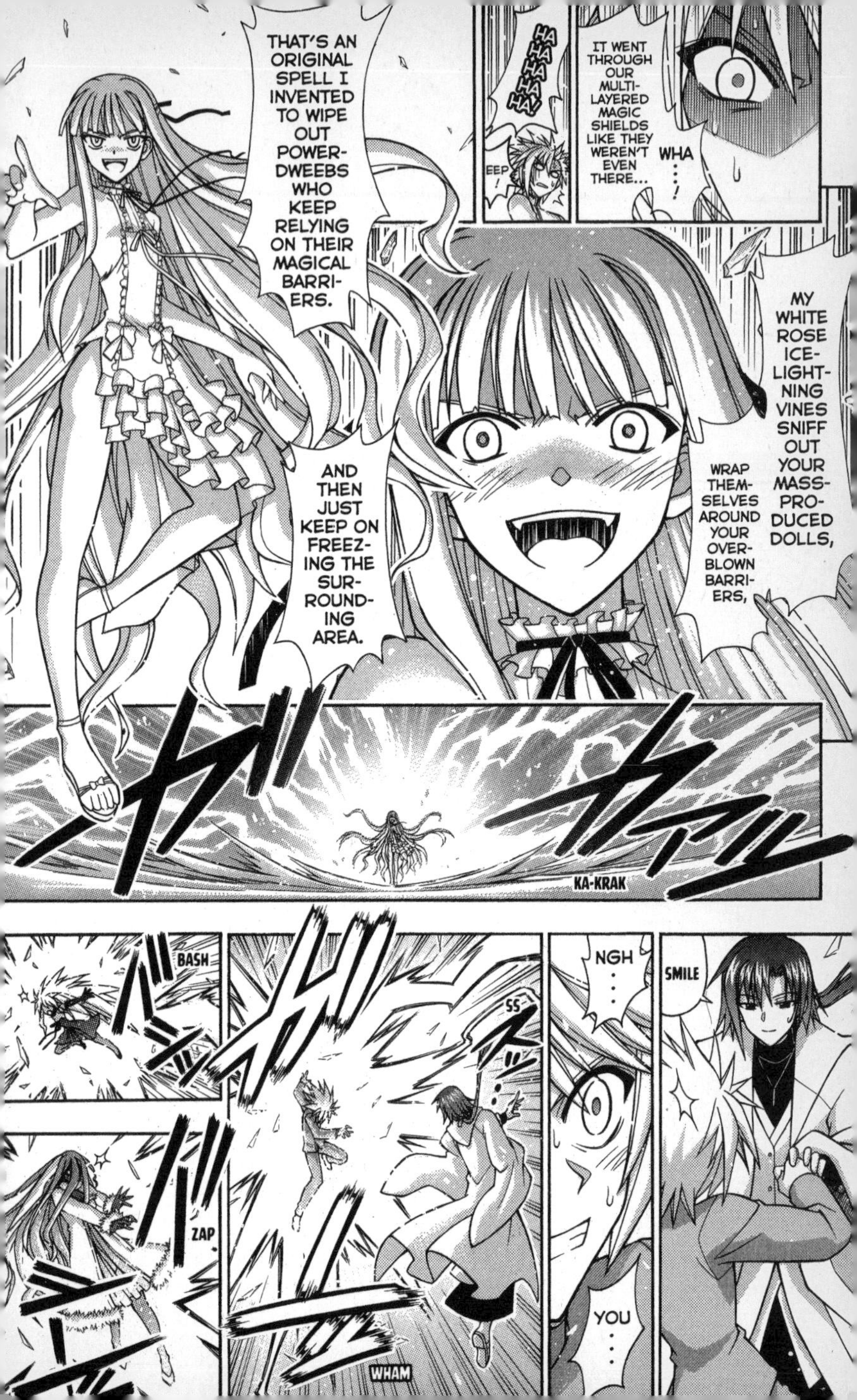
WHA
...!
IT WENT THROUGH OUR MULTI-LAYERED MAGIC SHIELDS LIKE THEY WEREN'T EVEN THERE...
HA HA HA HA HA!
EEP!
MY WHITE ROSE ICE-LIGHTNING VINES SNIFF OUT YOUR MASS-PRODUCED DOLLS,
WRAP THEMSELVES AROUND YOUR OVERBLOWN BARRIERS,
AND THEN JUST KEEP ON FREEZING THE SURROUNDING AREA.
THAT'S AN ORIGINAL SPELL I INVENTED TO WIPE OUT POWER-DWEEBS WHO KEEP RELYING ON THEIR MAGICAL BARRIERS.
KA-KRAK
SMILE
YOU...
NGH...
SS
WHAM
BASH
ZAP

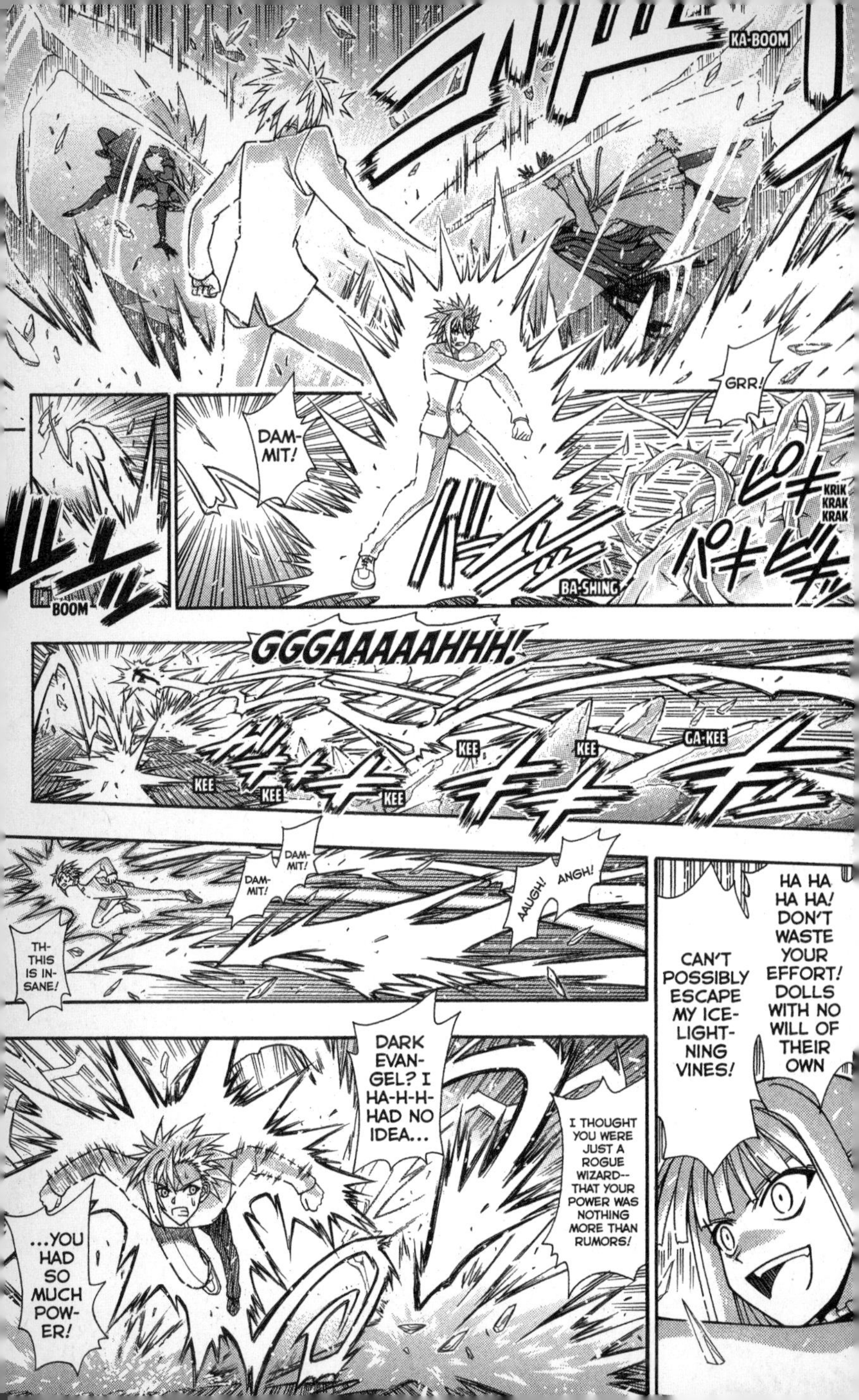
KA-BOOM
GRR!
KRIK KRAK KRAK
DAM-MIT!
BA-SHING
BOOM
GGGAAAAAAHHH!
GA-KEE
KEE
KEE
KEE
KEE
KEE
HA HA HA HA! DON'T WASTE YOUR EFFORT! DOLLS WITH NO WILL OF THEIR OWN
CAN'T POSSIBLY ESCAPE MY ICE-LIGHTNING VINES!
ANGH!
AAUGH!
DAM-MIT!
DAM-MIT!
TH-THIS IS IN-SANE!
I THOUGHT YOU WERE JUST A ROGUE WIZARD--THAT YOUR POWER WAS NOTHING MORE THAN RUMORS!
DARK EVAN-GEL? I HA-H-H-HAD NO IDEA...
...YOU HAD SO MUCH POW-ER!

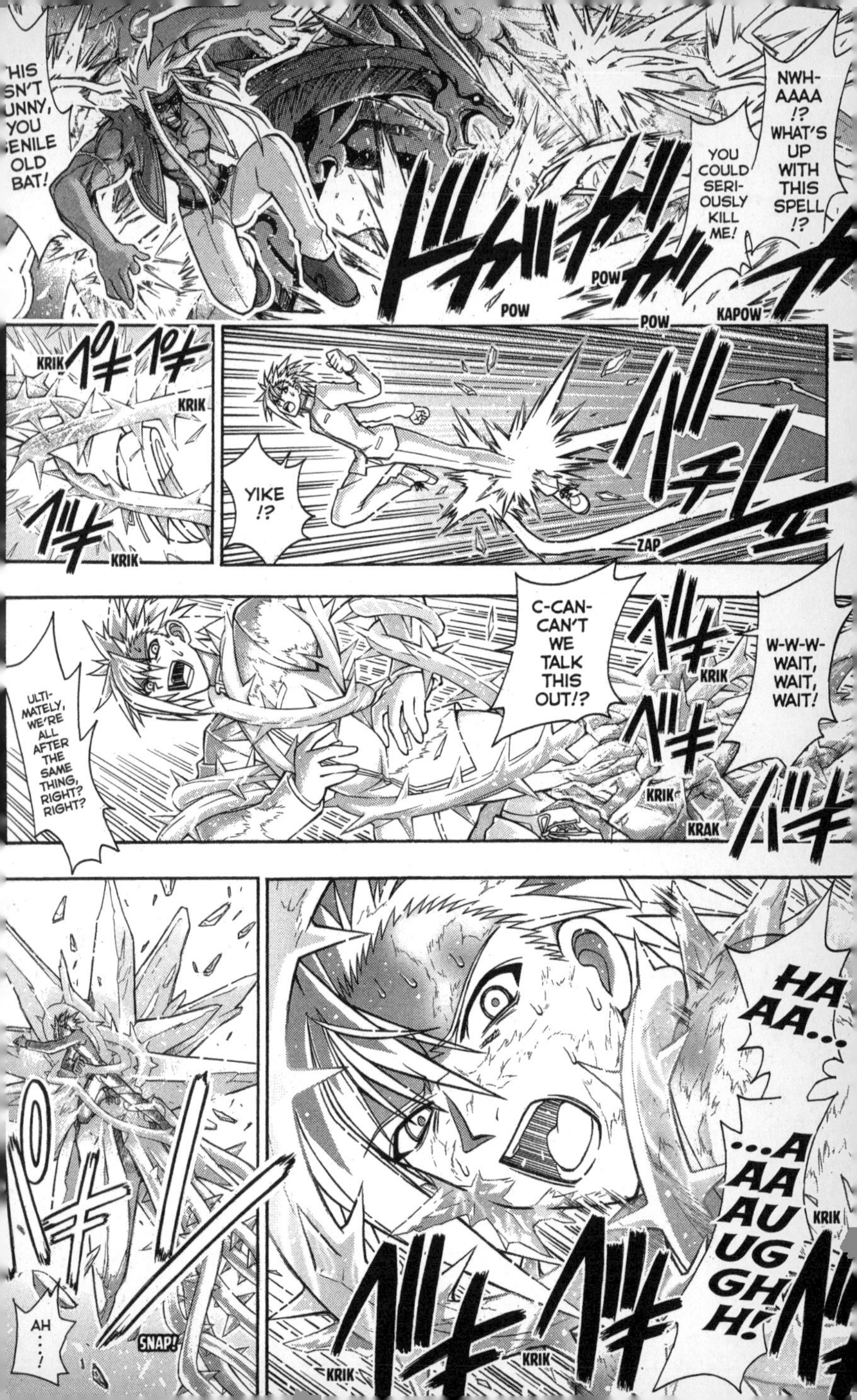
NWH-AAAA!? WHAT'S UP WITH THIS SPELL!?
YOU COULD SERI-OUSLY KILL ME!
THIS SN'T UNNY, YOU ENILE OLD BAT!
KAPOW
POW
POW
POW
ZAP
YIKE!?
KRIK
KRIK
KRIK
W-W-W-WAIT, WAIT, WAIT!
C-CAN-CAN'T WE TALK THIS OUT!?
KRIK
KRIK
KRAK
ULTI-MATELY, WE'RE ALL AFTER THE SAME THING, RIGHT? RIGHT?
HAAA...
...AAAAUGHGH!
KRIK
KRIK
KRIK
SNAP!
AH...!

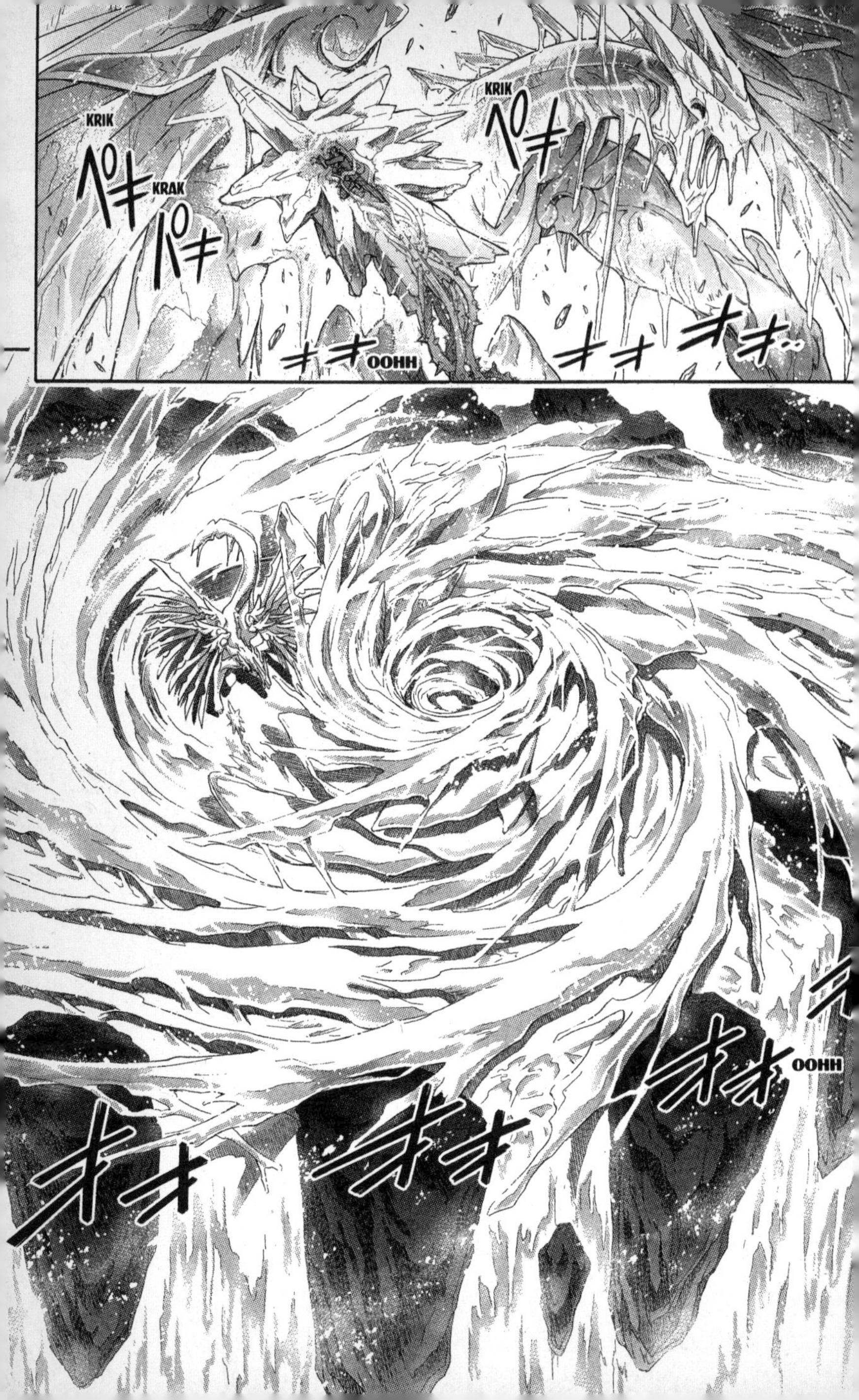
KRIK
ペキ
KRIK
ペキ
KRAK
パキ
オオオオォ
オオ
OOHH
OOHH
オオオオオオ

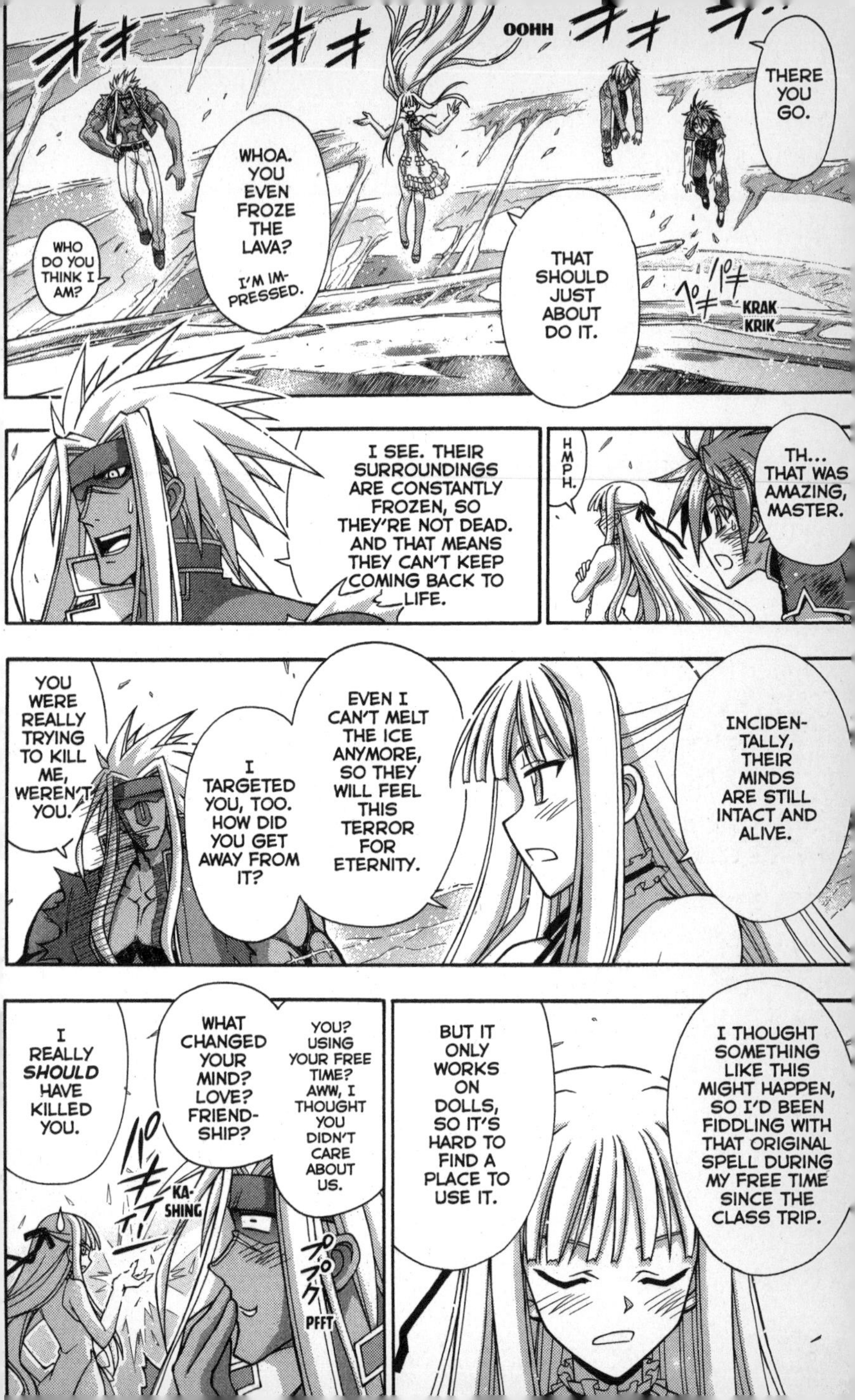
OOHH
THERE YOU GO.
THAT SHOULD JUST ABOUT DO IT.
KRAK KRIK
WHOA. YOU EVEN FROZE THE LAVA?
I'M IM-PRESSED.
WHO DO YOU THINK I AM?
TH... THAT WAS AMAZING, MASTER.
HMPH.
I SEE. THEIR SURROUNDINGS ARE CONSTANTLY FROZEN, SO THEY'RE NOT DEAD. AND THAT MEANS THEY CAN'T KEEP COMING BACK TO LIFE.
INCIDEN-TALLY, THEIR MINDS ARE STILL INTACT AND ALIVE.
EVEN I CAN'T MELT THE ICE ANYMORE, SO THEY WILL FEEL THIS TERROR FOR ETERNITY.
I TARGETED YOU, TOO. HOW DID YOU GET AWAY FROM IT?
YOU WERE REALLY TRYING TO KILL ME, WEREN'T YOU.
I THOUGHT SOMETHING LIKE THIS MIGHT HAPPEN, SO I'D BEEN FIDDLING WITH THAT ORIGINAL SPELL DURING MY FREE TIME SINCE THE CLASS TRIP.
BUT IT ONLY WORKS ON DOLLS, SO IT'S HARD TO FIND A PLACE TO USE IT.
YOU? USING YOUR FREE TIME? AWW, I THOUGHT YOU DIDN'T CARE ABOUT US.
PFFT
WHAT CHANGED YOUR MIND? LOVE? FRIEND-SHIP?
KA-SHING
I REALLY *SHOULD* HAVE KILLED YOU.

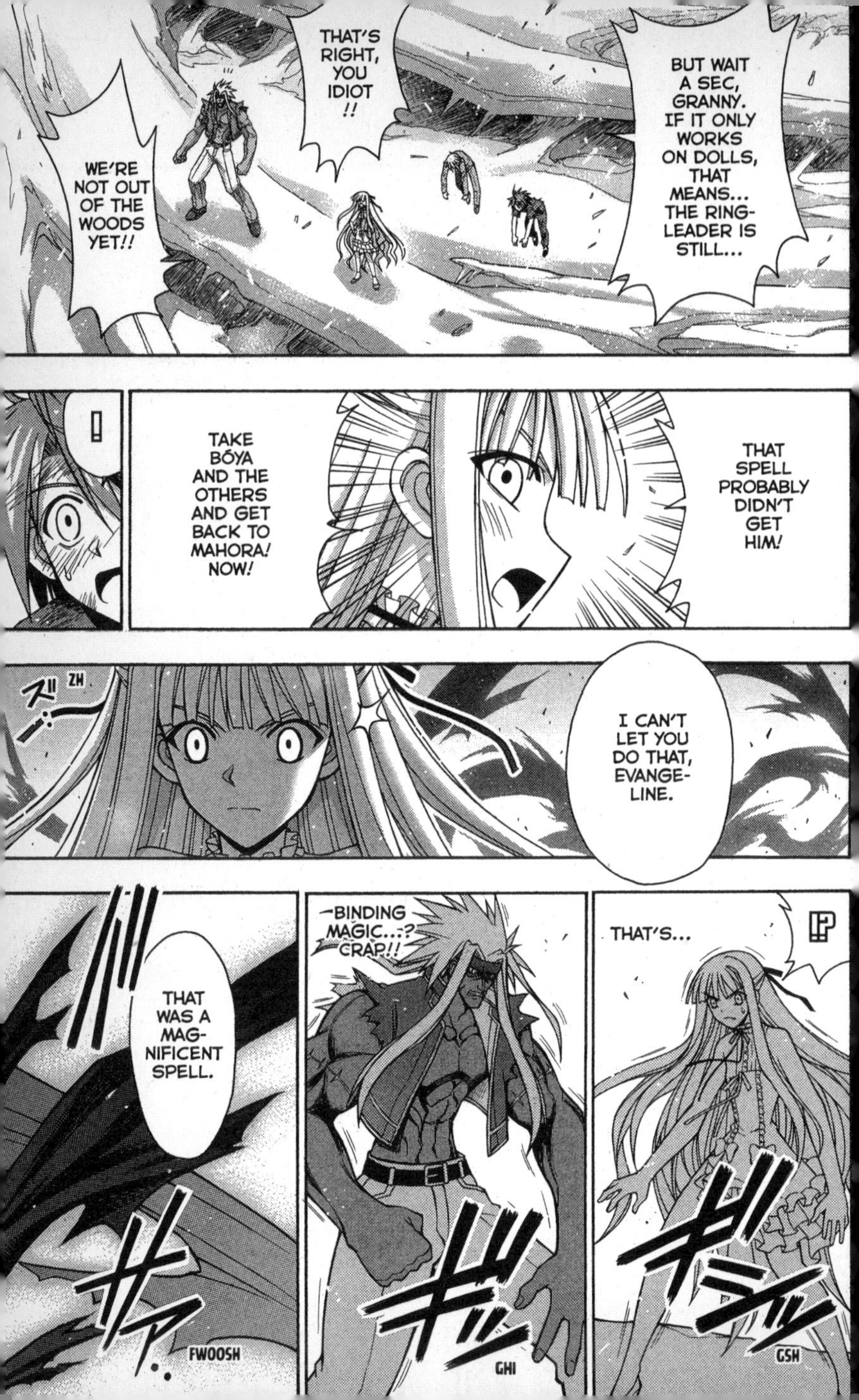
BUT WAIT A SEC, GRANNY. IF IT ONLY WORKS ON DOLLS, THAT MEANS... THE RING-LEADER IS STILL...
THAT'S RIGHT, YOU IDIOT!!
WE'RE NOT OUT OF THE WOODS YET!!
THAT SPELL PROBABLY DIDN'T GET HIM!
TAKE BŌYA AND THE OTHERS AND GET BACK TO MAHORA! NOW!
!
I CAN'T LET YOU DO THAT, EVANGE-LINE.
ZH
!?
THAT'S...
GSH
BINDING MAGIC...? CRAP!!
GHI
THAT WAS A MAG-NIFICENT SPELL.
FWOOSH

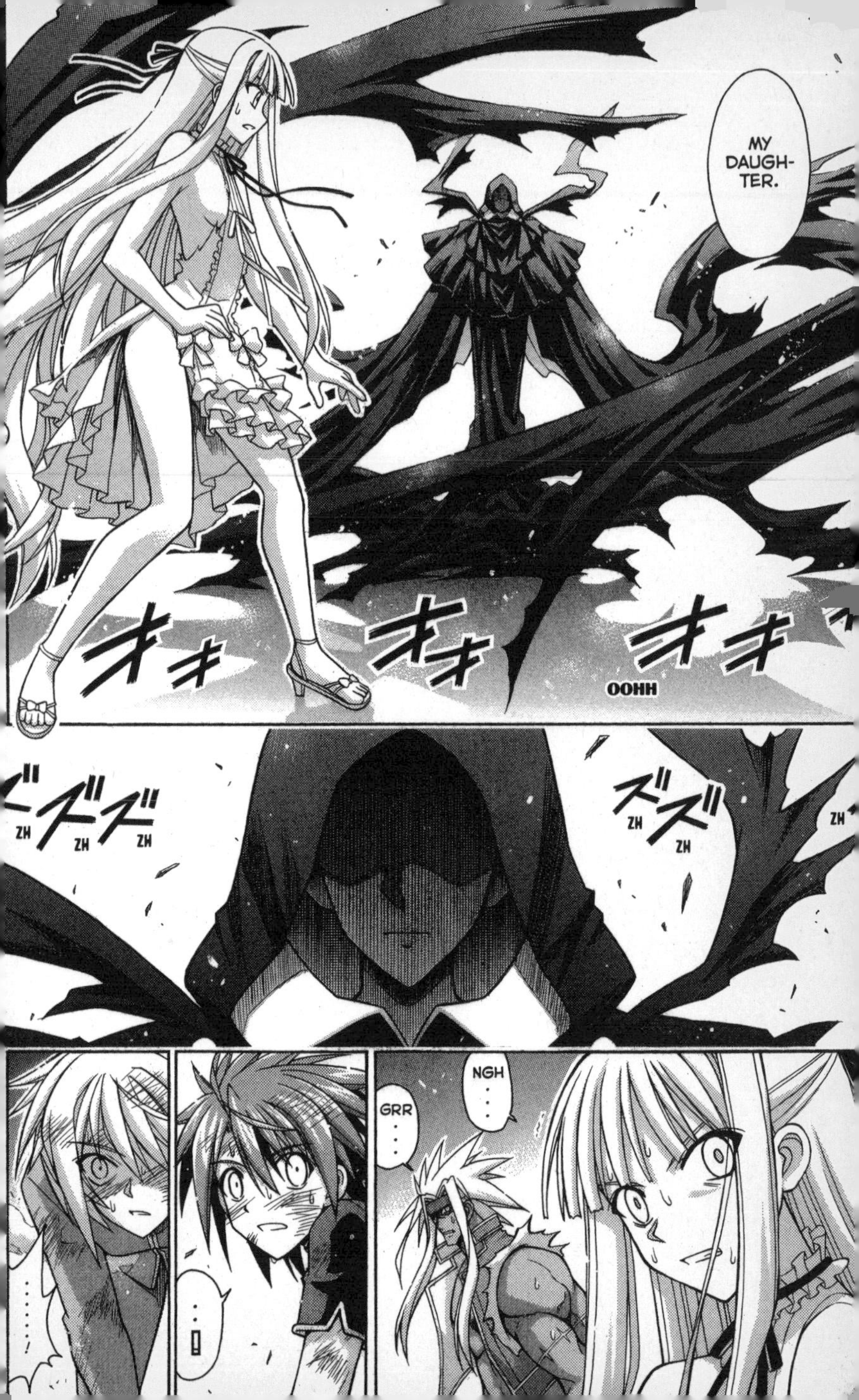
MY DAUGHTER.
オォオォオォ
OOHH
ズズズ
ZH ZH ZH
ズズ
ZH ZH ZH
NGH ...
GRR ...
...!
......!

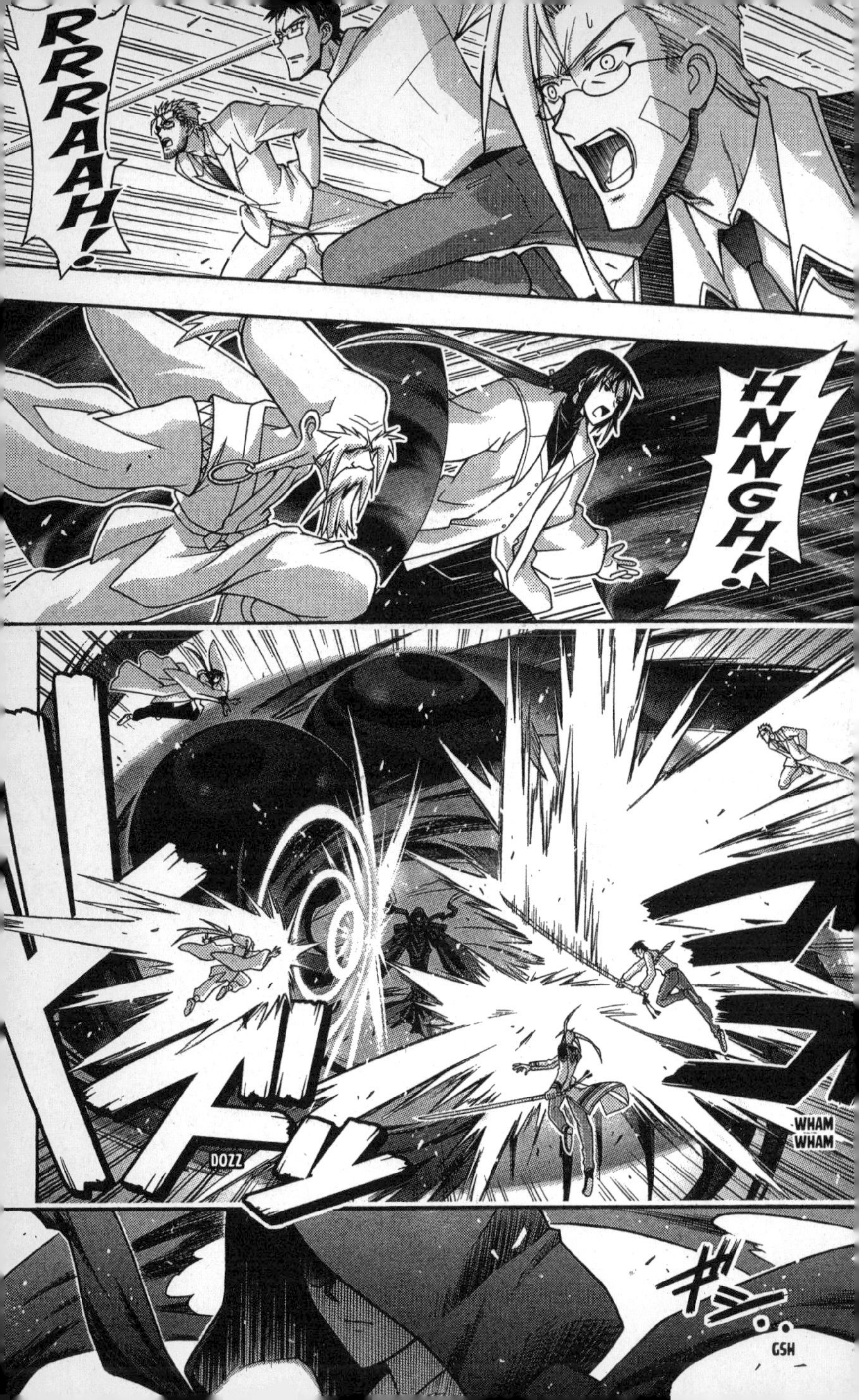
RRRAAH!
HNNGH!
WHAM
WHAM
DOZZ
GSH

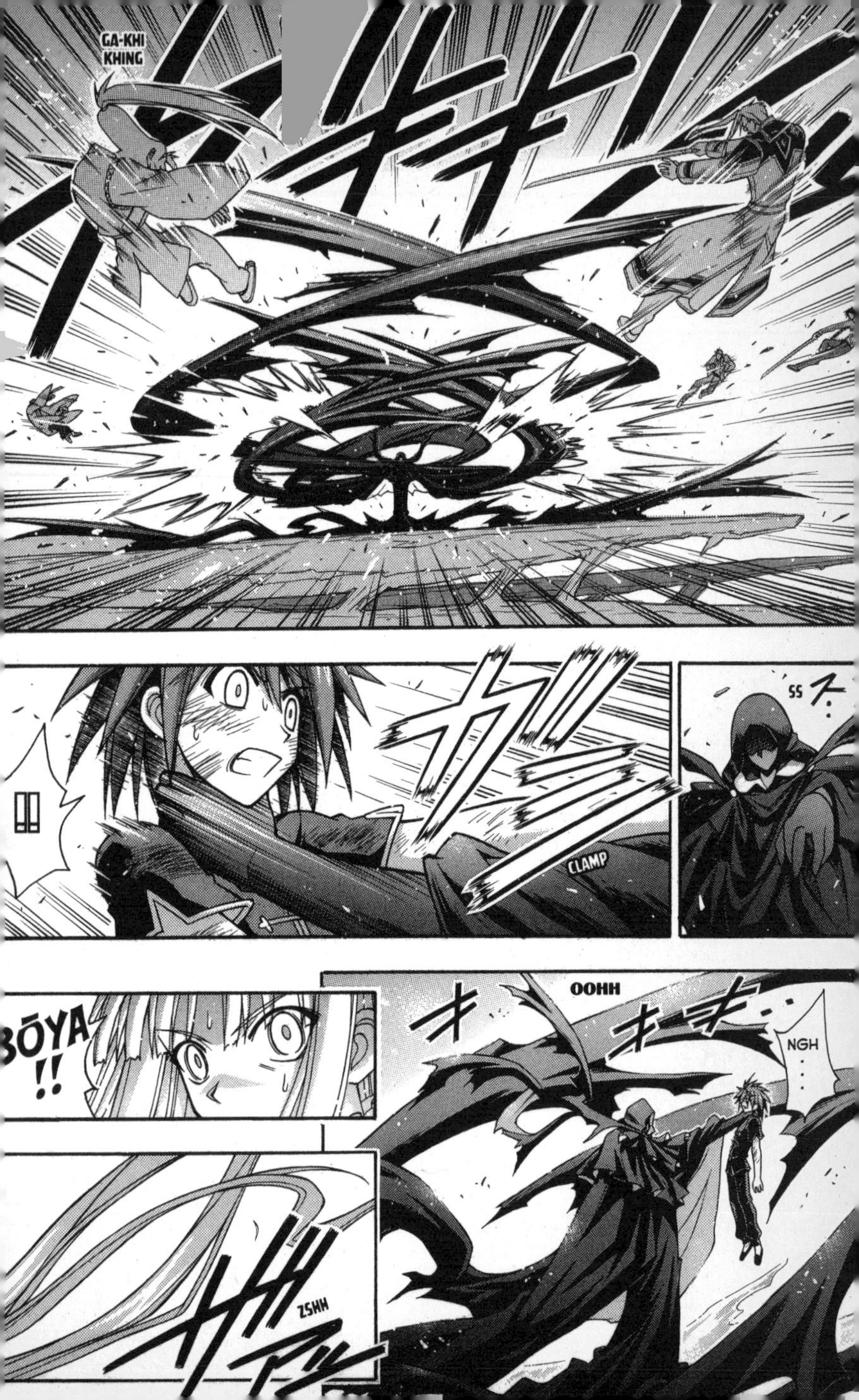
GA-KHI KHING
SS
CLAMP
!!
OOHH
NGH...
BŌYA!!
ZSHH

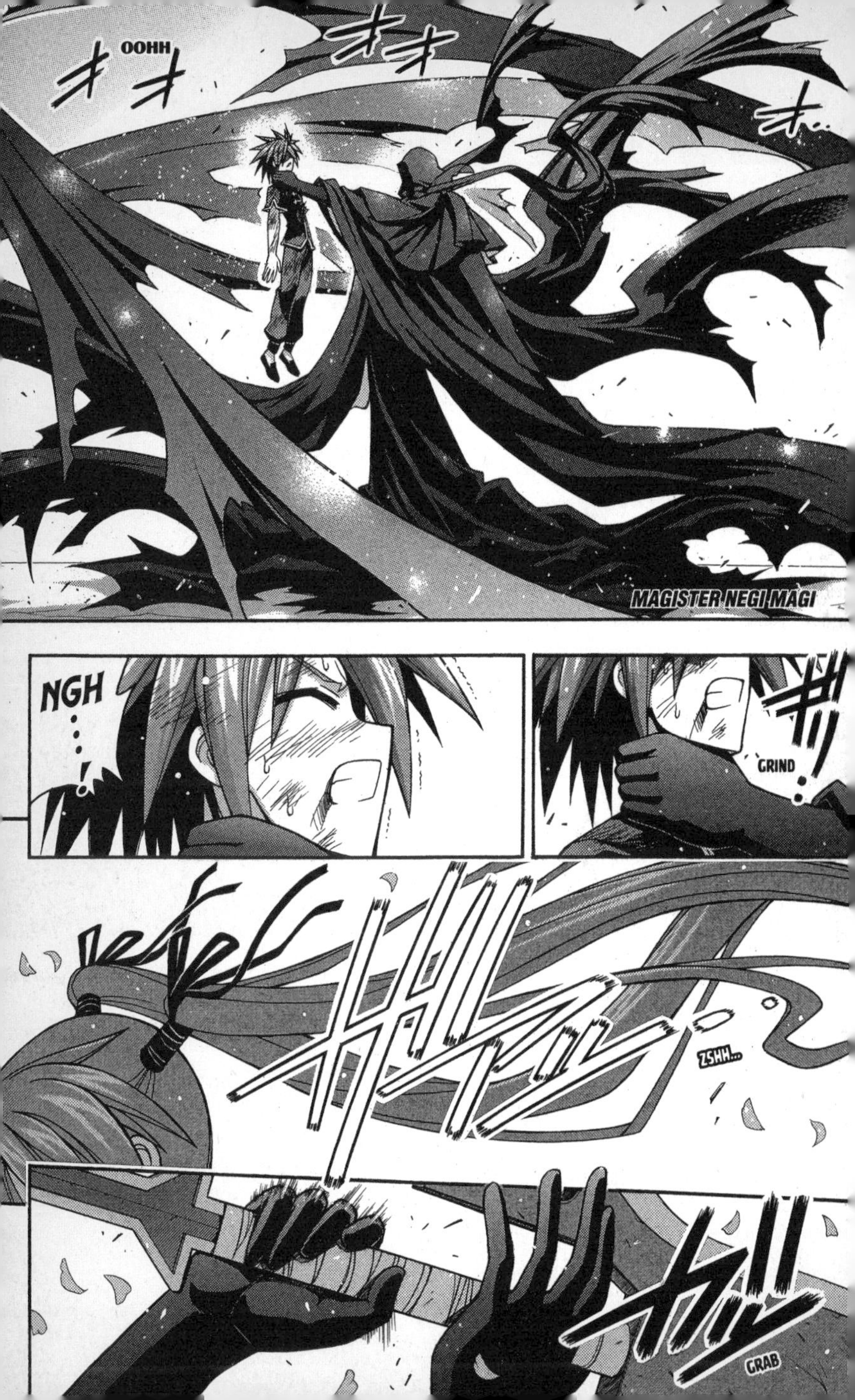
OOHH
MAGISTER NEGI MAGI
GRIND...!
NGH...!
ZSHH...
GRAB

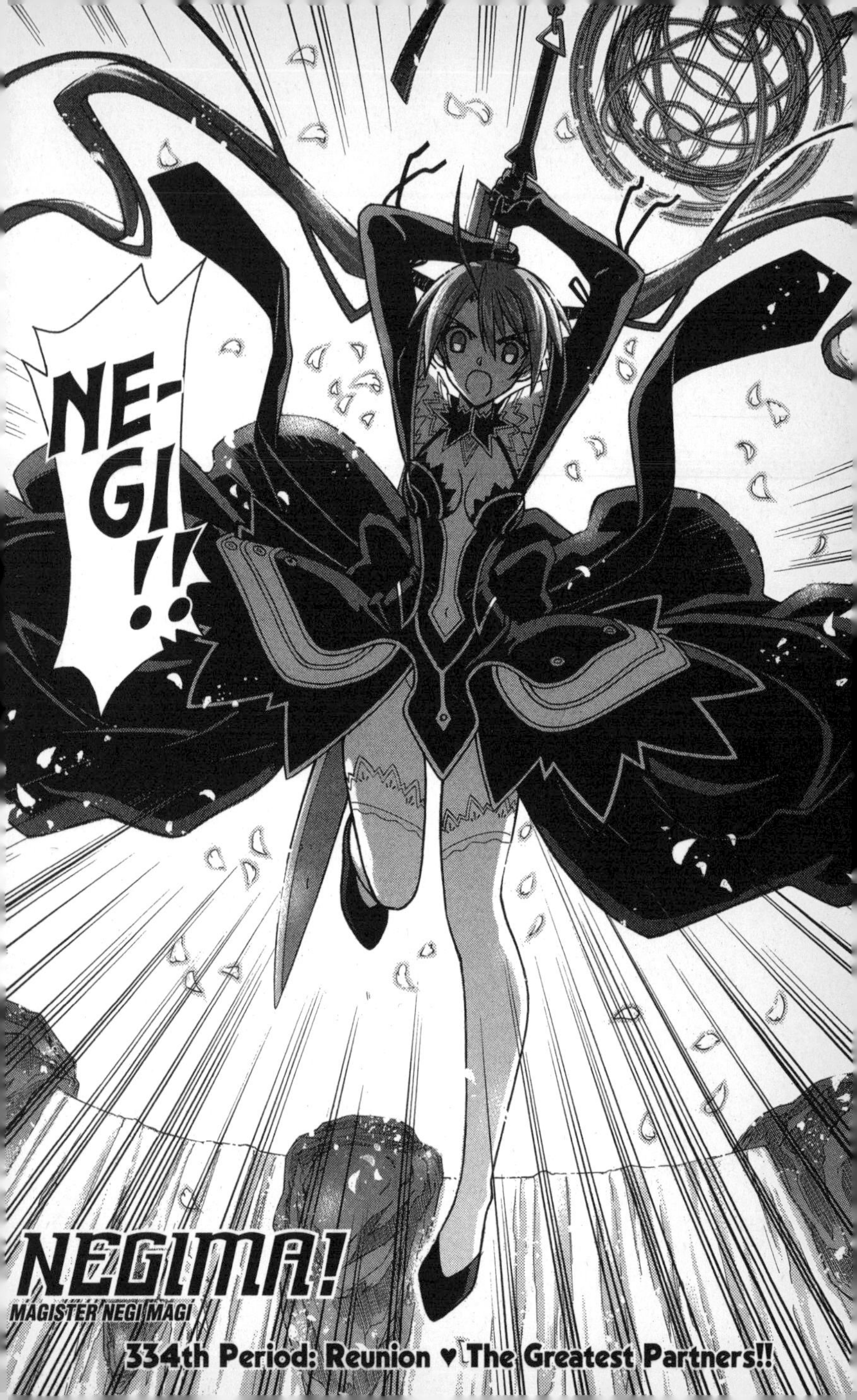
NE-GI!!
NEGIMA!
MAGISTER NEGI MAGI
334th Period: Reunion ♥ The Greatest Partners!!

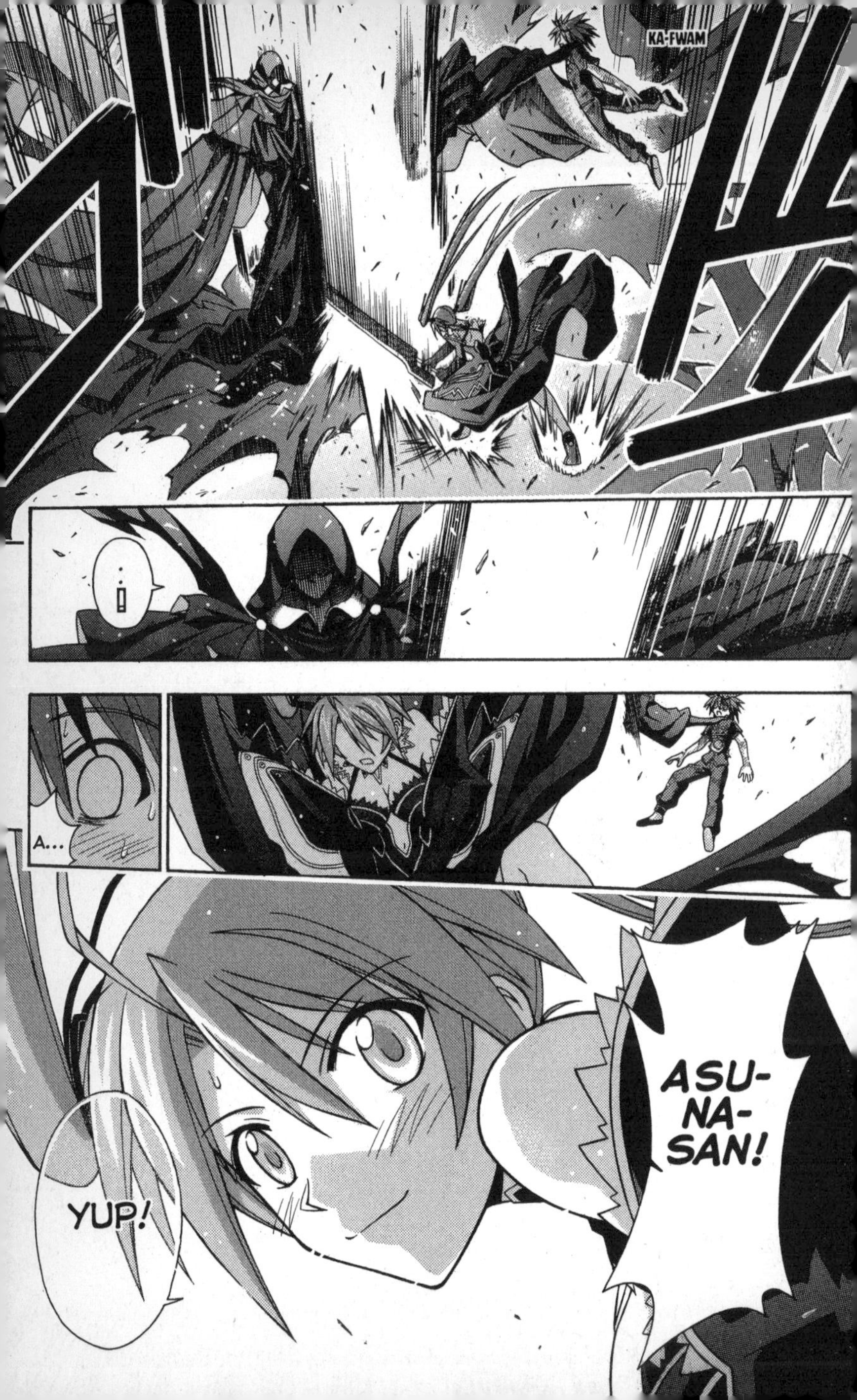
KA-FWAM
!
A...
ASU-NA-SAN!
YUP!

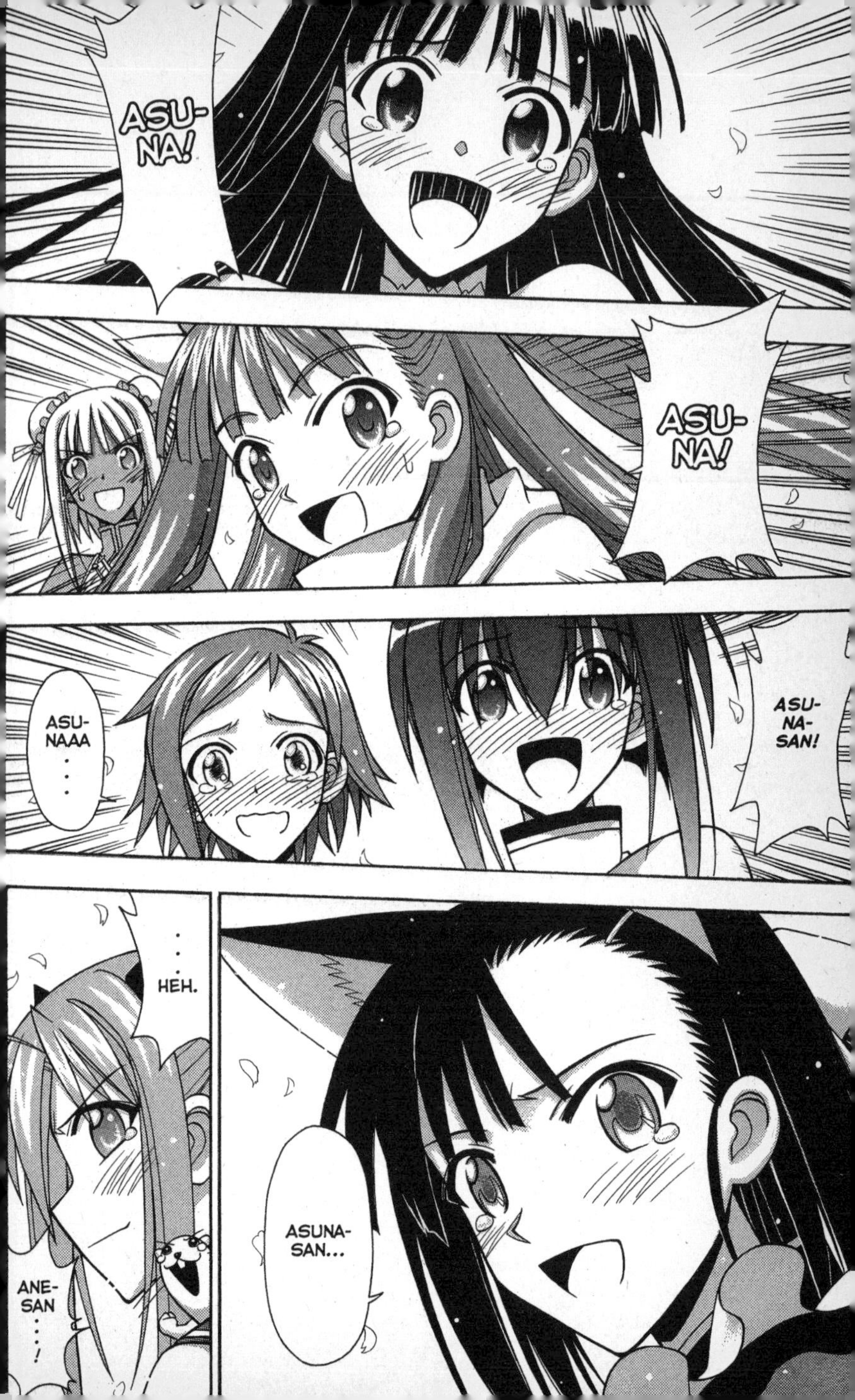
ASU-NA!
ASU-NA!
ASU-NA-SAN!
ASU-NAAA.....
ASUNA-SAN...
...HEH.
ANE-SAN...!

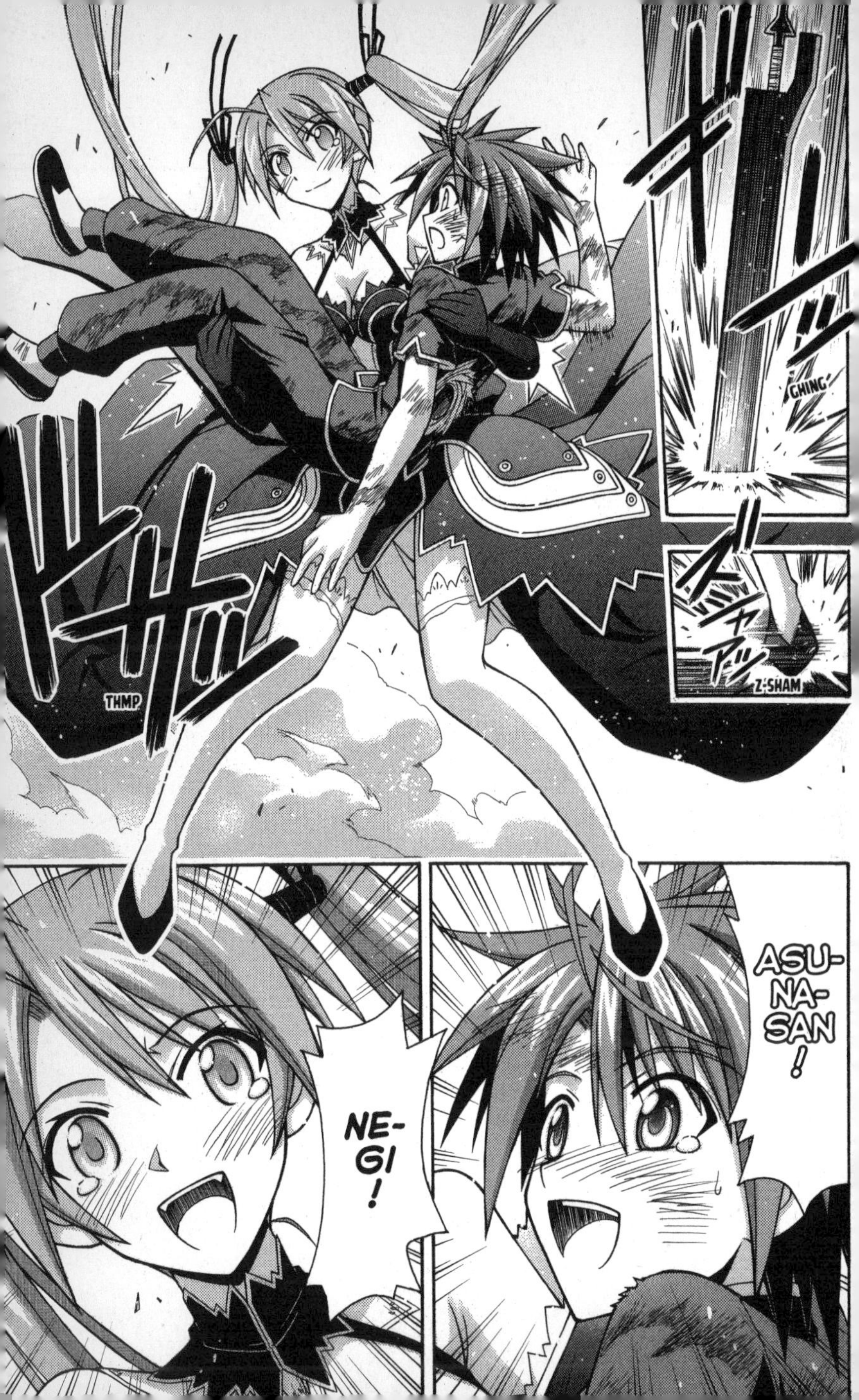
GHING
Z-SHAM
THMP
ASUNA-SAN!
NEGI!

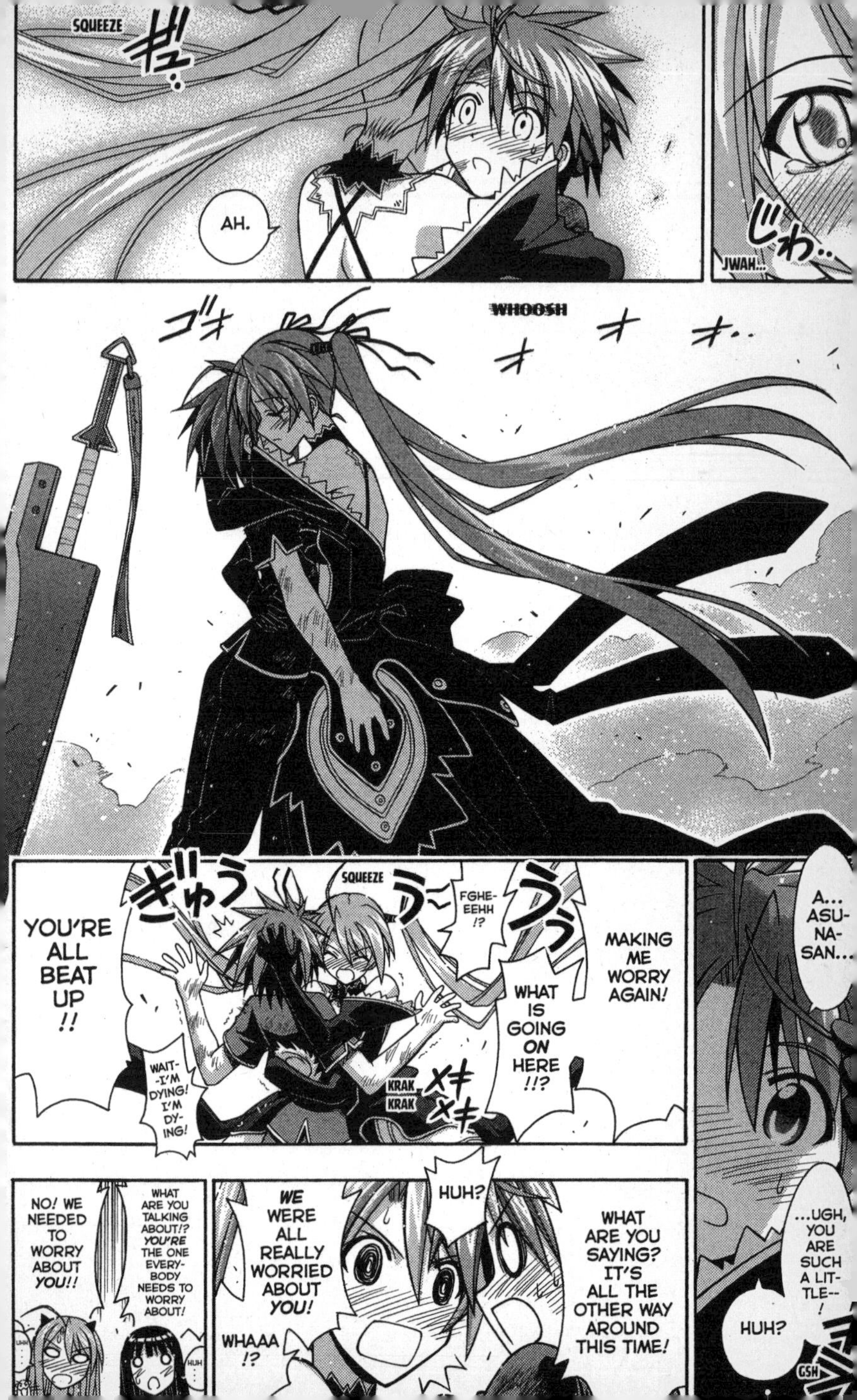
じわ…
JWAH...
SQUEEZE
AH.
WHOOSH
A... ASUNA-SAN...
...UGH, YOU ARE SUCH A LIT-TLE--!
HUH?
GSH
MAKING ME WORRY AGAIN!
WHAT IS GOING ON HERE!!?
FGHE-EEHH!?
SQUEEZE
YOU'RE ALL BEAT UP!!
WAIT-I'M DYING! I'M DY-ING!
KRAK KRAK
HUH?
WHAT ARE YOU SAYING? IT'S ALL THE OTHER WAY AROUND THIS TIME!
WE WERE ALL REALLY WORRIED ABOUT YOU!
WHAAA!?
WHAT ARE YOU TALKING ABOUT!? YOU'RE THE ONE EVERY-BODY NEEDS TO WORRY ABOUT!
NO! WE NEEDED TO WORRY ABOUT YOU!!
HUH
UHH

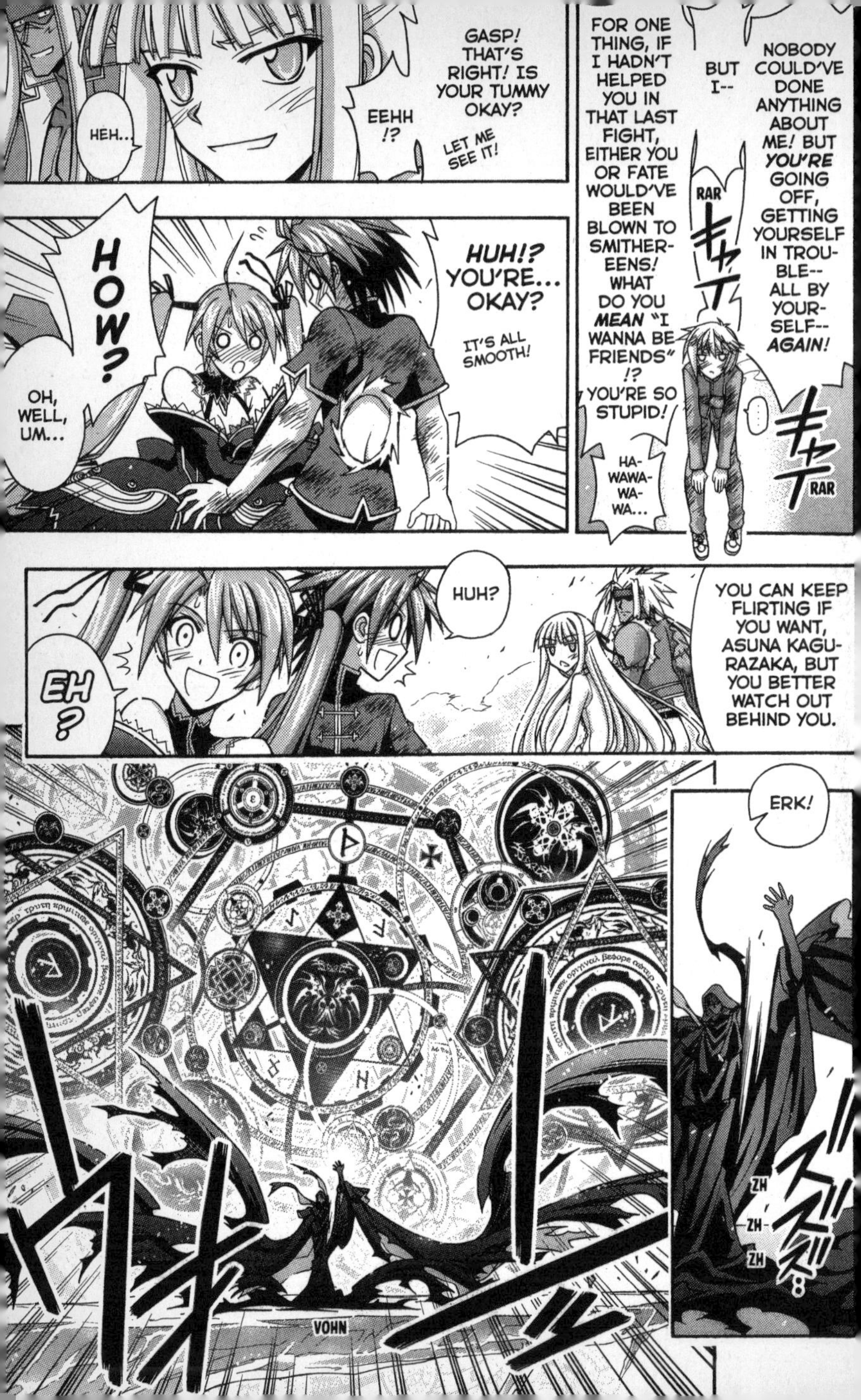
NOBODY COULD'VE DONE ANYTHING ABOUT ME! BUT YOU'RE GOING OFF, GETTING YOURSELF IN TROUBLE-- ALL BY YOURSELF-- AGAIN!
BUT I--
FOR ONE THING, IF I HADN'T HELPED YOU IN THAT LAST FIGHT, EITHER YOU OR FATE WOULD'VE BEEN BLOWN TO SMITHEREENS! WHAT DO YOU MEAN "I WANNA BE FRIENDS" !? YOU'RE SO STUPID!
RAR
...
RAR
HA-WAWA-WA-WA...
GASP! THAT'S RIGHT! IS YOUR TUMMY OKAY?
EEHH !?
LET ME SEE IT!
HEH...
HUH!? YOU'RE... OKAY?
IT'S ALL SMOOTH!
HOW?
OH, WELL, UM...
YOU CAN KEEP FLIRTING IF YOU WANT, ASUNA KAGURAZAKA, BUT YOU BETTER WATCH OUT BEHIND YOU.
HUH?
EH?
ERK!
ZH-ZH-ZH
VOHN

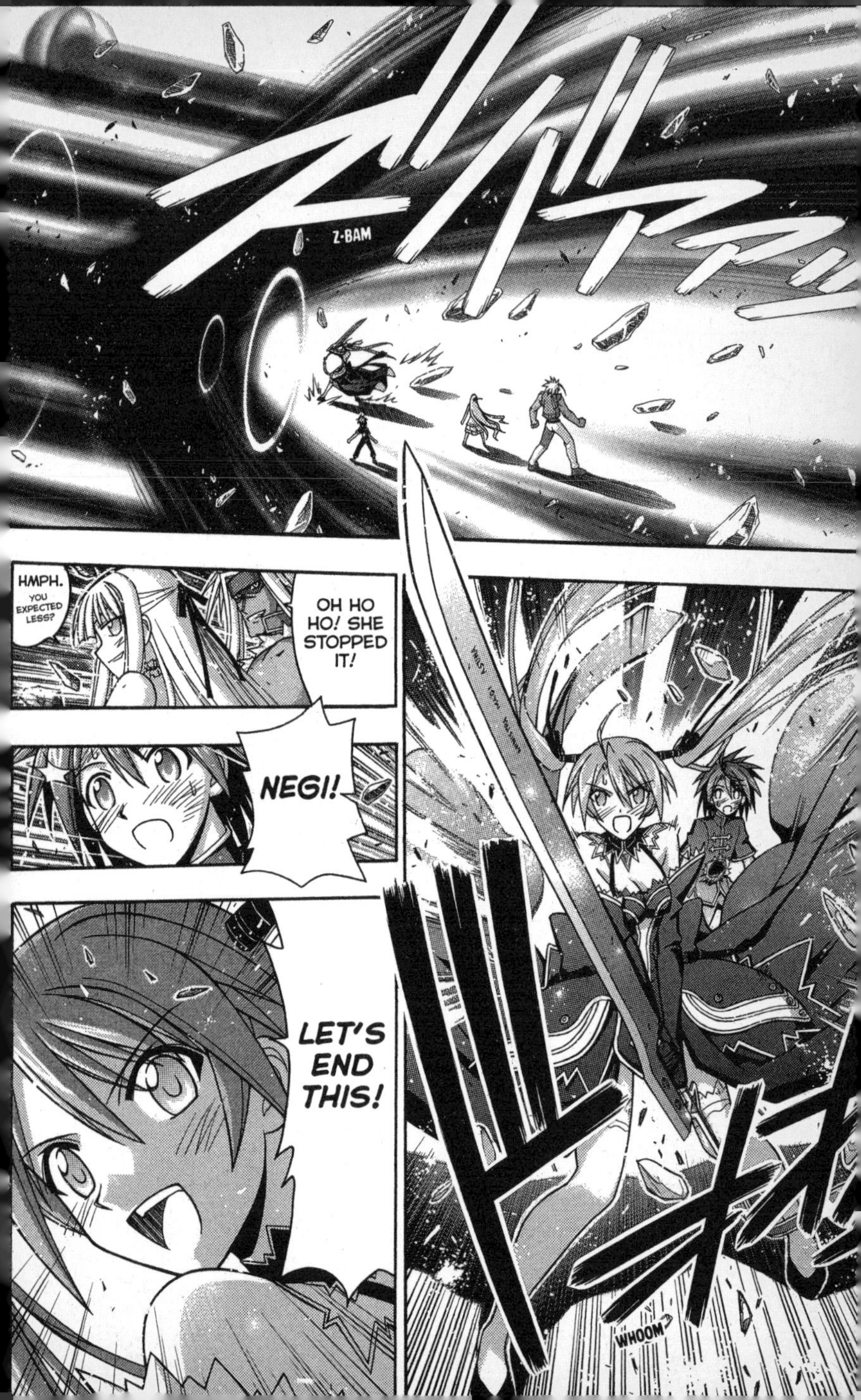

Z-BAM
WHOOM
OH HO HO! SHE STOPPED IT!
HMPH. YOU EXPECTED LESS?
NEGI!
LET'S END THIS!

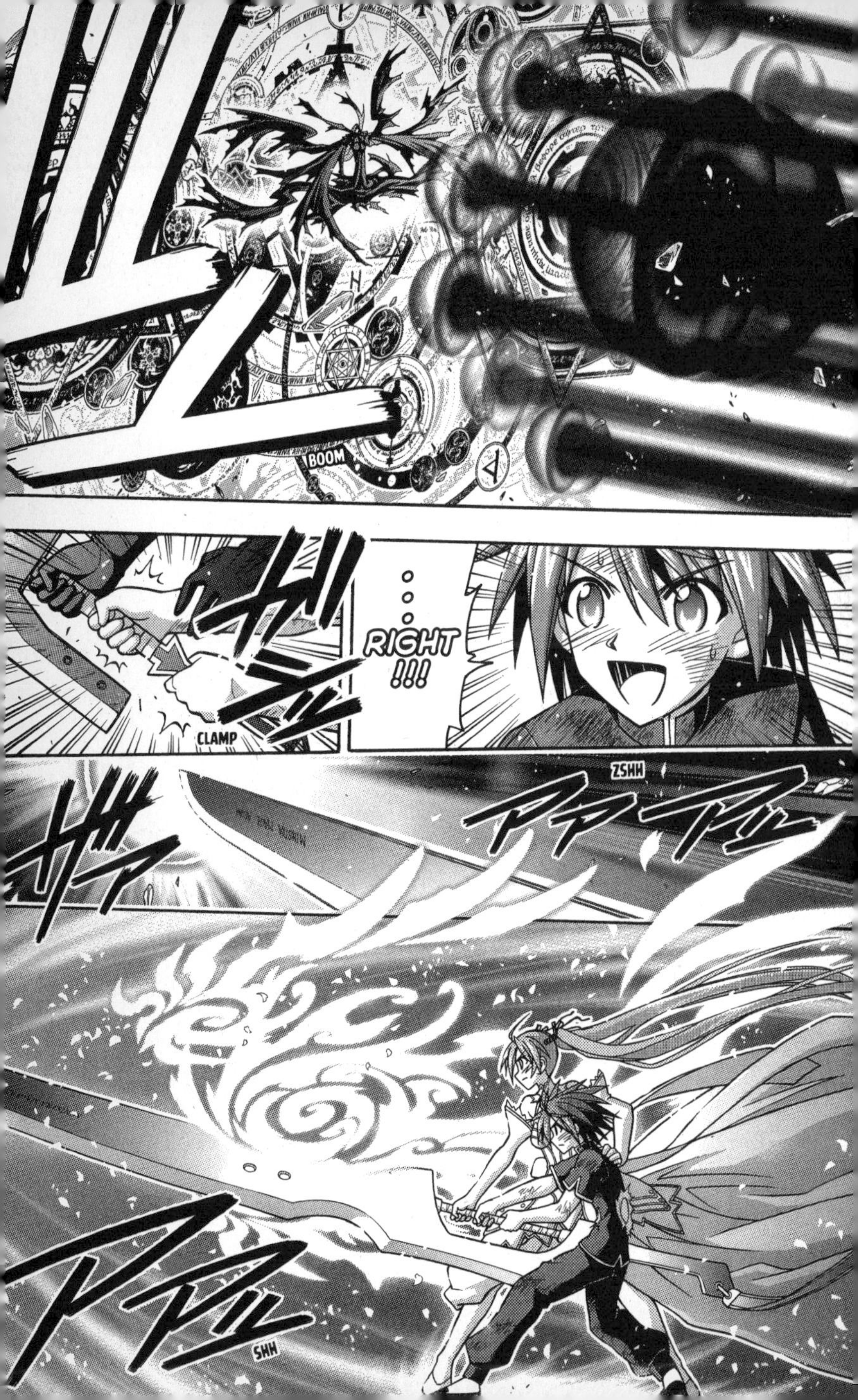
BOOM
.....RIGHT!!!
CLAMP
ZSHH
SHH

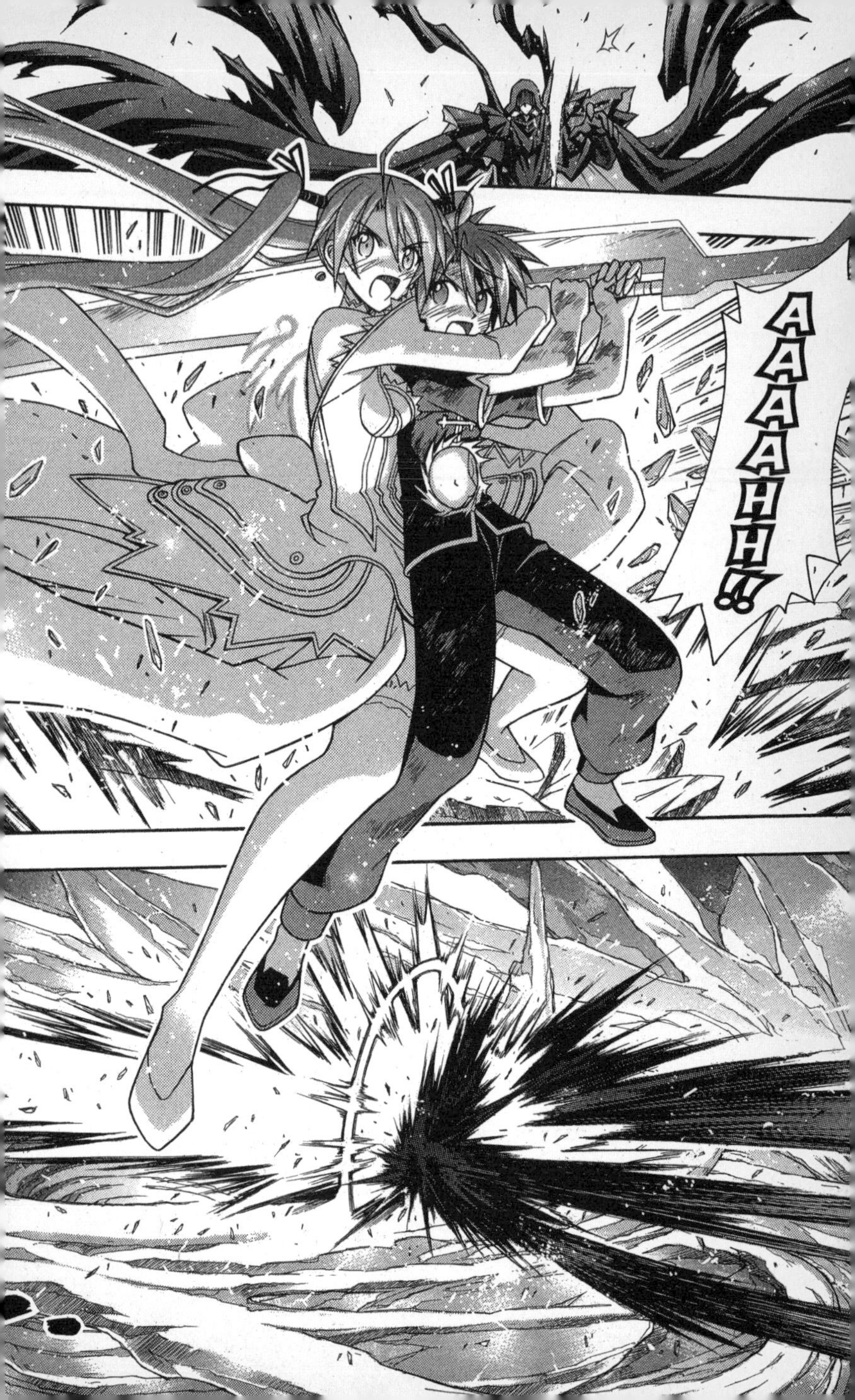
AAAAAAHH!!

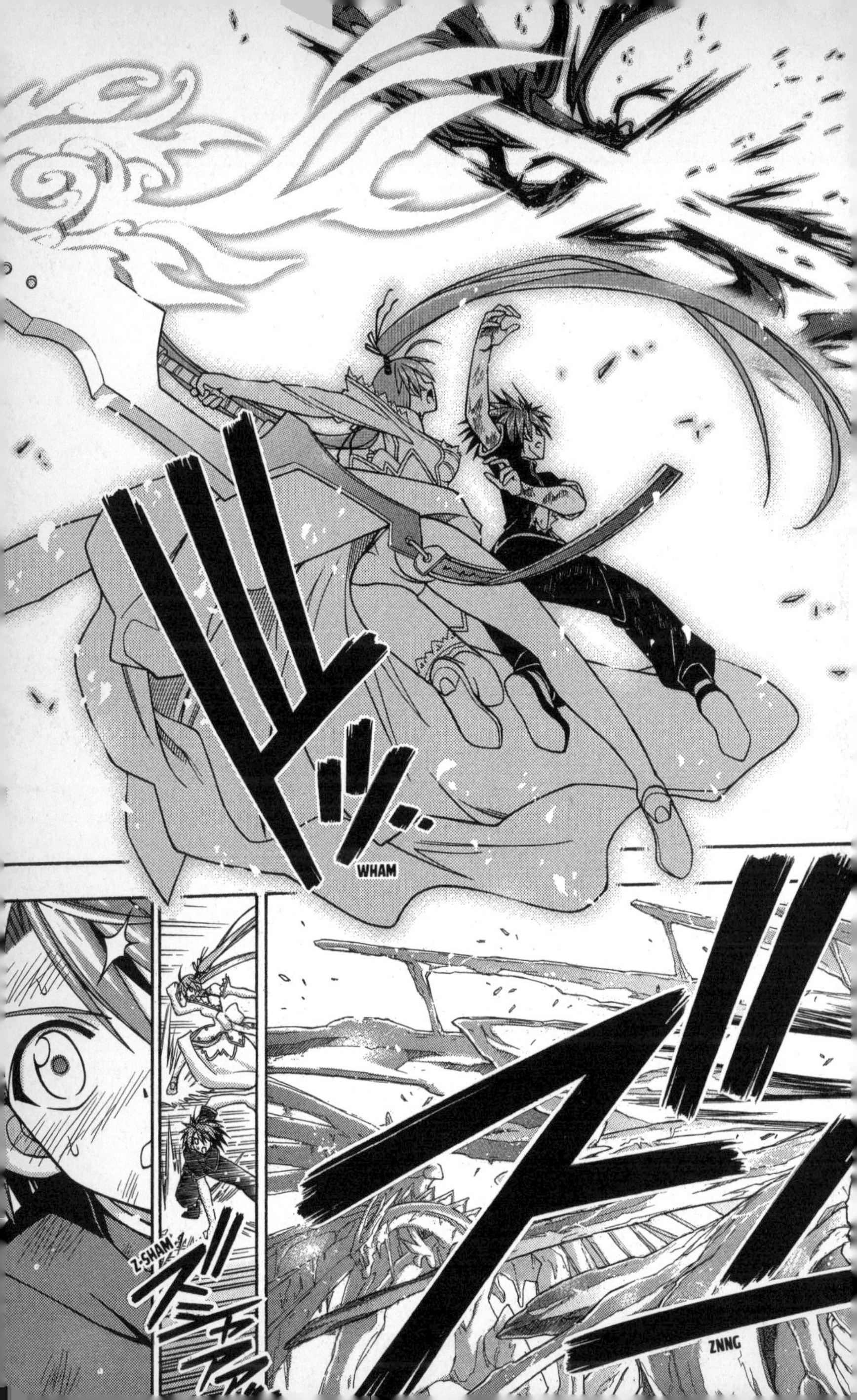
WHAM
ZNNG
Z-SHAM

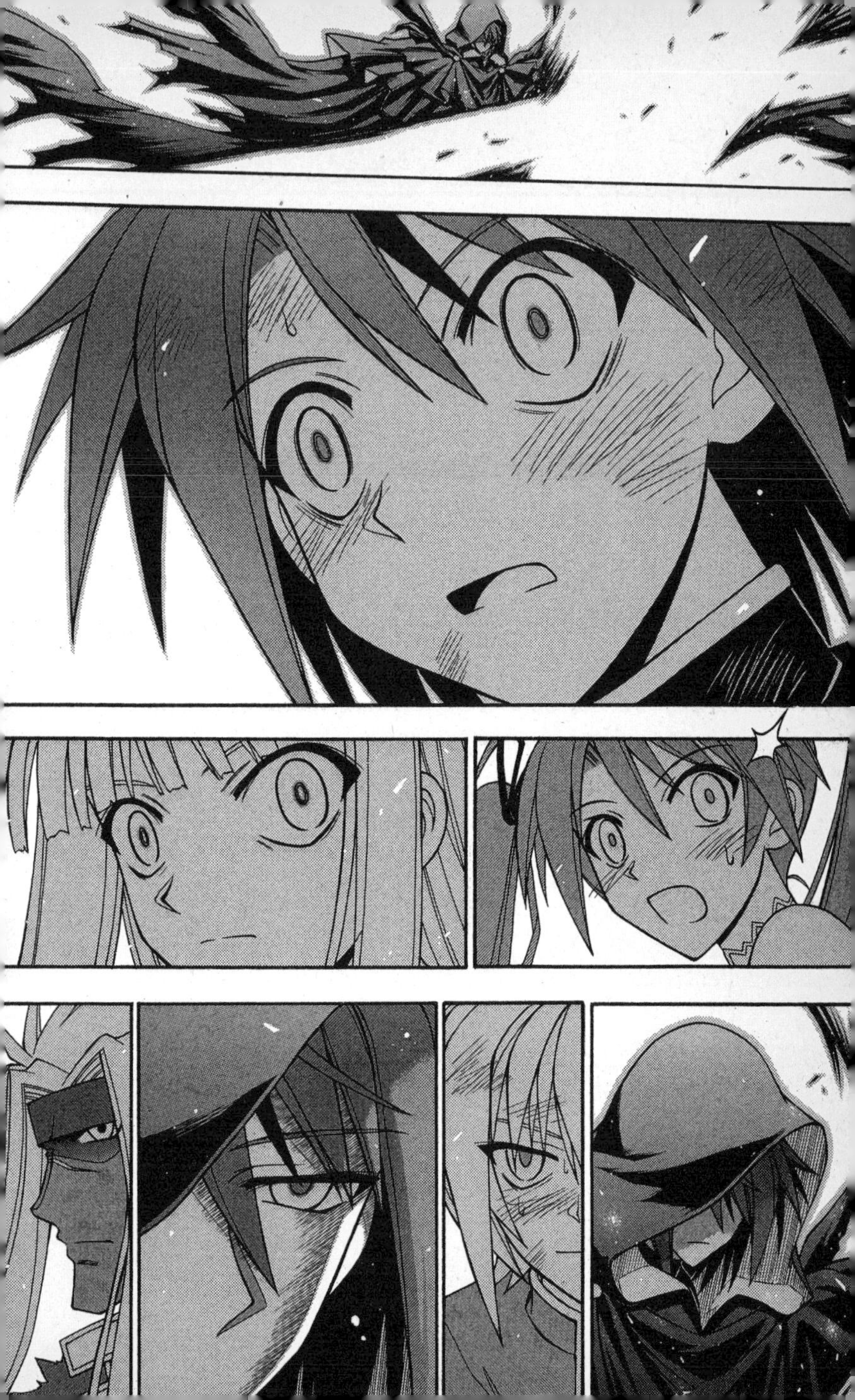

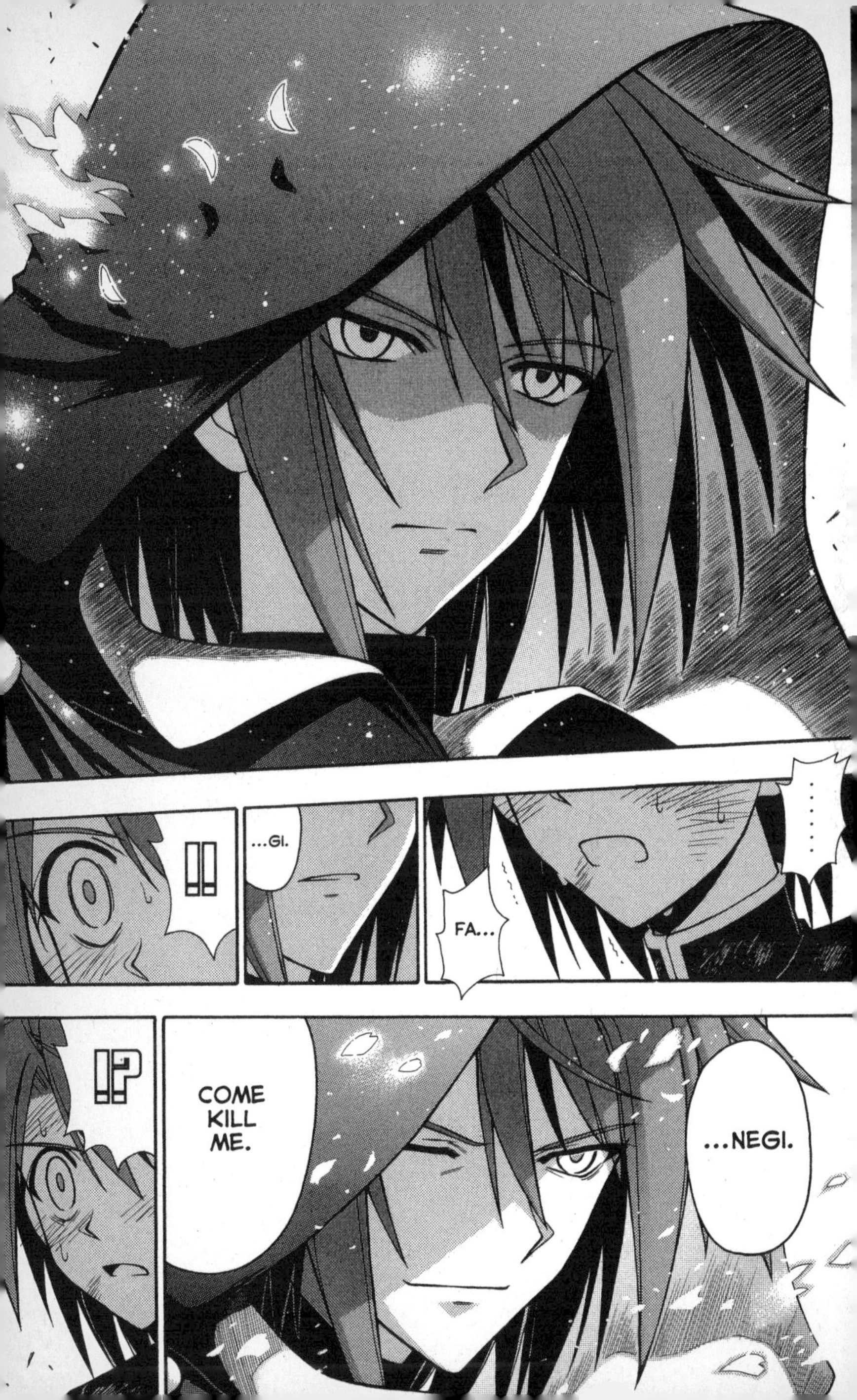
......
FA...
...GI.
!!
...NEGI.
COME KILL ME.
!?

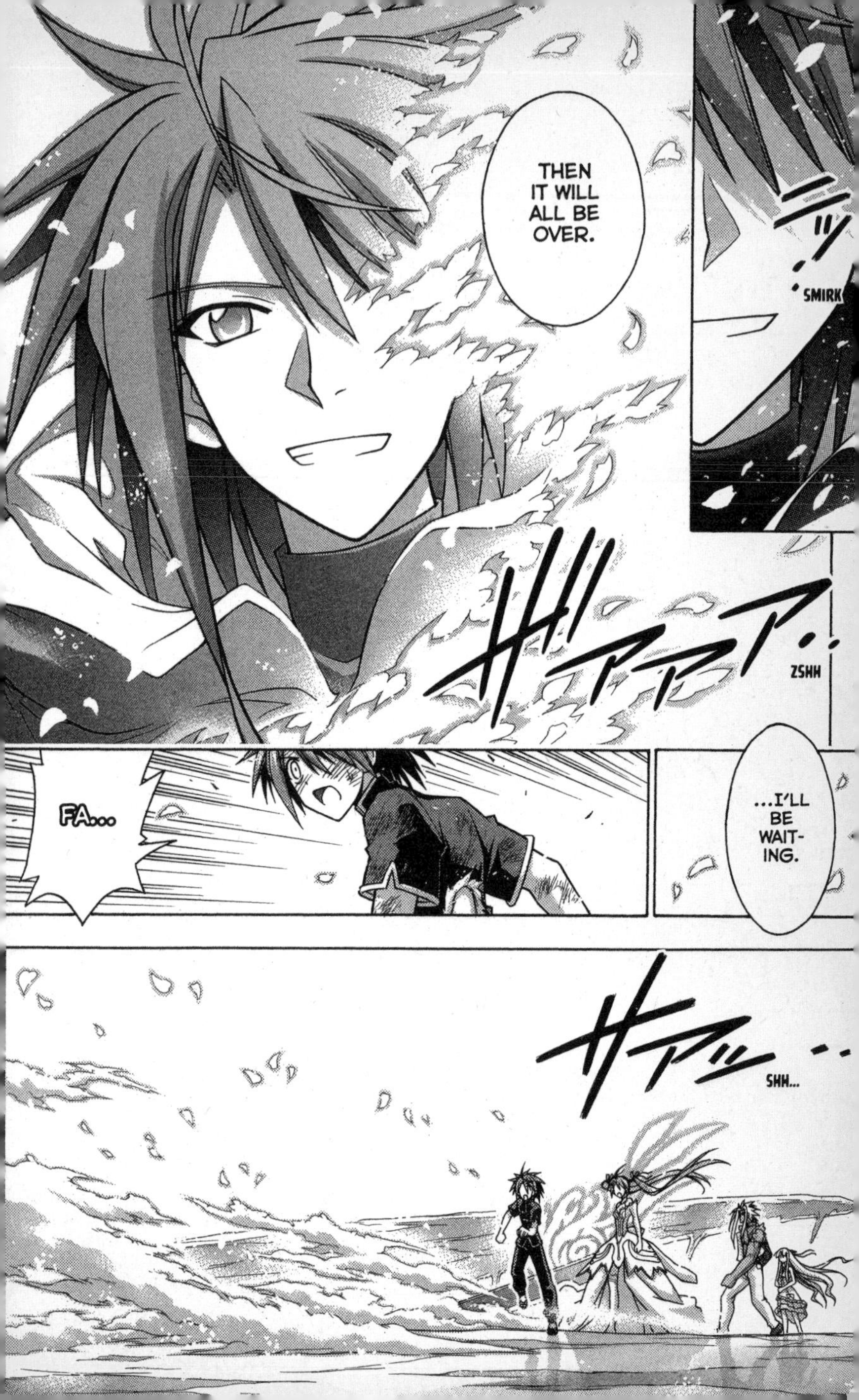
SMIRK
THEN IT WILL ALL BE OVER.
ZSHH
...I'LL BE WAIT-ING.
FA...
SHH...

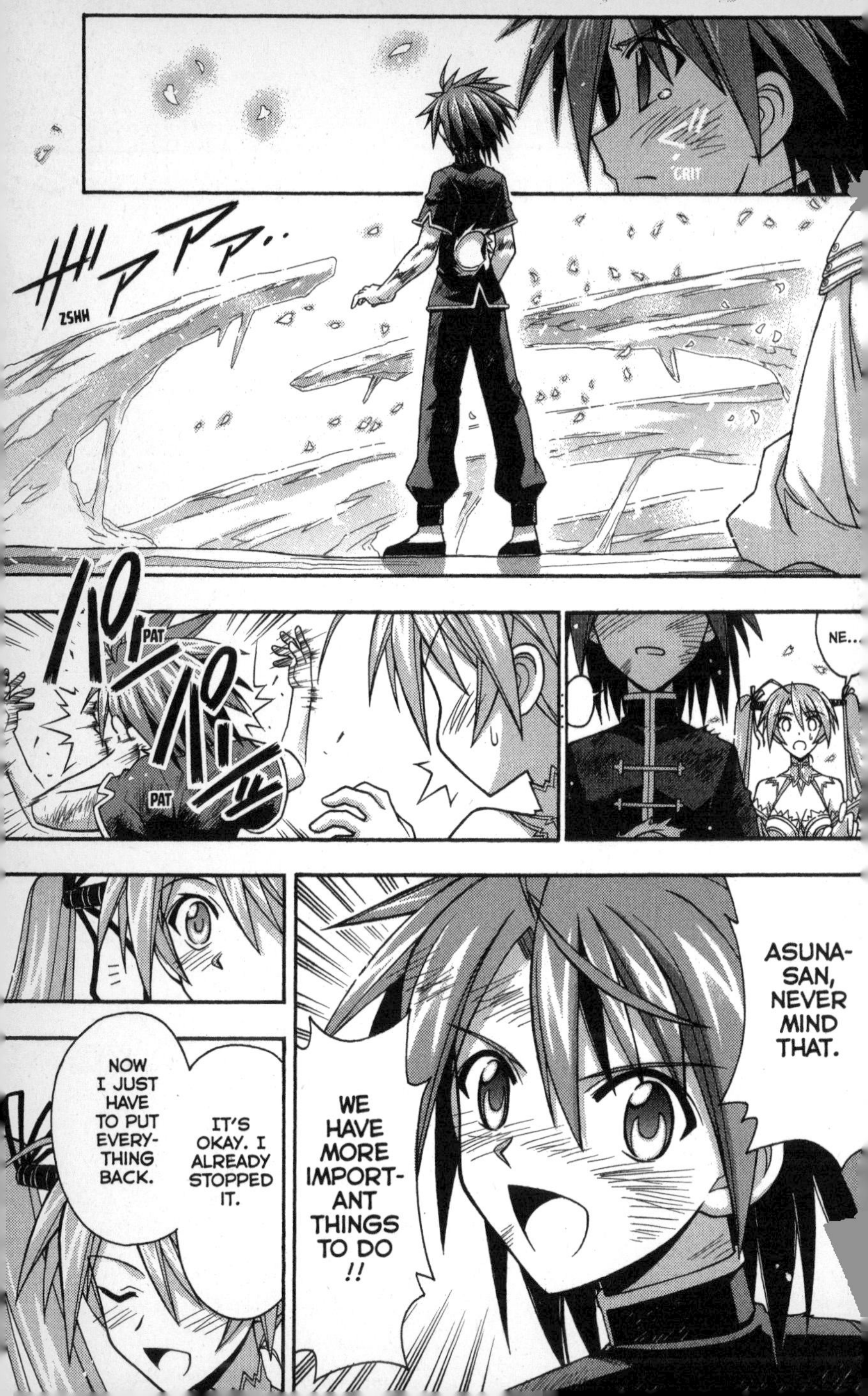
GRIT
ZSHH
NE...
PAT
PAT
ASUNA-SAN, NEVER MIND THAT.
WE HAVE MORE IMPORTANT THINGS TO DO!!
IT'S OKAY. I ALREADY STOPPED IT.
NOW I JUST HAVE TO PUT EVERYTHING BACK.

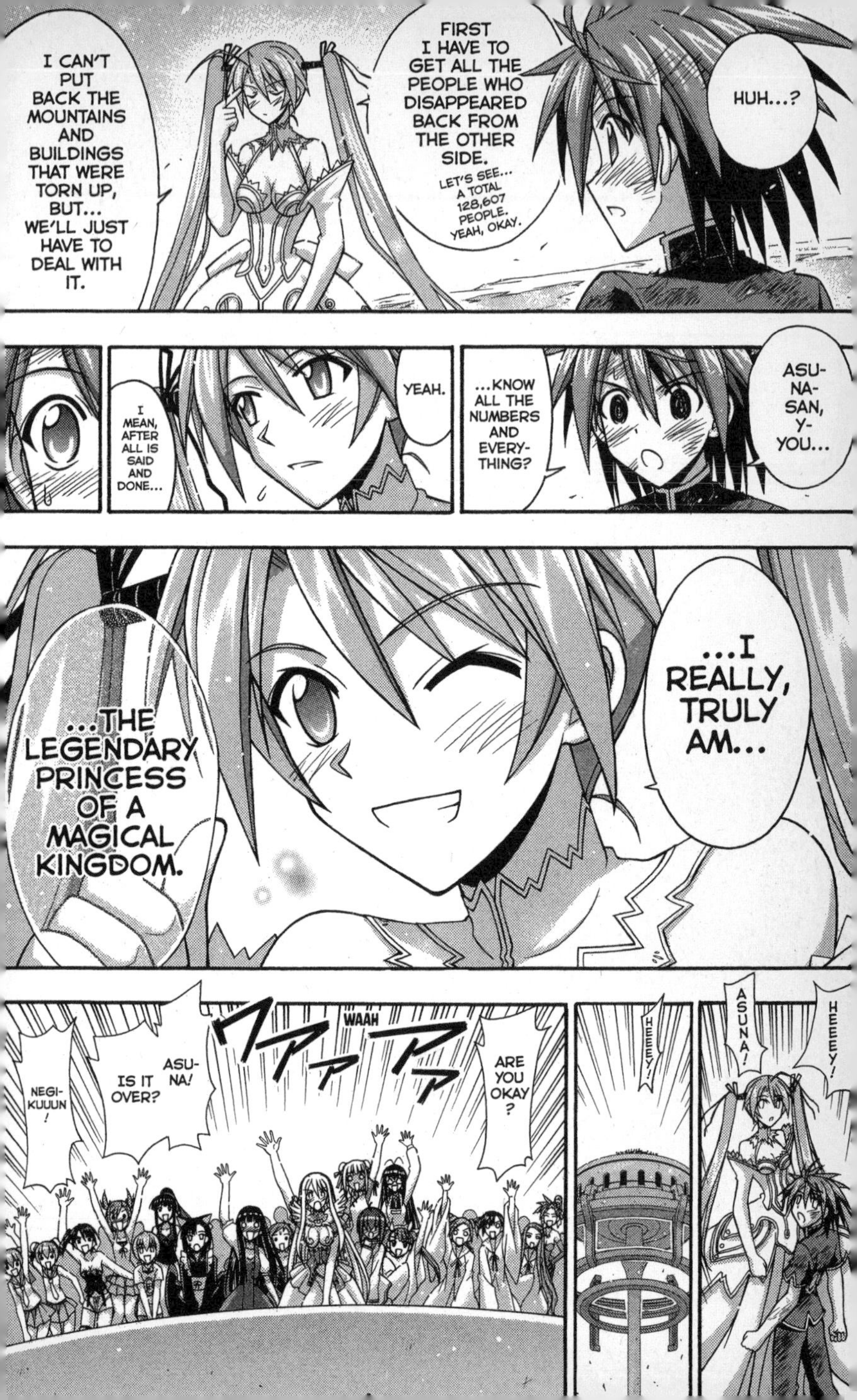
HUH...?
FIRST I HAVE TO GET ALL THE PEOPLE WHO DISAPPEARED BACK FROM THE OTHER SIDE.
LET'S SEE... A TOTAL 128,607 PEOPLE. YEAH, OKAY.
I CAN'T PUT BACK THE MOUNTAINS AND BUILDINGS THAT WERE TORN UP, BUT... WE'LL JUST HAVE TO DEAL WITH IT.
ASU-NA-SAN, Y-YOU...
...KNOW ALL THE NUMBERS AND EVERY-THING?
YEAH.
I MEAN, AFTER ALL IS SAID AND DONE...
...I REALLY, TRULY AM...
...THE LEGENDARY PRINCESS OF A MAGICAL KINGDOM.
HEEEY!
ASUNA!
HEEEY!
ARE YOU OKAY?
WAAH
ASU-NA!
IS IT OVER?
NEGI-KUUUN!

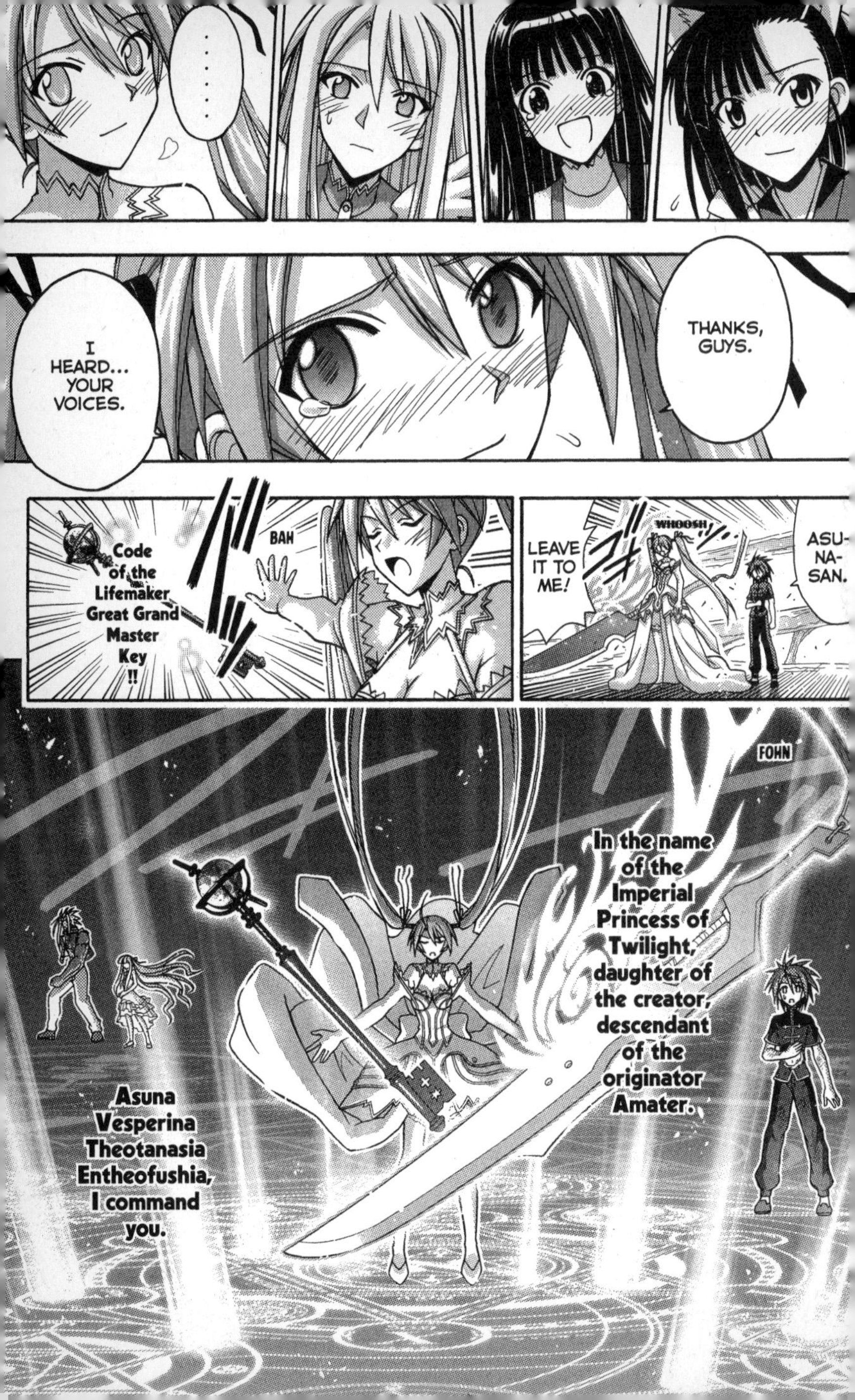

......
THANKS, GUYS.
I HEARD... YOUR VOICES.
ASUNA-SAN.
WHOOSH
LEAVE IT TO ME!
BAH
Code of the Lifemaker Great Grand Master Key!!
FOHN
In the name of the Imperial Princess of Twilight, daughter of the creator, descendant of the originator Amater.
Asuna Vesperina Theotanasia Entheofushia, I command you.

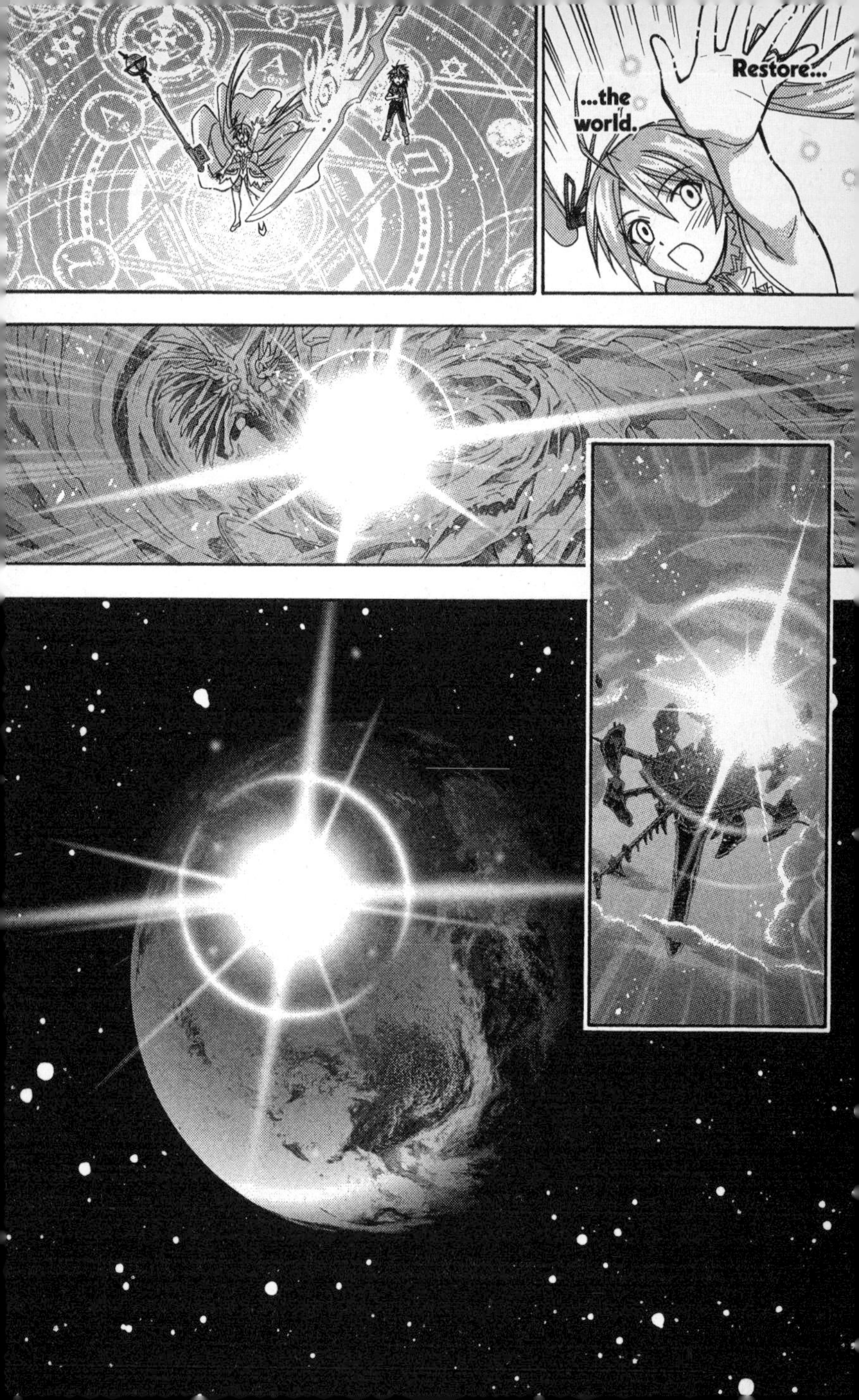
Restore...
...the world.

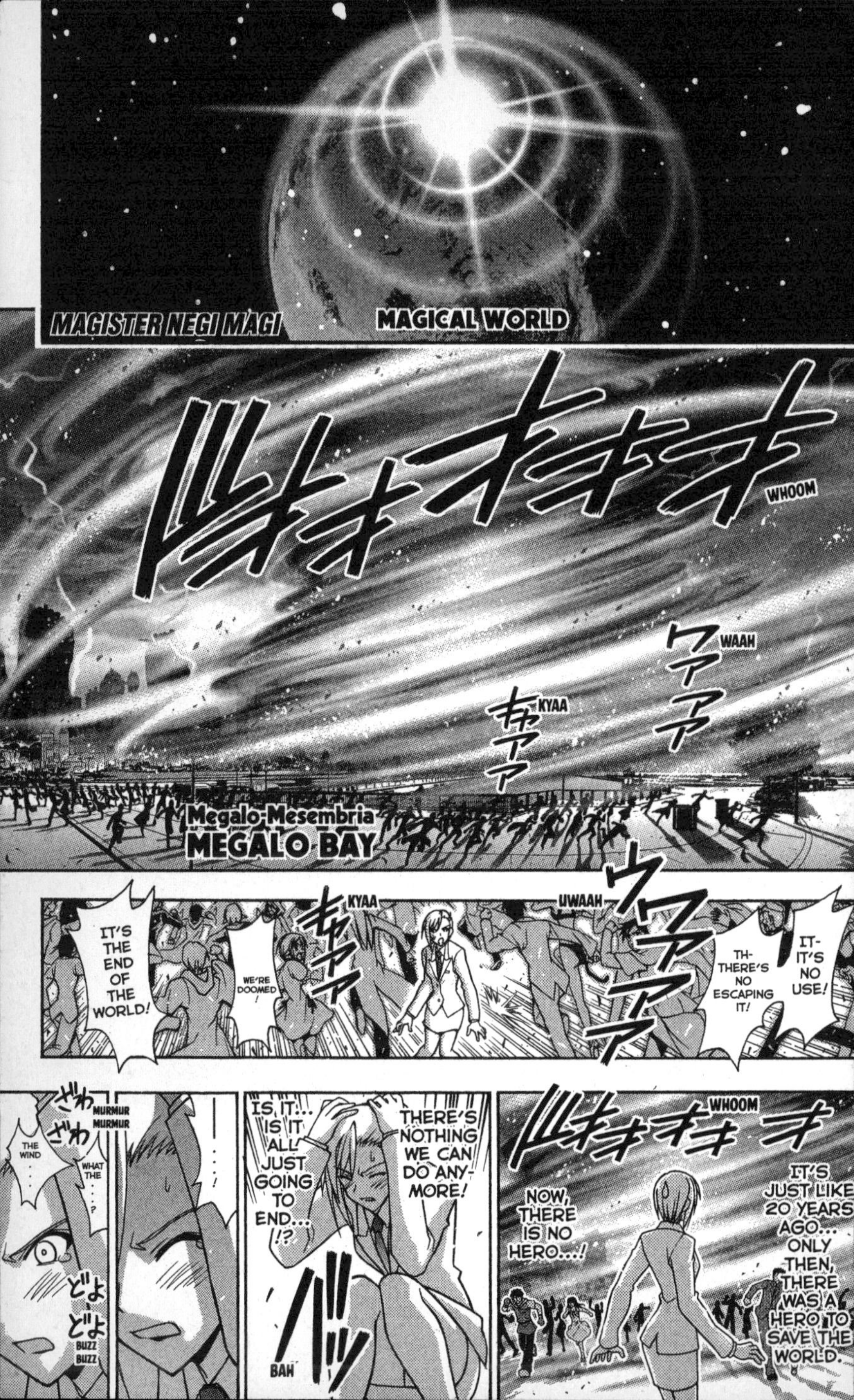
MAGICAL WORLD
MAGISTER NEGI MAGI
WHOOM
ワァァァ
WAAH
キャアア
KYAA
Megalo-Mesembria
MEGALO BAY
IT-IT'S NO USE!
TH-THERE'S NO ESCAPING IT!
UWAAH
KYAA
WE'RE DOOMED!
IT'S THE END OF THE WORLD!
WHOOM
IT'S JUST LIKE 20 YEARS AGO... ONLY THEN, THERE WAS A HERO TO SAVE THE WORLD.
NOW, THERE IS NO HERO...!
THERE'S NOTHING WE CAN DO ANYMORE!
IS IT... IS IT ALL JUST GOING TO END...!?
BAH
...!
ざわ ざわ
MURMUR MURMUR
WHAT THE...?
THE WIND...
どよ どよ
BUZZ BUZZ

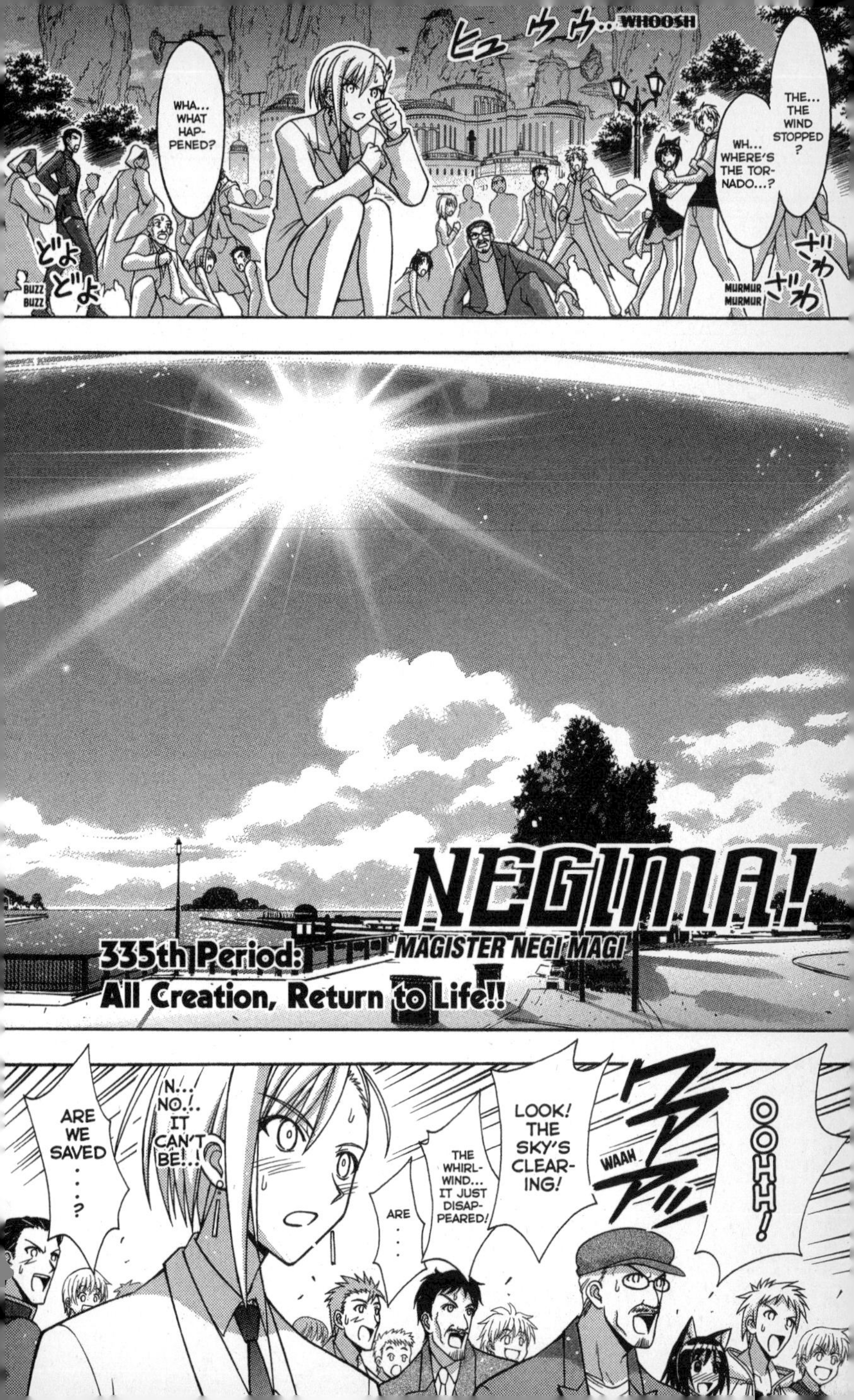
ヒュウウ.. WHOOSH
THE... THE WIND STOPPED?
WH... WHERE'S THE TORNADO...?
ざわざわ MURMUR MURMUR
WHA... WHAT HAPPENED?
どよどよ BUZZ BUZZ
NEGIMA!
MAGISTER NEGI MAGI
335th Period:
All Creation, Return to Life!!
OOHHH!
ワァッ WAAH
LOOK! THE SKY'S CLEARING!
THE WHIRLWIND... IT JUST DISAPPEARED!
ARE...
N... NO...! IT CAN'T BE...!
ARE WE SAVED...?

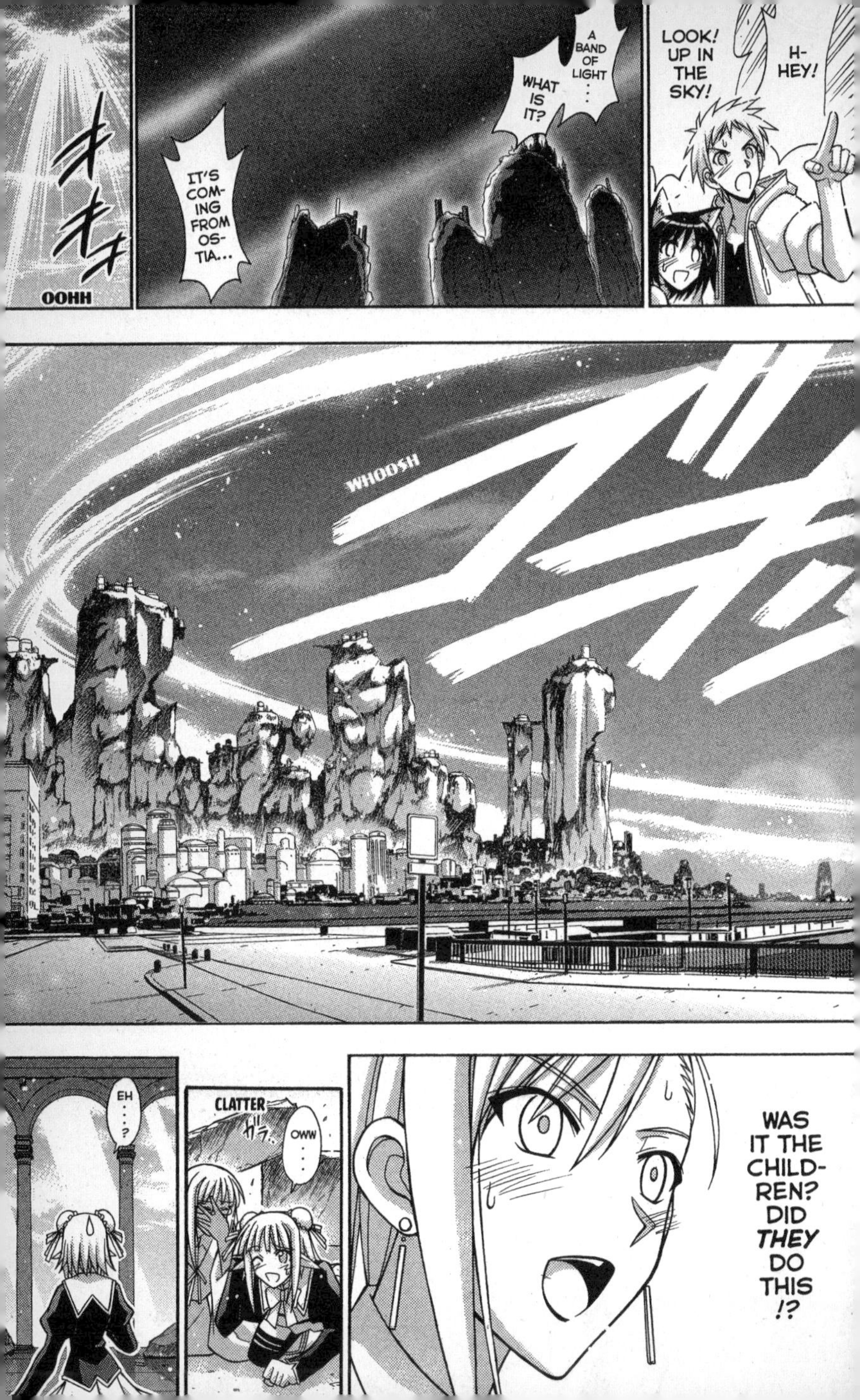
H-HEY!
LOOK! UP IN THE SKY!
A BAND OF LIGHT . . .
WHAT IS IT?
IT'S COMING FROM OSTIA...
OOHH
WHOOSH
WAS IT THE CHILDREN? DID *THEY* DO THIS!?
CLATTER
OWW . . .
EH . . . ?

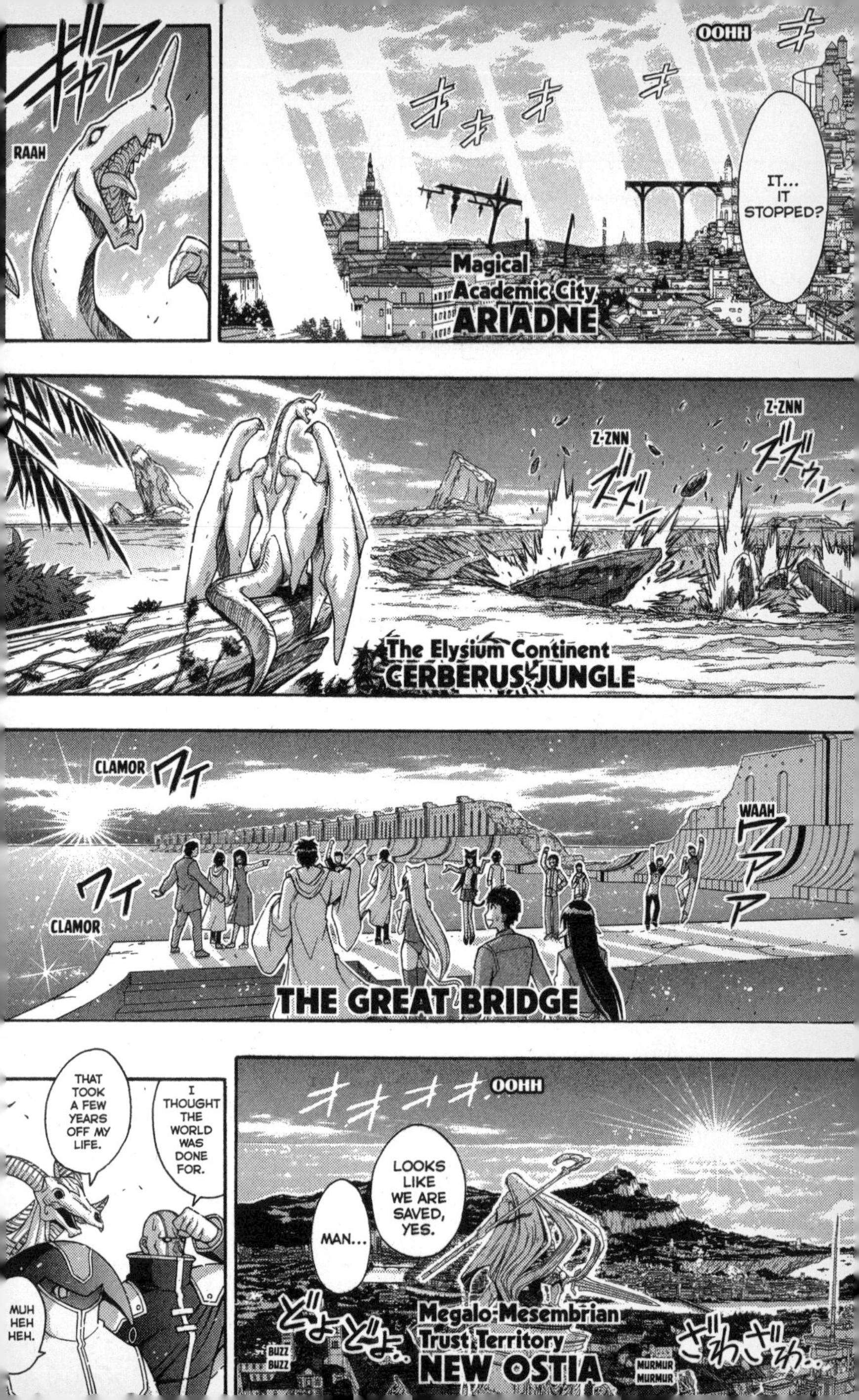
OOHH
IT... IT STOPPED?
Magical Academic City
ARIADNE
RAAH
Z-ZNN
Z-ZNN
The Elysium Continent
CERBERUS JUNGLE
WAAH
CLAMOR
CLAMOR
THE GREAT BRIDGE
OOHH
LOOKS LIKE WE ARE SAVED, YES.
MAN...
MURMUR MURMUR
Megalo-Mesembrian
Trust Territory
NEW OSTIA
BUZZ BUZZ
I THOUGHT THE WORLD WAS DONE FOR.
THAT TOOK A FEW YEARS OFF MY LIFE.
MUH HEH HEH.

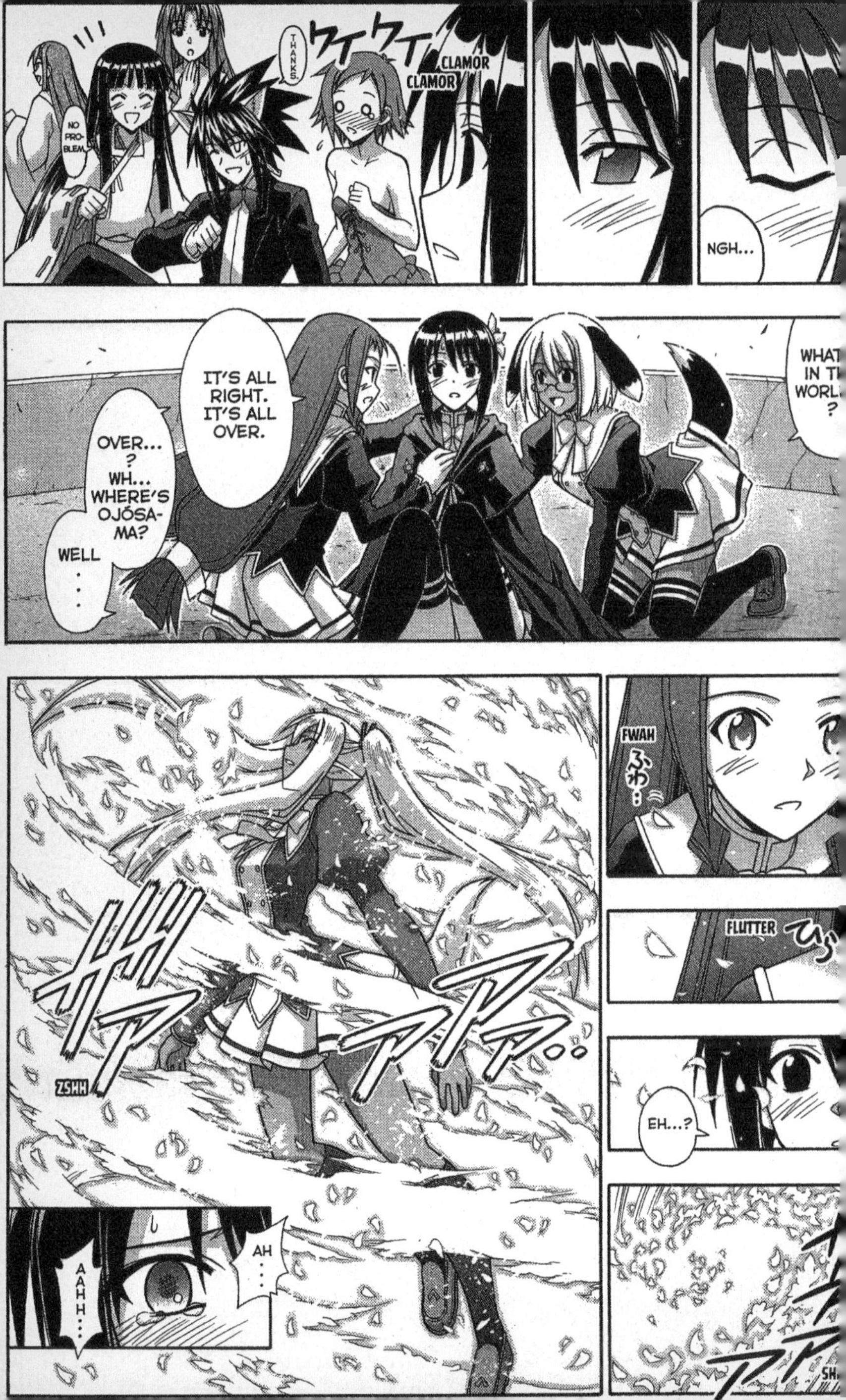
NGH...
CLAMOR
CLAMOR
ワイワイ
THANKS.
NO PROBLEM.
WHAT IN TH WORL ?
IT'S ALL RIGHT. IT'S ALL OVER.
OVER...? WH... WHERE'S OJŌSAMA?
WELL...
FWAH
ふわ…
FLUTTER
EH...?
ZSHH
AH...
AAHH...

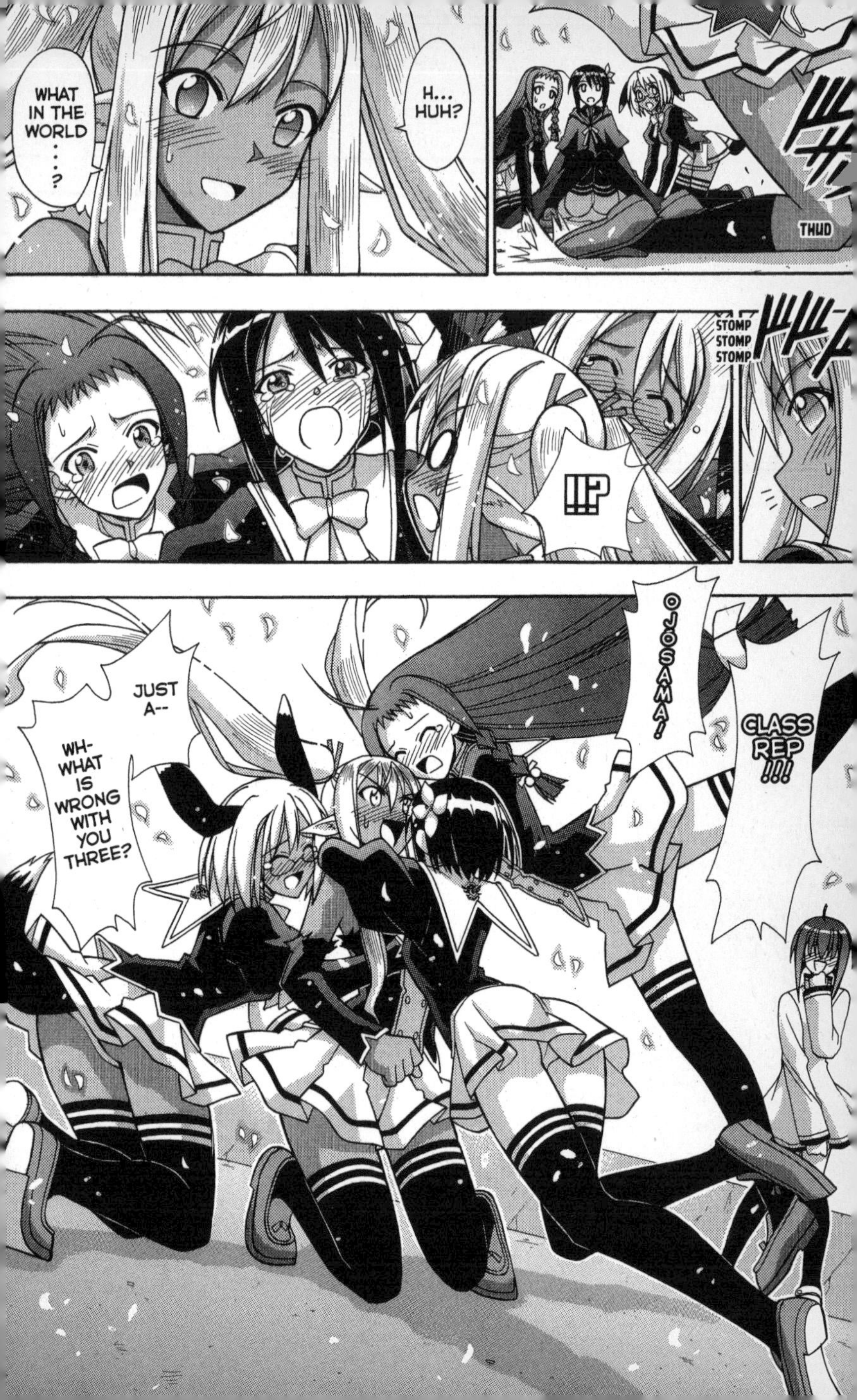
THUD
H... HUH?
WHAT IN THE WORLD ...?
STOMP STOMP STOMP
!!?
CLASS REP!!!
OJŌSAMA!
JUST A--
WH-WHAT IS WRONG WITH YOU THREE?

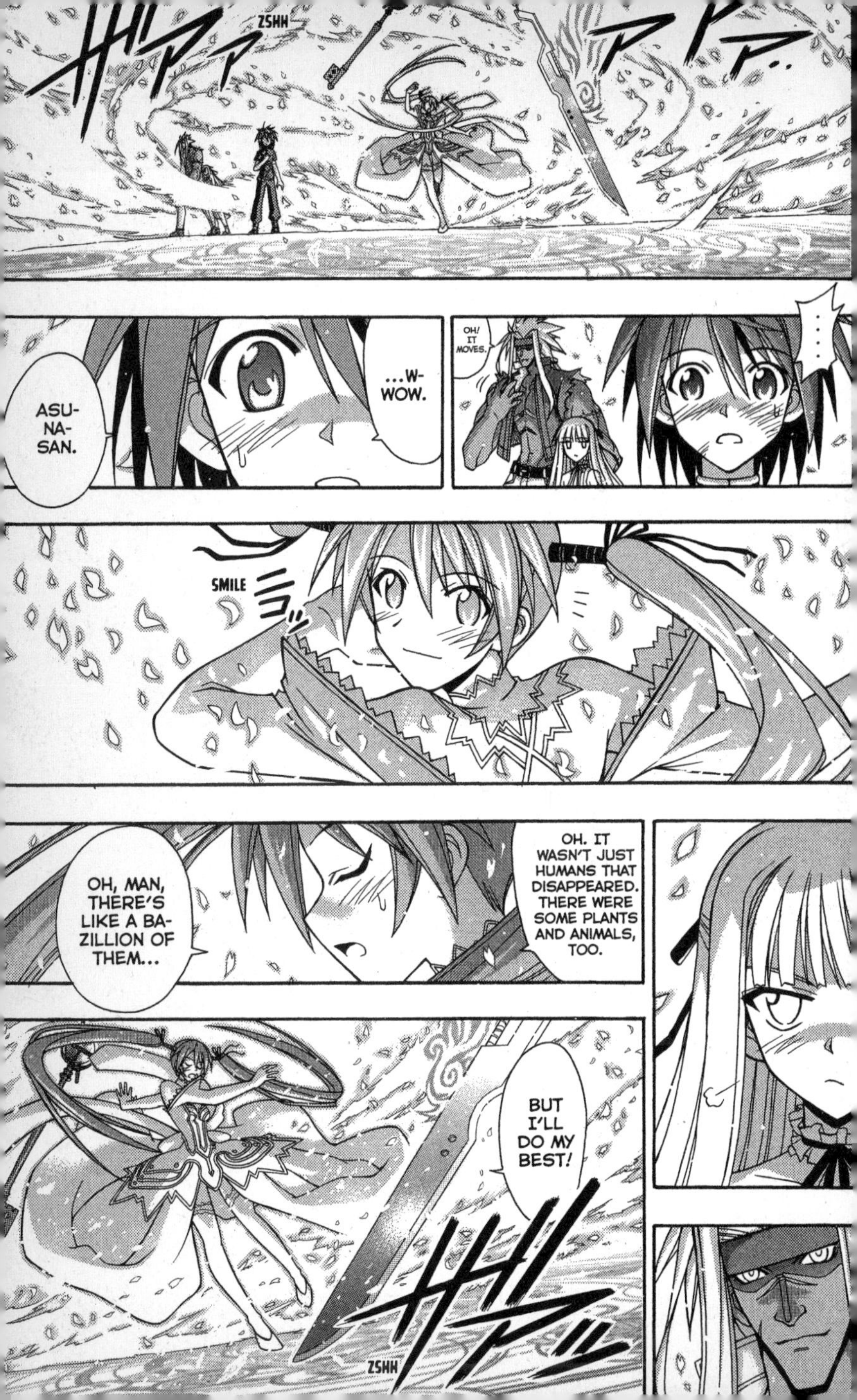
ZSHH
OH! IT MOVES.
...W-WOW.
ASUNA-SAN.
SMILE
OH. IT WASN'T JUST HUMANS THAT DISAPPEARED. THERE WERE SOME PLANTS AND ANIMALS, TOO.
OH, MAN, THERE'S LIKE A BAZILLION OF THEM...
BUT I'LL DO MY BEST!
ZSHH

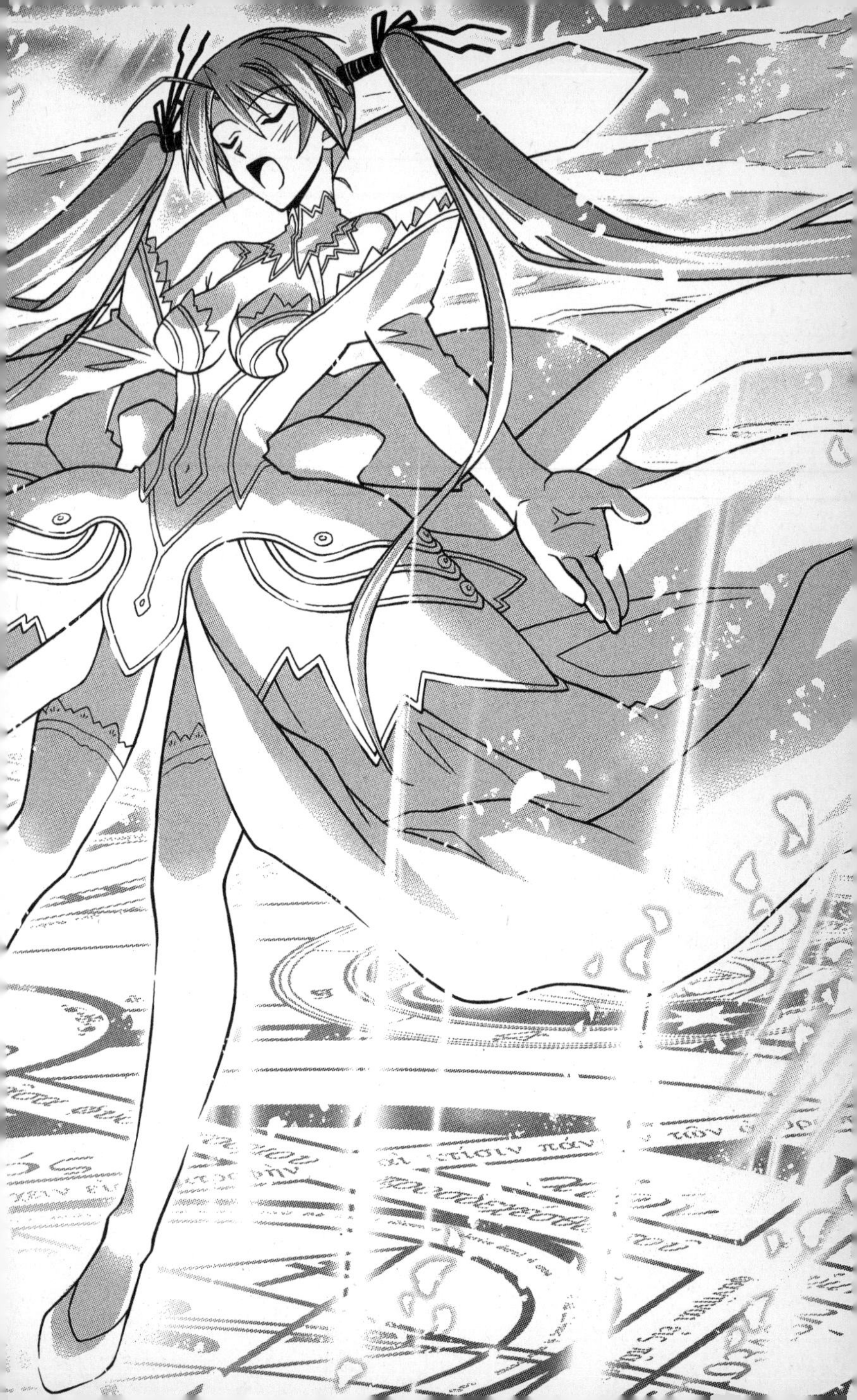

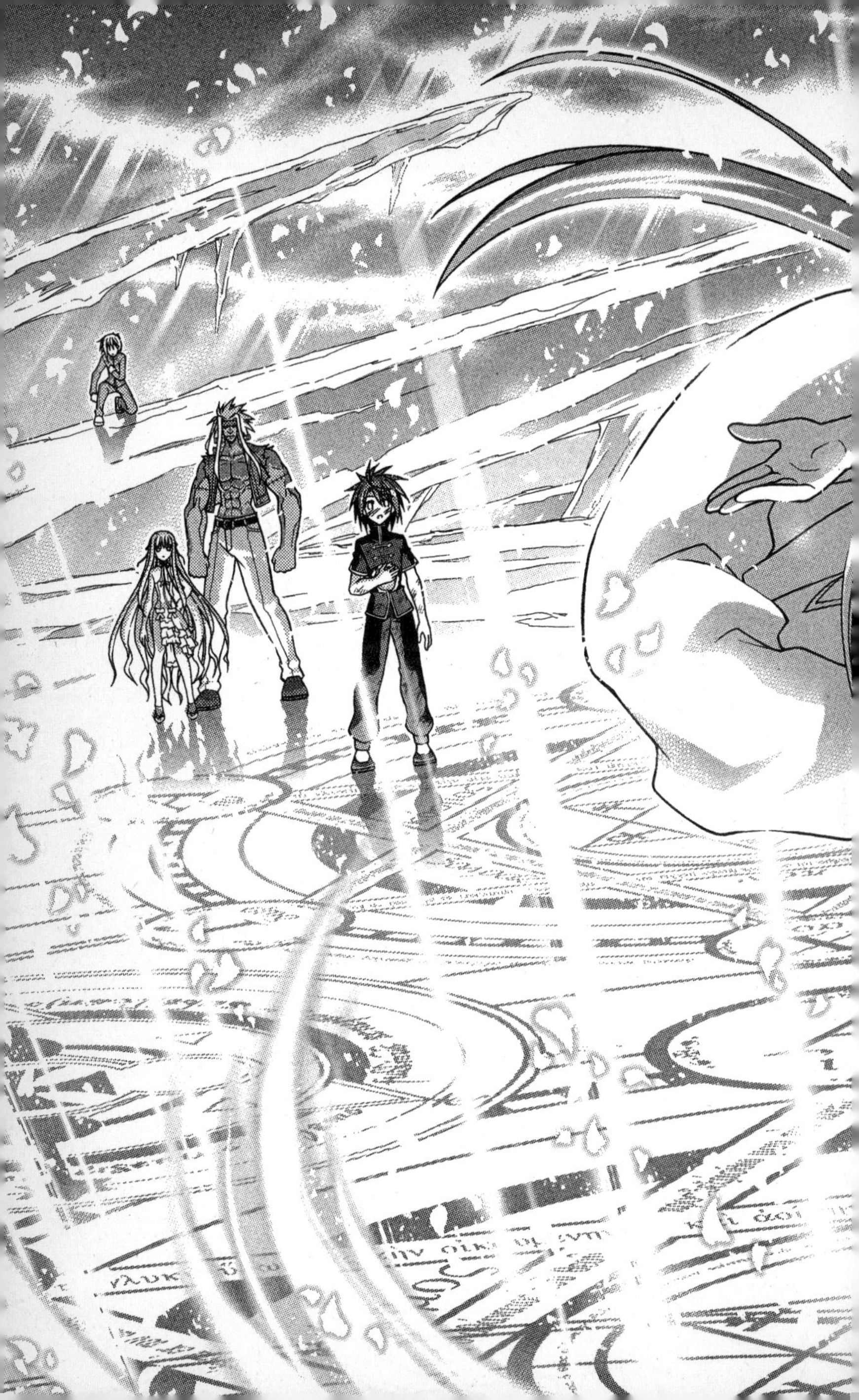

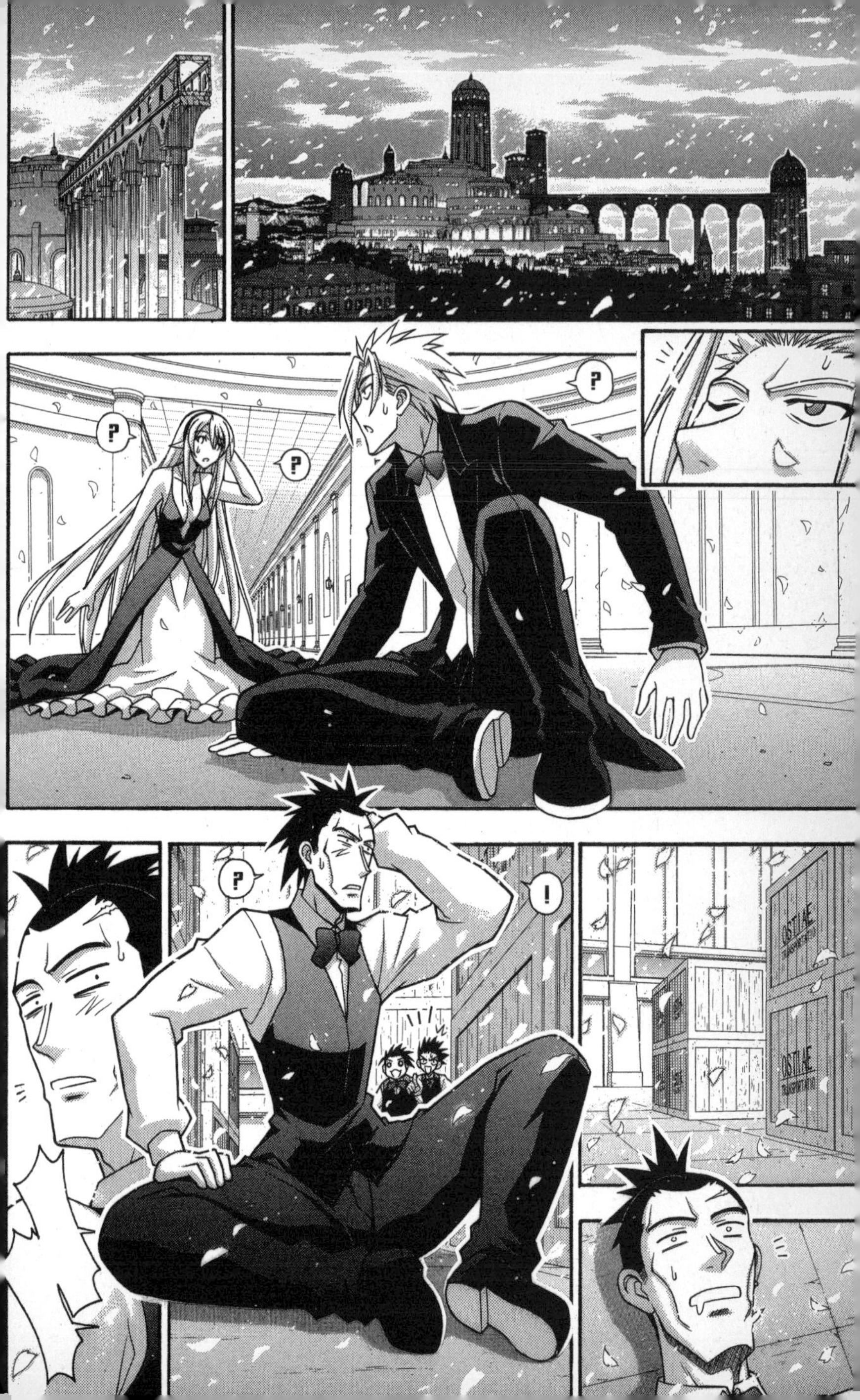
?
?
?
OSTIAE
OSTIAE
!
?

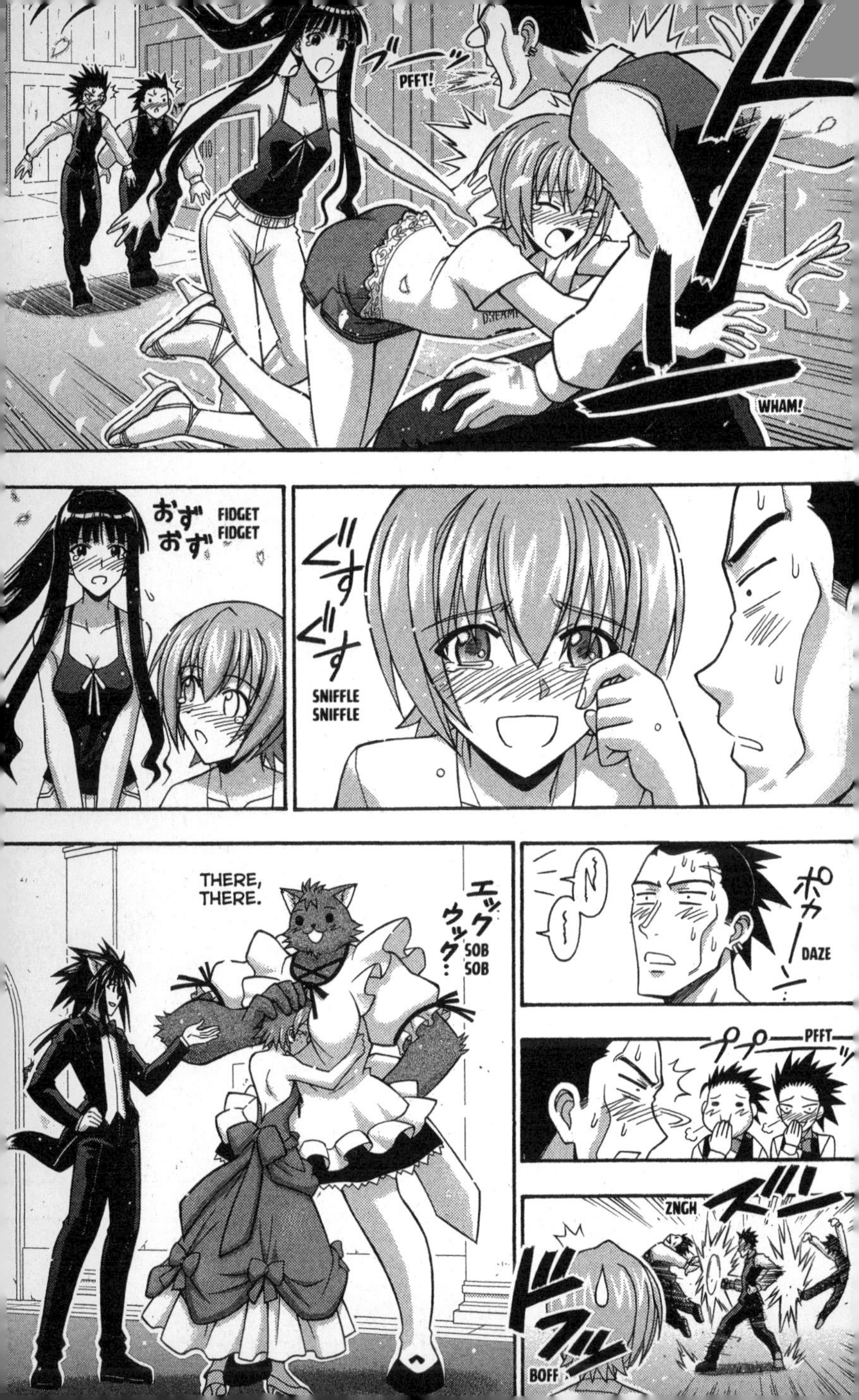

ブーッ
PFFT!
WHAM!
ぐすぐす
SNIFFLE SNIFFLE
おずおず
FIDGET FIDGET
N...
ポカーン
DAZE
PFFT
ZNGH
BOFF
THERE, THERE.
エックウック
SOB SOB

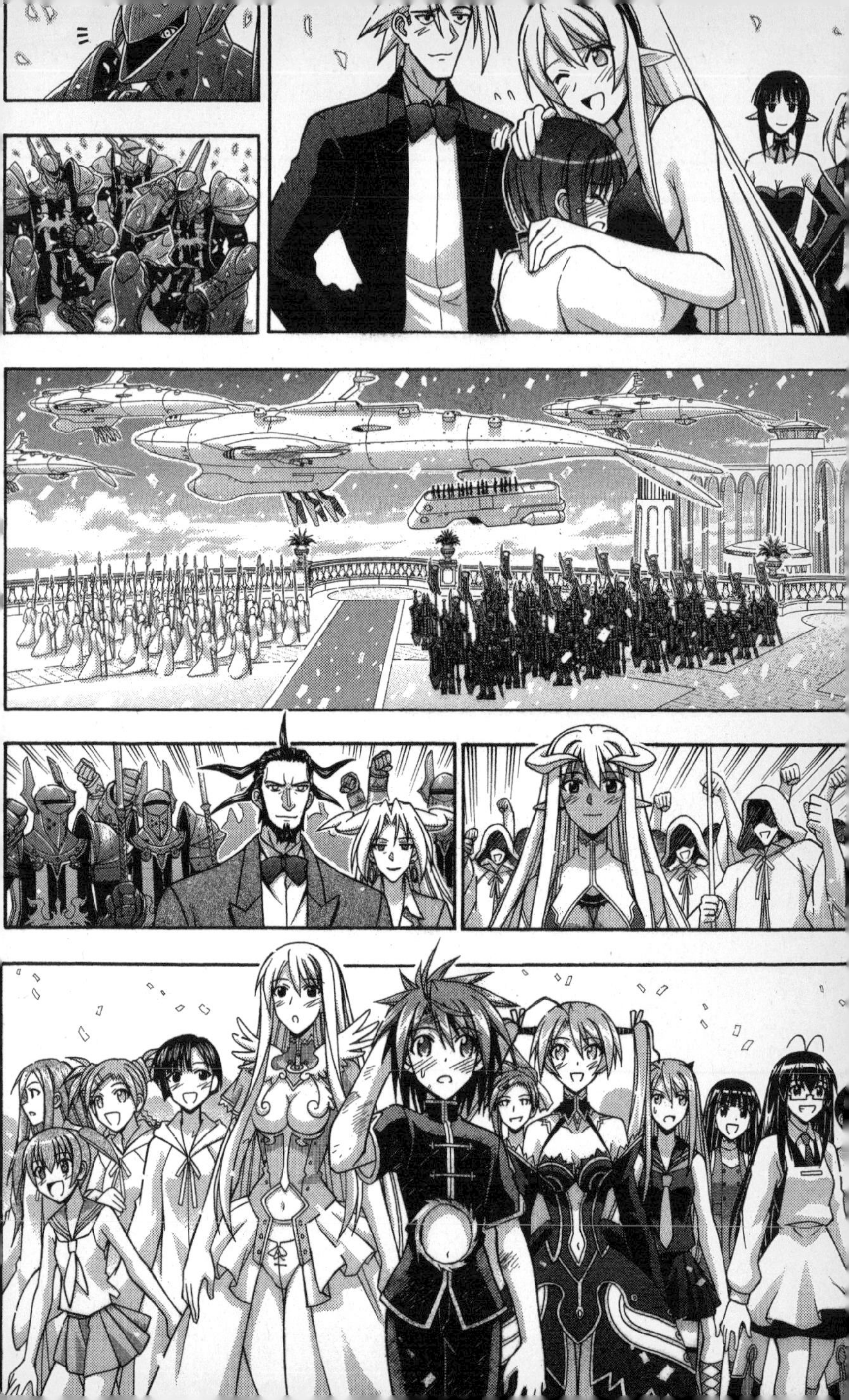

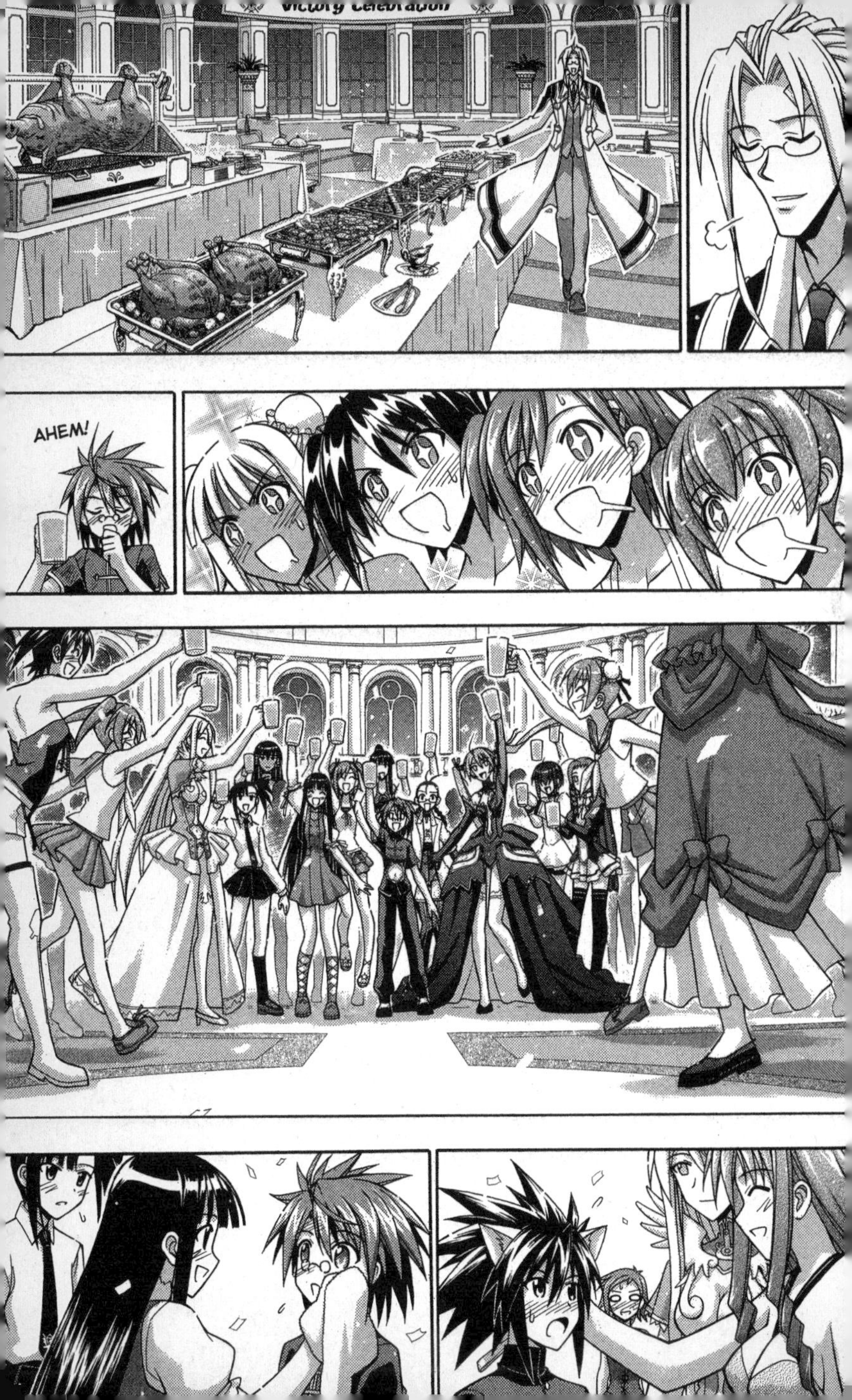
Victory Celebration
AHEM!

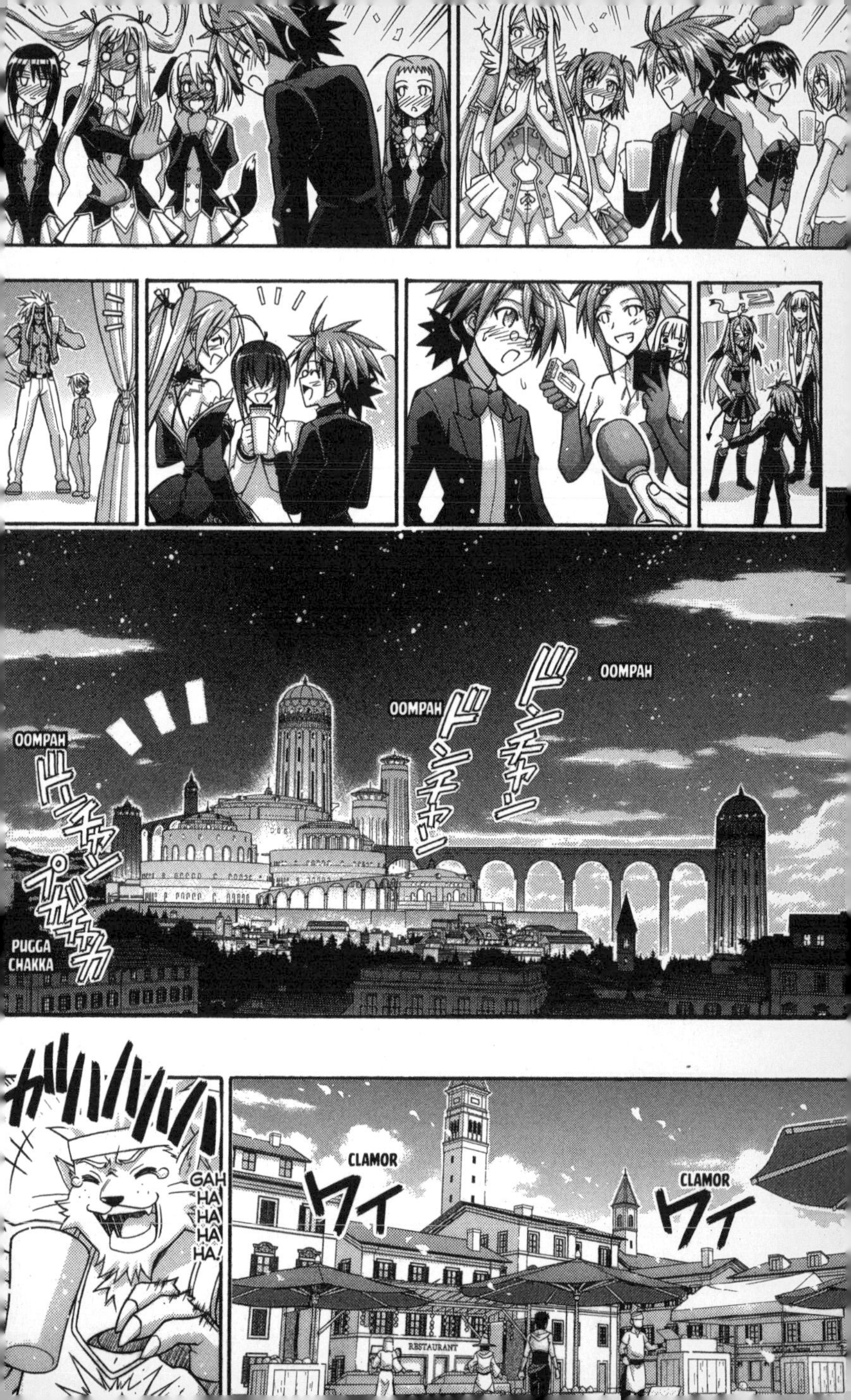
OOMPAH
OOMPAH
OOMPAH
PUGGA CHAKKA
CLAMOR
CLAMOR
GAH HA HA HA HA HA!

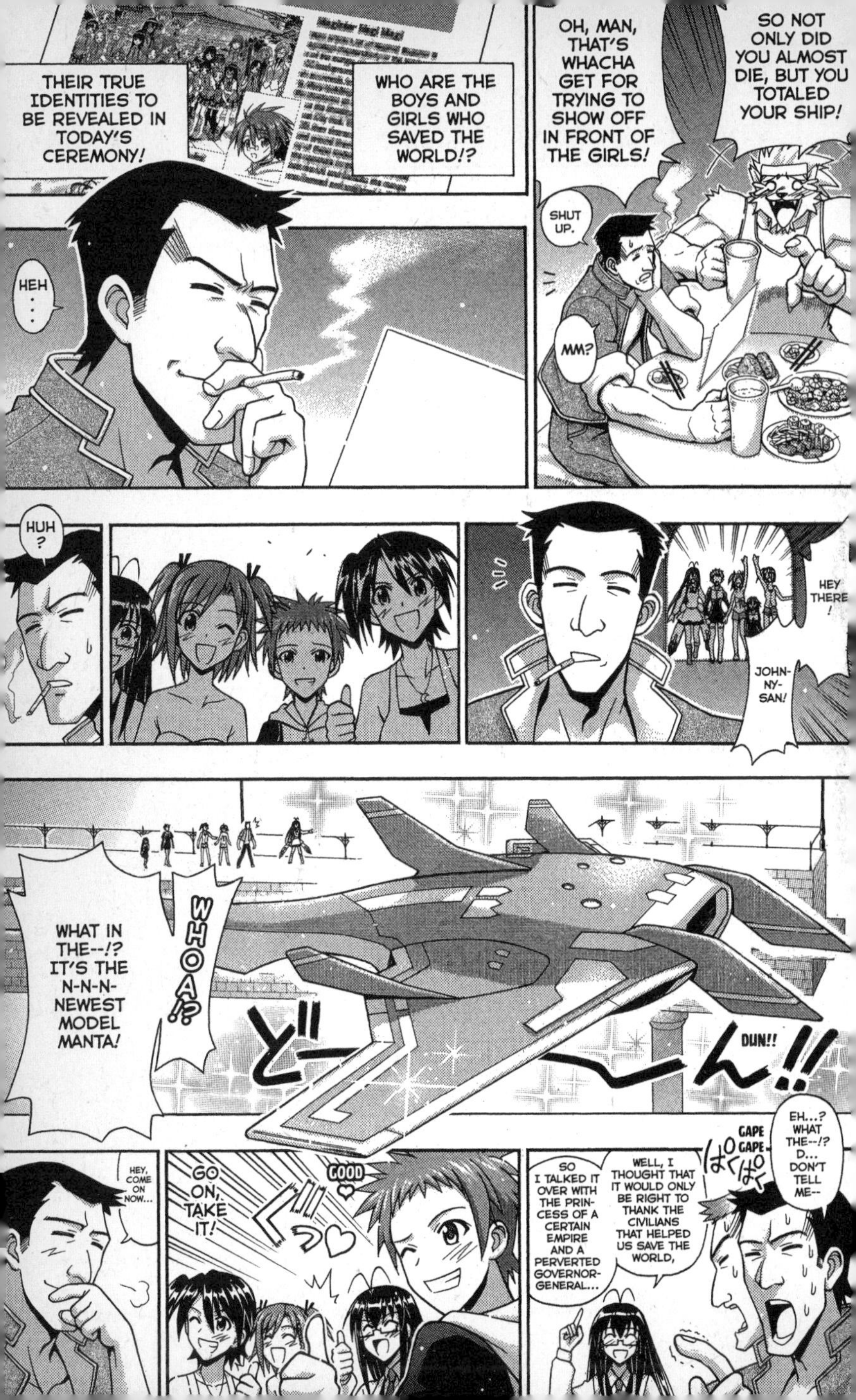
SO NOT ONLY DID YOU ALMOST DIE, BUT YOU TOTALED YOUR SHIP!
OH, MAN, THAT'S WHACHA GET FOR TRYING TO SHOW OFF IN FRONT OF THE GIRLS!
SHUT UP.
MM?
WHO ARE THE BOYS AND GIRLS WHO SAVED THE WORLD!?
THEIR TRUE IDENTITIES TO BE REVEALED IN TODAY'S CEREMONY!
HEH...
HEY THERE!
JOHN-NY-SAN!
HUH?
DUN!!
WHOA!?
WHAT IN THE--!? IT'S THE N-N-N-NEWEST MODEL MANTA!
EH...? WHAT THE--!? D... DON'T TELL ME--
GAPE GAPE
WELL, I THOUGHT THAT IT WOULD ONLY BE RIGHT TO THANK THE CIVILIANS THAT HELPED US SAVE THE WORLD,
SO I TALKED IT OVER WITH THE PRIN-CESS OF A CERTAIN EMPIRE AND A PERVERTED GOVERNOR-GENERAL...
GOOD
GO ON, TAKE IT!
HEY, COME ON NOW...

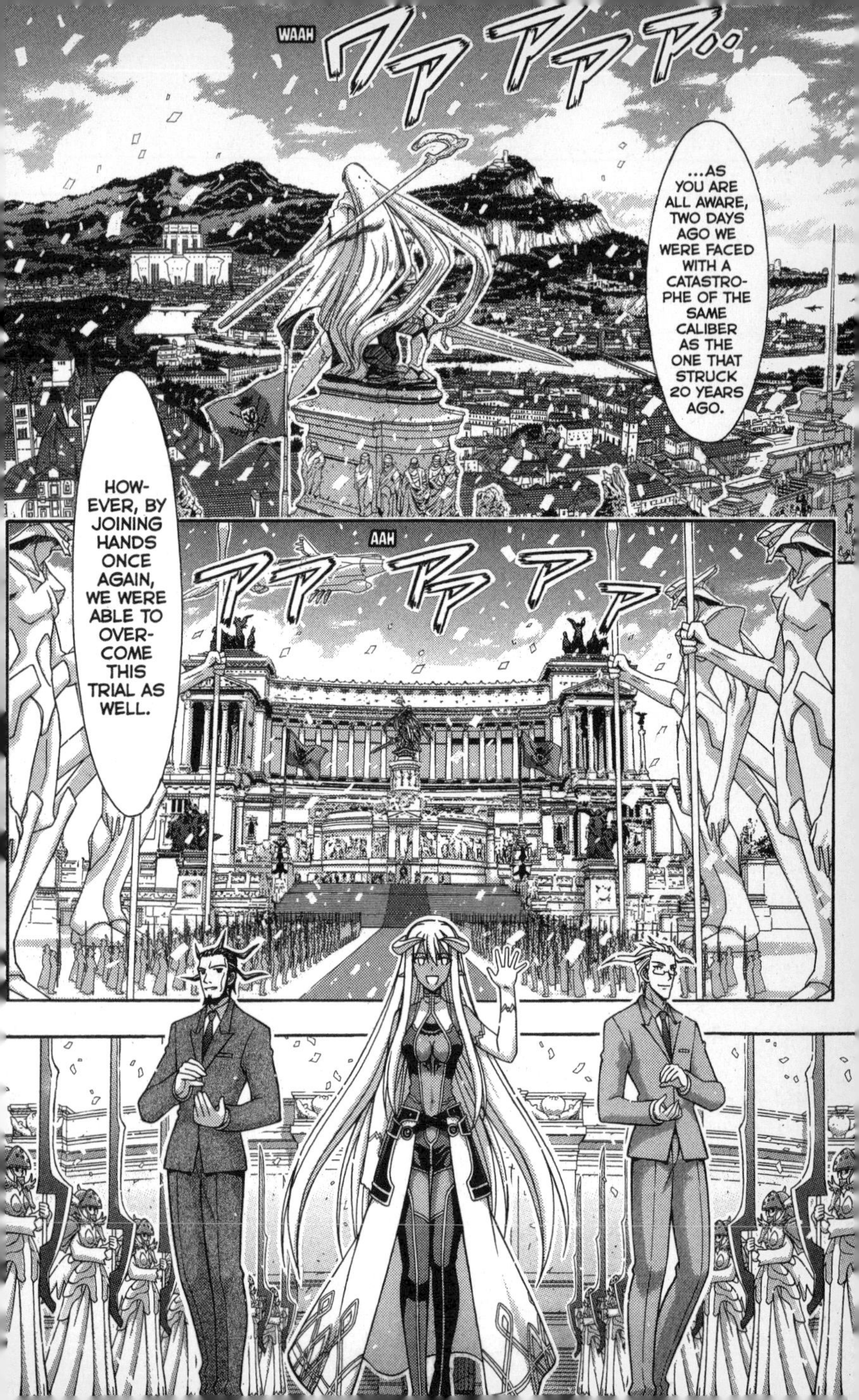
WAAH
...AS YOU ARE ALL AWARE, TWO DAYS AGO WE WERE FACED WITH A CATASTRO-PHE OF THE SAME CALIBER AS THE ONE THAT STRUCK 20 YEARS AGO.
HOW-EVER, BY JOINING HANDS ONCE AGAIN, WE WERE ABLE TO OVER-COME THIS TRIAL AS WELL.
AAH

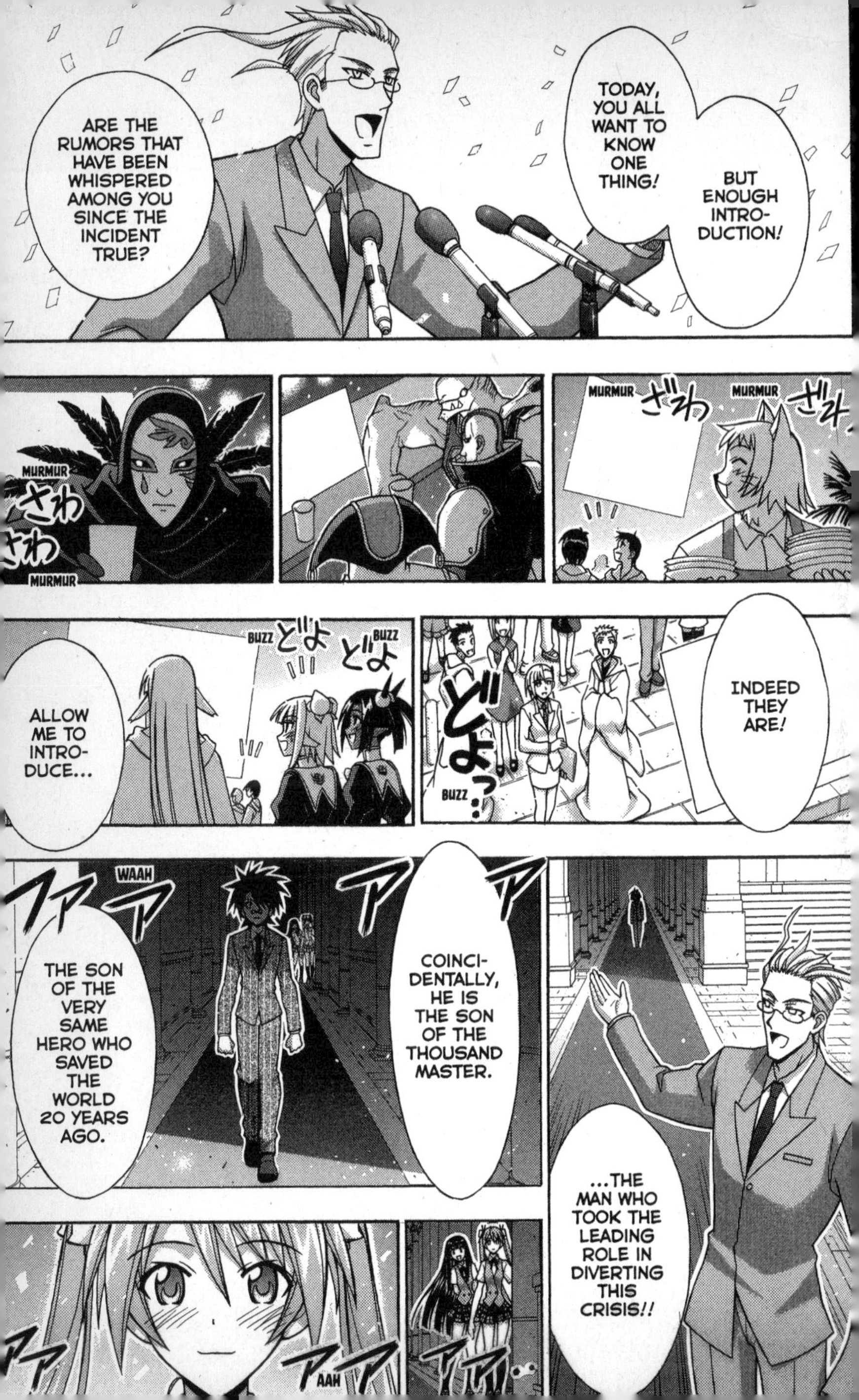
BUT ENOUGH INTRODUCTION!
TODAY, YOU ALL WANT TO KNOW ONE THING!
ARE THE RUMORS THAT HAVE BEEN WHISPERED AMONG YOU SINCE THE INCIDENT TRUE?
MURMUR ざわ
MURMUR ざわ
MURMUR さわ さわ MURMUR
INDEED THEY ARE!
どよっ BUZZ
BUZZ どよ
BUZZ どよ
ALLOW ME TO INTRODUCE...
...THE MAN WHO TOOK THE LEADING ROLE IN DIVERTING THIS CRISIS!!
ア
COINCIDENTALLY, HE IS THE SON OF THE THOUSAND MASTER.
ア
WAAH
ファア
THE SON OF THE VERY SAME HERO WHO SAVED THE WORLD 20 YEARS AGO.
アア AAH
アア

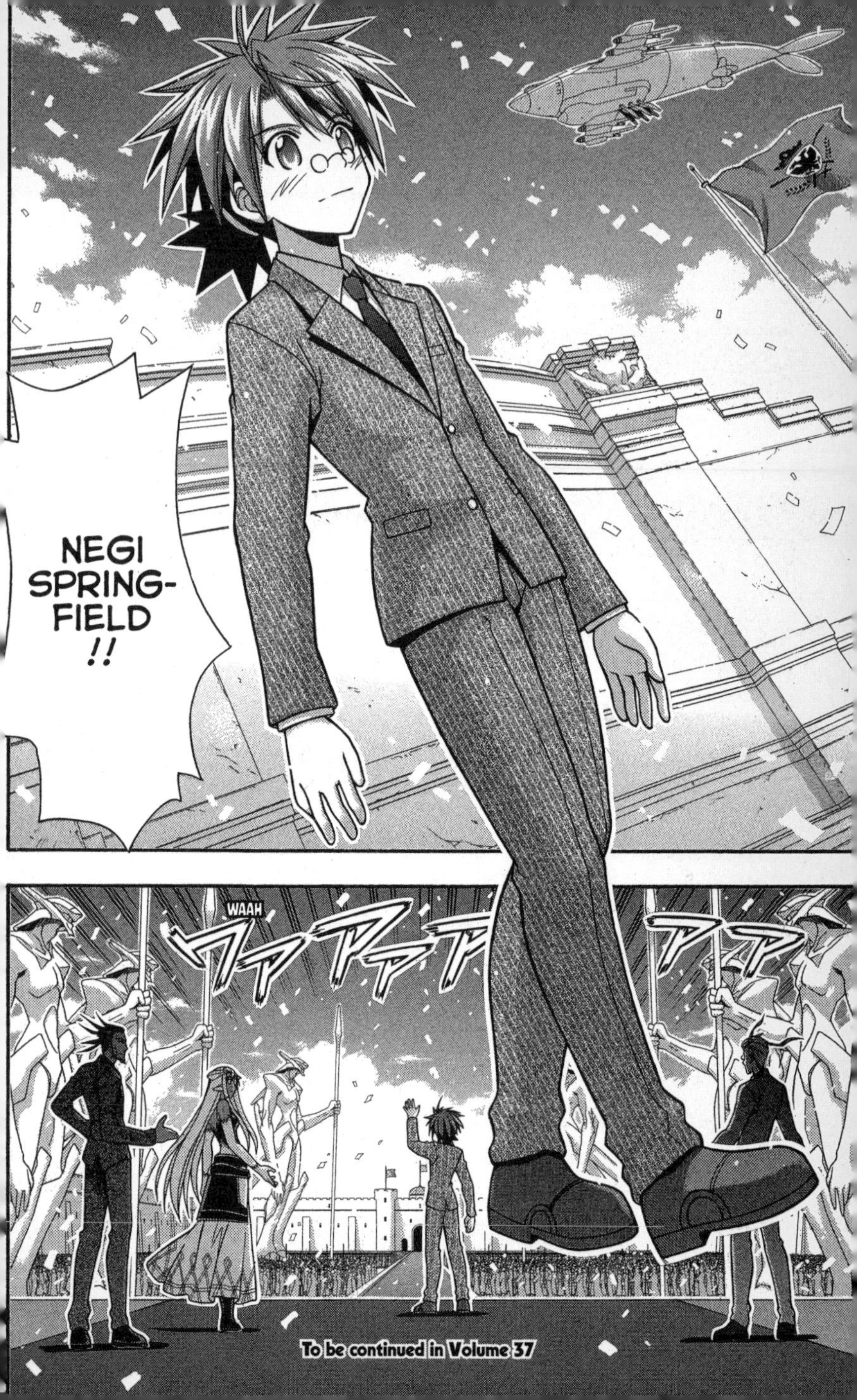
NEGI SPRING-FIELD !!
WAAH
To be continued in Volume 37

-STAFF-

Ken Akamatsu

Takashi Takemoto

Kenichi Nakamura

Keiichi Yamashita

Tohru Mitsuhashi

Yuichi Yoshida

Susumu Kuwabara

Thanks to
Ran Ayanaga

Character Profile

• Tsukuyomi

Setsuna's rival character, a Shinmei swords-woman who showed up in the Class Trip Arc.

She's very skilled with the sword, which is why she still looked so composed, even when up against Tatsumiya.

Technically, her glasses are supposed to be her weakness.

Like Tsuruko in LOVE HINA, she's even stronger when in demon mode, and easily overpowered Setsuna after obtaining the Demon Blade Hina. But in the end, she lost to the power of love.

THAT DOESN'T SOUND QUITE RIGHT! AND IS SHE DEAD OR WHAT!?

In the OADs, she is voiced by Rie Kugimiya-san. In the first anime series, she was voiced by Hiromi Tsunakake-san. They're such big names, it's a real shame she's in the anime so little!! (laugh)

Akamatsu

魔法先生ネギま!
MAGISTER NEGI MAGI

赤松 健
SHONEN MAGAZINE COMICS
KEN AKAMATSU

36

The What and Why of Negima!?

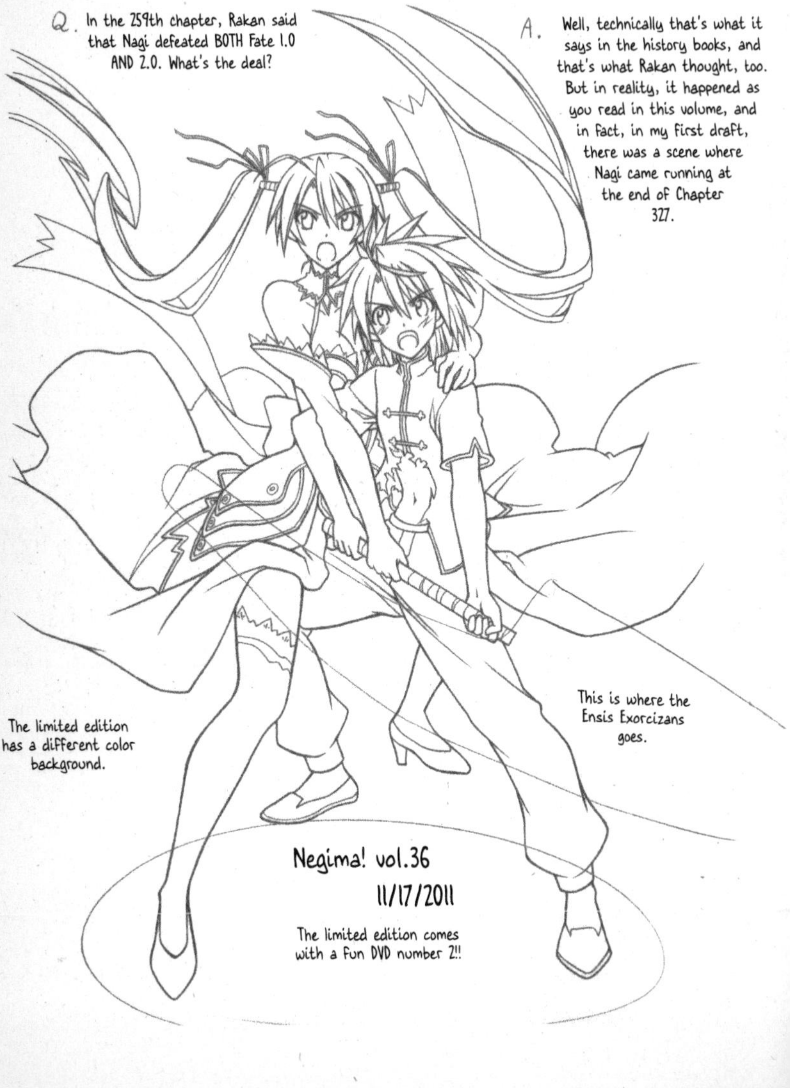
Q. In the 259th chapter, Rakan said that Nagi defeated BOTH Fate 1.0 AND 2.0. What's the deal?
A. Well, technically that's what it says in the history books, and that's what Rakan thought, too. But in reality, it happened as you read in this volume, and in fact, in my first draft, there was a scene where Nagi came running at the end of Chapter 327.
The limited edition has a different color background.
This is where the Ensis Exorcizans goes.
Negima! vol.36
11/17/2011
The limited edition comes with a fun DVD number 2!!

Translation Notes

Japanese is a tricky language for most Westerners, and translation is often more art than science. For your edification and reading pleasure, here are notes on some of the places where we could have gone in a different direction with our translation of the work, or where a Japanese cultural reference is used.

One-handshake deathmatch, page 9

A one-handshake deathmatch is a fight in which the combatants shake hands at the beginning, then, keeping hold of each other's hand, they fight to the death one-handed.

Mundus Gelans, page 31

Those of you well-versed in Latin may have noticed that this incantation is somehow familiar. The first half of the spell matches in translation the High Ancient spell Evangeline uses in volume six, "Ending World." The second half is the incantation to trap the caster's enemy in ice (as opposed to shattering the enemy). In other words, this is the Latin version of "Frozen World." As to why Septendecim chooses Latin over Greek, that remains a mystery, but as it is assumed that Ancient Greek is a superior language to Latin, we can only imagine that Evangeline's spell is more powerful.

Pontiki, page 64

It may seem like Nagi is making up names to call Fate, but in fact, a pontiki is a kind of toy in Japan. It's a type of construction set, where the pieces are used to build strange creatures, also known as pontiki. Since Fate keeps calling himself a doll and a puppet, it makes sense that Nagi would use the name of a toy as an insult.

APERANTOS LEFKOS OURANOS, page 145

The translators thought this spell would look cooler in Greek, so we left that way in the story. For anyone who's curious, here's the English translation: "Obey your contract and hear me, eternal queen of darkness and snow! Blooming white roses of ice, garden eternally in sleep! Come, everlasting darkness, eternal river of ice! Arrest the soulless toys in frigid lightning! Fantastic silence, white roses in bloom, endless prison! INFINITE WHITE HEAVEN!!"

Preview for Volume 37

Enjoy these preview pages from Negima! volume 37 and check www.kodanshacomics.com to see when it'll be available!

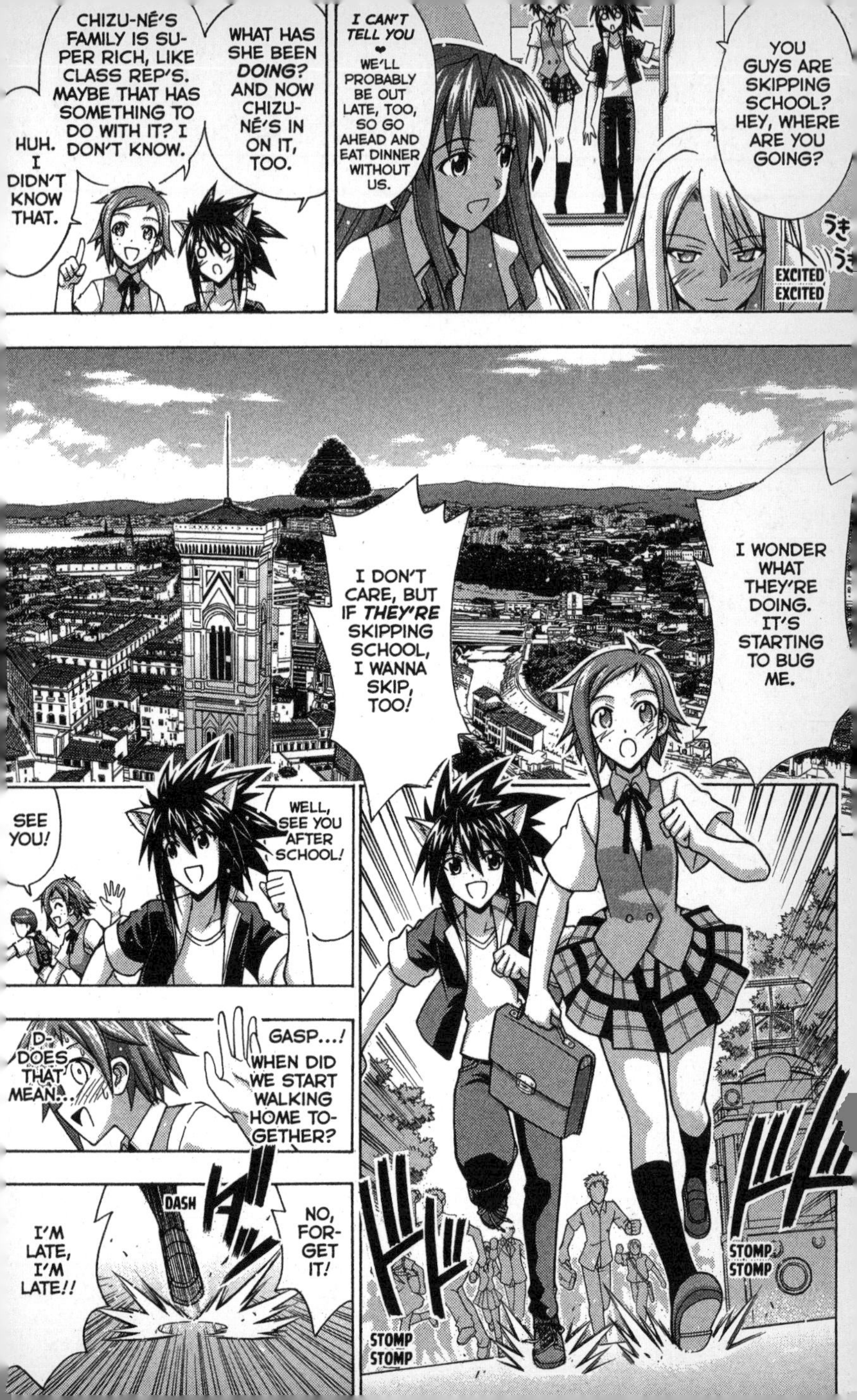
YOU GUYS ARE SKIPPING SCHOOL? HEY, WHERE ARE YOU GOING?
I CAN'T TELL YOU ❤ WE'LL PROBABLY BE OUT LATE, TOO, SO GO AHEAD AND EAT DINNER WITHOUT US.
EXCITED EXCITED
WHAT HAS SHE BEEN *DOING*? AND NOW CHIZU-NÉ'S IN ON IT, TOO.
CHIZU-NÉ'S FAMILY IS SUPER RICH, LIKE CLASS REP'S. MAYBE THAT HAS SOMETHING TO DO WITH IT? I DON'T KNOW.
HUH. I DIDN'T KNOW THAT.
I WONDER WHAT THEY'RE DOING. IT'S STARTING TO BUG ME.
I DON'T CARE, BUT IF *THEY'RE* SKIPPING SCHOOL, I WANNA SKIP, TOO!
STOMP STOMP
STOMP STOMP
WELL, SEE YOU AFTER SCHOOL!
SEE YOU!
GASP...! WHEN DID WE START WALKING HOME TOGETHER?
D-DOES THAT MEAN...
NO, FORGET IT!
DASH
I'M LATE, I'M LATE!!

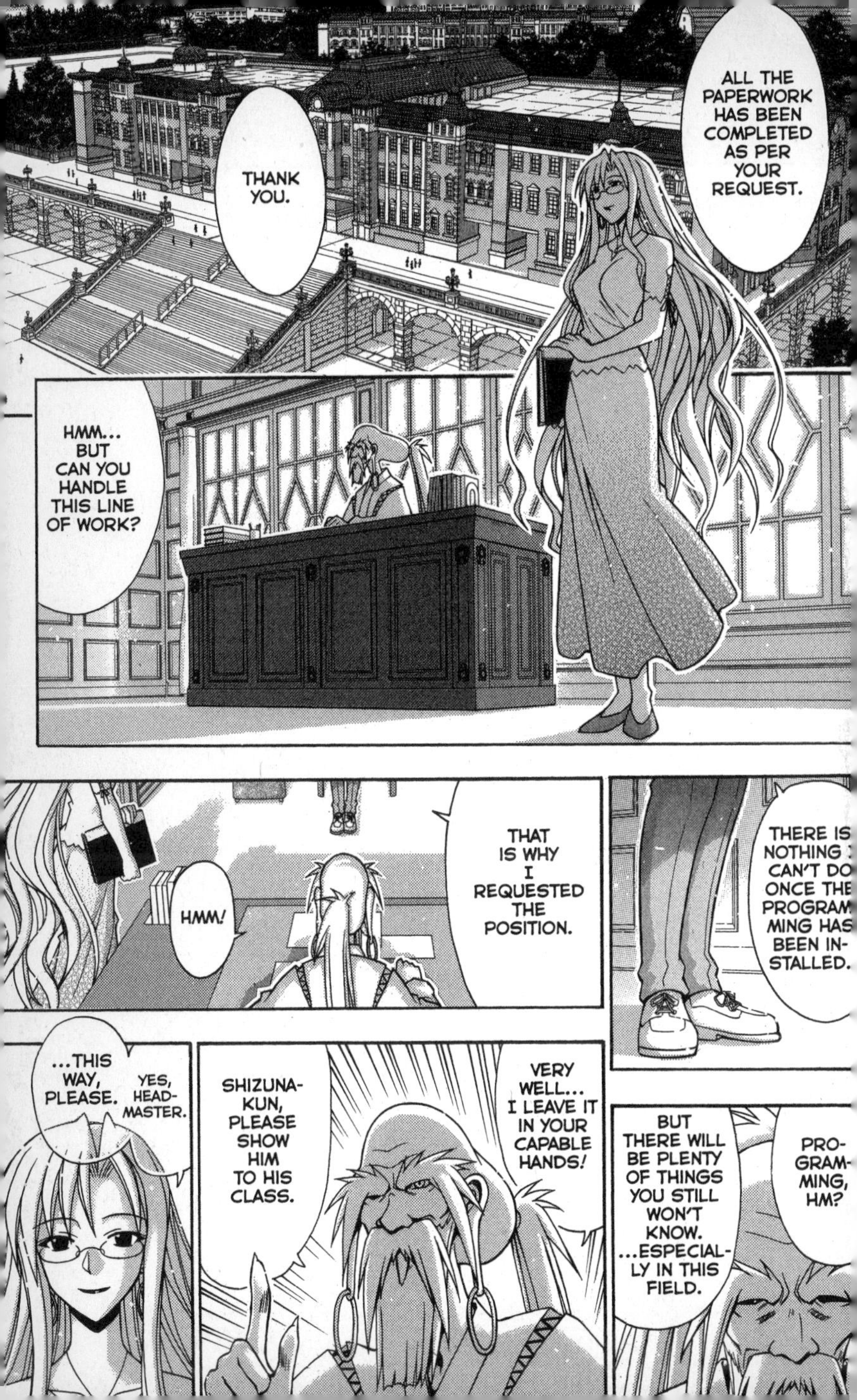
ALL THE PAPERWORK HAS BEEN COMPLETED AS PER YOUR REQUEST.
THANK YOU.
HMM... BUT CAN YOU HANDLE THIS LINE OF WORK?
THERE IS NOTHING I CAN'T DO ONCE THE PROGRAMMING HAS BEEN INSTALLED.
THAT IS WHY I REQUESTED THE POSITION.
HMM!
PROGRAMMING, HM?
BUT THERE WILL BE PLENTY OF THINGS YOU STILL WON'T KNOW. ...ESPECIALLY IN THIS FIELD.
VERY WELL... I LEAVE IT IN YOUR CAPABLE HANDS!
SHIZUNA-KUN, PLEASE SHOW HIM TO HIS CLASS.
YES, HEADMASTER.
...THIS WAY, PLEASE.

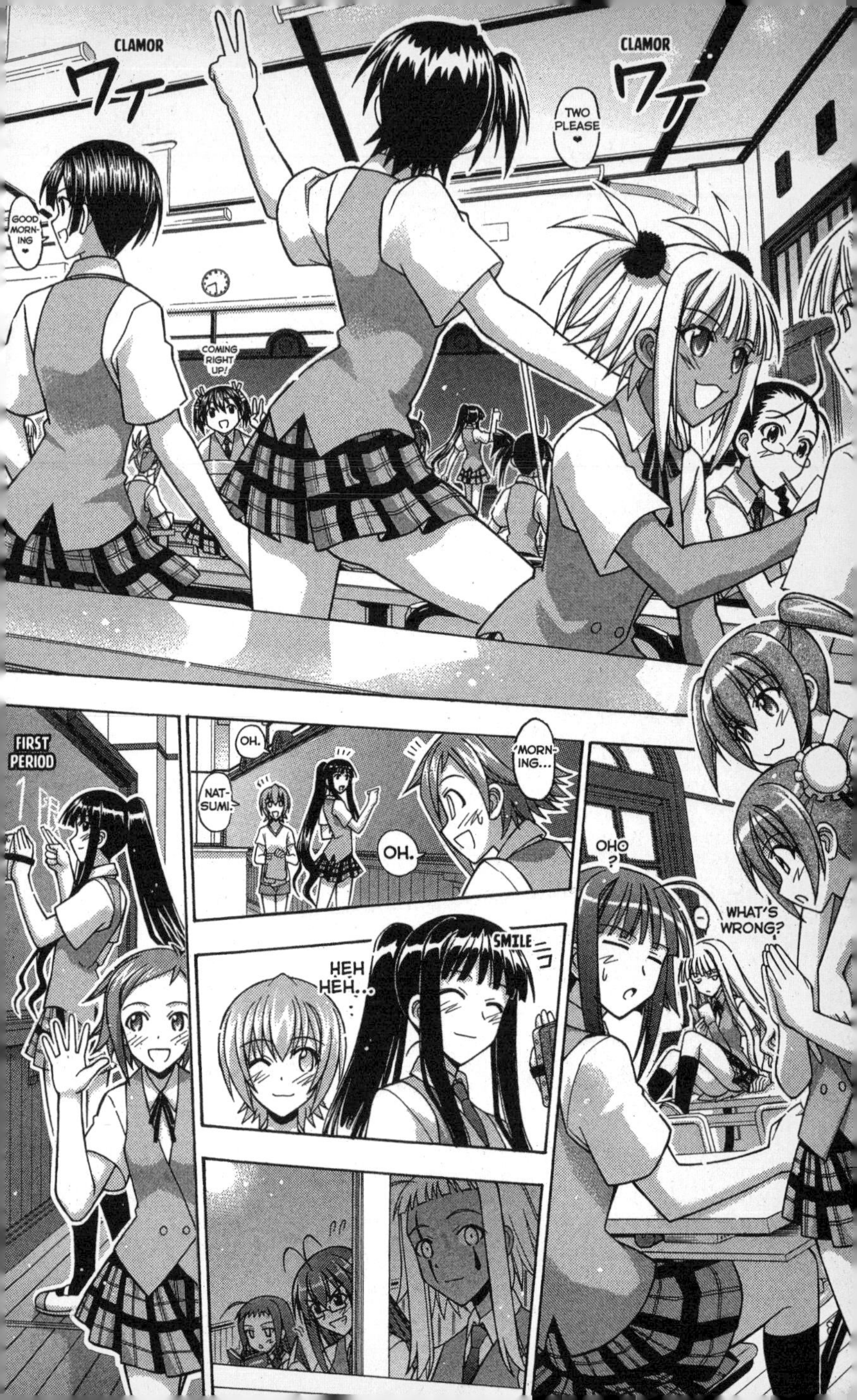
CLAMOR
ワイ
TWO PLEASE ❤
CLAMOR
ワイ
GOOD MORN-ING ❤
COMING RIGHT UP!
OHO ?
WHAT'S WRONG?
'MORN-ING...
OH.
NAT-SUMI.
OH.
SMILE
HEH HEH...
FIRST PERIOD

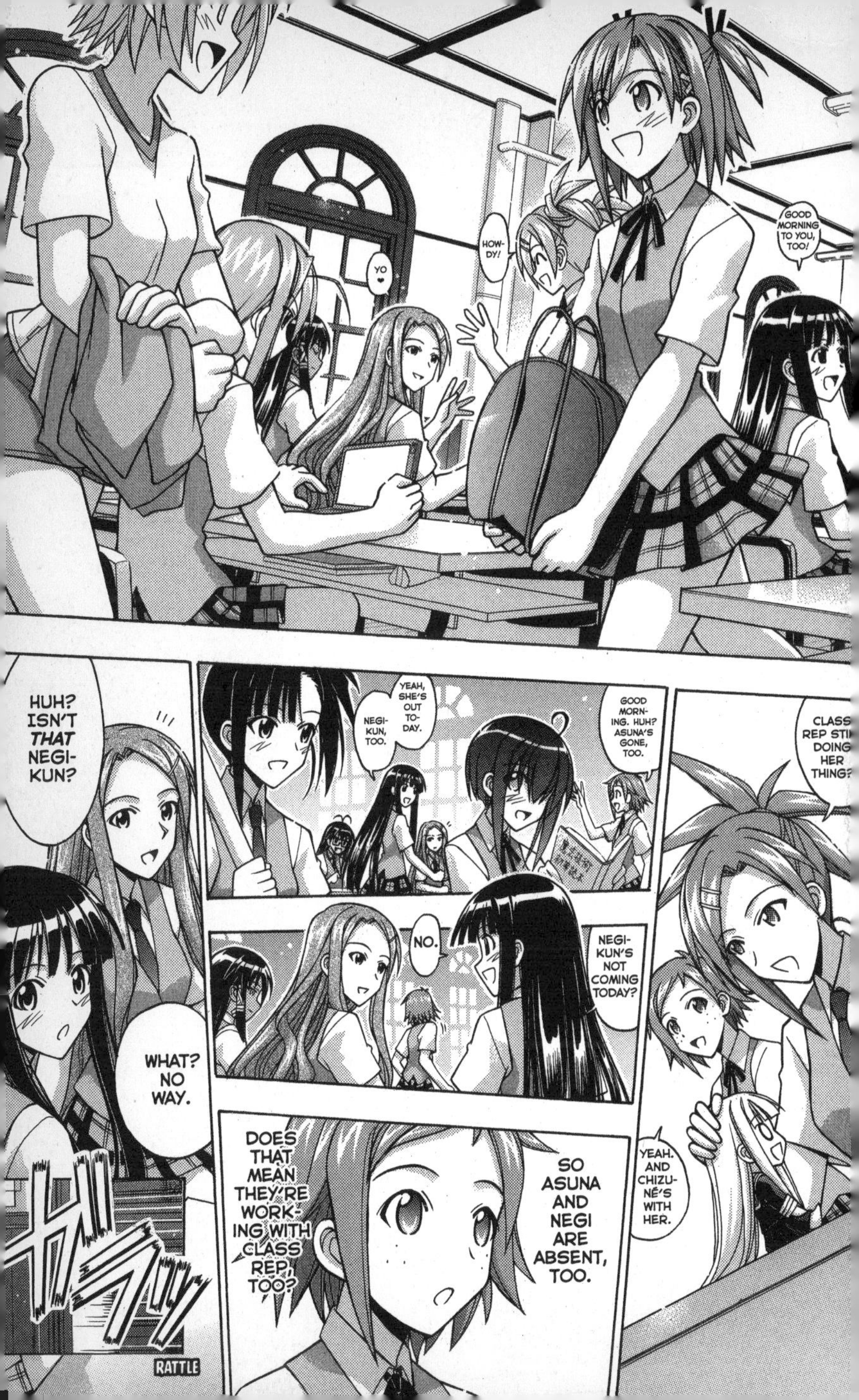
GOOD MORNING TO YOU, TOO!
HOW-DY!
YO ♥
CLASS REP STI DOING HER THING?
YEAH. AND CHIZUNÉ'S WITH HER.
GOOD MORNING. HUH? ASUNA'S GONE, TOO.
YEAH, SHE'S OUT TODAY.
NEGI-KUN, TOO.
NEGI-KUN'S NOT COMING TODAY?
NO.
SO ASUNA AND NEGI ARE ABSENT, TOO.
DOES THAT MEAN THEY'RE WORKING WITH CLASS REP, TOO?
HUH? ISN'T *THAT* NEGI-KUN?
WHAT? NO WAY.
RATTLE

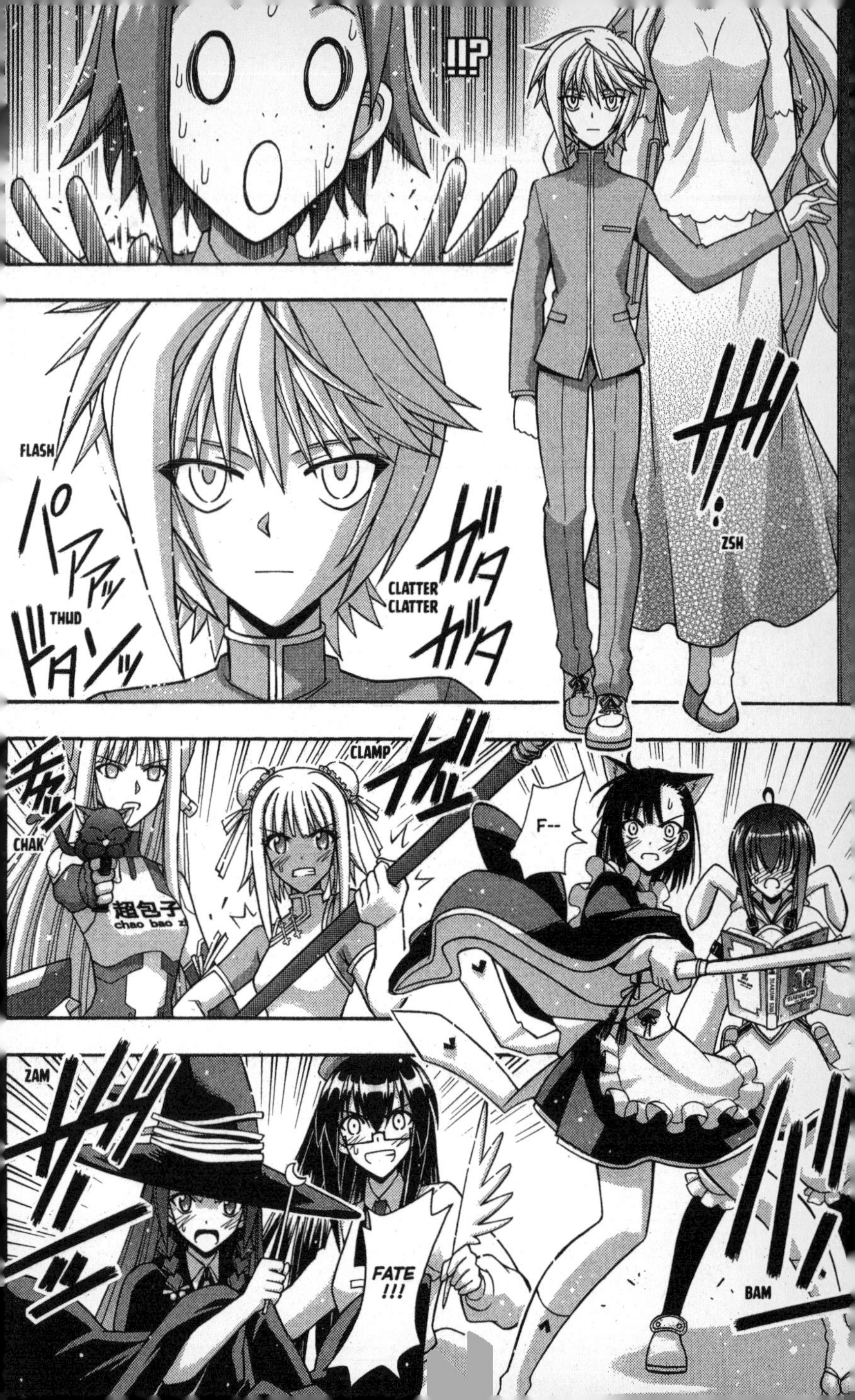

ZSH
!!?
CLATTER CLATTER
FLASH
THUD
CLAMP
F--
CHAK
超包子
chao bao zi
BAM
FATE !!!
ZAM

FROM HIRO MASHIMA, CREATOR OF RAVE MASTER

FAIRY TAIL

FAIRY TAIL 1
Hiro Mashima Creator of Rave Master

FAIRY TAIL 2
Hiro Mashima Creator of Rave Master

Lucy has always dreamed of joining the Fairy Tail, a club for the most powerful sorcerers in the land. But once she becomes a member, the fun really starts!

Special extras in each volume! Read them all!

RATING T AGES 13+

VISIT WWW.KODANSHACOMICS.COM TO:

- View release date calendars for upcoming volumes
- Find out the latest about new Kodansha Comics series

KC KODANSHA COMICS

ANIMAL LAND

BY MAKOTO RAIKU

In a world of animals, where the strong eat the weak, Monoko the tanuki stumbles across a strange creature the likes of which has never been seen before–a human baby! While the newborn has no claws or teeth to protect itself, it does have the special ability to speak to and understand all different animals. Can the gift of speech between species change the balance of power in a land where the weak must always fear the strong?

ANIMAL LAND 1

MAKOTO RAIKU

Ages 13+

Negima! volume 36 is a work of fiction. Names, characters, places, and incidents are the products of the author's imagination or are used fictitiously. Any resemblance to actual events, locales, or persons, living or dead, is entirely coincidental.

A Kodansha Comics Trade Paperback Original

Published in the United States by Kodansha Comics, an imprint of Kodansha USA Publishing, LLC, New York.

Publication rights arranged through Kodansha Ltd., Tokyo.

First published in Japan in 2011 by Kodansha Ltd., Tokyo, as *Maho sensei Negima!*, volume 36.

ISBN 978-1-61262-239-2

Printed in the United States of America

www.kodanshacomics.com

9 8 7 6 5 4 3 2 1

Translator/Adapter: Alethea Nibley and Athena Nibley
Lettering: Scott O. Brown

TOMARE!

[STOP!]

You're going the wrong way!

Manga is a completely different
type of reading experience.

To start at the *beginning*,
go to the *end*!

That's right! Authentic manga is read the traditional Japanese way—from right to left. Exactly the *opposite* of how American books are read. It's easy to follow: Just go to the other end of the book, and read each page—and each panel—from the right side to the left side, starting at the top right. Now you're experiencing manga as it was meant to be!